Part Two - The Handbook

Part Two - The Handbook

The Guide to
Maritime Environmental & Efficiency Management

Part Two - The Handbook

Authors: Catherine Austin and Isabelle Rojon

Expert Contribution and Review:
BIMCO Marine Department, coordinated by Jeppe Skovbakke Juhl
CSL Group coordinated by Jonathan White
Alison Jarabo, Fathom

Design: Ben Watkins

Published by: Fathom

Developed by:

Supported by:

ClassNK

First published in 2015 by Fathom.

Copyright 2015 BIMCO and Fathom Eco-Efficiency Consultants Ltd.

ISBN: 978-0-9568259-6-4

CONTENTS

Part Two - The Handbook

BIMCO

Efficient ship management is an increasingly demanding task – operating in compliance with international rules at all times is crucial to avoiding challenges from port state controls and other issues that could delay your ship's operation.

BIMCO and Fathom's latest Guide gives a practical, guided approach for shipping companies – providing the right knowledge and tools to implement an environmental and efficiency management system.

The Guide is comprehensive but simple to use – its 'workbook' design gives a step-by-step approach to successful implementation – from building a corporate environment vision and commitment to change – to generating viable ideas and action steps at all operational levels from boardroom to ship.

Whether a company is taking the first steps to implementing an efficiency and environmental management culture – or looking for a clear, recognisable structure to document and drive activities already taking place, the guide has the right tools to help them achieve it. This approach also helps companies to see opportunities for improvements and cost savings more easily – and the steps towards putting them in place.

I recommend this guide to ship owners and operators as an excellent tool to facilitate the efficient management of ships, with steps to tackle the great and complex environmental challenges they face on a daily basis. It can also assist companies in minimising the risk of global non-compliance issues, which can be very costly and inconvenient for owners and operators.

John Denholm
President of BIMCO

Today, greater awareness of the need to protect the marine environment combined with commercial demands for greater efficiency are driving tremendous changes in our industry. Yet, adapting to constantly changing technologies whilst operating in line with tightening regional and international regulations presents a major challenge for stakeholders throughout the industry, especially for shipowners and operators.

As a leading classification society, we play a central role in the development and safe implementation of new technologies, developing and applying our own independent technical rules to ensure the safety of ships, their crews, and the marine environment, as well as working on behalf of more than 100 flag administrations to implement international conventions and regulations on vessels around the world.

Moreover, our surveyors carry out surveys and audits for more than 9,000 ships on our register each year. These vessels total more than 230 million gross tons or roughly 20% of the world's merchant tonnage under class, so we know first-hand the challenges that new regulations pose for shipowners and operators throughout the maritime industry.

Just as technology has advanced and become more sophisticated so too have maritime regulations. Beyond just grasping the requirements and intentions of these new rules, implementing new management policies, procedures, and best practices are essential to ensuring that compliance is achieved both effectively and cost-efficiently.

Any attempt to address the challenges of new regulations, however, must begin with understanding, and it is for that reason that we are proud to work alongside BIMCO to publish the Guide to Maritime Environmental & Efficiency Management.

This essential publication provides shipowners, operators, managers and charterers with a simple, easy-to-follow framework on how to efficiently manage vessels while keeping in line with safety and environmental rules and regulations. Moreover, the Guide provides simple steps on how to plan, implement, monitor and improve management systems in order to provide a competitive advantage whilst ensuring the protection of the marine environment and strict compliance with international conventions.

We believe that publications like this one will be of great benefit to owners and operators as they seek to achieve safe, effective and environmental friendly compliance. We are honoured to have supported the Guide's production; we salute BIMCO, Fathom, and Canada Steamship Lines for their incredible contributions to its contents, and we hope that you will find it a useful tool in your efforts to ensure safer and greener shipping.

The shipping industry is without a doubt influenced by growing societal pressure to take the impact of shipping operations on society and the environment into account. Cargo owners, charter companies, banks, investors and insurers are increasingly demanding evidence of environmental and operational efficiency commitments when making contract decisions. A greater awareness of the need to conduct shipping operations with environmental impact and ship efficiency in mind is becoming a necessity.

In an industry that is evolving and growing in complexity, developing awareness and acting strategically upon such awareness requires effective planning, foresight and long-term thinking, a structured approach is needed.

The structured approach required can be provided through the development and application of environmental management systems.

However, the number of environmental management systems currently available to the shipping industry are limited. Those that are available may be complex, not easy to follow and have not been tailored for application to shipping operations.

Fathom believes that ship owners and operators should have the correct tools available that will enable them to implement an effective management system and exploit all the benefits that are created through its development and application to create a lasting competitive advantage.

As information specialists, Fathom catalysed the creation of a resource that offers a practical, guided approach to support shipping companies on their path to establishing an environmental management framework that is tailored specifically for shipping operations to suit the unique requirements of the industry.

Whether you are taking the first steps to implementing an efficiency and environmental culture or looking for a clear structure to document and drive activities already taking place – this publication will provide you with the tools to help you achieve your goals.

Catherine Austin
Director - Fathom

CANADA STEAMSHIP LINES

Customers and communities around the world expect shipping companies to conduct their operations in a sustainable, efficient and environmentally-responsible manner. As part of a global movement toward sustainable business practices, the marine transportation sector is accountable not only to regulatory bodies, but also to the ecosystems and communities in which it operates.

The CSL Group ("CSL") a leading provider of marine dry bulk cargo handling and delivery services, and the world's largest owner and operator of self-unloading vessels, strongly believes shipping companies must take a proactive approach to promote technologies, solutions and sound public policy to reduce the industry's environmental impact. In the past few years, CSL has made remarkable progress to improve the energy efficiency and environmental performance of its global fleet. In fact, environmental stewardship has become a natural extension of CSL's collective consciousness.

CSL is a leading advocate of short sea shipping, a critical segment of global trade and a significant contributor to reducing the environmental footprint associated with transporting large quantities of bulk cargo. Typically operating along coastlines and rarely transiting vast ocean distances, short sea ships play a key role in reducing greenhouse gas emissions, noise and congestion problems by competing directly with less efficient transportation modes such as truck and rail.

Despite its inherent economic and environmental advantages, short sea shipping is often overlooked by governments, and must comply with inadequate global regulatory requirements designed for deep sea shipping. The unintentional consequence is a modal shift to less efficient forms of transporting bulk cargo.

As part of a global solution to move cargo in an efficient and environmentally-responsible manner, short sea shipping must be defined, defended and promoted to support a viable and sustainable shipping industry. CSL is actively working to ensure short sea shipping is accorded an internationally recognized definition, with sound policy development and proper convention negotiation.

CSL is honoured to have participated in the development of the 'Guide to Maritime Environmental & Efficiency Management', in collaboration with BIMCO and Fathom. We hope the insight and knowledge contained in the guide will enhance the environmental management of shipping around the world and lead to global improvements in fleet efficiency.

CANADA STEAMSHIP LINES

ABBREVIATIONS

The abbreviations listed are solely for Part Two of this Guide.

A-C

Abbreviation	Meaning
AFS Convention	International Convention on the Control of Harmful Anti-Fouling Systems on Ships
AMS	Alternate Management System
AWT	Advanced Wastewater Treatment System
BCH Code	Code for the Construction and Equipment of Ships Carrying Dangerous Chemicals in Bulk
BDN	Bunker Delivery Note
Bunkers Convention	International Convention on Civil Liability for Bunker Oil Pollution Damage
BWE	Ballast Water Exchange
BWM	Ballast Water Management
BWM Convention	International Convention for the Control and Management of Ships' Ballast Water and Sediments
BWWG	Ballast Water Working Group (under GESAMP)
CAA 90	Clean Air Act Amendments of 1990
CARB	California Air Resource Board
CFC	Chlorofluorocarbon
cfu	colony forming unit
CO_2	Carbon Dioxide
CoF	Certificate of Fitness for the Carriage of Dangerous Chemicals in Bulk
COW	Crude Oil Washing
CRMS	Craft Risk Management Standard
CWA	Clean Water Act

D-G

Abbreviation	Meaning
DWT	Deadweight Tonnage
EAL	Environmentally Acceptable Lubricant
ECA	Emission Control Area
ECP	Environmental Compliance Plan
EEDI	Energy Efficiency Design Index
EEOI	Energy Efficiency Operational Indicator
EGCS	Exhaust Gas Cleaning System
EGR	Exhaust Gas Recirculation
EIAPP Certificate	Engine International Air Pollution Prevention Certificate
EPA	US Environmental Protection Agency
GESAMP	Group of Experts on the Scientific Aspects of Marine Environmental Protection
GHG	Greenhouse Gas
GT	Gross Tonnage

Abbreviation	Meaning
HCFC	Hydrochlorofluorocarbon
HCFC-22	Difluorochloromethane
HFO	Heavy Fuel Oil
HNS Convention	International Convention on Liability and Compensation for Damage in Connection with the Carriage of Hazardous and Noxious Substances by Sea
HSD Engine	High-Speed Diesel Engine
IAPP Certificate	International Air Pollution Prevention Certificate
IBC Code	International Code for the Construction and Equipment of Ships carrying Dangerous Chemicals in Bulk
IBTS	Integrated Bilge Water Treatment Systems
IEE Certificate	International Energy Efficiency Certificate
IGC Code	International Code for the Construction and Equipment of Ships Carrying Liquefied Gases in Bulk
IMDG Code	International Maritime Dangerous Goods Code
IMO	International Maritime Organization
IOPP Certificate	International Oil Pollution Prevention Certificate
IPCC	International Panel on Climate Change
ISGOTT	International Safety Guide for Oil Tankers & Terminals
ISM Code	International Safety Management Code
ISO	International Organization for Standardization
ISPP Certificate	International Sewage Pollution Prevention Certificate
LNG	Liquefied Natural Gas
MARPOL	International Convention for the Prevention of Pollution from Ships
MDO	Marine Diesel Oil
MEPC	Marine and Environment Protection Committee
MGO	Marine Gas Oil
mPa.s	Millipascal Seconds
MSD Engine	Medium-Speed Diesel Engine
MSDS	Material Safety Data Sheet
mt	Metric tonne
n/a	Not applicable
NDZ	No Discharge Zone
NLS Certificate	International Pollution Prevention Certificate for the Carriage of Noxious Liquid Substances in Bulk
nm	Nautical Mile
NMFS	National Marine Fisheries Service
NMVOC	Non-Methane Volatile Organic Compound
NO_x	Nitrogen Oxide

Abbreviation	Meaning
ODS	Ozone-Depleting Substance
OGV	Ocean-Going Vessel
OPRC Convention	Convention on Oil Pollution Preparedness, Response and Co-operation
OPRC-HNS Protocol	Protocol on Preparedness, Response and Co-operation to Pollution Incidents by Hazardous and Noxious Substances
ORB	Oil Record Book
PAH	Polycyclic Aromatic Hydrocarbon
P&I	Protection and Indemnity
PM	Particulate Matter
ppm	Parts Per Million
PSC	Port State Control
P/V Valve	Pressure/Vacuum Valve
RCW	Regulated California Waters
rpm	Revolutions Per Minute
SCR	Selective Catalytic Reduction
SDR	Special Drawing Right
SEEMP	Ship Energy Efficiency Management Plan
SMPEP	Shipboard Marine Pollution Emergency Plan
SOLAS	International Convention for the Safety of Life at Sea
SO_x	Sulphur Oxide
SO_2	Sulphur Dioxide
SO_3	Sulphur Trioxide
SO_4	Sulphate
SOPEP	Shipboard Oil Pollution Emergency Plan
SSD Engine	Slow-Speed Diesel Engine
TBT	Tributylin
USCG	United States Coast Guard
VCS	Vapour Control System
VECS	Vapour Emission Control System
VGP	Vessel General Permit
VOC	Volatile Organic Compound

CHAPTER ONE

CONTENTS

THE GUIDE TO THE GUIDE

THE GUIDE TO THE GUIDE

This Guide offers practical guidance and resources that will equip you with the knowledge and tools to develop and implement an organisation-specific environmental and efficiency management system. The aim is to help you improve your environmental performance, improve the efficiency of your ships and fleet - and therefore remain competitive in the changing business landscape.

This Guide is presented in three different parts.

1.1 Part One - The Framework

Part One provides guidance on how to develop an organisation- and maritime-specific environmental and efficiency management system, referred to throughout this Guide as the Environmental & Efficiency Management Framework. It will assist you in developing and implementing a management system in an easy way and exploit the benefits that stem from it to create a lasting competitive advantage.

The fundamental idea behind building your Framework is to use a modular approach. This will allow you to adapt your Framework to your organisation's specific needs and circumstances, link it to an existing management system or facilitate the development of a full management system.

In addition, Part One demonstrates how this resource and your resulting Framework links to other industry requirements, including the International Safety Management (ISM) Code and the Ship Energy Efficiency Management Plan (SEEMP). Your Framework can also be used to help deal with US enforcement action where the development and implementation of an Environmental Compliance Plan (ECP) can be imposed on a company. Part One also explains how your Framework relates to standards developed by the International Organization for Standardization (ISO), such as the Environmental Management Standard ISO 14001 and how it can be used to participate in the most common environmental evaluation schemes.

1.2 Part Two - The Handbook

Part Two is a compendium of technical and regulatory information, advisory resources and templates - the technical counterpart to Part One. It covers the entire spectrum of environmental issues related to ship operations, including:

- Oil pollution.
- Garbage.
- Sewage.
- Chemical pollution.
- Air pollution.
- Ballast water.
- Biofouling.
- Underwater noise.

Each Chapter within Part Two provides a brief introduction to each issue, explains what the associated environmental impacts are and describes related international and regional regulatory requirements. Each chapter also covers how your organisation can not only meet and comply with these regulatory requirements but move beyond them. Each Chapter also presents the potential business case for measuring your organisation's environmental performance.

1.3 Part Three - The Templates

The Maritime Environmental & Efficiency Templates (on the USB memory stick supplied) are an extensive library of templates in the form of logbooks, forms and data collection tools that supplement Part Two of this Guide.

Together, the three parts provide an essential resource that will support your organisation in developing an effective Environmental & Efficiency Management Framework that is specific to your organisation and operations and can be adapted to changing circumstances.

CHAPTER TWO

CONTENTS

OILY BILGE WATER

OILY BILGE WATER

2.1 Introduction

Oily bilge water is the mixture, from a variety of different sources, of water, oily fluids, lubricants, cleaning fluids, and other similar wastes that accumulate in the lowest part of a ship.

Oily bilge water differs from 'normal' bilge water because it originates in the machinery space. 'Normal' bilge water, on the other hand, refers to the water that collects in bilges placed in the cargo holds of the ship.

This Chapter deals with oily bilge water rather than 'normal' bilge water. You can also refer to Chapter 3 on operational discharges from oil tankers, including crude oil and tank washings.

Ship machinery spaces consist of, for example, tanks, pumps, flanges and valves, all of which are connected via piping and tubing. Although systems are designed to be leak-free, many leaks develop due to poor maintenance or the lack of maintenance, inadequate repair of failed seals, gaskets, pump shaft seals, machinery casing gaskets and other components.

Both the amount and type of leaking fluid can vary tremendously. This often results in a complex mixture of fluids which does not only contain oil and water, but also lubricating oil, hydraulic oil, oil additives, chemicals, detergents and particles.

2.2 Environmental Impact

Oily bilge water from the engine room is usually contaminated with oil leaking from engines and machineries as well as from engine maintenance activities, such as soaps, detergents, dispersants, and degreasers used to clean the engine room. These cleaning agents create an emulsion and prevent separation of oil and water. Thus, they are often incompatible with oily water separators and oil content monitors.

Regardless of the content, discharge of untreated oily bilge water poses a threat to the marine environment. It may poison or contaminate fish stocks and other marine organisms and cause widespread pollution of water and coastal areas.

2.3 International Regulation

Oily bilge water discharges are regulated under MARPOL 73/78 Annex I.

In general, the discharge of oil or oily mixtures into the marine environment is prohibited except when the strict discharge criteria are met. These discharge regulations depend on whether the ship is in or outside a 'Special Area'.

2.3.1 What Is A Special Area?

Resolution MEPC.117(52)

MARPOL Annex I defines certain sea areas as Special Areas in which, for technical reasons relating to their oceanographical and ecological condition and to their sea traffic, the adoption of special mandatory methods for the prevention of sea pollution is required.

These Special Areas are provided with a higher level of protection than other sea areas.

Resolution MEPC.117(52)
Resolution MEPC.154(55)

The sea areas that currently fall under this category are:

- Mediterranean Sea.
- Baltic Sea.
- Black Sea.
- Red Sea.
- Gulfs area[1].
- Gulf of Aden.
- Antarctic area.
- North West European Waters.
- Oman area of the Arabian Sea.
- Southern South African Waters.

The Red Sea, Gulf of Aden and Oman area of the Arabian Sea have been designated as Special Areas, but at the time of writing (*December 2014*) had not yet taken effect. This is because not enough of the MARPOL Parties whose coastlines border these Special Areas have notified the International Maritime Organization (IMO) on the existence of adequate reception facilities. This means that at the moment, these areas can be disregarded with regards to bilge water regulations for Special Areas.

---

[1] The Gulfs area means the sea area located north-west of the rhumb line between Ras al Hadd and Ras al Fasteh.

2.3.2

Resolution MEPC.117(52)

Discharge Requirements For Ships Outside Special Areas

Outside Special Areas, the discharge requirements for ships of 400 gross tonnage (GT) and above are:

- The ship is *en route* to ensure the discharge is spread over a great area.
- The oil content without dilution is less or equal to 15 parts per million (ppm).
- The ship is fitted with oil filtering equipment that ensures that any oily mixture discharged into the sea after passing through the filtering equipment has an oil content not exceeding 15 ppm.
- All ships above 10,000 GT additionally need to be equipped with an alarm system that shuts off discharge in the event it exceeds 15 ppm.
- On oil tankers, the oily mixture
  - does not originate from cargo pump-room bilges;
  - is not mixed with oil cargo residues.

All oil filtering equipment fitted onboard ships must be approved in accordance with resolution MEPC.107(49). However, the equipment on older ships approved in accordance with resolutions MEPC.60(33) and A.393(X) may also continue to be used.

If the instruments are calibrated, it is advised to keep the calibration certificate onboard.

2.3.3

Resolution MEPC.117(52)

Discharge Requirements For Ships Inside Special Areas

Inside Special Areas, the discharge requirements for ships of 400 GT and above are almost the same as those outlined in Section 2.3.2. The difference relates to the oil filtering equipment: within Special Areas, all ship of 400 GT and above must be provided with an oil filtering equipment with alarm arrangements and an automatic stopping device.

For ease of understanding, the discharge requirements for ships ≥ 400 GT inside Special Areas are listed below:

- The ship is *en route* which means that it is underway at sea on a course or courses, including deviation from the shortest direct route. This is to ensure the discharge is spread over a great area.
- The oil content without dilution is less or equal to 15 ppm.
- The ship is fitted with oil filtering equipment that ensures that any oily mixture discharged into the sea after passing through the filtering equipment has an oil content not exceeding 15 ppm. The oil filtering equipment must have an alarm system that shuts off discharge in the event it exceeds 15 ppm.
- On oil tankers, the oily mixture
  - does not originate from cargo pump-room bilges;
  - is not mixed with oil cargo residues.

All oil filtering equipment fitted onboard ships must be approved in accordance with resolution MEPC.107(49). However, the equipment on older ships approved in accordance with resolutions MEPC.60(33) and A.393(X) may also continue to be used.

Again, if the instruments are calibrated, it is advised to keep the calibration certificate onboard.

Resolution MEPC.117(52)

2.3.4   Discharges In The Antarctic Area

With respect to the Antarctic area, the discharge requirements are stricter than inside other Special Areas. Here, any discharge of oil or oily mixtures into the sea from any ship is strictly prohibited.

Resolution MEPC.117(52)

2.3.5   When Oily Bilge Water Does Not Meet Discharge Criteria

Oily bilge water that cannot be discharged into the sea in compliance with these provisions has to be kept onboard and discharged to shore-based reception facilities. Therefore, a standard discharge connection has to be fitted to the ship's discharge pipeline for residues from bilges and sludge tanks.

It is the duty of each signatory Party to MARPOL 73/78 Annex I to ensure the provision of adequate reception facilities at oil loading terminals and ports.

2.3.5.1   *Beware Of Regulatory Misinterpretations*

An unfortunate misinterpretation of MARPOL Annex I, Regulation 12, has shown that over the past years, ships have been built with one common pipe from the discharge pump. The discharge pipe and pump then transports both sludge and oily bilge disposals on its way to the joint deck manifold. Some systems even have a separate pipe to an incinerator sludge service tank attached to the common discharge pipe.

Such piping arrangements are in breach with the intentions of MARPOL Annex I. It must be clear that both sludge pumps and bilge pumps must have separated dedicated discharge connections. These dedicated lines must not be serviced by the other pumps.

Collecting oil residues from a bilge tank creates no problem - however transfer of sludge through the oily bilge system is not allowed. A screw-down non-return valve, arranged in lines connecting to common piping leading to the standard discharge connection, provides an acceptable means to prevent sludge from being transferred or discharged to the bilge system, oily bilge water holding tank(s), tank top or oily water separator.

In order to deal with the above breach, it is important to note that the revised MARPOL Annex I, Regulation 12 will enter into force 2017 and is to be applied retroactively to all ships in service based on a phase-in scheme lasting 5 years.

2.3.6   Managing Oily Bilge Water

Oily bilge water is a complex mixture of not only oil and water, but it also often contains lubricating oil, hydraulic oil, oil additives, chemicals and detergents – not to mention particles like soot and dirt.

During normal operation, all of these substances are channelled into the bilge water holding tank which is maintained at an elevated temperature. This high temperature facilitates separation due to the force of gravity in the bilge water tank. Oil rises to the top and particles settle on the tank bottom, generally dividing bilge water into three distinct layers in the tank:

- **Top layer:** This contains most of the oil and organic solvents and constitutes a small portion of the total tank volume. Skimming this top layer for separate treatment is recommended.
- **Middle, or main, layer:** This aqueous phase contains water polluted by oil, chemicals and particles in emulsified form. This is fed to the bilge water treatment system.
- **Bottom layer:** This contains solids and heavy sludge, which should also be removed for separate treatment.

While gravity is enough for this primary separation, it usually cannot provide the secondary treatment needed before oily bilge water can be discharged.

One of the principal reasons why the force of gravity is not sufficient to separate oily bilge water is the presence of emulsions. Emulsions are smooth and even mixtures of liquids that do not dissolve in one another. Emulsifiers - liquids similar to soap - reduce the ability of oil to separate from water by gravity alone and therefore should ideally be excluded from a ship's bilges since they will cause the oily water separator to malfunction. In addition, the mixture of several cleaning agents in the engine bilges should be avoided. Unfortunately it is difficult to predict what type of liquids enter the bilges and often, inadvertently, chemicals that act as emulsifiers end up in the ship's bilges, with resultant problems in bilge separation.

In order to deal with emulsions, several measures can be taken:

- The use of quick-separating detergents reduces problems caused by emulsions.
- After applying cleaning agents, it is recommended to allow some time (at least 30-60 minutes) before washing, preferably with hot water and utilising a high-pressure washing machine if available and where possible. After cleaning, any emulsion should remain in the bilge water holding tank or bilge water settling tank for a sufficient period of time before passing through the oily water separator.
- To destabilise emulsions, methods that induce flocculation or coagulation are most often used. Flocculation or coagulation are processes used to aggregate small particles into larger ones that settle more readily. Both processes can be encouraged by raising the temperature and pH value of the bilge water, by means of high centrifugal force or by adding chemicals, e.g. flocculants.

From the middle layer in the bilge water holding tank, oily bilge water is fed to the oily water separator. Often, this water is mixed with contaminants like particles and soot and many oil content monitors cannot differentiate between oil and such contaminants.

Unless the oily water separator is relatively new and, in accordance with resolution MEPC.107(49), equipped with an integrated large second-stage fine filter, the soot and particles will remain suspended in the water and the oil content monitor will not permit the water to pass through, as it will assume the water to be contaminated with oil. This problem can be mitigated by installing a large fine filter between the oily water separator and the oil content monitor.

Surveys And Certification

Every ship of 400 GT and above as well as every oil tanker of 150 GT and above must carry an International Oil Pollution Prevention (IOPP) Certificate onboard for inspection by port or flag States. The Certificate can last for up to five years.

In order to be granted an IOPP Certificate, the ship has to pass the following surveys:

- An initial survey, before the ship is put into service, or before an IOPP Certificate is issued for the first time.
- A renewal survey, before the end of every period of five years following the issue of an IOPP Certificate in respect of the ship.
- A minimum of one intermediate survey within 3 months before or after the second or third anniversary date of the IOPP Certificate.
- An annual survey.
- An additional survey whenever any important repairs or renewals are made.

These surveys are undertaken to ensure that the structure, equipment, systems, fittings, arrangements and material fully comply with the applicable requirements of MARPOL Annex I.

Monitoring And Reporting

Every oil tanker of 150 GT and above and every ship of 400 GT and above is required to carry an Oil Record Book (ORB) Part I onboard. Whenever any of the following machinery space operations takes place, entries must be made in the ORB Part I:

- Ballasting or cleaning of oil fuel tanks.
- Discharge of dirty ballast or cleaning water from oil fuel tanks.
- Collection and disposal of oil residues (sludge and other oil residues).
- Discharge overboard or disposal otherwise of bilge water which has accumulated in machinery spaces.
- Bunkering of fuel or bulk lubricating oil.

Each completed operation can be signed by the crew, however, the overall responsibility for the ORB entries always lies with the Master. The ORB must be ready for display upon official inspections and must be preserved for at least three years after the last entry has been made.

The form of the ORB is specified in Appendix III of MARPOL Annex I and included in the Maritime Environmental & Efficiency Templates on the USB memory stick. In addition, MEPC has issues a guidance document for the recording of operations in the ORB Part I (MEPC.1/Circ.736/Rev.2).

Questions to Consider

Under which circumstances am I allowed to discharge oily bilge water?
The table below shows the discharge requirements for ships ≥400 GT that need to be met for discharging oily bilge water.

Sea Area	Discharge Criteria
Outside Special Area	No discharge except when: • The ship is *en route*. • The oil content without dilution is ≤15 ppm.
	• The ship is fitted with oil filtering equipment that ensures that any oily mixture discharged into the sea after passing through the filtering equipment has an oil content ≤15 ppm. • All ships ≥ 10,000 GT additionally need to be equipped with an alarm system that shuts off discharge in the event it exceeds 15 ppm. • On oil tankers, the oily mixture does not originate from cargo pump-room bilges and is not mixed with oil cargo residues.
Inside Special Area	Same as outside a Special Area, however, the oil filtering equipment should be provided with alarm arrangements and arrangements that the discharge is automatically stopped when the content of the effluent exceeds 15 ppm.
Antarctic area	No discharge.

What do I do with the bilge water that I cannot discharge into the sea?
Bilge water that cannot be discharged into the sea in compliance with these provisions has to be kept onboard and discharged to shore-based reception facilities. To this end, a standard discharge connection has to be fitted to the ship's discharge pipeline for residues from bilges and sludge tanks.

2.4 Regional Regulation

Some national, regional and local authorities, especially those governing sensitive waters, have stringent regulations in place in addition to those governed through MARPOL Annex I.

2.4.1 United States

2013 VGP Part 2.2.2

Under the United States 2013 Vessel General Permit (VGP), ship owners and operators of ships built after 19 December 2013 that are greater than 400 GT must sample and analyse their bilge water effluent once per year for oil and grease content. The monitoring can be conducted as part of the ship's annual survey.

As an incentive for new oil pollution prevention equipment, the US Environmental Protection Agency (EPA) includes a means for reducing bilge water monitoring. If analytical results for oil and grease are less than 5 ppm for two consecutive years, it is not necessary to sample and analyse for the subsequent years of permit coverage if:

- The ship uses an oily water separator capable of meeting a 5 ppm oil and grease limit or you use an alarm which prevents the discharge of oil and grease above 5 ppm;
- the oil content monitor is calibrated annually; and
- the oil content monitor never reads above 5 ppm when discharging in waters subject to the VGP.

In the Clean Water Act (CWA) § 401 Certifications, Connecticut and New York prohibit the discharge of bilge water; Rhode Island requires the discharge of all bilge water prior to entering its waters.

2.4.2 Other National Requirements

Before discharging any oily bilge water into territorial waters, the Master should check the relevant national regulations. This is because some countries forbid discharges of oily waters within a certain distance from their shores.

Denmark, for example, prohibits discharge of oily bilge water within 12 nautical miles (nm) from the nearest point of land; Finland and Iceland within 4 and 3 nm, respectively.

National maritime authorities with responsibility for the environmental protection of their coastlines adopt a strict approach to the enforcement of MARPOL. Companies and seafarers need to understand that even the most minor violations of MARPOL will be handled severely by the authorities. In addition to large fines amounting to millions of dollars, both company management and seafarers can be liable to criminal prosecution and imprisonment for any deliberate or accidental violation of MARPOL requirements or falsification of records.

2.5 Going Beyond Compliance
2.5.1 Procedural Measures

Going beyond compliance is sometimes not only a matter of exceeding the standards set by the regulations but also ensuring that processes are in place to help comply with regulations and thus reduce the possibility of non-compliance.

Whilst there are technical solutions that can help go beyond compliance on bilge water regulations, much of it will come down to implementing best practices, control and maintenance measures.

Such items will include:

- Establishing and communicating formal procedures and company policies to ensure compliance.
- Establishing a confidential hotline to allow crewmembers to report suspected breaches anonymously.
- Determining the recommended procedures for maintenance of equipment and putting in appropriate schedule.
- Introducing expanded oily bilge water management procedures, including keeping the engine room clean, disposing oily bilge water to port reception facilities properly and regularly; securing or locking any overboard valves when the ship is operating within areas where discharges are not allowed.
- Reviewing and verifying the maintenance records and procedures at regular internal audits.

These are just a few examples. For more options, see the Box Out on the following page.

Guidance On Bilge Water Management[2]

Several industry associations have together produced a guidance document on the use of oily water separators. This document also covers the role of senior management onboard the ship which is outlined below.

The Master, Chief Engineer and engineers should:
- Promote awareness that any attempt to circumvent MARPOL requirements is totally unacceptable.
- Determine the most appropriate procedures to maintain equipment, machinery and systems.
- Minimise and if possible eliminate leakage through good housekeeping.
- Correctly maintain the ORB and the record of discharges of oily water separator effluent into the sea.
- Ensure that all routine shipboard safety meetings include time to discuss a specific agenda item on environmental matters.
- Use sign on/off check lists for duty personnel.

Use Of Oily Water Separators
The Master, Chief Engineer and engineers should:
- Instruct users of oily water separator equipment and verify the standard achieved.
- Verify that maintenance schedules are being followed.
- Ensure that internal audits include operational tests and a reconciliation of records.
- Ensure that scheduled tank sounding logs are maintained and signed for.
- Keep records of verification of correct operation through testing at sea.
- Ensure that onboard spares are adequate to meet the demand.
- Create a culture where complacency in operation and maintenance standards is unacceptable.

Record Keeping
The Master, Chief Engineer and engineers should:
- Ensure that all entries in the tank sounding log, ORB and incinerator logs are completed by the crew member who performed the task.
- Ensure that the ORB is examined and signed by the Master.
- Require signatures from those conducting overboard discharges and operational tests.
- Ensure that ship familiarisation procedures verify that company environmental policy and operability of equipment are understood and followed.
- Require the status of pollution prevention equipment to be recorded in the handover notes of the responsible engineer and the Chief Engineer.
- Record the independent verification of the correct operation of the oil discharge monitoring equipment.
- Raise awareness of the need for an open chain of command and accurate record keeping that can be substantiated with Port State Control (PSC).

Tracking Waste And Maintenance
The Master, Chief Engineer and engineers should:
- Conduct analyses of waste disposal records.
- Compare waste output to volumes purchased.
- Compare waste disposal records with maintenance records.
- Remove disincentives to offloading waste, or purchasing additional material or parts related to safety and the environment.

2.5.2 Meeting Future Requirements

Some classification societies anticipate the introduction of stricter regulatory requirements with regard to the discharge of oily bilge water, lowering the limit to 5 ppm.

The next step would thus be to further decrease the concentration of oil contained in discharged bilge water. This can be achieved by installing 5 ppm bilge water treatment and alarm systems.

2.5.3 Minimising The Generation Of Oily Bilge Water

Reducing the oily content of discharged bilge water is a great step towards protecting the marine environment from oil pollution, however it does not address the root of the problem: the contamination of bilge water with oily effluents and other hazardous materials. Minimising the generation of oily bilge water should thus be the ultimate goal.

Therefore, it is suggested to:

- Drain all waste oil to the sludge tank.
- Drain water from cleaning the air coolers to the sludge tank instead of the engine bilges.
- Avoid contaminating the bilges with purifiers and fuel oil transfer pump leaks. Arrange save-alls wherever possible and drain to the sludge tank.
- Avoid overflow to bilges when washing the exhaust boiler and make sure there is a collecting tank for the washing water. After settling, drain the water to the sludge tank or evaporate it, and collect the oily sludge remaining in the tank for legal disposal.
- Evaporate bilge water by surplus steam in a purposely built evaporating tank.
- Remove oil skims with paper or designated cloths.
- Route drain from the main engine air coolers to a separate tank. Water generated in the air cooler should not be routed directly overboard, even if it is clean, but should pass through the oil content monitor before being discharged.
- Transfer or drain residues from chemical cleaning in the engine into the sludge tank.

MEPC.1/Circ.642, as amended by MEPC.1/Circ.676 and MEPC.1/Circ.760

Furthermore, the IMO has proposed the introduction of Integrated Bilge Water Treatment Systems (IBTS). According to industry, the IBTS is probably the best system to use and the most reliable and effective. Such a system minimises the amount of oily bilge water generated in machinery spaces by treating the leaked water and oil separately and provides an integrated means to process the oily bilge water and oil residue.

IBTS are particularly efficient in regions of high humidity like Singapore or the Persian Gulf. When humidity is high, compressors, fans and the like produce large quantities of condensed water vapour. IBTS collect such water directly in a separate tank and treat it without cross-contaminating it with drains from e.g. the fuel oil system.

There are of course other alternatives to IBTS, e.g. bilge skimmers. However, the bilge is usually a structurally complex area of the ship which means that it may be difficult to get the required depth or width of access to allow full usage of the skimmers.

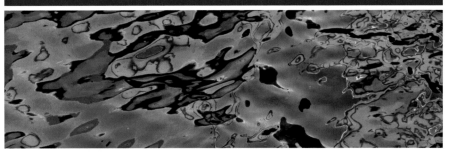

Questions to Consider

How do I avoid accidental discharge?

Ship operators have ultimate responsibility for establishing a compliance culture within their companies, and it is important that every effort is made to ensure that seafarers do not engage in any illegal conduct in the mistaken belief that it will benefit their employer. Every seafarer should be made fully aware of the severe legal consequences, both for the company and the seafarers themselves, of even minor non-compliance with environmental rules.

At first glance, the advice contained in the following questions may appear to contain nothing new; for the vast majority of shipping companies, these are issues which should already be fully addressed by their safety management systems, as required by the International Safety Management (ISM) Code. Nevertheless, it is recommended that the following guidance is carefully analysed by company management, and that a firm message of zero tolerance of non- compliance with MARPOL is circulated as widely as possible amongst seagoing personnel.

Many operators have implemented a kind of 'stop card' policy that anybody can use without any personal risk and a 'if you see it you own it' policy. This is frequently used in the offshore industry and is becoming more and more common in the shipping industry as well.

How can I improve my environmental performance?

Shipping companies should consider:
- Installing the latest equipment, or an upgrade in capability, if existing equipment does not perform to requirements.
- Upgrading related equipment to minimise the production of waste.
- The advantages of the pre-processing of waste.
- Increasing tank capacity for waste where possible.
- Modifying systems to facilitate in port testing of treatment systems.
- Implementing the periodic testing of the oil discharge monitoring equipment.
- The use of cleaning agents consistent with equipment capability.

Can I install control devices?

Shipping companies should consider:
- Fitting uniquely numbered environmental tags on flanges to prevent unauthorised by-passing.
- Using seals on overboard valves and cross-connections.
- Installing strategically placed placards concerning compliance with MARPOL onboard ship.
- Fitting surveillance cameras.
- Using tamper resistant recording systems, alarms and printouts to verify equipment operation, valve position, flow, oily water separator, incineration, ship's position etc.
- Installing locked boxes or cages over monitoring equipment.
- Fitting interlocks to prevent falsification of monitoring equipment inputs.
- Using meters to record equipment running time for all engine room pumps.

Important Note on Overboard Valves and Cross-Connections
Tags, locks and seals on relevant valves are an absolute must. The same is true for a proper seal log. A procedure should be in place in order to have a common recording system for sealing of overboard valves and flanges.

For more information, please see MEPC.1/Circ.736/Rev.2, examples number 26 and 27.

What is the role of shore management in ensuring and going beyond compliance?

- Assign environmental responsibility to senior management and ship superintendents, Masters and Chief Engineers onboard ships.
- Ensure adequacy of internal audits and implementation of corrective actions.
- Review maintenance records and procedures, log entries and handover notes.
- Monitor workloads imposed by the operation and maintenance of oily water separators, and assess the impact on crew priorities.
- Analyse waste streams to determine content, volume, means and capacity for storage, and estimate realistically the cost of treatment and disposal.
- Ensure that the operating budget for waste removal and spare parts is adequate.
- Establish comprehensive check lists for inspections/audits.
- Verify that tests have been performed to ensure the continued correct operation of oily water separators.
- Discuss findings and concerns with all levels of the engineering department.
- Explore the potential gains from the installation of new technology.
- Shore management staff must verify that the equipment onboard can in fact handle the bilge water.

How can I train the crew onboard to ensure MARPOL compliance?

- Ensure that training, whether shipboard, in-house or from an outside authority, is specific on relevant MARPOL requirements.
- Consider supplementary training on MARPOL issues.
- Document the training and assess its relevance.
- Establish formal policy documents and procedures on MARPOL compliance and training.

2.6 Business Benefits

Sometimes, the benefits are not so much a gain of positives but rather an avoidance of negatives. This is certainly the case with oily bilge water.

MARPOL Annex I is one of the most frequently violated environmental regulations in the shipping industry. Illegal discharges of oily bilge water are one of the reasons for this.

In the past, 'creative' engineering crew have devised ways to circumvent the oily water separator or the monitoring equipment in order to discharge oily water overboard seemingly unnoticed. Shipping companies engaging in such practices face heavy penalties.

In the United States, presenting a falsified ORB is a criminal offence and the maximum fine against the company under the US criminal sentencing guidelines is US$ 500,000. This fine may be doubled if the violation resulted in financial gain for the company. Penalties do not only include monetary fines for the company, but those responsible may also be prosecuted and put in jail. In the United States, the maximum penalty upon conviction for individuals is five years of incarceration and US$ 250,000 in fines.[3]

Furthermore, it should be noted that it is illegal in the United States to document a non-legal operation. In other words, it is forbidden to document something that is known to constitute a breach of regulations under the heading 'that it was done in good faith'.

Other countries are also taking a zero tolerance approach towards oily discharges. According to the European Ship Sources Pollution Directive, pollution caused by 'serious negligence' is deemed sufficient for criminal liability. In Canada, criminal liability is presumed unless proven otherwise and demonstrating that the accused took all reasonable steps to prevent the pollution.

This shows that while regulatory compliance does not provide any direct financial benefits per se, it prevents companies and individuals from prosecution and the concomitant public shaming.

Even going beyond compliance by effectively treating oily bilge water and avoiding its generation in the first place can have business benefits. This is the case because it reduces the need for and cost of waste disposal onshore.

2.7 Measuring Environmental Performance

The sludge and bilge water production, volume treated in the oily water separator, evaporating tank, incinerator or deliveries ashore, etc. of each ship should be monitored and reported to the shore-based office.

These reports can be processed automatically and warnings can be raised if volumes are above or below pre-set targets.

CHAPTER THREE

CONTENTS

MARINE LUBRICANTS

MARINE LUBRICANTS

3.1 Introduction

Lubricating oils are used throughout the ship to reduce friction in rotating and moving parts and extend the life of machinery.

Lubricating oils, commonly referred to as marine lubricants, are used across ship functions both underwater (e.g. stern tubes, controllable pitch propellers, thrusters and pods, steering gear and stabilisers) and above the waterline (e.g. cranes, davits, hatch covers and winches).

The composition of marine lubricants can vary significantly. All of the lubricants host carefully balanced blends of base oils and additives, with the base oil typically making up over 90% of the lubricant - although it can be as low as 70%.

Typically the base oil is either mineral or synthetic but it may be a blend. Mineral oils are derived through the distillation of crude oil stock whilst synthetic lubricants are essentially a chemically engineered product built to deliver precise required properties.

Historically, neither mineral nor synthetic lubricants have been 'biodegradable'. However, products that break down to natural compounds in a suitable time frame - as recognised by international standards - have been available to the maritime industry since 2002 and the range of products available to the market is growing in size.

NOTE: 'Biodegradable' is not an exact term and should be used with caution. There is no internationally accepted meaning.

Further information can be sourced from the publication 'Choosing Optimal Lubricant Solutions for Your Operation' published by Fathom in 2014. This publication is free to download from www.fathomshipping.com.

3.2 Environmental Impact

Traditional lubricants are a form of oil, based on petroleum products. Such petroleum-based oils form a thin film on the surface of seas upon contact due to their immiscibility which can drastically impede and reduce the localised level of oxygen in the water which in turn will have an adverse effect on marine life. It also has the potential to coat micro-organisms, plants and animals with which it comes into contact and cause difficulties to those animals and plant life.

Lubricants may leak into the sea during the course of a ship's operation life. The amount of marine oil pollution caused by leaking lubricants can be significant. For example, according to a study submitted to the International Maritime Organization (IMO), 80 million litres of oil-based lubricants are lost at sea annually from intact stern tubes alone.[1]

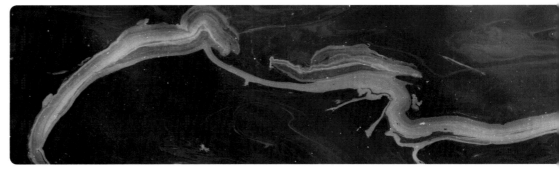

3.3 International Regulation

There are currently no international regulations that govern lubricant use.

3.4 Regional Regulation

There are regional requirements that enforce regulations around lubricant use for ships operating in United States (US) and Arctic waters.

3.4.1 United States Waters

In March 2013, the US Environmental Protection Agency (EPA) published the final version of its 2013 Vessel General Permit (VGP) which sets out the rules and regulations applicable for ships sailing in US waters.

2013 VGP Part 2.2.9

The revised VGP which came into force in December 2013 requires ships that are greater than 79 feet (24.079m) in length to use an Environmentally Acceptable Lubricant (EAL) across all oil-to-sea interfaces, unless technically infeasible.

EALs are defined by EPA as lubricants that are 'biodegradable', 'minimally toxic' and 'not bioaccumulative'.

According to the EPA, four major types of lubricants meet all the necessary required criteria to be approved as an EAL.

These are:

- Vegetable Oils (such as canola or soy oil based).
- Synthetic Esters (esters derived from bio-based sources).
- Polyalkylene Glycols (can be either water soluble or water insoluble).
- Water (referring to water lubricated and cooled stern tubes).[2]

2013 VGP Part 2.2.9

The VGP enforces that these 'bio-lubricants' must be used in all applications where the lubricant and the ocean come in to direct contact. This would include such areas of the ship as the controllable pitch propellers, stern tubes, rudder and thruster bearings, stabilisers, Azimuth thrusters, propulsion pod lubrication and wire rope and mechanical equipment that are subject to immersion.

By 'technically infeasible', the VGP is referring to:

- Pre-lubricated equipment such as some wire rope;
- when there is no EAL available that meets the manufacturer's lubricant specifications either on the market or at that specific dock; and
- if the process of switching over needs to be performed at the next drydocking.

This means that the full switch on all applications may not occur until the first drydocking post 19 December 2013. However, the use of non-compliance lubricant must be recorded in the ship's Annual Report and its usage justified.

2013 VGP Part 2.2.9

Furthermore, it is strongly encouraged – but not mandated - that ships use EALs in all above deck equipment and that new ships be designed to use seawater-based systems for their stern tube lubrication.

[2] EPA (2011) Environmentally Acceptable Lubricants

3.4.2   Arctic And Antarctic Waters

The IMO Guidelines for Ships Operating in Polar Waters state that stern tube bearings, seals and main propulsion components located outside the hull should not leak pollutants. Non-toxic biodegradable lubricants are not considered to be pollutants.

Questions to Consider

Do the VGP regulations affect my fleet?
If you are trading in US Waters, then the answer is yes.

However, it should also be considered to impact ships that may change operating pattern (for example change charterers).

Can I use 'environmentally safe' lubricants to comply with the VGP requirements?
Current products that claim to be 'Environmentally Safe' may not necessarily meet the stringent requirements for EALs set by EPA:
- 'No-Sheen' lubricants that are promoted as 'inherently biodegradable' should be queried.
- 'Food Grade' oils and greases may not meet the testing standards for bio-accumulation or chronic toxicity.
- Oils and greases with a specific gravity > 1.0 will not be allowed in unless they also achieve the environmental standards.

3.5   Going Beyond Compliance

Regulations regarding marine lubricant use are in their infancy, compared to other aspects of environmentally driven regulation. Therefore, there is ample opportunity for companies to go beyond the regulatory requirements.

3.5.1   Use EALs For Oil-To-Sea Interfaces On Ships That Do Not Enter US Regulated Waters

As currently the only regulations surrounding lubricant use apply to US waters, using EALs for ships that do not sail in US waters is certainly beyond compliance.

It should perhaps be considered that, as many ships will be affected by the VGP regulations, switching to EALs on just oil-to-sea interfaces may not be seen as a commitment to moving beyond compliance in future years, even when operating routes are not affected.

However, in the initial stages following the introduction of the legislation this would be a valid target for an environmental policy.

Remember: this can be undertaken in a phased manner with a target for the number of ships per year that are converted.

3.5.2 Use EALs Beyond Oil-to-Sea Interfaces

Pollution from the use of marine lubricants across ship machinery does not just occur from those applications in direct contact with the ocean.

Above waterline equipment is also a significant contributor, e.g. leaks from hydraulic deck machinery, greases from wire ropes, winches and anchor windlasses are washed down directly by rain and splash water. All of this goes overboard and 'pollutes' the sea.

Companies can undertake a risk-based maintenance programme for hydraulic deck machinery to mitigate these spills, conduct planned and periodic replacement of flexible hydraulic hoses used on deck machinery all of which reduce the risk and frequency of spills to the deck and to the sea from these types of machines.

In addition, companies could switch to the use of EALs on all deck equipment. Similarly, this can be effected in a phased manner.

3.5.3 Replace Oil Lubricated Bearings With Alternatives

3.5.3.1 *Below Waterline*

For stern tubes and rudder bearings, a simple way to completely eliminate oil pollution is to use seawater as the lubrication medium and proven non-metallic bearings in place of oil and white metal bearings. The seawater is pumped from the sea through the bearings and returned to the sea.[3]

Whilst this meets the VGP regulations, it could be considered that as stern lube oil leakage (biodegradable or not) is completely eliminated, this is a significant step beyond just compliance.

3.5.3.2 *Above Waterline*

There are alternative bearings for deck machinery made of thermoplastics that require no lubrication during their lifetime.

Typical applications include davit bearings, fairlead, sheave and pivot bearings, water tight door bushings, cargo ramp bushings and crane bearings.

[3] MEPC 58/INF.22 Use of seawater lubricated tube bearings to eliminate stern tube oil pollution from ships

Questions to Consider

How easy will it be to switch to EALs?
This mainly depends on your suppliers. If your company is already with a global lubricant supplier who has an EAL range, it will be relatively easy. If not, choosing a new supplier and negotiating the terms with him will require a bit more effort.

What will the cost implication of using EALs be?
Lubricants account for 20-30% to the running costs of most ships, so any factor that has the potential to add a premium to this is another challenge ship operators and managers must contend with in order to optimise the profitability of their ships.

One of the most comprehensive sources of information on the cost differential between traditional lubricants, sourced from cost data and retailers of marine lubricants and EALs, was provided via extensive market research performed by EPA prior to introducing the final 2013 VGP. This study found EALs to be on average 38% more expensive than mineral-based lubricants, but not necessarily more expensive than other synthetic lubricants.

Operating costs for using EALs are expected to increase modestly relative to conventional products, although there can be efficiency gains from longer life, e.g. reduced corrosive properties, enhanced water contamination performance.

Are other alternatives to EALs applicable and viable for our operation?
In the current market, the principal alternative would be seawater lubricated bearings and lubricant-free thermoplastic bearings.

What goals could I set to improve the company's environmental performance related to lubricant use?
Setting goals and targets strongly depends on your current environmental performance and other company-specific factors. Nonetheless, here are some example goals distinguished by whether you are trading in US waters or not.

Not trading in US waters:
- Conversion of each ship in the fleet to use EALs on all below waterline equipment (implemented at ship drydocking).
- Use of EALs on all deck equipment on two ships by the end of this coming year.
- Use of EAL's on all below and above waterline equipment on three further ships by the end of this coming year.

Trading in US Waters:
- Replacement of stern tube bearings with seawater lubricated bearings eliminating oil leakage.
- Use EALs on all above waterline equipment across the whole fleet by the end of the coming year.

How can I communicate the switch to EALs to my customers and stakeholders?

There is no definite answer to this question as the choice of communication channels will be specific to your company.

Consider which communication channels you are already using (e.g. environmental reports, your website, email communication with your clients) and how you could use them to transfer environmental information (e.g. announcement on your website, in your company newsletter, etc.).

Remember that this could make your ship offer more attractive to certain charterers.

3.6 Business Benefits

3.6.1 Reputational Risk Management

A lubricant spill is in essence an 'oil leakage'. The business impact of a spill should not be underestimated, particularly the financial cost of clean-up and the possible restrictions that may be placed upon the ship's tradability by charterers.

Internationally, authorities impose heavy fines for such pollution offences with the United States being particularly stringent.

With the cost of cleaning up the pollution, the impact upon your insurance premium, the loss of time due to suspension of operations, the human impact and the subsequent bad publicity, any significant oil leakage can amount to thousands of dollars and cause loss of business.

The use of bio-lubricants has been regarded as a mitigating factor by enforcement authorities in some cases of accidental leakage, resulting in lower penalties.

3.6.2 Demonstrating Environmental Leadership

The 2008 VGP encouraged the use of 'environmentally preferable lubricants' wherever possible. The 2013 VGP mandates it on all oil-to-sea interfaces. Therefore, today's encouragements are often tomorrow's requirements

The 2013 VGP now strongly encourages the use of EALs in all above deck equipment, so it might be wise to develop technical and operational EAL experience over the coming years in case the more widespread use of EALs across all above deck equipment becomes mandatory.

3.6.3 Lubricant Performance

EALs are synthetic lubricants. Synthetic lubricants are specifically designed in a laboratory to display certain characteristics. This is more variable in mineral oil lubricants. Therefore, they can offer better performance, longer fluid life and less machinery downtime.

NOTE: In order to get the value from synthetic lubricants, the correct operating conditions must be present.

3.6.4 Qualification For Environmental Class Notations

Several class notations as well as the Baltic Sea Position either recommend or require the use of biodegradable lubricants.

3.7 Measuring Environmental Performance

Determining your environmental performance is relatively straightforward. Lubricants leaked to sea have to be replaced by new lubricants, hence the amount of replaced lubricant less the operational usage represents the amount of leakage.

CHAPTER FOUR

CONTENTS

BUNKERING OPERATIONS

BUNKERING OPERATIONS

4.1 Introduction

Due to fluctuating bunker fuel prices and ever-increasing marine environmental protection awareness, the bunkering of ships, which was once a relatively low skill, low value activity, has evolved into a highly focused inter-ship/ship-to-shore operation in terms of regulatory compliance, quality and quantity assurance.

The principal drivers for regulation and governance around bunkering operations are the threat to the marine environment through the leakage of bunker fuels into the sea and the increased atmospheric pollution caused by out of specification bunker fuels.

4.2 Environmental Impact

4.2.1 Oil Spills During Bunkering

The International Tanker Owners Pollution Federation (ITOPF) has reported that a significant number of oil spills occur during the bunkering process. ITOPF maintains a database of oil spills from tankers, combination carriers, ore-bulk-oil carrier and barges. This contains information on accidental spillages since 1970.

For historical reasons, spills are generally categorised by size:

- Under seven tonnes;
- between 7-700 tonnes; and
- over 700 tonnes.

The majority of spills are small and fall within the first category: in total, 7,847 small oil spills occurred during 1974 and 2013, compared to 1,351 medium and 459 large oil spills. Of those small spills, 565 incidents - equivalent to 7.2% - took place during bunkering. Bunkering operations were responsible for 32 medium-sized spills and for one large oil spill. While oil spills occurring during discharge or loading of oil tankers still happened more frequently, these numbers demand that more attention is given to avoid oil spills during bunkering operations.[1]

4.2.2 Causes Of Oil Spills During Bunkering

Many of the bunker overflows and spillages that occur can be attributed to human error. Mistakes often happen when designated staff are distracted by other tasks and cannot devote their full attention to the bunkering procedure.

Some of the most frequently mentioned causes of oil spills during bunkering are:

- The failure to completely close a valve to a tank which had already completed bunkering.
- Exceeding the stipulated maximum loading rate.
- Non-adherence to the procedures for topping off tanks.
- Failure to regularly monitor the progression of loading.

The Box Out on the following page provides examples of oils spills that have occurred during bunkering operations.

[1] ITOPF (2013) Oil Tanker Spill Statistics 2013

> ### Examples Of Oil Spills During Bunkering
> 1. A 27,000 gross tonnage (GT) gas carrier was loading bunkers in Mexico. After fuelling had started, the bunker hose burst due to high pressure, spilling marine diesel over the ship and into the sea. When bunkering was eventually resumed, there was only a short interval before diesel oil began to gush from one of the tank vents, causing additional pollution. Investigation showed that the bunker pumping rate had been 582 metric tonnes (mt) per hour, which is far in excess of the safe bunkering rate. The owners of the facility detained the ship and demanded a guarantee of US$ 800,000 against the cost of the clean-up. Actual clean-up costs were estimated to be US$ 300,000.
> 2. A tanker was loading diesel oil as fuel in Genova. All tanks except the final tank were safely topped off at their intended ullage. The ordered amount would fit safely in the last tank, so the engineers stopped ullaging the tank. Unfortunately, the barge had onboard more fuel than had been ordered and decided to discharge it all to the tanker. The excess fuel overflowed the vent pipe on the port side and about 0.05m³ escaped to the sea.
> 3. In Rotterdam, a motorman was assigned to watch the filling tank of a tanker loading heavy fuel oil (HFO). The tank contained considerable 'mist' making the surface hard or impossible to see. The motorman was not provided with an ullaging tape and float, and was unable to measure the ullage. The tank overflowed via the ullage hatch and about 300 litres escaped from the tank to the sea.

4.3 International Regulation

Bunkering operations are governed under MARPOL Annexes I and VI as well as SOLAS Chapter VI and IX.

4.3.1 MARPOL Requirements

4.3.1.1 Oil Record Book

MARPOL Annex I governs the prevention of oil pollution. With regards to bunkering, it requires that every bunkering operation is recorded in the Oil Record Book (ORB) Part I. The place and time of bunkering as well as the type and quantity of fuel oil and the identity of tanks are to be reported.

4.3.1.2 Shipboard Oil Pollution Emergency Plan

Resolution MEPC.117(52)

In addition, MARPOL Annex I stipulates that every oil tanker of and above 150 GT and every other ship of and above 400 GT carry a Shipboard Oil Pollution Emergency Plan (SOPEP) onboard. The SOPEP conveys information from the owner to the Master on how to react in case of an oil spill. It lists what actions have to be taken under different scenarios and which people and organisations to contact in case of an oil spill.

4.3.1.3 Bunker Delivery Note

Resolution MEPC.117(52)

MARPOL Annex VI – although it regulates air pollution from ships - stipulates that information on the fuel oil quality is included in the Bunker Delivery Note (BDN).

4.3.2 SOLAS Requirements

4.3.2.1 Material Safety Data Sheet

Resolution MSC.239(83)

In addition, SOLAS Chapter VI Regulation 5.1 requires that a Material Safety Data Sheet (MSDS) be provided for oil products carried onboard ships. It is meant to assist the shipboard personnel in carrying out their duties under safe conditions.

Resolution MSC.286(86)

Prior to loading of oil products, information has to be provided on a number of factors, including:

- Hazards identification.
- First aid measures in case of exposure to oil leaking.
- Accidental release measures.
- Toxicological and environmental information.

For a full list of reporting requirements, please check resolution MSC.286(86) – Recommendations for Material Safety Data Sheets (MSDS) for MARPOL Annex I Oil Cargo and Oil Fuel.

4.3.2.2 International Safety Management Code

SOLAS Chapter IX entered into force in 1998 and made the International Safety Management (ISM) Code mandatory.

Resolution A.741(18), as amended by resolutions MSC.104(73), MSC.179(79), MSC.195(80), MSC.273(85), MSC.353(92)

The ISM Code requires a Safety Management System (SMS) to be established by the ship owner or any person responsible for the ship. A SMS refers to a structured and documented system that enables personnel to effectively implement the company's safety and environmental protection policy.

For certain key shipboard operations, including bunkering, the ISM Code also requires that procedures, plans and instructions, including checklists where appropriate, are put in place concerning the safety of the personnel, the ship and the protection of the environment. The various tasks must be defined and assigned to qualified personnel.

4.3.3 Bunkers Convention

The International Convention on Civil Liability for Bunker Oil Pollution Damage (Bunkers Convention) was adopted in March 2001 and entered into force in November 2008. Its aim is to make sure that persons who have been harmed by oil spills resulting from shipping operations are compensated in an adequate, prompt and effective way.

The Convention established that the ship owner is liable for all pollution damage caused by its bunker oil. Therefore, each registered owner of any ship of more than 1,000 GT and registered in a Party to the Convention must maintain insurance or other financial security to cover their liability for pollution damage. As a proof that insurance is in force, the State Party issues a Bunkers Convention Certificate that the ship must carry onboard.

The Bunkers Convention applies to damage caused on the territory, including the territorial sea, and in exclusive economic zones of States that are Party to the Convention.

Questions to Consider

How can I prepare for a potential accidental oil spill during bunkering?

You are required by law to keep a SOPEP. Furthermore, you need special SOPEP equipment. This equipment must be stowed in an easily accessible locker, clearly marked, and is to be brought on deck ready for immediate use, prior to all oil transfer operations.

Owners should ensure that the crew conduct regular bunker spill drills, that these drills are recorded and that any improvements which have been identified during the drill to the SOPEP or the contingency planning are considered and adopted as seen fit.

A list of items to be included in the SOPEP locker can be found in the document 'A Master's Guide To Using Fuel Oil Onboard Ships' by the Standard P&l Club and ABS.

What do I need to do in case of an accidental oil spill during bunkering?

In case of an accidental oil spill during bunkering, the procedures contained in the SOPEP should be followed. The SOPEP advises the Master how to react in case of an oil spill to prevent or at least mitigate negative effects on the environment.

You also need to report the oil spill. A list of people or organisation to be contacted should be included in the SOPEP.

Does the Bunkers Convention apply to my ships?

The Bunkers Convention applies to any ship over 1,000 GT. It includes floating production storage and off-loading units, floating storage units and floating production units as well as ships that carry bunker oil for the operation of generators or other equipment onboard.

If any of the above apply to your ships, then yes, the Bunkers Convention concerns you.

Who is liable under the Bunkers Convention for pollution damage?

The ship owner (including the registered owner, bareboat charterer, manager and operator) is liable under the Convention.

What is an acceptable form of security?

Security can be in the form of insurance policy or contract, a bank guarantee, letter of credit, etc. Most ships are insured with a Protection and Indemnity (P&I) Club, which issues a 'Blue Card' that represents coverages provided.

Under the Bunkers Convention, how much insurance coverage do I need?

The amount required is based on the Protocol of 1996 to the International Convention on the Limitation of Liability for Marine Claims, 1976.

Under Article 6(1)(b) of that Convention, the limit of liability is:

	Tonnage	SDR
Tonnage not exceeding	2,000	1,000,000 in full
AND for each ton from	2,000 - 30,000	400 per ton
AND for each ton from	30,001 - 70,000	300 per ton
AND for each ton from	70,001 and above	200 per ton

What are SDRs?

SDR stands for Special Drawing Right. The SDR is an international reserve asset, created by the International Monetary Fund in 1969, to supplement its member countries' official reserves. Its value is based on a basket of four key international currencies. SDRs can be exchanged for freely usable currencies and are a common unit used in international Conventions.

4.4 Regional Regulation

In addition to requirements by the International Maritime Organization (IMO), many States and some individual ports have their own regulatory regimes covering bunkering operations. It is therefore crucial to check the applicable requirements with the local agent and/or bulk prior to bunkering. Many companies incorporate the Bunkering Safety Checklist of the 'International Safety Guide for Oil Tankers & Terminals' (ISGOTT).

Many port authorities insist on ISGOTT procedures being implemented. More information about the ISGOTT Bunkering Safety Checklist can be found in the Box Out on the following page.

4.5 Going Beyond Compliance

Many of the bunker overflows and spillages can be attributed to human error. Mistakes often happen when designated staff are distracted by other tasks and cannot devote their full attention to the bunkering procedure.

Therefore, careful planning is key. Personnel involved in the bunkering operation onboard should have no other tasks and should remain at their workstations during topping-off.

For more information, please refer to the 'BIMCO & IBIA Bunkering Guide' available in Part Three supplied on the USB memory stick as well as on the BIMCO website.

For a comprehensive list of procedures applicable to oil tankers, we advise you to consult the Bunkering Safety Checklist of the 'International Safety Guide for Oil Tankers & Terminals' produced by ISGOTT.

The ISGOTT Safety Checklist

The ISGOTT Safety Checklist is primarily structured for loading bunkers from a barge, but it is also suitable for use when taking bunkers from a jetty or when loading bulk lubricating oil or gas oil from a road tanker. It is divided into four different sections, all of which have to be considered for ensuring the safety of operations. As responsibility and accountability for the safe conduct of bunkering operations is shared between the Masters of the vessel and the barge, all the statements have to be jointly checked.

1. Bunkers To Be Transferred

A joint agreement on the quantity and grades of bunkers to be transferred, together with agreed transfer rates and the maximum line back pressures.

2. Bunker Tanks To Be Loaded

An identification of the tanks to be loaded with the aim of ensuring that there is sufficient space to safely accommodate the bunkers to be transferred. Space is provided to record each tank's maximum filling capacity and the available volume.

3. Checks By Barge Prior To Berthing

- The barge has obtained the necessary permissions to go alongside the receiving vessel.
- The fenders have been checked, are in good order and there is no possibility of metal-to-metal contact.
- Adequate electrical insulating means are in place in the barge-to-ship connection.
- All bunker hoses are in good condition and are appropriate for the service intended.

4. Checks Prior To Transfer

- The barge is securely moored.
- There is a safe means of access between the ship and barge.
- Effective communications have been established between responsible officers.
- There is an effective watch onboard the barge and ship receiving bunkers.
- Fire hoses and fire-fighting equipment onboard the barge and ship are ready for immediate use.
- All scuppers are effectively plugged. Temporarily removed scupper plugs will be monitored at all times. Drip trays are in position on decks around connections and bunker tank vents.
- Initial line up has been checked and unused bunker connections are blanked and fully bolted.
- The transfer hose is properly rigged and fully bolted and secured to manifolds on ship and barge.
- Overboard valves connected to the cargo system, engine room bilges and bunker lines are closed and sealed.
- All cargo and bunker tank hatch lids are closed.
- Bunker tank contents will be monitored at regular intervals.
- There is a supply of oil spill clean-up material readily available for immediate use.
- The main radio transmitter aerials are earthed and radars are switched off.
- Fixed VHF/UHF transceivers and AIS equipment are on the correct power mode or switched off.
- Smoking rooms have been identified and smoking restrictions are being observed. Naked light regulations are being observed.
- All external doors and ports in the accommodation are closed.
- Material Safety Data Sheets (MSDS) for the bunker transfer have been exchanged where requested.
- The hazards associated with toxic substances in the bunkers being handled have been identified and understood.

4.6 Business Benefits

Many bunker spills are noticeably small in quantity. In comparison to the quantity spilled, the cost of preventing pollution and cleaning up after a pollution incident may appear disproportionate. Fines of US$ 40,000 or more are not uncommon, but much higher fines can be imposed at the discretion of port authorities.

> ### Fines For Spilling Oil During Bunkering
> In 2014, a German ship owner was fined NZ$ 30,000 for spilling 1,000 litres of HFO during bunkering into a New Zealand harbour. In his sentence, the judge took into account that the ship owner had already paid over NZ$ 17,000 in clean-up costs and had no prior relevant convictions. The maximum penalty for this type of offence would have been NZ$ 600,000.

With the entry into force of the Bunkers Convention in 2008 and the potential for even more stringent action by States that are not Party to the Convention, ship owners and operators will face even stricter rules for liability compensation.

In order to avoid potentially huge compensation claims, it makes good business sense for ship owners, operators and the crew to proceed with caution when conducting bunkering operations and ensure they are properly supervised and conducted carefully, until full conclusion.

4.7 Measuring Environmental Performance

Ship owners and operators should track and trend frequency and size of bunker spills within their fleet and trend the identified root causes and implement improvement plans as necessary.

CHAPTER FIVE

CONTENTS

TANK CLEANING & OPERATIONAL DISCHARGE FROM OIL TANKERS

TANK CLEANING & OPERATIONAL DISCHARGE FROM OIL TANKERS

5.1 Introduction

When oil is stored in cargo tanks, sludge may form and accumulate within the tank. Sludge that accumulates may restrict or block both the suction pipe lines and drain holes in the tank preventing the final draining of the oil tanks. It is therefore important to manage and remove cargo and sludge residue build-up.

Oil tankers may carry different grades of oil in the same cargo tanks on different voyages, which makes residue management important to avoid cross contamination and loss of carriage capability of the ship.

There are different ways of cleaning cargo oil tanks, one of which is Crude Oil Washing (COW). COW is a system whereby oil cargo is sprayed with pressure on tank walls and surfaces. This removes the sediments sticking to the tank and converts it into useful cargo which can be pumped out to the shore tanks.

Other tank washing methods are generally less complex than COW operations, but equally important both in terms of safety and environmental protection. In order to complete a tank cleaning operation, it is important to strip and drain all the involved tanks, pumps and the piping system by blowing or purging the entire cargo system with compressed air or inert gas to the shore. Alternatively, the remaining cargo that cannot be easily discharged from the cargo system can be drained or purged into a single tank (i.e. a slop tank) which can then be discharged and stripped to shore.

5.2 Environmental Impact

Accidental operational discharges and spills of oil from ships, especially tankers, is the most obvious and visible cause of oil pollution of the marine environment.

Ships cause about a third of marine oil pollution when washing out their tanks or illegally dumping their bilge water (see Chapter 2 on Oily Bilge Water). For example, washing out the tanks with seawater and discharging it overboard could mean losing as much as 200 tonnes of oil on a large tanker if the process is not managed correctly and within the law.

COW is a method of reducing the impact and protecting the marine environment from the oil pollution caused by washing out the cargo tanks of crude oil tankers. Another way is to properly carry out stripping and tank cleaning operations.

International Regulation

Crude Oil Washing

MARPOL Annex I requires every crude oil tanker of 20,000 deadweight tonnage (DWT) and above, delivered after 1 June 1982 to be fitted with a cargo tank cleaning system using COW. Existing tankers over 40,000 DWT must be fitted either with segregated ballast tanks or with COW systems.

COW installation and arrangements must comply with at least all of the provisions of the Specifications for the Design, Operation and Control of Crude Oil Washing Systems. These provisions can be found in resolution A.446(XI), as amended by resolutions A.497(XII) and A.897(21).

Every oil tanker operating with COW systems must have an Operations and Equipment Manual (COW Manual) that is approved by the Administration. The COW Manual details the system and equipment and specifies operational procedures. It must conform with the requirements set out in resolution A.446(XI), as amended by resolutions A.497(XII) and A.897(21). The standard format for the COW Manual can be found in resolution MEPC.3(XII), as amended by resolution MEPC.81(43).

If an alteration is made that affects the COW system, the Manual must be revised accordingly.

With respect to the ballasting of cargo tanks, ballast water may only be put into cargo tanks which have been crude oil washed.

5.3.2

Operational Discharge Of Oil And Oily Mixtures From Cargo Areas

MARPOL Annex I governs discharges of oil or oily mixtures from the cargo area of an oil tanker. Such oily mixtures include washing water, bilge, and ballast water containing cargo oil.

These regulations vary according to whether the tanker is in or outside a 'Special Area' (see Section 5.3.2.2 for further information).

Discharge Criteria

The regulatory requirements for oil tankers are relatively straightforward: no discharge of oil or oily mixtures from the cargo areas of an oil tanker is allowed unless all of the following criteria are met:

- The tanker is not within a Special Area;
- the tanker is more than 50 nautical miles (nm) from the nearest land;
- the tanker is proceeding *en route*;
- the instantaneous rate of discharge of oil content does not exceed 30 l/nm;
- the total quantity of oil discharged into the sea does not exceed 1/30,000 of the total quantity of the particular cargo of which the residue formed a part (for tankers delivered after 31 December 1979); and
- for oil tankers of 150 gross tonnage (GT) and above: the tanker has in operation an oil discharge monitoring and control system and a slop tank arrangement.

These provisions do not apply to the discharge of clean or segregated ballast.

Oil or oily mixture from the cargo area of an oil tanker that cannot be discharged into the sea in compliance with the provisions in MARPOL Annex I has to be kept onboard and discharged to shore-based reception facilities.

To this end, a standard discharge connection has to be fitted.

5.3.2.2
Resolution MEPC.117(52)

Regulatory Requirements In Special Areas

MARPOL Annex I defines certain sea areas as Special Areas in which, for technical reasons relating to their oceanographical and ecological condition and to their sea traffic, the adoption of special mandatory methods for the prevention of sea pollution is required. These Special Areas are provided with a higher level of protection than other sea areas.

Resolution MEPC.117(52)
Resolution MEPC.154(55)

The sea areas that currently fall under this category are:

- Mediterranean Sea.
- Baltic Sea.
- Black Sea.
- Red Sea.
- Gulfs area.[1]

- Gulf of Aden.
- Antarctic area.
- North West European Waters.
- Oman area of the Arabian Sea.
- Southern South African Waters.

The Red Sea, Gulf of Aden and Oman area of the Arabian Sea have been designated as Special Areas, but at the time of writing *(December 2014)* have not yet taken effect. This is because not enough of the MARPOL Parties whose coastlines border these Special Areas have notified the International Maritime Organization (IMO) on the existence of adequate reception facilities.

Resolution MEPC.117(52)

In Special Areas, any discharge of oil or oily mixture from the cargo area of an oil tanker is prohibited, except segregated or clean ballast water.

5.3.3
Resolution MEPC.117(52)

Slop Tank Arrangements

Slop tanks are tanks specifically designated for the collection of tank drainings, tank washings and other oily mixtures.

Oil tankers of 150 GT and above must be provided with slop tank arrangements. Oil tankers of 70,000 DWT and above must be fitted with at least two slop tanks. Furthermore, adequate means must be provided for cleaning the cargo tanks and transferring the dirty ballast residue and tank washings from the cargo tanks into a slop tank.

The arrangements of the slop tanks must have a capacity necessary to retain the slop generated by tank washings, oil residues and dirty ballast residues. The total capacity of the slop tank or tanks must not be less than 3% of the oil-carrying capacity of the ship. However, under certain circumstances, the Administration may accept a reduced capacity.

These circumstances are listed in resolution MEPC.117(52), Regulation 29.

---

[1] The Gulfs area means the sea area located north-west of the rhumb line between Ras al Hadd and Ras al Fasteh.

Resolution MEPC.117(52)

Equipment

Discharge Monitoring And Control Systems

Oil tankers of 150 GT and above must be equipped with an oil discharge monitoring and control system that is approved by the Administration. The system must have a recording device to provide a continuous record of the discharge. It must be in operation when there is any discharge of effluent into the sea and must ensure that the discharge stops automatically when the permitted discharge rate is exceeded.

The discharge monitoring and control system must comply with certain IMO guidelines. The applicable guideline depends on the building date of the oil tanker:

Building Date	Relevant Guideline
Before 2 October 1986	Resolution A.393(X)
On or after 2 October 1986	Resolution A.586(14)
On or after 1 January 2005	Resolution MEPC.108(49), as amended by resolution MEPC.240(65)

If the system fails, the discharge must be stopped. A manually operated alternative can then be used but the system must be repaired as soon as possible.

Resolution MEPC.117(52)

Oil/Water Interface Detector

Besides the discharge monitoring and control system, every oil tanker of 150 GT and above must be equipped with an oil/water interface detector. The detector must comply with the specifications of resolution MEPC.5(XIII).

Resolution MEPC.117(52)

Surveys And Certification

Every oil tanker of 150 GT and above must carry an International Oil Pollution Prevention (IOPP) Certificate onboard for inspection by port or flag States. The Certificate can last for up to five years.

In order to be granted an IOPP Certificate, the ship has to pass the following surveys:

- An initial survey, before the ship is put into service, or before an IOPP Certificate is issued for the first time.
- A renewal survey, before the end of every period of five years following the issue of an IOPP Certificate in respect of the ship.
- A minimum of one intermediate survey during the period of validity of the IOPP Certificate.
- An annual survey.
- An additional survey whenever any important repairs or renewals are made.

These surveys are undertaken to ensure that the structure, equipment, systems, fittings, arrangements and material fully comply with the applicable requirements of MARPOL Annex I.

Resolution MEPC.117(52)

5.3.6 Monitoring And Reporting

Every oil tanker of 150 GT and above must carry an Oil Record Book (ORB) Part II onboard.

Whereas the ORB Part I only concerns machinery space operations on all ships (considered in Chapter 2 on 'Oily Bilge Water'), Part II refers to cargo/ballast operations on oil tankers.

When any of the following cargo/ballast operations takes places, entries must be made in the ORB Part II:

- Loading of oil cargo;
- unloading of oil cargo;
- internal transfer of oil cargo during voyage;
- ballasting of cargo tanks and dedicated clean ballast tanks;
- cleaning of cargo tanks including COW;
- discharge of ballast except from segregated ballast tanks;
- discharge of water from slop tanks;
- closing of all applicable valves or similar devices after slop tank discharge operations;
- closing of valves necessary for isolation of dedicated clean ballast tanks from cargo and stripping lines after slop tank discharge operations; and
- disposal of residues.

The ORB Part II must be available at all times for examination by any port State when within the jurisdiction of that State. It must be preserved for three years from the date of the last entry.

A form of the ORB Part II is contained in Appendix III to resolution MEPC.117(52). It is provided in Part Three - The Maritime Environmental & Efficiency Templates on the USB memory stick.

5.4 Regional Regulation

Ports impose different requirements for tank cleaning, therefore ship owners and operators are urged to check which requirements apply prior to calling the port and performing tank cleaning.

5.5 Going Beyond Compliance

Going beyond regulatory compliance is sometimes not only a matter of exceeding the standards set by the regulations but also ensuring that simple and effective, easily understandable and executable processes and procedures are in place to aid compliance with regulations and thus reduce the possibility of non-compliance.

Such processes and procedures could take the form of the following:

Before starting the operation:

- Confirm crew are properly trained, experienced and competent.
- Confirm all pre-arrival checks are performed.
- Discuss the complete operation with ship and shore staff.
- Establish a communication channel between ship and shore facility.
- Discuss signals and emergency signs to stop the operation with shore and ship staff.
- Confirm that the inert gas system is working correctly and that the oxygen concentration is less than 5%.
- Check that the fixed oxygen analyser is working properly and is calibrated.
- Make portable oxygen analysers available and check they are working properly.
- Take the oxygen reading in swash bulkhead tanks from both sides.
- Confirm that the concentration of oxygen in the tank is below 8% by volume.
- Check all tanks for positive inert gas pressure.
- Assign duties to all responsible ship staff. One person should be responsible for checking the leakage in the pipe line system as soon as the operation starts.
- Check all the relevant equipment is working properly.
- Check and set the line and valves for ship to shore operation.

When the operation is under process:

- Check the inert gas values frequently, i.e. tank pressure and oxygen value.
- If COW operation, this must be done in the designated tanks as per the plan including the washing cycle.
- Make sure a responsible person is always present on deck.
- Check all deck lines and valves frequently for any leakages.
- Check parameters and running condition of all the machineries involved in the operation frequently.
- If COW operation, raise all ullage gauge floats for the tanks which are being washed.
- Make sure that trim is sufficient to assist in stripping and if COW, in the bottom washing of tanks.
- If COW operation, monitor the level of holding tanks for COW supply continuously to avoid overflow.

When the operation is finished:

- If COW operation, drain the tank wash line off crude oil.
- Shut all the valves in the line used for the operation.
- If COW operation, stop and drain all the machines involved in the operation.
- Drain all the cargo pumps after the operation is finished.

Stop the operation immediately if you suspect any kind of trouble such as failure of the inert gas system, increase of oxygen content or pressure drop in the cargo tank.

5.6 Business Benefits

Besides protecting the marine environment from oil pollution, COW and properly carried out stripping and tank cleaning also reduce the amount of retained cargo and thus increase cargo out-turn.

In addition, COW and properly carried out stripping and tank cleaning can:

- Reduce deadfreight as less oil-water slops are retained onboard.
- Reduce time and cost of tank cleaning.
- Reduce sludge build-up in cargo tanks.
- Reduce gas freeing time.
- Reduce tank corrosion due to water washing.
- Reduce bunker usage and emissions.
- Reduce need for tank coating maintenance.
- Avoid losses (time and money) in terms of tanks found unsuitable for next cargo by surveyors.
- Avoid vetting notations related to MARPOL Annex I compliance.

Avoiding operational discharges of oil from tankers also has direct and indirect financial benefits in that the ship owner avoids fines, other penalties as well as reputational damage through negative press and public shaming.

5.7 Measuring Environmental Performance

Properly carried out tank washing operations mean that the amount of tank cleaning slop disposed to shore-based reception facilities is reduced. This is recorded in the ORB.

CHAPTER SIX

CONTENTS

GARBAGE

GARBAGE

6.1 Introduction

Large quantities of waste and litter collect in the oceans from both land-based activities and maritime activities.

For the purpose of this Chapter, the term 'garbage' when used to refer to waste generated by the maritime industry, includes food wastes, domestic and operational wastes, all plastics, cargo residues, cooking oil, fishing gear, and animal carcasses.

6.2 Environmental Impact

Garbage from ships and other sources can be immensely damaging to marine life and ecosystems.

While many items can be degraded whilst in transit in the oceans, the process of degradation can take months or years. Some example degradation lengths are provided below.

Time taken for objects to dissolve at sea:

- Cotton cloth   1-5 months
- Rope   3-14 months
- Woollen cloth   1 year
- Painted wood   13 years
- Tin can   100 years
- Aluminium can   200-500 years
- Plastic bottle   450 years

The United Nations Environment Program estimates that every km² of ocean contains approximately 18,000 pieces of floating plastic. Every year, this plastic causes the deaths of up to one million seabirds, 100,000 marine mammals and countless fish.[1]

Larger species such as turtles, whales, seals and sea lions can be trapped in or get entangled by plastic items which may cause death by drowning, suffocation and/or strangulation.

Marine animals digesting plastic could even become dangerous for humans through biomagnification, i.e. higher-level predators (e.g. fish, birds and marine mammals) build up greater and more dangerous amounts of toxic materials than animals lower on the food chain. At some point, humans may then eat animals containing a significant concentration of toxins stemming from plastics or other waste materials.

Another danger stems from 'ghost fishing': fishing gear lost or left in the ocean can keep on trapping fish and crustaceans. Nets lost in calm waters may continue to 'fish' for decades and purposelessly kill off fish and crustaceans.

[1] UNEP (2006) Ecosystems and Biodiversity in Deep Waters and High Seas

> **The Marine Litter Express:**
> **The Incredible Journey Of The Rubber Ducks**
> Waste which enters the ocean can turn up anywhere in the world. In 1992 a
> container ship in the Pacific Ocean lost 30,000 rubber ducks off the coast of
> China. These ducks first travelled with the dominant currents in the direction of
> Australia, but 15 years later they turned up on the shores of the UK.
>
> An interesting story that illustrates perfectly how ship-source marine litter is a
> global problem.

6.2.1 Operational Impact

Marine litter can present numerous different risks for ships, a principal concern for ship
operation is the entanglement of nets, ropes and lines in equipment and ship structures.

Examples of the potential risks include:

- Fouling and entanglement of a ship's propeller and thruster, which can limit the
  ability to manoeuvre.
- Benthic and subsurface debris can foul anchors and equipment deployed from
  ships.
- Collisions with marine litter can damage a ship's propeller shaft seal.
- Clogging of seabays.
- Incidents may require divers to clear the debris and depending on the sea state,
  working in close proximity to the ship's hull may be highly risky.

The cost of emergency rescues to ships stricken by marine litter can be substantial and
most operations are commonly a result of entangled or fouled propellers.

6.3 International Regulation

Regulations for the prevention of pollution by garbage from ships are governed by
MARPOL Annex V which aims to eliminate and reduce the amount of garbage released
into the sea from ships.

MARPOL Annex V originally entered into force in December 1988, but underwent a
major review from 2006 to 2010. The revised Annex V was adopted in July 2011 and
entered into force on 1 January 2013. The revised guidelines for the implementation of
MARPOL Annex V were adopted in March 2012 by resolution MEPC.219(63).

Resolution MEPC.201(62)

Under MARPOL Annex V, the term garbage covers:

- Food wastes (excluding fresh fish);
- domestic wastes: means all types of wastes not covered by other MARPOL
  Annexes that are generated in the accommodation spaces onboard the ship, e.g.
  paper products, rags, glass, metal, bottles, crockery, etc. Domestic waste does not
  include grey water;
- operational wastes: means all solid wastes (incl. slurries) not covered by other
  MARPOL Annexes that are collected onboard during normal maintenance or
  operations of a ship, or used for cargo stowage and handling. Also include cleaning
  agents and additives contained in cargo hold and external washwater, but excludes
  grey water, bilge water, or other similar discharges essential to the operation of a ship;

Resolution MEPC.201(62)

- all plastics;
- cargo residues;
- incinerator ashes;
- cooking oil;
- fishing gear; and
- animal carcasses

…that are generated during the normal operation of the ship and are liable to be disposed of continuously or periodically.

NOTE: The Basel Convention on the Control of Transboundary Movements of Hazardous Wastes and their Disposal, which was adopted in 1989 and entered into force in 1992, does not regulate garbage and waste from ships. It regulates the import/export of hazardous and other wastes in terms of cargo only. This Chapter does not deal with the Basel Convention.

6.3.1 General Prohibition Of Discharges

Resolution MEPC.201(62)

Under the revised MARPOL Annex V, virtually all discharges of waste into the sea are prohibited. While there are certain exceptions to this rule (see Sections 6.3.2 to 6.3.5), the discharge of the following types of garbage is completely prohibited:

- Plastics.
- Domestic wastes.
- Cooking oil.
- Incinerator ashes.
- Operational wastes (except for cleaning agents and additives).
- Fishing gear.

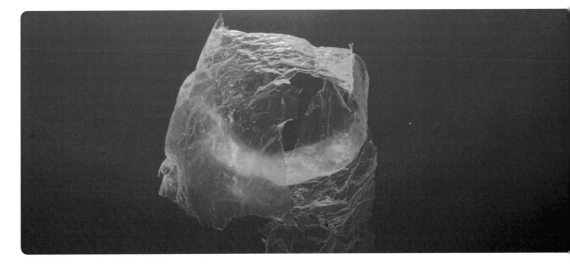

6.3.2 Exceptions To The No Discharge Rule

Resolution MEPC.201(62)

Depending on the type of garbage and the area in which the ship operates, there are certain exceptions to the general no discharge rule.

More specifically, a distinction is made between operations in and outside Special Areas (see Sections 6.3.3 and 6.3.4 for more information on Special Areas), as well as operations within 500 metres of offshore platforms.

The table on the following page summarises the garbage discharge requirements both outside and within Special Areas and from offshore platforms.

Type Of Garbage	Ships Outside Special Areas	Ships Within Special Areas	Offshore Platforms And All ships Within 500m Of Such Platforms
Food waste comminuted or ground[2]	Discharge permitted ≥3 nm from the nearest land and *en route*	Discharge permitted ≥12 nm from the nearest land and *en route* [3]	Discharge permitted ≥12 nm from the nearest land
Food waste NOT comminuted or ground	Discharge permitted ≥12 nm from the nearest land and *en route*	Discharge prohibited	Discharge prohibited
Cargo residues[4] NOT contained in washwater	Discharge permitted ≥12 nm from the nearest land and *en route*	Discharge prohibited	Discharge prohibited
Cargo residues[4] contained in washwater	Discharge permitted ≥12 nm from the nearest land and *en route*	Discharge only permitted in specific circumstances[5] and ≥12 nm from the nearest land and *en route*	Discharge prohibited
Cleaning agents and additives[4] contained in deck and external surfaces washwater	Discharge permitted	Discharge only permitted in specific circumstances[5] and ≥12 nm from the nearest land and *en route*	Discharge prohibited
Cleaning agents and additives[4] contained in cargo hold washwater	Discharge permitted	Discharge permitted	Discharge prohibited
Carcasses of animals carried onboard as cargo and which died during the voyage	Discharge permitted as far from the nearest land as possible and *en route*	Discharge prohibited	Discharge prohibited
All other garbage incl. plastics, domestic wastes, cooking oil, incinerator ashes, operational wastes and fishing gear	Discharge prohibited	Discharge prohibited	Discharge prohibited
Mixed garbage	When garbage is mixed with or contaminated by other substances prohibited from discharge or having different discharge requirements, the more stringent requirements shall apply.		

The discharge criteria are explained further in Sections 6.3.3 to 6.3.5.

6.3.3 Discharge Of Garbage Outside Special Areas

When ships are outside one of the MARPOL Annex V Special Areas they are permitted to discharge (according to the table provided in Section 6.3.2) when *en route* and at certain distances from land (although as far as possible from land is preferable).

The permitted discharges include:

- Food waste that has been comminuted or ground (i.e. able to pass through a screen with holes of no larger than 25 mm) when ≥3 nautical miles (nm) from the nearest land.
- Discharge of food wastes not ground or comminuted ≥12 nm from the nearest land.
- Cargo residues including hold washwater residues which cannot be unloaded using commonly available means and which are not harmful to the marine environment ≥12 nm from the nearest land.
- Discharge of animal carcasses at the maximum depth of water ≥100 nm from the nearest land and in accordance with IMO guidelines.
- If animal carcasses are discharged into the sea, they must be split or otherwise treated so that they sink immediately.

---

[2] Comminuted or ground food wastes must be able to pass through a screen with mesh no larger than 25 mm.
[3] The discharge of introduced avian products in the Antarctic area is not permitted unless incinerated, autoclaved or otherwise treated to be made sterile.
[4] These substances must not be harmful to the marine environment.
[5] According to Regulation 6.1.2 of MARPOL Annex V, the discharge shall only be allowed if: (a) both the port of departure and the next port of destination are within the Special Area and the ship will not transit outside the Special Area between these ports (Regulation 6.1.2.2); and (b) if no adequate reception facilities are available at those ports (Regulation 6.1.2.3).

Resolution MEPC.201(62)

- Discharge of cleaning agents which are not harmful to the marine environment (contained in cargo hold, deck and external surfaces washwater). There is no minimum distance for cleaning agents declared not to be harmful to the marine environment. This should be clear from the associated Material Safety Data Sheet (MSDS)/product information (declared as not HME[6] from supplier).

Resolution MEPC.219(63),
as amended by resolution
MEPC.239(65)

The definition of non-harmful in this respect requires that the cargo carried is not declared as being harmful to the marine environment under the criteria set out in MARPOL Annex III and that the cleaning material does not contain any carcinogenic, mutagenic or reprotoxic components.

NOTE: Where mixed garbage exists, the more stringent disposal criteria will always apply regardless of whether or not a ship is in a Special Area.

Resolution MEPC.201(62)

6.3.4 Special Areas And Garbage Disposal Regulations

Special Areas, as defined under MARPOL Annex V, are areas which have particular problems because of heavy maritime traffic or low water exchange caused by the land-locked nature of the sea concerned.

The following sea areas currently fall under this category:

- Mediterranean Sea.
- Baltic Sea Area.
- Black Sea Area.
- Red Sea Area.
- Gulfs Area.[7]
- North Sea.
- Wider Caribbean Region.
- Antarctic Area.

NOTE: Due to a lack of adequate shore reception facilities in the Black Sea and Red Sea, the Special Area requirements for these areas have not yet taken effect.

Given that Special Areas benefit from a higher level of environmental protection, most discharges of garbage are prohibited. However, the following is allowed:

- Discharge of comminuted or ground food waste only if ≥12 nm from the nearest land, if the ship is *en route* and if food waste can pass through a screen with openings no greater than 25mm.

NOTE: in the Antarctic Special Area the discharge of avian (bird) products including poultry is not permitted unless made sterile beforehand.

- If the ship is not transiting outside the Special Area between ports and no adequate reception facilities are available at those ports, discharge of cargo residues contained in washwater, cleaning agents and additives contained in cargo hold wash may occur ≥12 nm from the nearest land as long as the substances are not harmful to the marine environment.

---

[6] HME = cargoes declared as harmful to the marine environment
[7] The 'Gulfs area' means the sea area located north west of the rhumb line between Ras al Hadd (22°30'N, 59°48'E) and Ras al Fasteh (25°04'N, 61°25'E).

Resolution MEPC.201(62)

- Discharge of cleaning agents which are not harmful to the marine environment (contained in deck and external surfaces washwater). No distance from land or nearest ice shelf is specified.

NOTE: Where mixed garbage exists, the more stringent disposal criteria will always apply regardless of whether a ship is in a Special Area or not.

6.3.5 Discharges From Offshore Platforms And All Ships Within 500m Of Such Platforms

Resolution MEPC.201(62)

Most discharges of garbage from fixed or floating platforms and from any ship alongside or within 500 metres of these platforms are prohibited. The only exception are comminuted or ground food wastes which may be discharged if further than 12 nm away from the nearest land.

6.3.6 When Garbage Does Not Meet Discharge Criteria

Garbage that cannot be discharged into the sea has to be either kept onboard and discharged to shore-based reception facilities or in certain circumstance may be processed onboard, e.g. incinerated (see Section 6.3.7).

6.3.7 Garbage Processing

Resolution MEPC.219(63), as amended by resolution MEPC.239(65)

To reduce the space required for storing garbage and/or make it easier to discharge garbage at port reception facilities, certain garbage can be processed onboard the ship by means of compactors, incinerators, comminuters and other devices for garbage processing.

6.3.7.1 *Shipboard Incineration*

Shipboard incineration is regulated through MARPOL Annex VI.

According to MARPOL Annex VI, certain materials may not be incinerated at all. Furthermore, shipboard incinerators installed after 1 January 2000 must meet specific air pollution criteria and be type-approved taking into consideration the specifications for shipboard incinerators which are contained in resolution MEPC.244(66).

Permitted waste for a shipboard incinerator:

- Plastic, cardboard, wood.
- Rubber, cloth, oily rags, lube oil filters.
- Diesel engine scavenge scraping.
- Paint scraping.
- Food waste, etc.
- Sludge oil, waste lubrication oil.
- Hospital waste, female hygienic binds.
- Destruction of contaminated water.

Resolution MEPC.176(58)

Not permitted waste for shipboard incineration:

- MARPOL Annex I, II and III cargo residues and related contaminated packing materials.
- Polychlorinated biphenyls.
- Garbage contaminated with more than traces of heavy metals.[8]
- Refined petroleum products containing halogen compounds.
- Exhaust gas cleaning system (EGCS) residues.

Waste that is deemed unsuitable to incinerate includes: drink and food cans, plates, flatware, serving spoons/tray, hardware (nuts and bolts), structural pieces, wire rope, chains etc., flammable materials such as bottles or cans containing flammable liquids or gasses and aerosol cans. These products should be recycled instead.

---

[8] The following materials have a density placing them in the category of heavy metal- Mercury, Lead, Nickel, Vanadium, and Zinc.

Resolution MEPC.176(58)

Resolution MEPC.219(63), as amended by resolution MEPC.239(65)

The incineration of sewage sludge and sludge oil, generated during the normal operation of the ship, is allowed in main or auxiliary power plants or boilers under Annex VI, but incineration by such methods is banned in ports, harbours and estuaries.

As a general rule, shipboard incineration should not be undertaken when the ship is in port or at an offshore terminal and always has to comply with local and national legislation.

6.3.8 Port Reception Facilities

Resolution MEPC.201(62)

It is the duty of each signatory Party to MARPOL Annex V to ensure that adequate facilities for the reception of garbage are provided in ports.

In order to disseminate information on the availability of reception facilities and make it easier to report inadequacies of these facilities, an Internet-based Port Reception Facility Database was developed. This database is hosted and updated by the International Maritime Organization (IMO) and provides data on facilities for the reception of all categories of ship-generated waste.

For logistical reasons, some providers of port reception facilities require the ship to notify in advance if it intends to use the facility. To facilitate communication and record keeping, a standard Advance Notification Form as well as a standard Waste Delivery Notification have been developed (see MEPC.1/Circ.834).

6.3.9 Monitoring And Reporting Requirements
6.3.9.1 Garbage Record Book

Resolution MEPC.201(62)

To make it easier to check that the regulatory requirements are adhered to, a Garbage Record Book has to be kept onboard the following ships:

- All ships of and above 400 gross tonnage (GT).
- Ships certified to carry 15 persons or more.

All disposal and incineration operations have to be recorded in the Garbage Record Book. For each of these operations, the date, time, position of ship, description of garbage and the estimated amount incinerated or discharged must be logged and signed. The Garbage Record Book must be kept for a period of two years after the date of the last entry.

An appendix to MARPOL Annex V gives a standard form for the Garbage Record Book. A form for the Garbage Record Book is provided in Part Three - The Maritime Environmental & Efficiency Templates provided on the USB memory stick that accompanies this Guide.

Resolution MEPC.201(62)

6.3.9.2 Garbage Management Plan

In addition to keeping a Garbage Record Book, all ships of and above 100 GT, all ships certified to carry 15 persons or more and fixed and floating platforms must carry and implement a Garbage Management Plan. The Garbage Management Plan outlines the written procedures for collecting, storing, processing and disposing of garbage, including the use of equipment onboard.

Please refer to the IMO 2012 Guidelines for the Development of Garbage Management Plans which are contained in resolution MEPC.220(63).

Resolution MEPC.201(62)

6.3.9.3 Placards

Every ship of 12 metres in length or more and fixed or floating platforms are to display placards notifying crew and passengers of the discharge requirements.

The placards shall be written in the working language of the ship's crew and, for ships engaged in voyages to ports or offshore terminals under the jurisdiction of other Parties to the Convention, shall also be in English, French or Spanish.

6.3.10 Dumping Of Waste At Sea

MARPOL Annex V does only cover operational discharges from ships (waste generated onboard the ship while the ship is operating). However, marine pollution also stems from the deliberate dumping of waste from ships, e.g. sediments from dredging.

While the consequence from operational discharges and dumping may not be that different (marine pollution), the intention is completely different: dumping refers to waste carried to be deliberately dumped at sea. This can include waste generated on land. Dumping is therefore neither operational nor accidental, but intentional.

Dumping is governed internationally by the London Convention on Dumping of Wastes at Sea, 1972 revised by the Protocol of 1996 (London Protocol).

NOTE: The Basel Convention considers the transboundary movement of hazardous and other wastes only.

Under the Protocol, all dumping is prohibited, except for possibly acceptable wastes on the so-called 'reverse list'. This list includes the following:

- Dredged material.
- Sewage sludge.
- Fish wastes.
- Ships and platforms.
- Inert, inorganic geological material (e.g. mining wastes).
- Organic material of natural origin.
- Bulky items primarily comprising iron, steel and concrete.
- Carbon dioxide streams from carbon dioxide capture processes for sequestration.

'Generic Guidelines' and comprehensive 'Specific Guidelines' have been developed for all wastes included in the 'reverse list'. These guidelines provide step-by-step procedures to evaluate wastes being considered for sea disposal, including waste-prevention audits, assessment of alternatives, waste characterisation, and assessment of potential adverse environmental effects of dumping, disposal site selection, monitoring and licensing procedures.

Questions to Consider

Do I need to know how much garbage is generated onboard my ship(s)?
Yes. MARPOL Annex V requires that the amount of garbage is estimated each time garbage is discharged into the sea, to a reception facility, accidentally discharged, lost at sea or incinerated. The estimated amount of garbage (m³) must then be noted in the Garbage Record Book.

Do I need to have a policy with regard to the disposal of garbage?
Yes, all companies are required to have a Garbage Management Plan in place. The plan should be signed by all the ship's staff responsible for shipboard handling and discharge of garbage to acknowledge that they have read and understood it.

How often do I need to revise my Garbage Management Plan?
There is no general rule on how often you need to revise your Garbage Management Plan. However, you need to make sure that it is up-to-date with current regulatory requirements.

What signage and information about the Garbage Management Plan is there around the ship?
Every ship of 12 metres in length or more and fixed or floating platforms must display placards notifying crew and passengers of the MARPOL Annex V requirements.

In addition you could display information about your company specific requirements. Make sure the information is provided in the language(s) of the crew. To make recycling and waste disposal easier, your waste bins should be clearly marked and possibly colour-coded.

How can I make sure the crew and shore-based staff are informed about regulatory requirements?
Crew: You can organise meetings and training sessions. Routine drills conducted onboard will ensure that the ship's staff is familiar with garbage management procedures and with the use of the equipment onboard. You could even think about conducting tests. Positive incentives could be provided for good test results. Make sure to introduce new crew to the Garbage Management Plans before they start their duties onboard.

Shore-based staff: Inform your staff about the existence of the Garbage Management Plan, summarising its main requirements. Consider keeping an electronic version that can be accessed by everyone and communicate where it can be found. When communicating your plans, make sure that you only provide information that is relevant to shore-based staff to avoid an overload of information.

How do I make sure the Garbage Management Plan is implemented?
In the first place, you need to make sure the crew and other personnel onboard the ship are sufficiently informed to implement the plan. Regularly reviewing the entries in your Garbage Record Book will help you understand whether your plans are being implemented or not. It allows you to review operations onboard and adjust or change your Garbage Management Plan if necessary.

Furthermore, your company should perform regular checks or audits. These can be conducted either by company staff or – if you want an independent opinion – by external auditors.

6.4 Regional Regulation

6.4.1 European Union

Directive 2000/59/EC

In 2000, the European Community adopted Directive 2000/59/EC on port reception facilities, with the aim of substantially reducing discharges of ship generated waste and cargo residues into the sea. This is to be achieved by improving the availability and use of port reception facilities.

According to the Directive, EU Member States have to ensure the availability of adequate reception facilities and ports must develop and implement a waste reception and handling plan.

For ship operators it means that the Master of a ship has to notify the port of call at least 24 hours prior to arrival about its intention to deliver ship-generated waste and cargo residues.

Unless the Captain can prove that his ship has adequate storage capacity, all ships are required to deliver their ship-generated waste before leaving a European Union port. Ships that do not deliver their waste without providing valid reasons for exemption are not allowed to leave the port until such delivery has taken place.

All ships calling at a port located in an EU Member State have to pay a waste fee regardless of whether or not they use the port reception facilities. This both provides an incentive to ships not to discharge garbage at sea and also helps ports recover the costs for providing adequate waste reception facilities.

6.5 Going Beyond Compliance

International and European regulations currently set out rules regarding the discharge of ship-generated waste.

However, this should only be considered as the first step in waste management. In general, a waste minimisation policy for the shipping industry should follow the list of preferences in industrial waste management options:

- Waste avoidance.
- Reusing.
- Recycling.
- Treatment and disposal.

6.5.1 Reduce Waste

Reducing garbage makes sense environmentally and financially - less garbage produced, less garbage to dispose of.

It is a lifecycle issue and means limiting the amount of material that may become garbage from being brought onboard the ship.

6.5.1.1 Procurement

By considering what is being bought from a perspective of waste management, more waste-conscious procurement choices can be made.

Look at products in terms of the amount of garbage they will generate. Options to be considered include:

- Where possible use supplies that come in bulk packaging (e.g. switching from small containers to much larger containers that can be decanted). Remember to take into account factors such as adequate shelf-life to avoid increasing garbage associated with such products.
- Use supplies that come in reusable packaging and containers and order refills for these.
- Tell your ship chandler that you want products with limited (or if possible without any) packaging.
- Avoid supplies that are packaged in plastic, unless a reusable container is used.
- Avoid the use of disposable products, e.g. cups, utensils, dishes, towels.
- Try using suppliers with a strong environmental policy as much as possible.

6.5.1.2   Removal Of Unnecessary Packaging While In Port

Dunnage, lining and packaging materials generated in port during cargo discharge should preferably be disposed of at the port reception facilities and not retained onboard for discharge at sea.

6.5.1.3   Food And Beverage Waste

- A water purifier can be installed in the drinking water system of the ship, which will reduce the plastic mineral water bottle consumption and thus the usage of plastic bottles.
- Reusable bottles should be used for storage of water.
- Food should be cooked appropriately and in adequate quantity as per persons onboard so that unnecessary wastage can be reduced.

6.5.1.4   Technical Waste Management Solutions

There are a range of waste management solutions that reduce the actual volume of the waste produced.

The basic premise of these is that the waste is sorted in to different waste fractions. These can then be put through onboard processing. Compactors, shredders and crushers can all be used to reduce the volume of the dry waste. This reduces both the storage space required and can also reduce the cost of using port reception facilities if they charge for the volume of waste discharged.

Non-processed waste can be up to five times the volume of properly managed and compacted waste.

Dust Management At The CSL Group

Loading and discharging dry bulk cargo such as coal or grain produces dust which, if released into the environment, can cause air pollution. Dust originating from dry cargo can also cause dirt build-up, not only onboard ships and equipment but also inland by travelling through the air. Examples of risks associated with dust include:

- Prolonged exposure to certain types of dust – coal dust for example – can become a source of health problems for crews if inhaled in large amounts and/or repetitively.
- Dust produced by certain types of cargo, like grain and coal, may pose an explosion hazard, especially during loading, unloading and cleaning operations.
- Negative impact on the quality of life of portside residents as dust results in dirt build-up.

In order to reduce the formation of dust and its associated risks, CSL implemented a series of unique measures across its entire fleet a few years ago. Most CSL vessels are equipped with boom spill trays, boom enclosures and conveyor skirting to prevent dust from escaping into the environment. Advanced dust suppression equipment and fully enclosed or covered booms on many CSL vessels further reduce the potential for dust or spillage.

Since 2010, CSL Americas has utilised a chute assembly for the discharge boom which, combined with the non-toxic foam surfactant applied with water to the cargo upon discharge, eliminates the fugitive dust of the gypsum barge discharges from their vessels. In addition, ships now operate with instructions to maintain the chute assembly height no more than 1 to 2 feet above accumulating cargo, which results in virtually no dust emission other than during change of holds: over a total of 12 hour discharge operation, less than 10 minutes dust emission has been achieved.

CSL Australia has installed dust suppression units on the wharf at its largest cement discharge plant in Melbourne. New and improved units have been placed onboard the CSL Sams for her clinker discharge. A new enclosed hopper was installed by CSL Australia at Bulwer Island, Brisbane, to reduce dust levels when discharging limestone, clinker and slag.

CSL self-unloaders also ensure a clean ship, a clean dock and no dust pollution around the port as loading and unloading operations are carried out within a completely enclosed system.

6.5.2 Reuse And Recycle

Reusing and recycling products and materials that would otherwise be thrown away can be facilitated by separating garbage according to whether it can be reused, recycled or has to be disposed of.

Recycling is preferred to disposal as recycled waste reduces cost for disposal and is a valuable resource.

6.5.2.1 *Crew Training*

The most important aspect of recycling onboard is to encourage and educate the crew on recycling practices. They should be properly trained in what garbage to separate, how to separate it and where to take it for further processing.

NOTE: A key point for crew training is the appropriate separation of garbage.

If a single plastic is found in a bin full of paper, then the whole bin will be treated and charged as plastic by most port authorities. This would cost unnecessary more money.

Resolution MEPC.219(63), as amended by resolution MEPC.239(65)

The recommended garbage types that should be separated are:

- Non-recyclable plastics and plastics mixed with non-plastic garbage.
- Rags.
- Recyclable material:
    - Cooking oil.
    - Glass.
    - Aluminium cans.
    - Paper, cardboard, corrugated board.
    - Wood.
    - Metal.
    - Plastics (including styrofoam or other similar plastic material).
- Garbage that might present a hazard to the ship or crew (e.g. oily rags, light bulbs, acids, chemical, batteries, etc.).
- E-waste generated onboard (e.g. electronic cards, gadgets, instruments, equipment, computers, printer cartridges, etc.).

To further encourage recycling, you could provide incentives to crews that manage to reduce the amount of garbage generated onboard.

6.5.2.2 *Recycling Bins Onboard*

In order to make it as easy as possible for the crew to recycle, all of the company's ships should be equipped with recycling bins that are each clearly labelled and differently coloured.

In addition, waste management and processing stations should be located around the ship.

6.5.2.3 *Replace Disposal Materials With Reusable Materials*

Try to replace disposable materials with reusable ones.

In terms of materials used for stowage, securing and protection of cargo, the amount of garbage generated can be decreased by:

- Using permanent reusable coverings for cargo protection.
- Using stowage systems and methods that reuse dunnage, shoring, lining and packing materials.

6.5.3 Zero Discharge

Despite taking efforts to reduce, reuse and recycle materials, garbage may still be generated onboard the ship.

Implementing a 'zero discharge' approach lessens environmental impact and also avoids confusion as to what can legally be discharged and what cannot. All waste is simply discharged to port reception facilities.

Questions to Consider

How can I reduce the amount of garbage generated onboard the ship?
The first step is to identify the sources of wastes. Think about the garbage generated by a product, e.g. packaging, before buying it. Consider, when possible, maintenance before repair, and repair before replacement and procurement. When restocking provision, you can ask your suppliers to remove or reduce all packaging at an early stage. While this will not reduce garbage in general, it will limit the generation of garbage onboard your ships and thus reduce collection, processing and storing requirements.

Many materials can be reused or recycled which will not only save you money, but also reduce the ship's environmental impact.

More ideas on how to reduce garbage can be found in Section 6.5.1.

What do I need to consider for collecting garbage onboard the ship?
You should provide suitable garbage bins (e.g. drums, metal bins, cans, container bags, or wheelie bins) for collecting and separating garbage. When organising your waste collection, keep in mind what is going to happen with the garbage after collection. Which garbage do you want to process onboard the ship (e.g. incineration), what you can recycle, which garbage do you want to discharge at reception facilities and what are the requirements at reception facilities. This will inform you on how to separate waste.

To make sure the crew knows what goes in which bin, each bin should be clearly marked and distinguished by colour, size, graphics, shape or location.

Make sure enough garbage bins are available for each type of garbage. Consult your Garbage Record Book to get an idea of how many bins you will need.

You need to think about where to put the garbage bin. Ideally, they are located close to where the specific garbage is generated. This avoids long walking ways and encourages the collection of garbage. Suitable locations would be the engine room, mess deck, wardroom, galley, and other living or working spaces.

Any garbage bins on deck areas, poop decks, or areas exposed to the weather should be secured on the ship and have lids that are tight and securely fixed. All garbage bins should be secured to prevent loss or spillage of garbage.

Also think about potential fire hazards: Make sure your garbage is kept away from places where it could easily ignite or protect it appropriately. Garbage in the engine room, for example, should be in a sealed metal container.

It is recommended that garbage is not discharged into a ship's sewage treatment system unless it is approved for treating such garbage. Furthermore, garbage should not be stored in bottoms or tanks containing oily wastes. Such actions can result in faulty operation of sewage treatment or oily water separator equipment and can cause sanitary problems for crew members and passengers.

Crew responsibilities should be assigned for collecting or emptying garbage bins and taking the garbage to the appropriate processing or storage location. This will facilitate subsequent shipboard processing and minimise the amount of garbage which must be stored onboard ship for return to port.

Ask yourself if onboard staff will require further training or education programmes to facilitate collection of garbage and sorting of reusable or recyclable material. If you do not know what their level of knowledge is, you could distribute questionnaires onboard or perform random checks.

How can I encourage recycling onboard the ship?

Consider what you could do with the proceeds generated from the return of recycled materials. You could for example add them to the ship's recreational fund or divide them among crew members.

What do I need to consider when processing garbage?

There are different devices to process garbage such as incinerators, compactors and comminuters. Using these devices has several advantages. Amongst others, they reduce shipboard space requirements for storing garbage and make it easier to discharge garbage at port reception facilities.

Things to consider vary depending on the processing device, however we advise you to always:

- Identify the personnel responsible for operating the processing equipment.
- Identify available processing devices and their capacities.
- Identify the location of processing devices and processing stations.
- Identify the categories of garbage that are to be processed by each of the available processing devices.
- Identify standard operating procedures for the operation and maintenance of the equipment used to manage garbage.
- Identify training needs to facilitate the correct use of the processing device.

Also think about whether processing devices make sense for you and if so, which one. For example, ships operating primarily in Special Areas or within 3 nm of the nearest land or ice-shelf are greatly restricted in what they can discharge. These ships should choose between storage of either compacted or uncompacted material for discharging at port reception facilities or incineration with retention of ash and clinkers. The type of ship and the expected volume and type of garbage generated will determine the suitability of compaction, incineration, or storage options.

What do I need to consider when using grinders or comminuters?

A wide variety of food waste grinders is available on the market and most modern ships' galleys have the equipment needed to produce a slurry of food particles and water that washes easily through the required 25 mm screen. Output ranges from 10 to 250 litres per minute. The discharge from shipboard comminuters should be directed into an appropriately constructed holding tank when the ship is operating within an area where discharge is prohibited.

Even though larger food scraps may be discharged beyond 12 nm, it is recommended that comminuters be used even outside this limit because they accelerate assimilation into the marine environment. Because food wastes comminuted with plastics cannot be discharged at sea, all plastic materials must be removed before food wastes are ground up.

Size reduction of certain other garbage items can be achieved by shredding or crushing and machines for carrying out this process are available for use onboard ships.

It is recommended that the discharge from shipboard comminuters be directed into a holding tank when the ship is operating within an area where discharge is prohibited.

What should I consider when using compactors?

Think about the location of the compactor. There should be adequate room for operating and maintaining the unit and for storing the trash to be processed. It should be adjacent to the areas of food processing and commissary store-rooms. If not already required by regulations it is recommended that the space have freshwater wash down service, coamings, deck drains, adequate ventilation and hand or automatic fixed fire-fighting equipment.

Most garbage can be compacted to some degree. The exceptions include unground plastics, fibre and paper board, bulky cargo containers and thick metal items. Pressurised containers should not be compacted or shredded without the use of specialised equipment designed for this purpose because they present an explosion hazard in standard compactors.

Compaction reduces the volume of garbage. In most cases the output from a compactor is a block of material which facilitates the shipboard storage of garbage and the discharge of the material in a port facility.

NOTE: The output from a compactor might be subject to quarantine, sanitary or health requirements or other requirements from the port reception facilities and advice from local authorities should be sought on any standards or requirements which are additional to those set by the IMO.

If grinding machines are used before compaction, the compaction ratio can be decreased which reduces the storage space. However, not all compactors require grinding. Therefore, careful investigation of the appropriate compaction machine should be undertaken, based on the type and volume of material that will be compacted.

Compactors have options including sanitising, deodorising, adjustable compaction ratios, bagging in plastic or paper, boxing in cardboard (with or without plastic or wax paper lining) and baling. Compacted materials should be stored appropriately. While metal and plastic bales can get wet, paper and cardboard bales should be kept dry.

What do I need to consider when using incinerators?

Ash and clinkers from shipboard incinerators should be considered as operational waste and therefore as garbage that is not eligible for discharge into the sea.

Incineration conducted in a shipboard incinerator can significantly reduce the need to store garbage onboard the ship. Shipboard incinerators should be designed, constructed, operated and maintained in accordance with resolution MEPC.244(66) '2014 Standard Specification for Shipboard Incinerators'.

In general, shipboard incineration should not be undertaken when the ship is in port or at an offshore terminal. Some ports may have domestic laws that specify additional air emission restrictions, particularly those near high population areas. The use of a shipboard incinerator may require permission from the port authority concerned.

Each operator of the onboard garbage incinerator should be trained and familiar in the use of the equipment and the types of garbage that can be destroyed in the incinerator.

Some of the disadvantages of incinerators may include the possible hazardous nature of the ash or vapour, dirty operation, and excessive labour required for charging, stoking and ash removal. Some incinerators may not be able to meet air pollution regulations imposed in some ports and harbours or by flag and coastal States when such matters are subject to their jurisdiction. Some of these disadvantages can be remedied by automatic equipment for charging and stoking, though the additional equipment to perform automatic functions will require more installation space.

The incineration of garbage that contains a large amount of plastic involves very specific incinerator design such as higher oxygen injection and higher temperatures (850 - 1,200°C). If these special conditions are not met, depending on the type of plastic and conditions of combustion, some toxic gases can be generated in the exhaust stream, including vaporised hydrochloric and hydrocyanic acids. These and other intermediary products of combustion of waste containing plastics are toxic to humans and marine life.

Onboard incineration of garbage may reduce the volume of garbage subject to quarantine requirements in some countries. However, incinerator ash may still be subject to local quarantine, sanitary or health requirements. Advice should be sought from local authorities regarding requirements that are in addition to MARPOL. For example, higher temperatures and more complete combustion may be required to effectively destroy organisms that present a risk.

How should I store garbage and reusable or recyclable material?

When deciding how to store garbage and other material, think about what is going to happen next with it and when. Garbage that must be returned to port for discharge may require long-term storage depending on the length of the voyage or arrangements for off-loading (e.g., transferring garbage to an offshore ship for subsequent transfer ashore). Garbage which may be discarded overboard may require short-term or no storage.

In all cases, garbage should be stored in a manner which avoids health and safety hazards and take into account occupational health and safety requirements.

For each storage location, identify the intended use, and the capacities of available storage stations for each category of garbage or reusable or recyclable material. Sufficient storage space and equipment (e.g. cans, drums, bags or other containers) should be provided. Where space is limited, ship operators are encouraged to install compactors or incinerators. To the extent possible, all processed and unprocessed garbage which must be stored for any length of time should be in tight, securely covered containers.

Furthermore, consider the conditions under which the garbage will be stored (for example, 'food – frozen'; 'cans – compacted and stacked'; 'paper – compacted and should remain dry'). The ship should use separate cans, drums, boxes, bags or other containers for short-term (disposable garbage) and trip-long (non-disposable garbage) storage. Food wastes and associated garbage which are returned to port and which may carry diseases or pests should be stored in tightly covered containers and be kept separate from garbage which does not contain such food wastes. Both types of garbage should be stored in separate clearly marked containers to avoid incorrect discharge and treatment on land. Disinfection and both preventative and remedial pest control methods should be applied regularly in garbage storage areas.

What should I do if garbage is accidentally lost to sea or if I see garbage in the ocean?

If it is safe to do so, seafarers are encouraged to recover persistent garbage from the sea during routine operations. However, think safety first! The recollected garbage should be retained onboard for discharge to port reception facilities.

Accidental losses have to be recorded in the Garbage Record Book.

6.6 Business Benefits

There are several business benefits to correct garbage management.

Crew members illegally discharging garbage into the sea risk being fined. Complying with relevant regulations, recording waste discharges and documenting waste management procedures thus avoids criminal charges. These would usually come with negative press and public shaming.

Going beyond regulatory compliance by reducing, reusing and/or recycling materials can also result in significant cost savings.

Limiting the amount of materials brought onboard ship and processing any waste properly saves garbage handling costs. In certain ports where charges for waste disposal are based on the amount discharged, it can also reduce disposal fees. Ultimately, reducing the amount of materials used while maintaining the same level of operations means increased efficiency which in itself is a common business goal.

Furthermore, enhanced garbage management practices, including reducing the amount of waste generated and increasing recycling rates, are required by environmental class notations and help companies achieve a higher rating in environmental evaluation schemes, e.g. the Green Award.

6.7 Measuring Environmental Performance

Estimating the amount of garbage onboard a ship is a regulatory requirement. Every time garbage is discharged into the sea, to a reception facility, accidentally discharged, lost at sea or incinerated, the estimated amount of garbage must be noted in the Garbage Record Book.

The amount of garbage onboard should be estimated in m^3, if possible separately according to category. Of course, these are only rough estimates which depend on interpretation. Furthermore, volume estimates differ before and after processing. Some processing procedures may not allow for a usable estimate of volume at all, such as the continuous processing of food waste.

Nonetheless, the entries in the Garbage Record Book are a good indicator for the amount of garbage generated at sea.

CHAPTER SEVEN

CONTENTS

SEWAGE & GREY WATER

SEWAGE & GREY WATER

7.1 Introduction

Untreated sewage, also known as 'black water', generally refers to human body wastes and wastes from toilet facilities. It can also refer to drainage from spaces containing living animals. As a ship always contains crew and staff members, the generation of sewage is unavoidable.

The volume of sewage generated per ship is dependent on the number of people or the amount of livestock onboard. For example, one person can generate approximately 38 litres per day and when considering ships such as cruise or ferries, immense volumes of sewage can be generated over the course of a voyage.

Besides sewage, grey water is generated onboard ships. This is generally understood to be waste water from sinks, showers, dishwashing and washing machines.

7.2 Environmental And Health Impact

The discharge of raw sewage into the sea is a thing of the past. Regulations now prohibit this activity due to the potential threat to both the environment and human health.

7.2.1 Environmental Impact

Sewage contains nutrients which can lead to an excessive growth of algae (algal blooms), the growth of which can deplete oxygen levels and pose a threat to marine flora and fauna. Some algal blooms are toxic and pose a greater threat to the marine ecosystems.

7.2.2 Health Impact

Human waste contains different *e.coli* bacteria. While most strains of bacteria present in sewage are harmless, some can cause adverse health effects such as diarrhoea, severe anaemia or kidney failure.

Sewage may also contain a range of chemicals and other specialised wastes including industrial chemicals, nutrients, heavy metals, pharmaceuticals, medical wastes, oils and greases, resulting in additional threats to human health.

7.3 International Regulation

The International Maritime Organization (IMO) currently regulates discharges of sewage but not of grey water.

Regulations governing the prevention of pollution by sewage are contained in Annex IV of MARPOL which entered into force in September 2003. A revised Annex IV entered into force on 1 August 2005.

Resolution MEPC.115(51)

The Annex applies to the following ships engaged in international voyages:

- Ships of 400 gross tonnage (GT) and above.
- Ships of less than 400 GT which are certified to carry more than 15 persons.

7.3.1 Discharge Of Sewage

Resolution MEPC.115(51)

As a general rule, the discharge of sewage into the sea is prohibited. However, there are certain circumstances under which it is allowed.

This is the case when the ship:

- Has in operation an approved sewage treatment plant; or
- is discharging comminuted and disinfected sewage using an approved system at a distance of more than 3 nautical miles (nm) from the nearest land; or
- is discharging sewage which is not comminuted or disinfected at a distance of more than 12 nm from the nearest land.

Resolution MEPC.164(56)

Any sewage that has been stored in holding tanks or sewage originating from spaces containing living animals may only be discharged at a moderate rate when the ship is *en route* and not slower than 4 knots.

Resolution MEPC.157(55)

The maximum permissible discharge rate has to be calculated according to resolution MEPC.157(55). It depends on a ship's average speed, its draft and breadth. By multiplying these factors, the swept volume of the ship is calculated. The maximum permissible discharge rate may not exceed 1/200,000 of swept volume.

7.3.2 Sewage Systems

Resolution MEPC.115(51)

MARPOL Annex IV requires ships to be equipped with:

- An approved sewage treatment plant. The sewage treatment plant has to meet the requirements set out in resolution MEPC.227(64); or
- an approved sewage comminuting and disinfecting system; or
- a sewage holding tank for the retention of all sewage for discharge ashore.

7.3.3 When Sewage Does Not Meet Discharge Criteria

Resolution MEPC.115(51)

Sewage that cannot be discharged into the sea in compliance with these provisions must be kept onboard and discharged to shore-based reception facilities.

To enable pipes of reception facilities to be connected with the ship's discharge pipeline, both lines must be fitted with a standard discharge connection. The standard dimensions of flanges for discharge connections are set out in Regulation 10 of resolution MEPC.115(51).

It is the duty of each signatory Party to MARPOL 73/78 Annex IV to ensure the provision of adequate facilities at ports and terminals for the reception of sewage.

Resolution MEPC.200(62)

7.3.4 Discharge Of Sewage From Passenger Ships In Special Areas

On 1 January 2013, new discharge requirements for passenger ships operating in a Special Area entered into force.

A Special Area under MARPOL Annex IV is defined as:

> "*a sea area where for recognized technical reasons in relation to its oceanographical and ecological condition and to the particular character of its traffic the adoption of special mandatory methods for the prevention of sea pollution by sewage is required.*"

Currently, there is only one Special Area under MARPOL Annex IV: the Baltic Sea.

Within a designated Special Area, the discharge of sewage from a passenger ship is prohibited:

- As of 1 January 2016 for new passenger ships; and
- as of 1 January 2018 for existing passenger ships

…unless the ship is equipped with a sewage treatment plant which meets the requirements set out in resolution MEPC.227(64). Furthermore, the effluent shall not produce visible floating solids nor cause discoloration of the surrounding water.

New passenger ships are those:

- For which the building contract is placed on or after 1 January 2016; or
- in the absence of a building contract, the keel of which is laid on or after 1 January 2016; or
- regardless of the building contract signing date or keel laying date the delivery of which is on after 1 January 2018.

Resolution MEPC.115(51)

7.3.5 Survey And Certification

Every ship covered by MARPOL Annex IV must carry a valid International Sewage Pollution Prevention (ISPP) Certificate onboard for inspection by port or flag States. The Certificate can last for up to five years.

In order to be granted an ISPP Certificate, the ship has to pass the following surveys:

- An initial survey, before the ship is put into service, or before a Sewage Certificate is issued for the first time.
- A renewal survey, before the end of every period of five years following the issue of a Sewage Certificate in respect of the ship.
- An additional survey after a repair following an accident to the ship or when a defect is discovered which substantially affects the integrity of the ship or the efficiency or completeness of its sewage equipment. An additional survey is also required after an important repair or renewal is made. It ensures that the necessary repairs or renewals have been effectively made, that the material and workmanship of such repairs or renewals are in all respects satisfactory and that the ship complies in all respects with the requirements of this Annex.

These surveys are undertaken to ensure that the required sewage equipment fitted to the ship is in good working order and the necessary infrastructure of the ship to support the proper functioning of that equipment is in a satisfactory condition.

A model ISPP Certificate is included in the Appendix to MARPOL Annex IV provided in Part Three - The Maritime Environmental & Efficiency Templates provided on the USB memory stick that accompanies this Guide.

7.4 Regional Regulation

In addition to international standards as established under MARPOL Annex IV, there are some regional regulations that govern sewage discharges.

7.4.1 United States

In the United States, sewage and other ship discharges are regulated through the Clean Water Act (CWA) by the US Environmental Protection Agency (EPA).

Under Section 312 of the CWA, ship sewage is generally controlled by regulating the equipment that treats or holds the sewage (marine sanitation devices), and through the establishment of areas in which the discharge of sewage from ships is not allowed - No Discharge Zones (NDZs).

7.4.1.1 No Discharge Zone

Clean Water Act, Section 312

A NDZ is an area in which both treated and untreated sewage discharges from ships are prohibited. Within NDZ boundaries, ship operators must retain their sewage discharges onboard and wait to dispose them either at sea, i.e. beyond three nautical miles from shore, or at a pump-out facility onshore.

A list of States with NDZs can be found on the EPA website. The biggest NDZ is currently in California where the new ban applies to all coastal waters out to three nautical miles from the coastline and all bays and estuaries subject to tidal influence.

7.4.1.2 Marine Sanitation Device

A marine sanitation device is defined as:

"any equipment for installation onboard a ship which is designed to receive, retain, treat, or discharge sewage, and any process to treat such sewage."

All commercial and recreational ships with installed toilet facilities that are operating in US waters are required to have marine sanitation devices.

There are three different types of marine sanitation devices that can be certified by the US Coast Guard (USCG):

- Type I marine sanitation devices use chemicals to disinfect the raw sewage prior to discharge and must meet a performance standard for fecal coliform bacteria of not greater than 1,000 per 100 ml and no visible floating solids.
- In Type II marine sanitation devices, the waste is either chemically or biologically treated prior to discharge and must meet limits of no more than 200 fecal coliforms per 100 ml and no more than 150 mg/l of suspended solids.
- Type III marine sanitation devices store wastes and do not treat them; the waste is pumped out later and treated in an onshore system or discharged outside US waters.

Type I marine sanitation devices are generally only found on recreational vessels or others under 65 feet (20m) in length. Large vessels use either Type II or Type III marine sanitation devices.

7.4.1.3 Grey Water Regulations

US regulations also cover grey water from ships. The 2013 Vessel General Permit (VGP) includes requirements on grey water discharges and monitoring.

Grey Water Discharges

2013 VGP Part 2.2.15

All ships must minimise the discharge of grey water while in port and when within 1 nm from shore

All ships of 400 GT and above may only discharge grey water:

- When they are underway and further away from shore than 1 nm; or
- when the grey water meets the treatment standards and other requirements that are applicable to cruise ships.[1]

Grey Water Monitoring

2013 VGP Part 2.2.15

The 2013 VGP includes monitoring requirements for grey water. Ship owners and operators must collect and analyse two samples per year, at least 14 days apart.

Samples must be taken for biochemical oxygen demand, fecal coliform, suspended solids, pH, and total residual chlorine. Ship owners and operators may choose to conduct monitoring for *e.coli* in lieu of fecal coliform. Sampling and testing shall be conducted according to 40 CFR Part 136. The results of analysis should be included as part of your annual report.

[1] The discharge requirements for cruise ships are contained under Parts 5.1.1, 5.1.2 (large cruise ships) or 5.2.1, 5.2.2 (medium cruise ships) of the 2013 VGP.

7.5 Going Beyond Compliance

Considering that it is not possible to reduce the amount of sewage generated during a ship's operation, going beyond regulatory requirements means further reducing the amount of pollutants, nutrients and other harmful contaminants contained in discharged sewage. This can be achieved by further reducing the rate of discharge, the concentration of harmful substances contained in sewage or by reducing the amount of black and grey water generated.

7.5.1 Reducing The Amount Of Discharged Sewage

The most obvious and effective measure to reduce the amount of sewage discharges is to discharge all sewage effluents to shore-based reception facilities. If this is not possible, the following measures should be taken:

- No discharges of untreated sewage.
- Extend the distance to the nearest land beyond IMO requirements when discharging sewage.
- Reduce the rate of discharges beyond IMO requirements with due regard to the treatment plant's operational performance limitations.
- Ensure that the ship's sewage treatment system has sufficient holding tank capacity taking into account ship size, type and trade.
- No discharges of sewage in or near to areas designated as Particularly Sensitive Sea Areas by the IMO.
- No discharges of sewage in or near to other sensitive areas (e.g. coral reefs, bathing beaches, water bodies with restricted circulation, flushing or inflow, marine protected areas, breeding grounds, near large population centres).

7.5.2 Reducing The Concentration Of Harmful Substances In Black And Grey Water

7.5.2.1 *Advanced Wastewater Treatment System*

Resolution MEPC.227(64) establishes effluent standards a sewage treatment plant has to meet. These effluent standards can be further improved by installing an Advanced Wastewater Treatment system (AWT).

AWTs generally provide improved screening, biological treatment, solids separation (using filtration or flotation), and disinfect sewage with ultraviolet light. According to a study conducted by EPA, they can reduce the amount of pathogens almost completely and have overall high removal rates for nutrients, metals and other pollutants.[2] The installation of AWTs is thus advisable.

Important criteria for selecting an AWT are the number of people onboard and the area your ship is mainly operating in (e.g. mostly deep-sea where discharge regulations are less strict or mainly around ports where stricter discharge requirements prevail).

7.5.2.2 *Minimising The Polluting Content Of Grey Water*

There are several ways to ensure that your grey water is less harmful to the environment.

For example, cooking oils, greases and dairy products such as milk and cream decrease the performance of an onboard wastewater treatment system. Therefore, try to prevent these products going down the sink and into an onboard treatment system.

Another way is to procure and use low-nitrogen and no-phosphorus detergents onboard and encourage your crew to use all soaps and cleaners sparingly.

[2] EPA (2008) Cruise Ship Discharge Assessment Report. Section 2: Sewage

7.5.3 Reducing The Amount Of Black And Grey Water

There are several ways to reduce the amount of sewage and grey water generated. These are shown in the table below:

Aim	Technologies
Reduce the amount of water used in toilets	• Low-volume flush toilets. • Vacuum toilets. • Urine-separating toilets. • Composting toilets. • Waterless urinals.
Reduce the amount of grey water	• Low-flow shower heads. • Low-volume washing machines. • Aerated tap faucets. • Controlled-flow tap valves. • Pressure-reducing valves.

Additionally, it might be possible to recycle and reuse pre-treated grey water before it becomes wastewater, for example by using water from the shower for flushing the toilets.

7.6 Business Benefits

Apart from the environmental and health benefits, complying with sewage discharge requirements has one principal benefit for businesses: avoiding criminal and civil penalties.

Punishments depend on the waters, but can be hefty. Under Danish law, imprisonment can be up two years, and in Canadian waters, under the Canada Shipping Act, the penalty for violation is a fine of up to C$1 million, imprisonment for up to three years, or both.

The detection of such criminal offences is usually covered by the press, bringing shame and a bad reputation upon the company.

A major advantage of adhering to the strictest sewage and grey water standards is that it allows you to operate compliantly everywhere in the world.

Classification societies also promote the use of sewage treatment systems as well as grey water treatment by offering environmental class notations, e.g. ClassNK's notation 'Environmental Awareness'.

7.7 Measuring Environmental Performance

It is not common for ship owners and operators to measure their sewage generation. Discharge rates, however, can be determined based on the sewage pump capacity or treatment plant capacity.

The sewage pump capacity or treatment plant capacity can be used to calculate the actual discharge rates.

CHAPTER EIGHT

CONTENTS

TRANSPORT OF LIQUID CHEMICALS

TRANSPORT OF LIQUID CHEMICALS

8.1 Introduction

The chemical industry is at the heart of the global economy and requires major flows of goods from production sites to consumption areas. The global production of chemicals is increasing and compared to 2000, is expected to double by 2024. Similarly, the volumes shipped are on the rise, with maritime chemical transport having more than tripled in the past 20 years.[1]

Whether chemicals are being shipped in bulk and carried by chemical tankers or in packaged form e.g. in drums and stowed in a container carried by a container ship, planning chemical shipments can be very complex.

This is due to the different properties of the chemicals that need to be accounted for. For example:

- Relative temperature sensitivity.
- Semi-gases.
- Relative sensitivity to water.
- Potential to react with each other.
- Flammability.
- Toxicity.
- Environmental hazard.

It is imperative that careful technical and logistical planning take place to ensure safety of the crew, the ship, operations and the environment.

The release of chemicals at sea can cause severe environmental, health and safety hazards and have negative economic implications such as time off-hire, fines for cleaning up and environmental restoration costs.

The most common causes of chemical pollution by ships are:

- Structural failure or lack of maintenance of the ship, causing a crack in the hull or damage in the machine room.
- Incidents during navigation (leading to collision or grounding).
- Incidents during cargo loading/unloading and tank cleaning operations.
- Incidents during cargo carriage, such as inappropriate cargo mixing resulting in chemical reactions and even explosions, or containers breaking loose or leaking.

8.2 Environmental Impact

The release of chemicals into the sea can be very harmful to marine ecosystems. Impacts may vary depending on the type and toxicity of chemical, the severity and duration of exposure, and the susceptibility of the organisms exposed.

Chemicals can have direct effects such as poisoning and killing flora and fauna, but they can also cause more indirect destruction by damaging their reproductive, hormone and immune systems. This can reduce biodiversity and productivity in entire marine ecosystems.

---

[1] Marine Board-ESF (2011) Chemical Pollution in Europe's Seas; Transport Canada (2012) Understanding Chemical Pollution at Sea. Learning Guide.

8.2.1 Health And Safety Impact

Chemical leakage is not only harmful to the marine environment but can also pose risks to human health and safety.

Some chemicals react violently with other products or when they come into contact with an element in the environment, e.g. water and air. These reactions can cause explosions, fire or the release of toxic vapours.

Chemicals can enter the human body and cause serious damage. This can happen through contact with the skin or other mucous membranes, through inhalation or ingestion. The negative effects depend on the toxicity of the chemical and are very different. Generalised effects can include severe cardiac, respiratory, and central nervous system conditions which can, in the worst case, lead to death.

8.3 International Regulation

The International Maritime Organization (IMO) regulates the carriage of liquid chemicals by ships through SOLAS Chapter 7, MARPOL 73/78 Annexes II and III, the International Bulk Chemical Code (IBC Code)/Code for the Construction and Equipment of Ships Carrying Dangerous Chemicals in Bulk (BCH Code) and the International Maritime Dangerous Goods Code (IMDG Code).

These regulations cover chemicals carried in bulk and chemicals carried in packaged form.

8.3.1 Liquid Chemicals Carried In Bulk

The regulatory requirements for chemicals carried in bulk can be found under SOLAS Chapter VII and MARPOL Annex II and the IBC Code/BCH Code as applicable.

The IBC Code applies to chemical tankers constructed on or after 1 July 1986, whereas the BCH Code applies to chemical tankers constructed before 1 July 1986. This Chapter deals predominantly with the IBC Code.

The principal regulatory requirements concerning the bulk carriage of chemicals by ships relate to ship construction and equipment, discharge of noxious liquid substances, survey and certification, and monitoring and reporting.

Just as the properties and hazard levels of chemicals carried by ship differ, so do the construction, equipment and discharge requirements. For this purpose, MARPOL Annex II distinguishes between chemicals using different pollution categories.

8.3.1.1 Categorisation Of Noxious Liquid Substances

Resolution MEPC.118(52)

Depending on the hazard they represent to human health and the marine environment, noxious liquid substances are divided into four categories:

- **Category X:** these substances are deemed to present a major hazard to either marine resources or human health. They may not be discharged into the marine environment.
- **Category Y:** these substances are deemed to present a hazard to either marine resources or human health or cause harm to amenities or other legitimate uses of the sea. The quality and quantity of substances that may be discharged is thus limited.
- **Category Z:** these substances are deemed to present a minor hazard to either marine resources or human health. The restrictions on the quality and quantity of discharges are therefore less stringent.
- **Other Substances (OS):** these substances are considered to present no harm to marine resources, human health, amenities or other legitimate uses of the sea. Their discharge is therefore not regulated under MARPOL Annex II.

Chapter 17, 18 and 19 of the IBC Code identify the category to which a chemical belongs. An agreement between ship owners, ship builders and classification societies has established interim provisions for categorising liquid substances as well.

The GESAMP Hazard Profiles as well as the Guidelines for the Categorisation of Noxious Liquid Substances contained in Appendix I of MARPOL Annex II, give further guidance and information.

In addition to presenting a pollution hazard, noxious liquid substances can also present a safety hazard. Categories X, Y and Z substances with a safety hazard are listed as such in Chapter 17 of the IBC Code, whereas Category Z substances that do not present a safety hazard and OS substances are listed in Chapter 18 of the IBC Code. To avoid 'double listing', substances are either included in Chapter 17 or 18 of the IBC Code.

Tankers carrying chemicals included in Chapter 17 are required to comply with the International Code for the Construction and Equipment of Ships Carrying Dangerous Chemicals in Bulk (IBC Code). The IBC Code does not apply to chemicals listed in Chapter 18; ships carrying these chemicals still fall under the regulations set out in MARPOL Annex II.

The International Certificate of Fitness for the Carriage of Dangerous Chemicals in Bulk, issued under the requirements of the IBC Code, lists the products from Chapter 17 that a ship is approved to carry. In the event the ship is required to carry a chemical that is not listed, an application to the ship's flag State should be made so that the chemical may be included on the ship's International Certificate of Fitness before it is carried.

8.3.1.2
Resolution MSC.176(79), as amended by resolution MSC.340(91)

Design, Construction And Equipment Requirements

The IBC Code provides detailed standards for the construction and equipment of three types of chemical tankers (Types 1, 2 and 3).

A Type 1 ship is a chemical tanker intended for the transportation of products considered to present the greatest overall hazard, and Types 2 and 3 for products of progressively lesser hazards. Accordingly, a Type 1 ship must be constructed in such a way so as to survive the most severe damage and its cargo tanks must be located at the maximum prescribed distance inboard from the shell plating.

There are a few liquid chemicals (e.g. ammonium nitrate solution, diethyl ether, hydrogen peroxide solutions) which require additional construction requirements as specified in Chapter 15 of the IBC Code. If such requirements apply, cross-check with Chapter 17 of the IBC Code, containing references to Chapter 15.

8.3.1.3
Resolution MEPC.118(52)

Pumping, Piping, Unloading Arrangements And Slop Tanks

Stripping is the process to remove the maximum amount of chemical residue from the ship's tanks. MARPOL Annex II provides for the permitted volumes of chemicals that may remain in tanks following stripping. For older ships, volumes are higher, but for newer ships which make use of improved stripping methods, the permitted limits are lower (see table).

Date Of Ship Construction	Permitted Residues In Tanks (In Litres)		
	Category X	Category Y	Category Z
Before 1 July 1986	300	300	900
On or after 1 July 1986 but before 1 January 2007	100	100	300
On or after 1 January 2007	7	75	75

Regardless of the date of construction, the efficiency of the ship's cargo pumping system must be tested in accordance with Appendix V of MARPOL Annex II.

In addition, ships certified to carry substances of Category X, Y or Z must have an underwater discharge outlet – unless they were constructed before 1 January 2007 and are certified only to carry substance in Category Z in which case it is not mandatory.

Operational Discharges Of Chemical Residues

The discharge of chemicals assigned to Category X, Y or Z or ballast water, tank washings or other mixtures containing these chemicals is only allowed if specific requirements are met. These requirements depend on the category under which the substance falls.

The following operational discharge requirements are dependent on the category under which the chemical falls:

Category X
- Discharge of Category X residues to the sea is not permitted. The ship must carry out a prewash as specified in Addendum B of MARPOL Annex II and all washings must be discharged to reception facilities prior to departure from the unloading port.
- Any water subsequently introduced into the tank may be discharged into the sea in accordance with the discharge standards described in MARPOL Annex II, Regulation 13.2 (*en route*, speed, underwater overboard discharge, distance, water depth).

Category Y
- For Category Y, a further distinction is made, namely between solidifying or high-viscosity residues and non-solidifying or low-viscosity residues.
    - A solidifying substance is a substance having a melting point <15°C whose unloading temperature is <5°C above the melting point, or a substance having a melting point ≥15°C whose unloading temperature is <10°C above the melting point.
    - A high-viscosity substance is a substance included in Category X or Y with a viscosity ≥50 millipascal seconds (mPa.s) at the unloading temperature.
- Solidifying substances and high-viscosity substances require the shipper to provide details about the melting point and viscosity at 50 mPa.s as indicated in column 'o' of Chapter 17.
- Discharge of solidifying or high-viscosity Category Y residues is not permitted. The ship must carry out a prewash as specified in Addendum B of MARPOL Annex II. All washings must be discharged to reception facilities prior to departure from the unloading port.
- Any water subsequently introduced into the tank may be discharged into the sea in accordance with the discharge standards described in MARPOL Annex II, Regulation 13.2 (*en route*, speed, underwater overboard discharge, distance, water depth).
- Non-solidifying or low viscosity Category Y residue tank washings may be discharged into the sea in accordance with the discharge standards described in MARPOL Annex II, Regulation 13.2 (*en route*, speed, underwater overboard discharge, distance, water depth).

Category Z
- Category Z residue tank washings may be discharged to the sea in accordance with the discharge standards described in MARPOL Annex II, Regulation 13.2 (*en route*, speed, underwater overboard discharge, distance, water depth).

Resolution MEPC.118(52)

Discharge Standards

Where the provisions of MARPOL Annex II permit the discharge of residues of Category X, Y or Z substance, the following discharge standards have to be met:

- The ship is proceeding *en route* at a minimum speed of 7 knots if it is a self-propelled ship or at 4 knots if it is not self-propelled;
- the discharge is made below the waterline through the underwater discharge outlet and does not exceed the maximum rate for which the underwater discharge outlet is designed; and
- the discharge is made at least 12 nautical miles (nm) away from the nearest land and in a minimum depth of water of 25 metres.

In the Antarctic area, any discharge into the sea of noxious liquid substances or mixtures containing such substances is prohibited.

Each Party to MARPOL Annex II undertakes to ensure that adequate facilities for the reception of chemical residues and mixtures containing such residues are provided in ports involved in ships' cargo handling.

However, some ports do not have reception facilities for Annex II pre-wash disposal. In this case, MARPOL Annex II has provisions for exemption for a prewash. In practice, disposal of pre-wash at a port other than the port of discharge can have operational difficulties as it is difficult to find approved vendors.

8.3.1.5 *Surveys And Certification*

NLS Certificate

Resolution MEPC.118(52)

MARPOL Annex II requires that any ship carrying noxious liquid chemical substances in bulk must have a valid International Pollution Prevention Certificate for the Carriage of Noxious Liquid Substances in Bulk (NLS Certificate) onboard. The Certificate is valid for up to five years.

In order to be granted a NLS Certificate, the ship has to pass the following surveys:

- An initial survey, before the ship is put into service, or before a NLS Certificate is issued for the first time.
- A renewal survey, before the end of every period of five years following the issue of a NLS Certificate.
- A minimum of one intermediate survey during the period of validity of the NLS Certificate.
- An annual survey.
- An additional survey after a repair following an accident to the ship or when a defect is discovered which substantially affects the integrity of the ship or the efficiency or completeness of its equipment. An additional survey is also required after a major repair or renewal is made.

These surveys are undertaken to ensure that the structure, equipment, systems, fittings, arrangements and material fully comply with the requirements of MARPOL Annex II and are in good working order.

A model NLS Certificate is included in Appendix 3 to MARPOL Annex II. It is also provided in Part Three - The Maritime Environmental & Efficiency Templates provided on the USB memory stick that accompanies this Guide.

International Certificate Of Fitness For Chemical Tankers

Under the IBC Code, every chemical tanker is required to carry an International Certificate of Fitness for the Carriage of Dangerous Chemicals in Bulk. The International Certificate of Fitness certifies that the tanker complies with the construction and equipment requirements of the IBC Code, but also that it complies with the provisions set out in MARPOL Annex II. This means that a separate NLS Certificate is not required.

The International Certificate of Fitness can last for up to five years. In order to be granted a Certificate, the tanker has to pass the following surveys:

- An initial survey before the ship is put in service.
- A periodical survey not exceeding 5 years.
- A minimum of one intermediate survey during the period of validity of the Certificate.
- A mandatory annual survey.
- An additional survey after a repair following an accident to the ship or when a defect is discovered which substantially affects the integrity of the ship or the efficiency or completeness of its equipment.

Both cargoes from Chapter 17 and 18 can be listed in the International Certificate of Fitness if the ship is approved to carry them.

8.3.1.6

Monitoring And Reporting Requirements

MARPOL Annex II requires ships carrying substances of Category X, Y or Z to carry a Procedures and Arrangements Manual and a Cargo Record Book, together with the NLS Certificate – or the International Certificate of Fitness.

Procedures And Arrangements Manual

Resolution MEPC.118(52)

Every ship certified to carry substances of Category X, Y or Z must have a Procedures and Arrangements Manual onboard which is approved by the flag Administration. The standard format for the Manual is given in Appendix 4 to MARPOL Annex II.

The main purpose of the Manual is to identify the arrangements and equipment required to enable compliance with Annex II and to identify for the ship's officers all operational procedures with respect to cargo handling, tank cleaning, slops handling, residue discharging, ballasting and deballasting, which must be followed in order to comply with the requirements of MARPOL Annex II.

Cargo Record Book

Resolution MEPC.118(52)

Every ship to which MARPOL Annex II applies has to carry a Cargo Record Book onboard. All of the following operations must be recorded in the Cargo Record Book:

- Cargo loading and unloading.
- Internal transfer of cargo.
- Mandatory prewash.
- Cleaning of cargo tank.
- Discharge into the sea of tank washings.
- Ballasting of cargo tanks.
- Discharge of ballast water from cargo tanks.
- Accidental or other exceptional discharge.

The Cargo Record Book must be readily available for inspection onboard the ship and must be retained onboard for a period of three years after the last entry has been made.

Resolution MEPC.118(52)

8.3.1.7 *Prevention Of Pollution Arising From An Incident Involving Noxious Liquid Substances*

Every ship of 150 gross tonnage (GT) and above certified to carry noxious liquid substances in bulk must carry onboard a Shipboard Marine Pollution Emergency Plan for Noxious Liquid Substances approved by the ship's flag Administration.

Resolution MEPC.85(44), as amended by resolution MEPC.137(53)

The plan must be based on the Guidelines for the Development of Shipboard Marine Pollution Emergency Plans of Oil and/or Noxious Liquid Substances.

8.3.2 Chemicals (Dry Or Liquid) Carried In Packaged Form

The regulatory requirements for chemicals carried in packaged form can be found in Part A of SOLAS Chapter VII and in MARPOL Annex III.

NOTE: MARPOL Annex III is a voluntary Annex and Parties to MARPOL are not automatically required to also ratify Annex III. Therefore ships registered in countries which are not Party to MARPOL Annex III may not be required to comply, however under the 'no more favourable treatment' principle they will be required to comply with these requirements when calling at ports in countries which are Party to Annex III.

The regulations of Part A of SOLAS Chapter VII and of MARPOL Annex III apply to all ships carrying dangerous goods (SOLAS) or harmful substances (MARPOL) in packaged form. The main difference between both regulations is that Part A of SOLAS Chapter VII covers all substances which are considered dangerous to transport, whereas the scope of MARPOL Annex III is narrower, and only applies to those substances considered harmful to the marine environment.

Both regulations prohibit the carriage of these goods in packaged form except under certain conditions as provided for by the regulations.

8.3.2.1 *International Maritime Dangerous Goods Code*

SOLAS Chapter VII Part A requires that the carriage of dangerous goods in packaged form must comply with the IMDG Code.

The IMDG Code was developed as a uniform international code for the transport of dangerous goods by sea, and covers such matters as cargo classification, packing, consignment procedures and documentation, dangerous goods and stowage paying particular attention to the segregation of incompatible substances.

Resolution MSC.122(75)

The IMDG Code divides dangerous goods into nine classes according to their properties and potential hazards. These properties and potential hazards determine the way in which different classes of dangerous goods should be handled during transport, for example:

- The type of packaging.
- The grouping of different dangerous goods.
- The storage onboard the ship and in port.

Many of the substances assigned to classes 1 to 9 are deemed as being marine pollutants. It is these marine pollutants which are considered as 'harmful substances'. The Appendix to MARPOL Annex III contains criteria for harmful substances.

For an overview of the nine classes, divisions and packaging groups, see the Box Out below.

The IMDG Code is not freely available, but can be purchased from the IMO Publications Section on the IMO's website or from various maritime or nautical bookstores. It is constantly evolving and reissued every two years to accommodate amendments adopted by the IMO MEPC and MSC. It is important to ensure that the most up-to-date version is used when planning the carriage of chemicals in packaged form.

The segregation of chemical tanks on container ships can also be done using the 'Storck Guide' (Storck Verlag Hamburg) which is also updated every two years in line with the IMDG Code.

Classes, Divisions, Packing Groups In The IMDG Code

Substances (including mixtures and solutions) and articles subject to the provisions of this Code are assigned to one of the classes 1-9 according to the hazard or the most predominant of the hazards they present. Some of these classes are subdivided into divisions. These classes or divisions are as listed below:

Class 1 Explosives
- Division 1.1: Substances and articles which have a mass explosion hazard
- Division 1.2: Substances and articles which have a projection hazard but not a mass explosion hazard
- Division 1.3: Substances and articles which have a fire hazard and either a minor blast hazard or a minor projection hazard or both, but not a mass explosion hazard
- Division 1.4: Substances and articles which present no significant hazard
- Division 1.5: Very insensitive substances which have a mass explosion hazard
- Division 1.6: Extremely insensitive articles which do not have a mass explosion hazard

Class 2 Gases
- Class 2.1: Flammable gases
- Class 2.2: Non-flammable, non-toxic gases
- Class 2.3: Toxic gases

Class 3 Flammable Liquids

Class 4 Flammable Solids; Substances Liable To Spontaneous Combustion; Substances Which, In Contact With Water, Emit Flammable Gases
- Class 4.1: Flammable solids, self-reactive substances and desensitised explosives
- Class 4.2: Substances liable to spontaneous combustion
- Class 4.3: Substances which, in contact with water, emit flammable gases

Class 5 Oxidizing Substances And Organic Peroxides
- Class 5.1: Oxidizing substances
- Class 5.2: Organic peroxides

Class 6 Toxic And Infectious Substances
- Class 6.1: Toxic substances
- Class 6.2: Infectious substances

Class 7 Radioactive Material

Class 8 Corrosive Substances

Class 9 Miscellaneous Dangerous Substances And Articles

8.3.2.2 Packaging

Resolution MEPC.193(61), as amended by resolution MEPC.246(66)

SOLAS Chapter VII Part A

IMDG Code Section 4

MARPOL Annex III requires that packages are adequate to minimise the risk of causing harm to the marine environment, considering their contents. They must be marked with durable labels (i.e. resisting >3 months of immersion in seawater) and be marked and labelled in accordance with MARPOL Annex III, SOLAS Part A Chapter VII and the relevant provisions of the IMDG Code.

Empty packaging which previously contained harmful substances must be treated as harmful substances themselves unless adequate precautions have been taken to clean out any residue that is harmful to the marine environment.

8.3.2.3 Loading And Stowage

Resolution MEPC.193(61), as amended by resolution MEPC.246(66)

According to MARPOL Annex III, certain harmful substances may, for sound scientific and technical reasons, need to be prohibited for carriage altogether or be transported only in limited quantities.

MARPOL Annex III further provides that harmful substances must be properly stowed and secured so as to minimise the hazards to the marine environment without impairing the safety of the ship and persons onboard.

Part A of SOLAS Chapter VII requires that all cargo, cargo units and cargo transport units are loaded, stowed and secured throughout the voyage in accordance with the Cargo Securing Manual. The preparation of the Cargo Securing Manual must be in line with the guidelines contained in resolution MSC.1/Circ.1353.

8.3.2.4 Documentation

Resolution MEPC.193(61), as amended by resolution MEPC.246(66)

SOLAS Chapter VII Part A

Both Part A of SOLAS Chapter VII and MARPOL Annex III require documentation of the dangerous or harmful substances carried in packaged form in accordance with the relevant provisions of the IMDG Code. Amongst others, both require a signed certificate or declaration that the shipment offered for carriage is properly packaged and marked, labelled or placarded, and each ship shall be provided with a list of all dangerous goods onboard including their location.

8.3.2.5 Reporting Of Incidents Involving Dangerous Goods

Resolution A.851(20), as amended by resolution MEPC.138(53)

Any incident involving the (likely) loss of dangerous goods in packaged form into the sea must be reported immediately to the nearest coastal State. In doing so, refer to the Guidelines for Reporting Incidents Involving Dangerous Goods, Harmful Substances and/or Marine Pollutants.

8.3.2.6 Jettisoning

Resolution MEPC.193(61), as amended by resolution MEPC.246(66)

MARPOL Annex III completely prohibits jettisoning of harmful substances carried in packaged form unless it is necessary for securing the safety of the ship or saving life at sea.

8.3.3 Response To Marine Chemical Pollution

At an international level, there is one main instrument to respond to marine chemical pollution: the Protocol on Preparedness, Response and Co-operation to pollution Incidents by Hazardous and Noxious Substances, 2000 (OPRC-HNS Protocol).

The OPRC-HNS Protocol was adopted in 2000 to expand the scope of the 1990 International Convention on Oil Pollution Preparedness, Response and Co-operation (OPRC Convention 1990) to apply to pollution incidents by hazardous substances other than oil. It entered into force on 14 June 2007.

The OPRC-HNS Protocol aims to provide a global framework for international co-operation in combating major incidents or threats of marine pollution. Parties to the Protocol are required to establish measures for dealing with pollution incidents, either nationally or in co-operation with other countries. Ships are required to carry a Shipboard Pollution Emergency Plan to deal specifically with incidents involving hazardous and noxious substances.

In addition to the OPRC-HNS Protocol, the International Convention on Liability and Compensation for Damage in Connection with the Carriage of Hazardous and Noxious Substances by Sea (HNS Convention) was adopted in 1996. However, it has not yet been ratified by sufficient Parties to enter into force.

—— Questions to Consider ——

What information and publications can be consulted for more information on any cargo offered for carriage (non-exhaustive list)?

- IBC Code.
- MEPC.2 for provisional categorisation of liquid substances (Tripartite Agreement).
- IMDG Code.
- MARPOL Annex I, II and/or III.
- SOLAS.
- Ship's International Certificate of Fitness for the Carriage of Dangerous Chemicals in Bulk.
- Ship's Procedure & Arrangement Manual.
- Shipper's voyage instructions.
- Material Safety Data Sheet (MSDS).
- Cargo tank coating compatibility information.
- FOSFA List of Banned Immediate Previous Cargoes.
- Shipboard Marine Pollution Emergency Plan (SMPEP).
- Tanker Safety Guides.
- Tank Cleaning Guides.
- Chemical Data Guide for Bulk Shipment by Water and compatibility chart contained therein.
- Ship's Loading and Stability Manual.
- FOSFA (for oils, seeds and fats).
- CHRIS Guide (US Coast Guard).Please be aware that for special trades and products, further information may be required.

Am I allowed to discharge chemicals at sea?
As a general rule of thumb, the answer is no. However, there are some permitted discharges for cargo residues.

To determine whether or not you may be allowed to discharge chemicals at sea, you first need to know under which category – X, Y, Z, or OS – the chemical in question falls:

- Category X: these substances present a major hazard to either marine resources or human health. They may not be discharged into the marine environment.
- Category Y: these substances present a hazard to either marine resources or human health. The quality and quantity of substances that may be discharged is thus limited.
- Category Z: these substances only present a minor hazard to either marine resources or human health. The restrictions on the quality and quantity of discharges are therefore less stringent.
- Other Substances (OS): these substances are considered to present no harm to marine resources or human health. Their discharge is therefore allowed.

To identify the category under which a chemical falls, please check the GESAMP Hazard Profiles as well as the Guidelines for the Categorisation of Noxious Liquid Substances contained in MARPOL Annex II, Appendix I.

No matter what the category, the following discharge standards always have to be met:

- The ship is proceeding *en route* at a minimum speed of 7 knots if it is a self-propelled ship or at 4 knots if it is not self-propelled;
- the discharge is made below the waterline through the underwater overboard discharge and does not exceed the maximum rate for which the underwater overboard discharge is designed; and
- the discharge is made at least 12 nm away from the nearest land and in a minimum depth of water of 25 metres.

Exemptions to discharge a chemical cargo into the sea are defined in MARPOL ANNEX II, Regulation 3, which relate to the safety of the ship or safety of life.

Where do I find updated information on the categorisation of liquid substances?

Before a bulk liquid product can be carried onboard ship, it has to be covered by a Tripartite Agreement between the involved stakeholders, namely the loading port, ship's flag Administration and the unloading port.

The Tripartite Agreement is seen as part of the initial proposal for including new entries in the product list in Chapter 17 or 18 of the IBC Code. Updated lists of Tripartite Agreements are published by the IMO in annual MEPC.2 Circulars issued in the month of December each year.

The circular contains the following annexes:

- Annex 1: List 1: Pure or technically pure products.
- Annex 2: List 2: Pollutant only mixtures containing at least 99% by weight of components already assessed by IMO.
- Annex 3: List 3: (Trade-named) mixtures containing at least 99% by weight of components already assessed by IMO, presenting safety hazards.
- Annex 4: List 4: Pollutant only mixtures containing one or more components, forming more than 1% by weight of the mixture, which have not yet been assessed by IMO.
- Annex 5: List 5: Substances not shipped in pure form but as components in mixtures.
- Annex 6: Synonyms for vegetable oils.
- Annex 7: Country abbreviations.
- Annex 8: Tripartite contact addresses.
- Annex 9: Manufacturers authorised to conduct pollutant-only assessments by calculation.
- Annex 10: Cleaning additives.
- Annex 11: Biofuels recognised under the 2011 Guidelines for the Carriage of Blends of Petroleum Oil and Biofuels.

How do I know what to do in case of an accidental discharge of chemicals into the sea or on deck?

Every ship of 150 GT and above certified to carry noxious liquid substances in bulk must carry onboard a Shipboard Marine Pollution Emergency Plan for Noxious Liquid Substances.

This Emergency Plan provides a detailed list of what to do and whom to contact in case of an accidental discharge of chemicals.

How do I make sure everybody onboard knows what to do in case of a chemical spill?

To ensure that everybody knows what to do in case of a spill and is familiar with the Shipboard Marine Pollution Emergency Plan, drills should be carried out at regular intervals. Such exercises should be as realistic as possible and should include mitigation exercises.

How should I stow chemicals in packaged form?

First of all, check if you are allowed to carry the chemical in question, and if so, how much of it. This is because MARPOL Annex III prohibits or limits the carriage of certain harmful substances.

You need to be particularly careful when stowing chemicals in packaged form onboard the ship. Any dangerous cargo presented for loading must be accompanied by a proper manifest and declaration as required by international regulations. Above all, you need to consider the properties of and interrelationships between the different chemicals, as they may react with one another and possibly with their environment. All cargo, cargo units and cargo transport units must be loaded, stowed and secured throughout the voyage in accordance with the Cargo Securing Manual

Also make sure that all containers containing chemicals are clearly marked to easily identify the content.

On a container ship, reference should be made to the Dangerous Goods Document of Compliance.

What do I need to do if a container with chemicals goes overboard?

Any incident involving the (likely) loss of dangerous goods in packaged form into the sea must be reported immediately to the nearest coastal State. In doing so, refer to the Guidelines for Reporting Incidents Involving Dangerous Goods, Harmful Substances and/or Marine Pollutants. These can be found in resolution A.851(20), as amended by resolution MEPC.138(53).

8.4 Regional Regulation

Regional and national requirements for the prevention and control of chemical pollution may be in place. These should be checked in advance to ensure compliance can be achieved accordingly. Some examples of regional and national regulations include:

- Special routes for ships carrying dangerous cargoes in certain areas (for example along the west cost of Spain, Portugal, English Channel, North Sea).
- Special reporting requirements (mandatory and non-mandatory) for ships carrying dangerous goods in some areas (for example West European Waters, English Channel).
- Requirements to carry specific pollution response plans, monitoring and control of operational discharges and associated reporting requirements.
- Special precautions during tank cleaning and requirements regarding the discharge of tank washings within 200 nm or the exclusive economic zone, which may include prohibition on discharge.

Other regional and national requirements for the prevention and control of pollution may be in place. It is recommended that appropriate checks through port agents are made in advance in order to ensure compliance.

8.5 Going Beyond Compliance

Even though Part A of SOLAS chapter VII makes the IMDG Code mandatory for the carriage of dangerous goods in packaged form, certain parts of the Code are only recommended instead of being mandatory. Therefore, to go beyond regulatory requirements, some or all of the points below could be acted upon.

This is the case with the provisions of the following parts of the IMDG Code:
- Chapter 1.3: Training.
- Chapter 2.1: Explosives, Introductory Notes 1 to 4 only.
- Chapter 2.3: Section 2.3.3: Determination of flashpoint only.
- Chapter 3.2: Columns 15 and 17 of the Dangerous Goods List only.
- Chapter 3.5: Transport schedule for Class 7 radioactive material only.
- Chapter 5.4: Section 5.4.5: Multimodal dangerous goods form, insofar as layout of the form is concerned.
- Chapter 7.3: Special requirements in the event of an incident and fire precautions involving dangerous goods only.

As the IMDG Code says, it is recommended to comply with these requirements to make sure the transport of dangerous cargo, whether in bulk or in packaged form, is safe and causes no harm to neither human health nor the environment.

8.6 Business Benefits

Apart from avoiding potentially serious environmental, health and safety hazards, the careful carriage of chemicals can also be beneficial for your business. This will be especially true once the HNS Convention enters into force. Under this Convention, ship owners would be liable for any damage caused by chemicals leaking from their ship into the marine environment and would have to pay to compensate for this damage.

In order to avoid potentially huge compensation claims, it makes good business sense for ship owners and the crew to proceed with caution when transporting chemicals.

From a health perspective, the implementation of additional protective measures would limit both the short- and long-term possible effect of crew's exposure to chemicals and any associated sick leave.

8.7 Measuring Environmental Performance

Implementing a process of regular performance monitoring can help identify trends and changes in performance levels, and examples of good and poor performance which can be further investigated. Some examples of 'leading' performance indicators might include:

- Provision of onboard training.
- Completion of non-statutory training courses on chemical pollution prevention.
- Results of voluntary or industry-standard audits and inspections (e.g. ISO 14001, vetting).

'Lagging indicators' might include the frequency of spills per port call, or the volume of spills per cargo operation - both of which should be monitored for a period of time so that performance can be compared with like-for-like past performance. Such records can allow for the setting of performance improvement targets, as well as benchmarking against industry results that may be available via safety forums and other industry initiatives.

If incidents do happen, it is valuable to investigate the causes of the incident to determine what corrective actions and preventative actions may be beneficial in the future, and to share these lessons through incident reports and other fleet updates, helping to raise awareness and improve understanding of pollution prevention. It is useful to differentiate between 'spills to water' and those which can be considered as a 'contained spill' (i.e. are either confined onboard or are prevented from reaching the water through response effort), and to evaluate the severity of the incident in terms of impacts to people (e.g. fatalities, injuries), environment (quantity, chemical type, receiving environment) and business (lost time, repair/clean-up costs).

CHAPTER NINE

CONTENTS

CARBON DIOXIDE

CARBON DIOXIDE

9.1 Introduction

Carbon dioxide (CO_2) is a compound gas that is naturally present in the Earth's atmosphere. It plays an important role in regulating the Earth's temperature, however, the balance of atmospheric CO_2 concentration is delicate.

According to leading scientists, the anthropogenic generation of CO_2, via the combustion of hydrocarbon-based fuels such as wood, oil and coal can significantly alter the atmospheric CO_2 concentration balance. CO_2 can be removed from the atmosphere by so-called natural sinks, e.g. forests, but human activities have and continue to destroy vast areas of these, thus reducing their absorption ability.

The transportation sector and heavy industry are often in the spotlight when it comes to CO_2 emissions, and the shipping industry is no exception.

Although shipping is the most energy efficient mode of freight transportation, due to the economy of scale factor, the global shipping fleet does generate significant volumes of CO_2 principally through the combustion of hydrocarbon-based fuels.

In 2012, international shipping released around 800 million tonnes of CO_2 representing just over 2% of global CO_2 emissions, and these emissions are expected to increase significantly in the next few decades.[1]

9.2 Environmental Impact

Greenhouse gases (GHGs), including CO_2, absorb infrared radiation emitted from the Earth's surface and reradiate it back, thus contributing to the greenhouse effect – commonly known as global warming or climate change.

In their 2013 assessment report, the International Panel on Climate Change (IPCC) has established that with 95% certainty, humans have been the dominant cause of global warming since the 1950s. The earth's climate has got successively warmer over the last three decades and these decades have all been warmer than any of the preceding decades since 1850. This has already resulted in changes in the global water cycle, reductions in snow and ice, global mean sea level rise and in changes in some climate extremes. These effects are very likely to exacerbate unless serious mitigation measures are taken.[2]

[1] IMO (2014) Third IMO GHG study
[2] IPCC (2013) Working Group I Contribution to the IPCC Fifth Assessment Report. Climate Change 2013: The Physical Science Basis - Summary for Policymakers.

9.3 International Regulation

CO_2 emissions are governed by MARPOL Annex VI.

In July 2011, a new chapter - Chapter 4 – was added to MARPOL Annex VI, introducing mandatory requirements to enhance ships' energy efficiency, including:

- Energy Efficiency Design Index (EEDI) applicable to new ships.
- Ship Energy Efficiency Management Plan (SEEMP) applicable to all ships.
- International Energy Efficiency (IEE) Certificate applicable to all ships.

Resolution MEPC.203(62)

The regulations contained in Chapter 4 apply to all ships of and above 400 gross tonnage (GT) and entered into force 1 January 2013.

9.3.1 The Energy Efficiency Design Index

The development and enforcement of the EEDI is intended to drive the design and construction of more energy efficient ships. This design-centric regulatory instrument quantifies the amount of CO_2 that a ship emits in relation to its transport work.

The EEDI is a performance-based mechanism that requires certain minimum energy efficiency benchmark values to be attained by new ships, depending on their year of build.

9.3.1.1 Scope

Resolution MEPC.203(62)

The EEDI applies to all new ships above 400 GT. It also affects existing ships above 400 GT but at the moment only those which have undergone a major conversion[3] that is so extensive that the ship's flag State regards the ship as newly constructed.

Resolution MEPC.203(62)
Resolution MEPC.231(65)

The EEDI applies to the following ship types:

- Bulk carrier.
- Gas carrier.
- Tanker.
- Container ship.
- General cargo ship.
- Refrigerated cargo carrier.[4]

- Combination carrier.
- Ro-Ro cargo ship.
- Ro-Ro passenger ship.
- LNG carriers.
- Cruise ships.

Resolution MEPC.203(62)

At present, ships with steam turbine, diesel-electric and hybrid propulsion are excluded from the EEDI requirements.

9.3.1.2 Energy Efficiency Requirements Under The EEDI

The energy efficiency requirements enforced by the EEDI regulations under MARPOL Annex VI are defined by 'attained EEDI' and 'required EEDI'. We distinguish and describe both of these in the next sections.

Attained EEDI

The attained EEDI is the actual EEDI of a ship. It is specific to each ship and indicates the estimated performance of the ship in terms of energy efficiency. It must be calculated according to guidelines by the International Maritime Organization (IMO) contained in resolution MEPC.245(66).

Resolution MEPC.245(66)

To calculate the attained EEDI, the following formula must be used:

$$\frac{\left(\prod_{j=1}^{n} f_j\right)\left(\sum_{i=1}^{nME} P_{ME(i)} \cdot C_{FME(i)} \cdot SFC_{ME(i)}\right) + (P_{AE} \cdot C_{FAE} \cdot SFC_{AE}{}^*) + \left(\left(\prod_{j=1}^{n} f_j \cdot \sum_{i=1}^{nPTI} P_{PTI(i)} - \sum_{i=1}^{neff} f_{eff(i)} \cdot P_{AEeff(i)}\right)C_{FAE} \cdot SFC_{AE}\right) - \left(\sum_{i=1}^{neff} f_{eff(i)} \cdot P_{eff(i)} \cdot C_{FME} \cdot SFC_{ME}{}^{**}\right)}{f_i \cdot f_c \cdot f_l \cdot Capacity \cdot f_w \cdot V_{ref}}$$

Admittedly, this formula looks rather intimidating, but it basically just means the following:

$$EEDI = \frac{CO_2 \text{ emission}}{\text{transport work}}$$

[3] For a definition of 'major conversion', check resolution MEPC.203(62), Regulation 2.
[4] Juice tankers are categorised as refrigerated cargo ships. Furthermore, ice-breaking cargo ships exceeding Finnish/Swedish ice-class '1A Super' are excluded from the EEDI regime.

Resolution MEPC.245(66)

The CO_2 emissions represent total CO_2 emissions from combustion of fuel, including propulsion and auxiliary engines and boilers, taking into account the carbon content of the fuels in question. If energy efficient mechanical or electrical technologies are incorporated onboard a ship, their effects are deducted from the total CO_2 emission.

The transport work is calculated by multiplying the ship's capacity - deadweight tonnage (DWT) - as designed, with the ship's design speed measured at the maximum design load condition and at 75% of the rated installed shaft power.

NOTE: You can calculate your ship's EEDI via a tool hosted on BIMCOs website.

Required EEDI

Resolution MEPC.203(62)

The required EEDI indicates how energy efficient the design of a ship must be in order to comply with Chapter 4 of MARPOL Annex VI. Accordingly, the attained EEDI of a ship must be equal to or less than the required EEDI for that ship type.

The required EEDI is a function of the reference line value which depends on a ship's type and size, and a reduction factor X:

$$Required\ EEDI = (1-X/100) \cdot Reference\ line\ value$$

The reference line values depend on certain parameters and the DWT of the ship. They are calculated as follows:

$$Reference\ line\ value = a \cdot b^{-c}$$

The parameters needed for determining reference line values for different ship types are shown in the table below:

Resolution MEPC.251(66)

Ship Type	a	b	c
Bulk carrier	961.79	DWT of the ship	0.477
Gas carrier	1120.00	DWT of the ship	0.456
Tanker	1218.80	DWT of the ship	0.488
Container ship	174.22	DWT of the ship	0.201
General cargo ship	107.48	DWT of the ship	0.216
Refrigerated cargo carrier	227.01	DWT of the ship	0.244
Combination carrier	1219.00	DWT of the ship	0.488
Ro-Ro cargo ship (vehicle carrier)	$(DWT/GT)^{-0.7}$ $\cdot$ 780.36 where $DWT/GT < 0.3$	DWT of the ship	0.471
	1812.63 where $DWT/GT \geq 0.3$		
Ro-Ro cargo ship	1405.15	DWT of the ship	0.498
Ro-Ro passenger ship	752.16	DWT of the ship	0.381
LNG carrier	2253.7	DWT of the ship	0.474
Cruise passenger ship having non-conventional propulsion	170.84	GT of the ship	0.214

Resolution MEPC.203(62)

If the design of a ship allows it to fall into more than one of the above ship type definitions, the required EEDI for the ship shall be the most stringent (the lowest) required EEDI.

Reduction factors increase over time so that every five years, the energy efficiency design requirements become more stringent. This is expected to stimulate continued innovation and technological development of all the components influencing the fuel efficiency of a ship from its design phase.

The reduction factors for different ship types and sizes are shown in the following table:

Resolution MEPC.203(62)

Resolution MEPC.251(66)

Ship Type	Size	Phase 0 1 Jan 2013 – 31 Dec 2014	Phase 1 1 Jan 2015- 31 Dec 2019	Phase 2 1 Jan 2020- 31 Dec 2024	Phase 3 1 Jan 2025 And Onwards
Bulk carrier	20,000 DWT and above	0	10	20	30
	10,000 - 20,000 DWT	n/a	0-10*	0-20*	0-30*
Gas carrier	10,000 DWT and above	0	10	20	30
	2,000 - 10,000 DWT	n/a	0-10*	0-20*	0-30*
Tanker	20,000 DWT and above	0	10	20	30
	4,000 - 20,000 DWT	n/a	0-10*	0-20*	0-30*
Container ship	15,000 DWT and above	0	10	20	30
	10,000 - 15,000 DWT	n/a	0-10*	0-20*	0-30*
General cargo ships	15,000 DWT and above	0	10	15	30
	3,000 - 15,000 DWT	n/a	0-10*	0-15*	0-30*
Refrigerated cargo carrier	5,000 DWT and above	0	10	15	30
	3,000 - 5,000 DWT	n/a	0-10*	0-15*	0-30*
Combination carrier	20,000 DWT and above	0	10	20	30
	4,000 - 20,000 DWT	n/a	0-10*	0-20*	0-30*
LNG carrier***	10,000 DWT and above	n/a	10**	20	30
Ro-Ro cargo ship (vehicle carrier)***	10,000 DWT and above	n/a	5**	15	30
Ro-Ro cargo ship***	2,000 DWT and above	n/a	5**	20	30
	1,000 - 2,000 DWT	n/a	0-5***	0-20*	0-30*
Ro-Ro passenger ship***	1,000 DWT and above	n/a	5**	20	30
	250 - 1,000 DWT	n/a	0-5***	0-20*	0-30*
Cruise passenger ship*** having non-conventional propulsion	85,000 GT and above	n/a	5**	20	30
	25,000 - 85,000 GT	n/a	0-5***	0-20*	0-30*

* Reduction factor to be linearly interpolated between the two values dependent upon ship size. The lower value of the reduction factor is to be applied to the smaller ship size.

** Phase 1 commences for those ships on 1 September 2015.

*** Reduction factor applies to those ships delivered on or after 1 September 2019, as defined in paragraph 43 of Regulation 2.

n/a means that no required EEDI applies.

The required EEDI for Phase 0 applies to all ships defined in the table above for which:

- The building contract date is placed in Phase 0, and the delivery is before 1 January 2019; or
- the building contract is placed before Phase 0 and the delivery is on or after 1 July 2015 and before 1 January 2019; or
- in absence of a building contract, the keel is laid or which is at similar stage of construction on or after the 1 July 2013 and before 1 July 2015 and delivery is before 1 January 2019.
- In absence of a building contract, the keel is laid or which is at similar stage of construction before the 1 July 2013 and the delivery is on or after 1 January 2015 and before 1 January 2019.

The required EEDI for Phase 1 applies to all ships defined in the table above for which:

- The building contract date is placed in Phase 1, and the delivery is before 1 January 2024; or
- the building contract is placed before Phase 1 and the delivery is on or after 1 July 2019 and before 1 January 2024; or
- in absence of a building contract, the keel is laid or which is at similar stage of construction on or after the 1 July 2015 and before 1 July 2020 and delivery is before 1 January 2024.
- In absence of a building contract, the keel is laid or which is at similar stage of construction before the 1 July 2015 and the delivery is on or after 1 January 2019 and before 1 January 2024.

The required EEDI for Phase 2 applies to all ships defined in the table above for which:

- The building contract date is placed in Phase 2, and the delivery is before 1 January 2029; or
- the building contract is placed before Phase 2 and the delivery is on or after 1 July 2024 and before 1 January 2029; or
- in absence of a building contract, the keel is laid or which is at similar stage of construction on or after the 1 July 2020 and before 1 July 2025 and delivery is before 1 January 2029.
- In absence of a building contract, the keel is laid or which is at similar stage of construction before the 1 July 2020 and the delivery is on or after 1 January 2024 and before 1 January 2029.

The required EEDI for Phase 3 applies to all ships defined in the table above for which:

- The building contract date is placed in Phase 3, or
- in absence of a building contract, the keel is laid or which is at similar stage of construction on or after 1 July 2025, or
- delivery is after 1 January 2029.

At the beginning of Phase 1 and at the midpoint of Phase 2, the IMO will review the status of technological developments and, if necessary, amend the time periods and the EEDI reference line parameters for relevant ship types and reduction rates.

NOTE: The installed propulsion power must not be less than the propulsion power needed to maintain the manoeuvrability of the ship under adverse conditions. In order to determine this minimum propulsion power, the IMO has adopted interim guidelines which can be found in resolution MEPC.232(65), as amended by resolution MEPC.255(67).

Resolution MEPC.203(62)

Survey And Certification Of The EEDI

According to Chapter 4 of MARPOL Annex VI, the attained EEDI must be verified.

Resolution MEPC.214(63),
as amended by resolutions
MEPC.234(65) and
MEPC.254(67)

EEDI verification requires input from the shipyard, ship owner and the verifier and is performed at two stages:

1. Preliminary assessment of the EEDI at the design stage to demonstrate the estimated EEDI prior to construction.
2. Final assessment of the EEDI at final stage of construction to verify the attained EEDI before delivery.

For further information, please refer to the IMO Guidelines on Survey and Certification of the EEDI which are contained in resolution MEPC.214(63), as amended by resolutions MEPC.234(65) and MEPC.245(67).

Resolution MEPC.203(62)

Ship Energy Efficiency Management Plan

As of 1 January 2013, all ships over 400 GT on international voyages are required to carry a ship-specific SEEMP onboard, detailing the operational and technical measures that will be implemented onboard to improve energy efficiency.

The SEEMP may form part of the ship's safety management system. It must be developed taking into account the IMO guidelines which can be found in resolution MEPC.213(63).

Resolution MEPC.213(63)

The IMO guidelines identify a process consisting of four different stages: planning, implementation, monitoring, self-evaluation and improvement. It is an ongoing process, with the results of each cycle feeding into the next iteration of the SEEMP. Thereby, the SEEMP allows for gradual improvements in energy efficiency over time.

Resolution MEPC.213(63)

The Four Stages Of SEEMP

1. **Planning**

   The planning stage should establish the current energy usage patterns of the ship, including its overall baseline efficiency. Both ship-specific and company-wide measures to save energy should be identified, together with any personnel training requirements that follow from these measures, goals for efficiency improvement, and the data requirements and measurement procedures that will underpin effective monitoring and evaluation.

2. **Implementation**

   Implementation of the measures set out in the SEEMP is not mandatory and there is no regulatory procedure for checking that measures have actually been put into practice. Bear in mind, however, that without implementing any energy-saving measures, you will also not be able to reap any of the various benefits, the most obvious being reduced energy costs.

3. **Monitoring**

   The monitoring stage comprises ensuring that measures have been carried out as well as collecting and collating the efficiency performance data identified at the first stage in order to calculate the ship's overall efficiency. To this end, the Energy Efficiency Operational Indicator (EEOI) can - but does not have to be – used.

4. **Evaluate**

   Self-evaluation and improvement is the final stage identified by the IMO guidelines and forms the basis for planning the next iteration of a SEEMP. The data collected should be assessed to understand how effective energy-saving measures have been, and where there is room for further improvements.

Resolution MEPC.176(58)

9.3.2.2 *Enforcement*

SEEMP is not an onerous regulation. All ships are required to carry a SEEMP, but this is all that is necessary for compliance. It need only 'take account' of the relevant IMO guidelines, and neither the Administration or Port State Control (PSC) can check that the contents of the SEEMP adhere to these guidelines, or that a ship is implementing the measures contained in its SEEMP. Enforcement powers are limited to verifying that a SEEMP exists – and even here, its continuing existence is not directly verified – the presence of SEEMP is attested by means of the IEE Certificate (see Section 9.3.3.2) which is issued once for the life of the ship.

9.3.3 Surveys And Certification – MARPOL Annex VI

9.3.3.1 *General Certification Requirements Applicable To All Air Pollutants*

Every ship covered by MARPOL Annex VI must carry a valid International Air Pollution Prevention (IAPP) Certificate onboard for inspection by port or flag States.

Usually, the IAPP Certificate is valid for five years – provided that no change of flag takes place. The basic prerequisite to obtain an IAPP Certificate is that the ship complies with the requirements of the applicable regulations of MARPOL Annex VI. This has to be proven through an initial survey.

After the IAPP Certificate has been issued for the first time, each ship has to undergo periodical surveys in order to avoid the Certificate cease to be valid. These are:

- Annual surveys within a time window of ± three months of the anniversary date of the IAPP Certificate.
- One intermediate survey either after 2 or 3 years after issuance of the IAPP Certificate.
- A renewal survey before the end of every five-year period after issuance of the IAPP Certificate.
- An additional survey after a repair following an accident to the ship or when a defect is discovered in a ship, either of which substantially affect the integrity of the ship or the efficiency or completeness of the equipment of the ship. An additional survey is also required after an important repair or renewal is made.

A model IAPP Certificate is included in Appendix I to MARPOL Annex VI. It has been amended by resolution MEPC.194(61). This model certificate is also included in Part Three - The Maritime Environmental & Efficiency Templates provided on the USB memory stick.

International Energy Efficiency Certificate

Every ship covered by Chapter 4 of MARPOL Annex VI must carry a valid IEE Certificate onboard for inspection by port or flag States. The Certificate is valid throughout the life of the ship unless the ship is withdrawn from service, changes to the flag of another State or following major conversion of the ship.

In order to be granted an IEE Certificate, the ship has to pass the following surveys:

- An initial survey before a new ship is put in service to verify that the ship meets the applicable EEDI requirements and carries a SEEMP onboard.
- A general or partial survey after a major conversion of a ship. The survey shall ensure that the attained EEDI is recalculated and is equal to or below the required EEDI.
- If the major conversion of a ship is so extensive that the Administration regards it as a newly constructed ship, it is up the Administration to determine if an initial survey on the attained EEDI is necessary.
- For existing ships, the verification that a SEEMP is onboard takes place at the first intermediate or renewal survey on or after 1 January 2013.

A model IEE Certificate is included in appendix VIII to MARPOL Annex IV, as amended by resolution MEPC.203(62). It is also included in Part Three - The Maritime Environmental & Efficiency Templates provided on the USB memory stick.

Any port State inspection is limited to verifying, when appropriate, that there is a valid IEE Certificate onboard.

Questions to Consider

Do energy efficiency regulations affect my fleet?

At IMO level, there are currently two main regulatory requirements for a ship's energy efficiency: the EEDI and the SEEMP.

The EEDI affects new ships above 400 GT and applies to the ship types mentioned in Section 9.3.1.1.

Passenger ships, Ro-Ro cargo ships and Ro-Ro passenger ships are not initially subject to any limits on energy consumption. However, the attained EEDI still needs to be calculated. At present, the EEDI excludes ships with steam turbine, diesel-electric and hybrid propulsion.

The requirement to carry a ship-specific SEEMP onboard applies to all ships over 400 GT on international voyages.

What is the purpose of the EEDI?

The IMO's rationale behind the EEDI is to provide an incentive for improving the design and construction of new ships so that future generations of ships built under the EEDI will be more energy efficient that the existing fleet resulting in overall reduction of GHG emissions over time.

What is the difference between the attained and the required EEDI?

The attained EEDI is the actual EDDI of a ship. It is specific to each ship and indicates the estimated performance of the ship in terms of energy efficiency.

The required EEDI indicates how energy efficient the design of a ship must be in order to comply with Chapter 4 of MARPOL Annex VI. It is a function of the reference line value and a reduction factor X.

The attained EEDI of a ship must be equal to or less than the required EEDI for that ship type.

What is meant by reference lines?

Reference lines help determine the required EEDI limits. They refer to average values of EEDI for global shipping and are based on data for the existing global fleet.

EEDI limits, which are defined by these reference lines, will be lowered gradually in the future using reduction factors (percentages of the original reference lines).

What are the proposed reduction factors for the required EEDI?

The reduction factors are specific to each applicable ship type. For bulk carriers, gas tankers, tankers, container ships and combination carriers, the EEDI reduction will be 0% from 1 January 2013, 10% from 1 January 2015, 20% from 1 January 2020 and 30% from 1 January 2025. For general cargo ships and refrigerated cargo carriers the same will apply with the exception of 15% reduction from 1 January 2020.

What happens if the attained EEDI from the result of the sea trial could not achieve the EEDI required?

This is an unusual case and would be a matter of 're-certification'. However, if a ship initially failed compliance with the required EEDI, then it would not be allowed to sail until this was rectified. In this case, re-doing speed trial would be considered an expected solution after remedying the efficiency of the ship to meet required EEDI value.

But in general, there is no need to worry about this as it is the obligation of the shipyard to make sure your ship complies with the EEDI requirements, so the shipyard would have to fix the matter

Are EEDI reduction measures ship dependent?

Some measures for reducing fuel consumption might not be efficient for all ship sizes. For example, heat recovery will only be efficient for a larger installed power.

Will the EEDI affect my ship's speed?

Ship speed is the most sensitive criterion in the EEDI formula. The aim is to define acceptable safety margins in terms of manoeuvrability capabilities in adverse environmental conditions. It was suggested that for some ship types (e.g. tankers, bulk carriers and container ships) manoeuvrability capabilities in adverse environmental conditions should also include the ballast loading condition. The regulation addresses the requirement to have a minimum installed power albeit the definition of this term is still under development.

However, please remember that the EEDI is intended to promote the use of a wider range of technologies and design improvements that will ensure ships meet the regulation. Reduction in ship speed, whilst an option, is not the only factor.

What are the main differences between the EEDI and the SEEMP?

The EEDI applies to new ships over 400GT, whereas the SEEMP applies to all ships, newbuild and existing, over 400 GT.

The EEDI is a technical measure and concerns the design of the ship. The SEEMP, however, is an operational measure establishing a mechanism to improve the energy efficiency of a ship in a cost-effective manner.

The EEDI establishes mandatory minimum energy efficiency requirements for new ships depending on ship type and size. While it is legally required for a ship over 400 GT to carry a SEEMP onboard, the implementation of energy efficiency measures mentioned in the SEEMP is voluntary and not being controlled.

What is the purpose of the SEEMP?

The SEEMP provides an approach for monitoring ship and fleet efficiency performance over time, and encourages the ship owner to consider new technologies and practices at each stage of the plan.

How are the SEEMP requirements verified and enforced?

All ships are required to carry a SEEMP. The presence of SEEMP is attested by means of the IEE Certificate, which is subject to the usual MARPOL surveys (initial, renewal, intermediate, annual etc.).

However, this is all that is necessary for compliance. The relevant IMO guidelines only need to be taken account of, and neither the Administration nor PSC can check that the contents of the SEEMP adhere to these guidelines, or that a ship is implementing the measures contained in its SEEMP.

Is there a standard form or template that I need to use for the SEEMP?

No. It is up to each company to develop their own SEEMP in conformity with the Guidance provided in MEPC.213(63). This guidance document contains a sample template that each SEEMP can be based upon, but it does not have to be used.

BIMCO and Fathom have developed the 'Step-by-Step Ship Energy Efficiency Plan Manual' to guide owners and operators through the process of creating their own SEEMPs in-house with ease.

Can I just create a generic SEEMP for each of my ships?

The whole purpose of the SEEMP is to be ship-specific. The risk of having a generic SEEMP is that some of the energy efficiency measures may not apply to other ships or may be too generic and impractical to implement. That is why the SEEMP should be ship-specific and only contain those energy efficiency measures which can be implemented for that specific ship.

How often do I need to review the SEEMP?

This is entirely at your discretion. However, it should be done on a regular basis to help ensure that the SEEMP remains relevant and has a positive effect on onboard energy efficiency. You could integrate the SEEMP review into your already established timeline, so for example at the same time as the intermediate, annual or renewal surveys of your IAPP Certificate.

The results of each review should feed back into the next planning phase of the SEEMP which is why the SEEMP should be considered as a 'live' document that never stops evolving.

Do I need to use the EEOI as the monitoring tool?

You can, but you don't have to. While an international standard such as the EEOI should preferably be used, other tools or Key Performance Indicators can be used as well.

If I want to sell a ship, do I have to pass on the SEEMP to the new owner?

No. It is the responsibility of the company who owns/operates the ship to develop their own SEEMP for each ship, noting the requirement to incorporate the broader corporate energy strategy that relates to that company.

9.4 Regional Regulation

9.4.1 The French CO_2 Regulation

Since 1 October 2013, ships calling at French ports must report how much CO_2 the ship has emitted during its voyage.

France's CO_2 reporting scheme forms part of a national strategy to reduce CO_2 emissions. The purpose of providing CO_2 information for transport services is to make stakeholders in the transport chain aware of their contribution to GHG emissions and help them make informed choices towards less-emitting solutions.

9.4.1.1 *Scope*

The new CO_2 emission disclosure requirement applies to:

> *"any public or private persons organising or selling transport services for passengers, goods or moving purposes, carried out using one or several means of transport, departing from or travelling to a location in France, with the exception of transport services organised by public or private persons for their own behalf"*
> - including ships transporting passengers or cargo to or from French ports.

The requirement does not apply to ships:

- Transiting French waters;
- making stops for refuelling or making other technical stops in France; and
- with no goods or passengers departing from or transporting to a location in France.

9.4.1.2 *Monitoring Requirements*

Ships calling at French ports must report how much CO_2 the ship has emitted during its journey.

The amount of CO_2 emitted is calculated by multiplying the fuel consumed for a particular leg of the journey by the relevant emission factor. The values of emissions factors are defined by the Minister of Transport. They take into account all emissions generated during both the upstream and the operating phase. The upstream phase corresponds to the activities implemented to supply the means of transport with its energy source, e.g. extracting the oil, refining it and distributing the fuel from the refinery to the pump. The operating phase refers to the combustion of the energy source.

For example, the emission factors for heavy fuel oil (HFO) are 0.46 kg of CO_2 per litre for the upstream phase and 3.12 kg of CO_2 per litre for the operating phase. Therefore, the overall emissions generated for one litre of HFO are:

$$0.46 \text{ kg} + 3.12 \text{ kg} = 3.58 \text{ kg of } CO_2.$$

More detailed information on the different emission factors, CO_2 calculations and reporting requirements can be found in the 'Methodological guide on CO_2 information for transport services' provided by the French Ministry of Ecology, Sustainable Development and Energy.

9.5 Going Beyond Compliance

In order to go beyond regulatory compliance you must first monitor a ship or fleet's CO_2 emissions and then consequently reduce the ship or fleet's CO_2 emissions.

9.5.1 Monitoring CO_2 Emissions

Decisions regarding the implementation of CO_2 reduction measures should always be based on comprehensive monitoring of CO_2 emissions. In the absence of a comprehensive monitoring framework and baseline data, it will be impossible to ascertain what your starting point is, and what impact any possible measure taken will have on ship performance.

Furthermore, accurate and regular monitoring of energy or fuel consumption for a ship or indeed across a fleet can highlight inefficiencies and provide a mechanism for continual improvement.

To monitor CO_2 emissions you should:

- Record and archive fuel consumption data.
- Complete an annual inventory of CO_2 emissions for all ships within the company fleet.

To make sure these measures are adhered to, documenting fuel consumption data should become an integral part of the company's strategy.

NOTE: The methodology for estimating CO_2 emissions is detailed in Section 9.7.

9.5.2 Reducing CO_2 Emissions

CO_2 emissions are proportional to fuel consumption, for this the approximate 3:1 ratio of CO_2 tonnes emitted to fuel tonnes consumed can be applied. This conversion rule recognises that for every tonne of HFO combusted, three tonnes of CO_2 are produced as a bi-product.

Therefore, a reduction in fuel consumption equates to a significant reduction in CO_2 emissions. Increasing the energy efficiency of a ship, or streamlining operations is the primary activity that can be undertaken to reduce CO_2 emissions, i.e. doing the same amount of work with less energy.

Another strategy to reduce CO_2 emissions would be to utilise alternative sources of fuel that produce less CO_2, or no CO_2 as a bi-product of combustion. This is considered to be more of a long-term option in comparison to simply reducing standard fuel consumption, due to the potential high investment required and change to the ship's machinery.

NOTE: This Guide does not include all energy saving measures or strategies – please refer to Fathom-CTech.com for more information on the available measures.

9.5.2.1 Increasing Energy Efficiency

Measures to increase the energy efficiency of your ship can be divided into operational and technical measures:

- Operational measures relate to the way in which the ship is maintained and operated.
- Technical measures aim to enhance the energy efficiency by improving the hardware (equipment) of the ship. They are linked to the design and building of the ship (e.g. hull design), to optimisation of the propulsion system, to the control and efficient operation of the main and auxiliary engines, and to retrofits on existing ships.

Operational measures generally have low investment requirements with a moderate increase in operating costs. If you are only starting to look into your ship's energy performance, we advise you to consider these measures first. Please consult Section 9.5.2.1 for further information on operational measures.

Once you have picked these low-hanging fruits, but want to continue improving your energy efficiency, you can move on and look into technical retrofit solutions. Some of these will give you quick wins, i.e. high energy savings requiring little investments, whereas others will be more elaborate.

Technical measures, often referred to as 'solutions', do require investment and this can range from low to moderate to high levels of financing depending on the technical solution in question. Technical measures can be considered both for new ships and existing ships. However, taking efficiency into account at the design stage could be of greater financial benefit with regards to investment due to the lessened drydocking costs and out of service periods for the ship that would be demanded from retrofitting an existing ship with technical solutions. Since the introduction of the EEDI, designing new ships with energy efficiency considerations in mind is mandatory, however, retrofitting existing ships with technical measures is becoming more and more attractive as fuel prices are continually fluctuating.

Operational Measures

A ship operator's most direct and useful tools for managing ship performance are the operational decisions made on a daily basis on how to conduct a voyage, perform regular maintenance and control onboard power usage. This should be done in agreement with the involved parties, e.g. in the charter party.

NOTE: BIMCO produces a wide variety of standard contracts, which are either issued by BIMCO or by another organisation and adopted by BIMCO. Sample copies of these contracts are available to download free of charge from BIMCO's website along with comprehensive explanatory notes.

Voyage Performance Management

Every voyage offers the opportunity to optimise speed, find the safest route through calm seas and make sure the ship is sailing at the best draft and trim and tuned to keep course efficiently.

We detail voyage performance management factors below:

- **Speed Optimisation**

    'Slow steaming' reduces propulsion power requirements significantly. In general, it is said that reducing ship speed by 10% can achieve savings of around 20% in fuel. However, slow steaming may also come at a cost when the volume of cargo being transported within the same time frame is unchanged. It may therefore require more ships to sail ensuring that the same volume of freight is delivered on time. In addition, as most ships are optimised for a certain speed, steaming at lower speeds might have negative consequences in terms of engine maintenance and fuel consumption. The optimum speed on any voyage will therefore be a function of several factors, including the charter rate, scheduled arrival time (and any flexibility in allowable arrival time), engine rating and condition, ship design speed, current fuel price and potentially the need to avoid adverse weather conditions.

- **Weather Routing**

    Avoiding areas of heavy weather not only reduces safety risks but can also significantly reduce fuel consumption. In some circumstances, it may be possible to take advantage of prevailing winds or currents to reduce propulsion power demand. There are a number of commercial providers of weather information and routing services of varying degrees of sophistication. Even when these are not used, the Master should assess the possibility for saving fuel through routing that takes account of weather conditions, and both oceanic and local currents when preparing the Voyage Plan.

- **Optimisation Of Ballast And Trim**

    Sailing a ship at its optimum trim for current speed, loading and sea state reduces its hydrodynamic resistance to the minimum possible, reducing propulsion energy requirements and hence fuel consumption. Following good cargo loading procedures, regularly checking the ballast and trim and if necessary adjusting them while at sea can therefore provide fuel savings at low costs. In addition, a variety of software packages are available that offer advice on optimising trim.

    NOTE: Trim adjustments must be carried out in accordance with the ship's Ballast Water Management Plan and recorded in the ship's Ballast Water Record Book.

- **Minimising Rudder Adjustments**

  Rudder movements can add drag to the hull and increase resistance. Therefore, minimising the number of times the rudder is used and the amount of rudder angle that is applied to maintain or change a course will save fuel. Adaptive autopilots and integrated systems are frequently used for this purpose.

- **Increasing Cargo Load Factor**

  Ensuring that ships voyage with the highest volume of cargo possible will reduce the fuel consumption per tonne-kilometre. The volume, timing and location of transport demand will determine the extent to which operators can increase current load factors, but improved logistical analysis may yield savings for some operators. Software programmes can ensure optimal loading and bunkering.

- **Optimum Berthing/Virtual Arrival**

  Some shipping segments have already begun and others could start using the concept of Virtual Arrival. Where it is known that the destination port is suffering congestion, this information can be relayed to the ship, which then sails slower, rather than proceeding at normal speed and waiting at anchor until a berth becomes available. This radically reduces bunker fuel consumption and emissions, while easing congestion and enhancing safety, but has to be done in agreement with involved parties, e.g. in the charter party.

  Even though the Virtual Arrival concept has been developed for and pioneered in the oil tanker sector, it is also suitable for adoption in other trades where the required time of arrival at a destination port is not fixed or is subject to change due to operational or commercial reasons.

- **Total Voyage Performance Management Systems**

  These systems integrate some or all of the above-mentioned voyage performance aspects. The more capable systems use predictive models with all these factors to plan the most efficient voyage – what route to take, what speeds to use on each leg, what trim to use, how much ballast to carry, and what autopilot strategies to use given the weather.

Hull And Propeller Condition Management

Hull fouling – the accretion of marine organisms on the hull surface – reduces the ship's hydrodynamic performance, increases fuel consumption and decreases top speed and range. In addition to hull fouling, propeller surface degradation will also reduce propulsive efficiency.

The process of biofouling can be moderated through the application of advanced paint coatings as well as by cleaning and polishing the hull and propeller.

- **Advanced Hull And Propeller Coatings**

  For a ship's hull the principal anti-fouling practice is the application of low friction paint coatings. The most advanced hull coatings have considerable potential for efficiency savings and can be quickly applied as a retrofit measure. Following the ban on tributyltin (TBT)-based coatings in 2008, research on alternative options increased tremendously. Copper acrylate-based self-polishing copolymers are now widely used. However, from an environmental perspective, the most desirable approach is to use non-toxic, low surface energy coatings, and a number of silicone-based foul release options are now available. Given the wide variety of products available and the range of savings claims by manufacturers, operators may wish to trial one or more coatings on individual ships before applying the measure more widely across the fleet.

- **Hull And Propeller Cleaning/Polishing And Condition-Based Monitoring**

  In-service cleaning of the propeller and the hull helps to keep the ship's underwater surfaces smooth. It can be undertaken at regular intervals, however, where ships have irregular trade patterns, hull fouling may occur at different rates. Knowing when to clean the hull and the propeller is the goal of condition-based hull and propeller maintenance. This can be done in two ways: observe and inspect actual hull and propeller fouling; or use performance-based systems that track changes in ship speed and required power (or using fuel consumed as a proxy for required power) to identify degrading surface conditions.

Onboard Power Management

Most modern ships in the global fleet host a vast array of power-consuming equipment onboard: pumps, fans, heating and cooling equipment and hydraulic machinery in the working areas of the ship, lighting, air conditioning and appliances in the accommodation block, to name but a few. Any item that consumes power is wasting energy if it is running (or on standby power) when not needed, or working at a higher load than necessary. Therefore, a ship-wide audit of all energy-consuming equipment should be conducted in order to identify and implement power-saving opportunities. The ship-wide audit should:

- Prioritise the heaviest power consumers (likely to be pumps and heating/cooling equipment and larger machinery).

- Involve a crew-wide exercise to ensure that all those responsible for operating particular equipment can give input (both to identify areas of potential saving and to ensure all operational requirements are borne in mind).

- Adhere at all times to manufacturers' guidelines for safe operation of equipment, and the ship's safety management system.

- Draw up a list of specific measures and best practices, identifying roles and responsibilities for implementing them and a monitoring/evaluation schedule.

The opportunities vary and will be different on every ship, but could include:

- **Cargo Heating:** Tanker and liquid bulk operators can save energy by not heating cargo to the discharge temperature specified in the charter throughout the whole of the voyage. Any planned change to cargo temperatures must take account of the applicable safety considerations, and of any effects on the condition of cargo itself. For applicable trades, operators may specify in the SEEMP that a voyage-specific cargo heating plan should be drawn up. Heating requirements may also be reduced by improving insulation of cargo areas and heating pipes, and by stowing cargoes with similar heating requirements together.

- **Bunker Heating:** Ships may also benefit from voyage-specific bunker heating plans that identify the most economical method of maintaining fuel at the optimum temperature for safety and engine performance. Factors to be considered include tank layout and volumes, the capacity and energy consumption of heating equipment, and the range of ambient and sea temperatures likely to be encountered *en route*.

- **Fans And Pumps:** Fans and pumps should not be run when not required.

- **Accommodation:** Crew should identify and agree on energy-saving measures within the accommodation, for instance switching off unnecessary lights, using electric appliances in the most efficient manner, and minimising loading on air conditioning/heating e.g. by closing blinds/curtains where possible.

In addition to these operational measures, ship owners and operators should consider investing in improved insulation, low-energy lighting, more efficient space heating /air conditioning and appliances etc. Optimising hotel functions is of paramount importance on passenger ships, where they consume a much greater proportion of energy than on cargo ships.

Creating An Energy-Saving Culture

Reducing fuel consumption is not just about using energy-saving technologies, but also about people and their willingness to engage in energy-saving practices. Creating a corporate culture that explicitly encourages such behaviour both across shore-based and onboard operations is therefore an important part of energy management.

Next to creating awareness, developing and communicating vision statements and targets, this could be achieved by providing incentives and bonuses for energy savings. These could take various forms – for example sharing part of the saved costs through a crew bonus for every percent improvement in the operational energy efficiency, or a competition among sister ships for the most improved performance. Training on energy-saving practices and a fuel-monitoring system will be useful so that the crew can make an impact and see the results.

See the Box Out below for a company's experience with crew competitions to improve energy efficiency.

Crew Competition To Improve Energy Efficiency

North European ferry operator DFDS organises a quarterly internal bunker prize competition which encourages crew on DFDS ships to compete for bunker fuel savings. In the second quarter of 2012, the winner was the Petunia Seaways. By employing a number of operational tweaks, engine room staff of the Petunia Seaways have reduced bunker consumption year on year for the first half of 2012, equivalent to annual savings of 179.2 metric tonnes (mt) of fuel oil and 100.8 mt of marine gas oil (MGO). DFDS estimates that this equates to annual savings of DKK 1,568,500 (US$ 255,536) at current bunker prices.

In general, the bunker prize competition seems to be a hit for DFDS. According to an internal newsletter, engine room crews across the fleet are *"all extremely focused on saving fuel by testing new and creative ideas and they are never satisfied with what they have achieved, but always looking for further improvements"*.

Technical Measures

NOTE: In this section we do not detail each technical measure due to the vast number of technical measures available to the market. For a comprehensive database of all technical measures please visit Fathom-Ctech.com.

A variety of technical measures can increase ship efficiency and reduce fuel consumption and the market of technical measures that can be retrofitted to existing ships is as vast as those that can be considered at the design stage.

For example, a variety of devices and modifications are available that improve the inflow of water to the propeller, the propulsive efficiency of the propeller itself, reduce drag or recover energy from the wake vortex. Many such devices have been extensively tested in-service over several decades and offer well established fuel savings, although ship-specific modelling is advisable before installation as benefits vary widely with hull form, ship speed etc.

In addition to ship propulsion, the optimal functioning of the main engine is a pivotal factor to consider when acting upon CO_2 reduction as this machinery is the vector for fuel combustion and CO_2 emission production. Ensuring the optimal functioning of the main engine is critical to ensuring efficient sailing. While operators will already have procedures for managing engine performance as part of their safety management system, processes should be established to review and extend these procedures as appropriate, with a view to ensuring fuel efficient as well as safe operations.

As a minimum, the following engine parameters should be monitored:

- Cylinder pressure.
- Scavenge air cooler.
- Fuel pumps and injectors.
- Turbocharger.

For new ships, a holistic approach to ship design takes at least the following aspects into account:

- **Hull Form:** Optimising the ship's capacity, its service speed and principal dimension.
- **Hull Resistance:** Optimising the hydrodynamic performance of a ship's hull form, also considering added resistance due to waves and wind.
- **Propulsion Efficiency:** Optimising the propeller(s) for the flow from the hull and installed machinery; designing and arranging the rudder in relation to the propeller and flow lines.
- **Construction Materials:** Using higher strength steel to reduce weight.

——— Questions to Consider ———

What can I do to increase the energy efficiency of my ship(s)?
There are a variety of measures to increase the energy efficiency of your ships. In general, one distinguishes between operational and technical measures. While operational measures relate to the way in which the ship is maintained and operated, technical measures aim to enhance the energy efficiency by improving the hardware (equipment) of the ship.

For a general and non-exhaustive overview of measures, please consult Section 9.5.2.1.

How do I determine which measures I should take to increase my ship's energy efficiency?
The choice of measures may depend on a variety of factors, including the ship's type, size, route, etc.

However, as a general rule of thumb, operational measures are easier to implement as technical measures because they require less upfront investments and have moderate operating costs.

Will energy saving devices be type-approved based on their respective quantifiable benefits?
It is currently very difficult to accurately and consistently demonstrate the benefits provided by individual performance improving devices. Given their dependency on variables which are not consistent between applications - e.g. ship type, hull form, operational mode, environmental conditions, etc. - the benefits vary greatly. However, it is possible to assess the benefits of a specific application for each individual ship.

Efficiency Retrofits On Canada Steamship Lines 'Forebodies' Self-Unloaders

Canada Steamship Lines (CSL) currently operates 20 vessels on the Great Lakes and the Saint-Lawrence River, four of which are Forebody class vessels.

Built in the 1980s and converted in the early 2000s, the Forebody vessels were extremely inefficient vessels that used electricity for heating water and fuel. The heat loads required for this heating operation by electricity produced 0.7g of CO_2 equivalent/kWh.

In order to increase energy efficiency, CSL's technical team investigated various Waste Heat Recovery Systems (WHRS) to employ waste energy form the main engine and auxiliary engines:

1. Retrofit installation of exhaust gas boilers to produce steam for heating.
2. Utilise the heat energy from the engines' cooling water systems.

The calculations carried out showed that option 1 would not produce a sufficient return of investment (ROI). Therefore, it was decided to install a WHRS utilising the cooling water system of both main engines to recover part of the jacket water waste heat via a simple hot water loop. The waste heat water loop is heated to and controlled at 75°C and it was calculated that the energy transferred through a series of heat exchangers to various consumers and producers could produce a potential of 400kW heat capacity.

One of the issues with this project was that when operating on the Great Lakes and within the St. Lawrence Seaway, the vessels only travel at full speed 48% of the time, which reduces the potential heat transfer capacity. However, in compliance with regulations, two auxiliary engines must be running at all times during most of the Seaway passage, so the auxiliary engine cooling water system was designed to connect to the WHRS. The added advantage is that the generators can be used in port to provide waste heat energy. Furthermore, the WHRS keeps the diesel engines at the optimum temperature for starting when they are stopped and uses them as heat sources when they are running. This resulted in a savings of 72kW of electrical energy (12kW/auxiliary engines and 60kW/both main engines) that had previously been used to keep the engines warm when in stand-by mode.

The WHRS is used to provide additional heat to crew accommodations. The temperature in crew accommodations is controlled using an electric load monitoring system due to the primary heating system being electrically powered. The 'set point' temperature of individual crew cabins is variable, allowing an electrical heating load of approximately 10kW for all accommodations. When the electric heat load increases above this point, the WHRS is activated to provide additional heating to the cabins. In maintaining the electric load at the set point of 10kW, the electrical load was reduced from 90kW, thereby saving 80kW.

Through extending the system to provide pre-heating for the lubricating oil purifiers, fuel oil purifiers, sludge tank heating and the domestic hot water system, an estimated additional reduction of 150kW in electrical heating load has been calculated.

All in all, the installation of WHRS has reduced CSL's greenhouse gas (GHG) emissions by 560 tonnes of CO_2e per year/vessel, saving a total of 2,240 tonnes of CO_2e annually for those four vessels alone. The switchboard electrical load was reduced from 410kW to 290kW. This does not include further reductions from bunker tank heating which still have to be calculated.

In addition to the WHRS, a further review of potential reductions of electrical power was carried out which would also assist in the heat capacity of the engine cooling systems through the control of the flow of seawater through the jacket water coolers. This involved the removal of the standard electric drive motors for the seawater cooling water pumps and the installation of Variable Speed Drive motors using variable frequency drives (VFDs) and an innovative constant Delta T temperature control. This allows the individual pumps to be operated at the optimum speed and adjusted constantly dependent on the seawater temperature and main engine load variation without the operator's intervention. One PID differential temperature controller is used.

Prior to the modifications of the pump drives, the main seawater pumps (2 off) were consuming 76kW of electrical load. Each vessel is now operating running with one pump at 5kW on average to cool both main engines. This has further reduced CO_2e emissions by over 200 tonnes per year per vessel. The ROI for this project was calculated at less than one year.

On two of the vessels, the 1980s Pielstick engines were changed and modern MAK engines installed, resulting in a reduction of CO_2e emissions by another 1,600 tonnes per year/vessel and decreasing the Energy Efficiency Operational Indicator (EEOI) from 12.16 g/t nm to 9.3 g/t nm.

Both projects combined have resulted in a considerable reduction of GHG emissions and they clearly show that modifications to increase efficiency can be beneficial even on old vessels built in the 1980s with calculated ROIs of approximately 2 years:

- Cost for WHRS: CAN$185,000
- Cost for VFDs, motors and controllers: CAN$86,000
- Total estimated electrical load reduction: 120kW average
- Total estimated CO_2e reduction (WHRS & VFD): 560- 800 tonnes CO_2e
- Total fuel reduction (WHRS & VFD): 190-290 tonnes MDO compared to 2011.

Alternative Energy Sources

Liquefied Natural Gas

LNG is potentially an attractive energy source for certain types of ships. It has a lower carbon to hydrogen ratio than diesel or HFO, so it generates up to 25% lower CO_2 emissions per unit of energy output when burned. Combusting LNG also significantly reduces sulphur oxides (SO_x), nitrogen oxides (NO_x) and particulate matter (PM) emissions which is important for complying with emission regulations for ships sailing within Emission Control Areas (ECAs).

A challenge to consider is that LNG bunker tanks typically require 2-3 times more space than a fuel oil tank. Based on recent experience, the new-build cost of LNG-fuelled ships is between 10-15% higher than for equivalent diesel-fuelled ships.

Currently, LNG bunkering infrastructure is limited. However, a significant increase in the number of bunkering terminals is expected in the coming decades, especially within ECAs.

Biofuel

The most favourable biofuels for ships are biodiesel and crude plant oil. Biodiesel is most suitable for replacing marine distillate, and plant oil is suitable for replacing residual fuels. In principle, existing diesel engines can run on biofuel blends. Challenges with biofuel include fuel instability, corrosion, susceptibility to microbial growth, and poor cold flow properties. Although these technical challenges can be resolved, widespread use of biofuel in shipping will depend on price, other incentives, and availability in sufficient volumes.

Furthermore, not all biofuels are carbon-friendly. The lifecycle carbon savings from biofuels compared to fossil fuels vary widely depending on the material used to produce biofuels, the refining process, and particularly any changes to land-use that are made to grow the fuel (i.e. if rainforest is cleared to plant biofuel crops, this will almost certainly have a negative impact on the climate).

Wind Power

Wind power is an attractive option for the shipping industry due to the fact that it is both cost and emission-free. However, with the exception of very few for smaller ships, none of the designs currently under consideration within the industry would completely replace a ship's engine, only supplement it.

Wind-assisted propulsion involves using rigid or soft sails, kites, or Flettner rotors to convert energy from the wind to thrust forces.

Solar Energy

Solar cells on a ship's deck can reduce fuel consumption by providing onboard power. However, with current solar cell technology, only a small fraction of auxiliary power can be met, even if the entire deck area were to be covered with photovoltaic cells which would of course only be possible with certain ship types. Moreover, since solar power is not always available (e.g. at night), backup power would be needed. Therefore, solar power appears to be of interest primarily as a complementary source of energy.

9.6 Business Benefits

9.6.1 Reducing Operating Costs

Bunker fuel represents a significant part of a ship's operating costs, thus any reduction in fuel consumption translates into reduced operating costs. In the current market, the reduction in operating costs can give you an advantage over competitors in the market and buffer profit margins.

9.6.2 Meeting Future CO_2 Emission Regulations

At present, the energy efficiency requirements for new ship designs are considered to be quite tame with regards to promoting CO_2 reduction and for existing ships are non-existent, but this is going to change in the future. EEDI enforcements for new ships will become harder to satisfy.

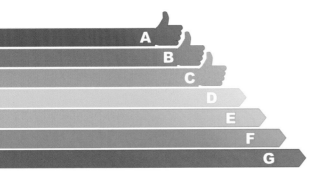

9.6.3 Attracting New Customers And Satisfying Existing Ones

Mitigating climate change is one of today's biggest challenges and in recent years, public awareness and attention for this topic has grown dramatically. Cargo owners increasingly have to account for and improve their environmental performance. Many of them have started passing environmental performance requirements, mostly, but not only related to CO_2 emissions, onto their suppliers. This process is called Green Supply Chain Management.

Improving your environmental performance, especially energy efficiency, can help you satisfy the demands of your existing customers, and could also result in attracting more customers who want to benefit from your good environmental performance.

9.6.4 Participating In Incentive Schemes

There are a number of voluntary environmental evaluation schemes specifically developed for the shipping industry. While the scope of these evaluation schemes differs, virtually all of them include CO_2 and energy efficiency. The advantages from participating in these schemes range from direct financial benefits (e.g. reduced port dues) to reputational gains due to increased transparency of your environmental performance. An overview of such schemes is provided in Part One - The Framework.

9.7 Measuring Environmental Performance

9.7.1 Measuring CO_2 Emissions

CO_2 emissions can be measured directly in exhaust gas stacks (funnels). However, this measurement method is still in its infancy both within the maritime sector and in most land-based industries. It will also require substantial investments since additional equipment is needed, including a supporting IT infrastructure both onboard and possibly onshore.

Emission = Fuel consumed x Emission factor

Multiply the fuel consumption data in tonnes by the CO_2 emission factor (see Section 9.7.2.1) to obtain an emission estimate.

9.7.2 Measuring Fuel Consumption

All ships have a record of the amount of fuel carried at certain points in time, and many ships record fuel consumption on a daily basis, although not all ships have equipment needed for measuring fuel consumption directly. The main data sources that are available to monitor fuel use are:

1. **Total amount of fuel purchased by (or on behalf of) the ship:** This information is normally contained within the budgets, accounts and records kept at a ship operator. The difficulty with this method is that the amount purchased within a certain time frame can differ from the amount of fuel used within the same time frame. This means that in addition, fuel tank levels have to be measured to establish a period inventory of fuel consumption.

2. **Total amount of fuel bunkered:** Ship owners and operators are required to record the quantity and type of fuel bunkered in the Bunker Delivery Note (BDN). These records need to be combined with tank readings, e.g. periodic sounding or ullage measurements of fuel tanks. The fuel at the beginning of the period, plus deliveries, minus fuel available at the end of the period, together constitute the fuel consumed over the period.

3. **Ullage:** Fuel tank levels are commonly measured onboard ships. In modern ships, tank soundings are normally taken using built-in automatic systems (e.g. pitot tubes, radar tank level indication systems) which transmit readings to the engine control room. Additionally, tank soundings can be manually taken with a measuring tape and digital thermometer via sounding pipes.

4. **Measuring fuel flow:** Net fuel flow to the engine can be measured directly using various types of fuel flow meters. Flow meters record the actual fuel used on any voyage. The installation of flow meters onboard ships is not routine practice, although some ship operators have experience of such systems and they are often included in modern fuel consumption monitoring systems. These systems incorporate electronic fuel flow meters and are the most accurate and reliable method of measuring fuel consumption in marine diesel engines.

It may be beneficial to combine manual with electronic fuel consumption measurements, i.e. doing tank soundings and using fuel flow meters. This gives you a high level of redundancy, serves as a back-up and can help you find out if or when your flow meters need to be calibrated.

The data on fuel consumption is recorded in daily noon reports and log books. If more sophisticated measuring systems, e.g. electronic fuel flow meters, are used, fuel consumption can be monitored continuously and data can be automatically communicated to shore-based offices.

9.7.2.1 CO_2 Emission Factor

The CO_2 emission factor depends on the kind of fuel used and is given in the table below:

Fuel Type	CO_2 Emission Factor (kg emitted/tonne of fuel)
HFO	3,114
MDO/MGO	3,206
LNG	2,750

Source: IMO (2014) Third IMO GHG Study

9.7.3   Determining Average Operational Energy Efficiency

In order to determine the efficiency of a ship in operation, the IMO suggests using the EEOI. The calculation of the EEOI is based on the amount of CO_2 emitted by an individual ship and data on the achieved transport work, e.g. cargo mass, number of passengers carried, etc. This results in a figure of CO_2 emissions per tonne nautical mile (nm):

$$\text{EEOI} = \frac{\text{Mass of } CO_2 \text{ emitted}}{\text{Transport work}} = \frac{\text{Fuel} \cdot CO_2 \text{ conversion factor}}{\text{Cargo quantity} \cdot \text{Distance}}$$

The parameters that the ship needs to record are:

- The fuel type.
- The mass of consumed fuel.
- The fuel mass to CO_2 mass conversion factor for the given fuel.
- EITHER cargo carried OR work done (number of TEU or passengers) OR gross tonnes for passenger ships.
- The distance in nautical miles corresponding to the cargo carried or work done.

The data sources for the parameters listed above can usually be found quite easily, e.g. in a ship's log-book, bridge log-book, engine log-book, deck log-book and in other official records.

As the goal is to reduce the energy consumption of the ship over time, it may be considered advantageous to record the EEOI value daily and monitor the rolling average or the average at set points in time, e.g. month-end average.

For further guidance on the EEOI, calculation formulas and examples, please check the IMO Guideline MEPC.1/Circ.684.

CHAPTER TEN

CONTENTS

SULPHUR OXIDES & PARTICULATE MATTER

SULPHUR OXIDES & PARTICULATE MATTER

10.1   Introduction

The term sulphur oxides (SO_x) is applied in reference to a variety of sulphur and oxygen containing gaseous compounds. The principal compounds under the spotlight in all transportation sectors globally are sulphur dioxides (SO_2), sulphur trioxides (SO_3) and sulphate (SO_4). SO_4 is known to have a radiative effect to sunlight thereby countering global warming (the Albedo effect). While SO_2 and SO_3 are short-lived gases staying only a few days in the atmosphere, SO_4 can form clouds which can remain for 10 days or more in the atmosphere.

Although some SO_x emissions occur naturally from seismic activity, sulphur is also naturally present to a greater or lesser extent in all crude oils. The combustion of these crude oils forms SO_x compounds.

Particulate matter (PM) refers to a mixture of solid particles and liquid droplets present in the air. Some particles, such as dust, dirt, black carbon (also known as soot), or smoke, are large or dark enough to be seen with the naked eye. Others can only be detected via the use of an electron microscope.

In conventional diesel engines, the formation of PM is dependent on the efficiency and completeness of the combustion process, the amount of hydrocarbons, sulphur and ash in the fuel and the amount of lubricating oil used. This is why PM and SO_x emissions are generally grouped together.

Compared with land-based power installations, the lower fractions of crude oil-based fossil fuels traditionally favoured for use by the shipping industry have a high sulphur content, up to 3.5%. These high sulphur levels in fuel, converted to SO_x during combustion, contribute significantly to the overall amount of global SO_x emissions at sea and in port areas.

International shipping is estimated to emit 10.6 million tonnes of SO_x annually, which amounts to about 12% of global SO_x emissions. In 2012, PM emissions from international shipping were estimated to be 1.3 million tonnes.[1]

10.2 Environmental And Health Impact

10.2.1 Human Health Implications

Both SO_x and PM emissions can cause negative health effects.

High exposure to SO_x can lead to respiratory problems, illness and can even initiate or worsen respiratory and cardiovascular diseases. People with asthma or chronic lung or heart diseases are the most sensitive to SO_x.

PM from exhaust emissions, especially the finer particles, can lodge in the respiratory system and mobilise into the bloodstream, leading to cardiovascular and pulmonary disease. According to a study from 2007, PM emissions from ships cause approximately 60,000 cardiopulmonary and lung cancer deaths annually, with most deaths occurring near coastlines in Europe, East Asia and South Asia.[2]

10.2.2 Environmental Impact

One of the components of PM emissions is black carbon. Black carbon contributes to global warming in two ways - through direct absorption of heat in the top of the atmosphere, and by depositing on snow or ice where the darker particles reduce the reflectivity of the lighter surfaces (also known as albedo effect). Reduced albedo means less solar radiation is reflected back into space and will instead be absorbed, thereby heating the Earth's surface and speeding up the melting of ice and snow.[3]

In the past few years, the environmental impact of black carbon from shipping, especially in the Arctic, has been a heavily discussed agenda item at the International Maritime Organization (IMO), in particular the definition of the term. A recent study has estimated the contribution of international shipping towards black carbon emissions globally and in the Arctic. Accordingly, international shipping contributes just 1% to the total global emissions of black carbon and about 2% of black carbon emissions in the Arctic.[4]

10.3 International Regulation

SO_x and PM emissions are governed by MARPOL Annex VI.

The principal approach taken by the IMO to control SO_x emissions is to limit the maximum sulphur content of the fuel oils used. The limits are subject to staged reductions, giving the industry and bunker suppliers time to plan for and adjust to the changes. Furthermore, lower limits to the fuel oil sulphur content apply, with their own sequence of reduction, in areas termed Emission Control Areas (ECAs).

In ECAs, a higher level of protection is required due to such factors as prevailing winds, the proximity of shipping routes to centres of population and the natural susceptibility of an area to acid deposition. Countries or regions applying for ECA status must provide evidence that lowering SO_x emissions from shipping activities will have a measurable and positive effect on human health and the environment.

10.3.1 Global SO_x And PM Emission Controls

For the purpose of this Chapter, any areas that are not within the boundaries of an ECA are considered to be globally regulated. Therefore, the international IMO rulings around sulphur apply.

Resolution MEPC.176(58)

Globally, the maximum sulphur limits are:

- 3.50% on and after 1 January 2012.
- 0.50% on and after 1 January 2020.

The 0.50% limit is subject to a global review of the availability of low sulphur fuel oils, distillates or alternatives. The review must be completed by 2018 and may recommend the postponement of the 0.50% limit until 2025.

[2] Corbett, J.J. et al (2007) Mortality from ship emissions: A global assessment, Environmental Science & Technology, 41(24), pp. 8512-8518
[3] Reddy, S.M. and Boucher, O. (2006) Climate imapct of Black Carbon Emitted from Energy Consumption in the World's Regions, Geophysical Research Letters, 34.
[4] Browse, J., Carslaw, K.S., Schmidt, A. and Corbett, J.J. (2013) Impact of future Arctic shipping on high-latitude black carbon deposition, Geophysical Research Letters, 40.

10.3.2 Emission Control Areas

Resolution MEPC.176(58)

Under MARPOL Annex VI, an ECA is defined as:

> *"an area where the adoption of special mandatory measures for emissions from ships is required to prevent, reduce and control air pollution from NO_x, or SO_x and particulate matter or all three types of emissions and their attendant adverse impacts on human health and the environment."*

Within ECAs, the maximum permitted limits for marine fuel sulphur content are:

- 1.00% on and after 1 July 2010.
- 0.10% on and after 1 January 2015.

10.3.2.1 Where Have ECAs Been Established Already?

Resolution MEPC.176(58)
Resolution MEPC.190(60)
Resolution MEPC.202(62)

At the time of writing *(December 2014)*, there are four established ECAs:

- Baltic Sea.
- North Sea.
- North American ECA.
- US Caribbean Sea.

The Baltic Sea and North Sea ECAs only enforce limits for SO_x and PM emission controls, whereas the North American and US Caribbean Sea ECAs additionally enforce limits for NO_x emissions.

Resolution MEPC.202(62)

NOTE: In the North American and US Caribbean Sea ECAs, prior to 1 January 2020 ships built on or before 1 August 2011 that are powered by propulsion boilers not originally designed for continued operation on marine distillate fuel or natural gas will not be required to comply with the ECA fuel oil sulphur requirements.

10.3.3 Options For Compliance

Resolution MEPC.176(58)

In order to comply with lower marine fuel sulphur content levels required under MARPOL Annex VI and those enforced within the various ECAs as presented above, ship owners and operators can either choose to use marine fuels with lower sulphur content or so-called 'equivalents' which provide other means to achieve the required SO_x and PM emission levels.

MARPOL Annex VI allows for the application of these 'equivalents', provided these are:

- At least as effective in terms of required emission reductions;
- approved by the Administration (the ship's flag State) taking into account any relevant IMO guidelines.

'Equivalents' can be divided into 'primary' and 'secondary' controls. Primary controls prevent the pollutant being formed in the first instance, whereas with secondary controls the pollutant formed is removed to the extent required before the exhaust gas stream is discharged to the atmosphere.

One possible 'equivalent' primary control option would be onboard blending of a non-compliant fuel oil with a lower-sulphur fuel oil in order to produce a sulphur-compliant blend. While it would be possible to meet the 1.00% as well as the 0.50% limits by this means, there are no IMO guidelines at this time covering onboard blending and therefore no direction for Administrations to approve it as an equivalent arrangement. It is not considered to be a feasible option for meeting the 0.10% limit, in force within the four designated ECAs as of 1 January 2015.

Secondary controls involve the use of exhaust gas cleaning systems (EGCS) or 'scrubbers' which clean the exhaust gas stream prior to discharge to the atmosphere. This strategy is detailed further in Section 10.3.3.2.

10.3.3.1 Low-Sulphur Fuels

Compliance with SO_x and PM emission restrictions are based upon the fuel oils used onboard. This includes all fuel oils used, both in main and auxiliary engines together with items such as boilers and inert gas generators.

For operation within ECAs, there are a number of options based on the fuel oil used:

- Sulphur-controlled residual fuel oil, up to 1 January 2015.
- Sulphur-controlled distillates, either marine diesel oil (MDO) or marine gas oil (MGO).
- Natural gas, typically loaded and stored onboard in a liquefied state (LNG).
- Alternative fuels from non-petroleum sources, i.e. biodiesel.

Although an operator is free to use ECA-compliant fuel when operating outside an ECA, the price differential between those fuels and higher sulphur residual fuel oils (such as IFO-180, IFO-380), normally dictates that fuel-switching between the grades occurs in preparation for entering an ECA and also when exiting an ECA.

Fuel-Switching

Currently, the most common ECA compliance option is fuel-switching: changing over to a lower-sulphur fuel, a process which must be complete before entry to an emissions-regulated zone, and changing back to the original, higher-sulphur fuel after the ship has left the zone.

Resolution MEPC.176(58)

A ship is required to have fully changed over to using ECA compliant fuel oil prior to entering the ECA from an area outside the ECA. Similarly, change-over from the ECA compliant fuel oil is not to commence until after the ship has exited the ECA.

Ships using separate fuel oils to comply with SO_x emission regulations are required to carry a written procedure showing how the fuel oil change-over is to be done. This must be specific to the ship.

In addition, records must be kept to demonstrate that the fuel oil change-over was fully completed prior to entry into the ECA, and that the change back was not begun until after the ship left the ECA. This record must include as a minimum the volume of low-sulphur fuel oils in each tank as well as the date, time and position of the ship when the fuel oil change-over operation was completed (prior to entering the ECA) or commenced (after exiting the ECA).

Ensuring Compliance When Switching Fuel

In order to ensure compliance with the MARPOL Annex VI sulphur limits when switching fuels, ship owners are recommended to consider the below.

Consult the engine, machinery and boiler manufacturers on:
- Considerations for specific types of engines, machineries and boilers.
- Appropriate and specific fuel-switching guidance.
- Any needs for fuel system modifications or safeguarding.

Check the existing fuel systems in terms of:
- Functional operation of system alarms, indicators, sensors, transmitters, etc. on all relevant fuel types.
- Compatibility of gaskets, filters, seals, valves, etc. with the relevant fuel types.
- Need for cleaning fuel tanks and the associated piping and treatment system.

Develop detailed and ship-specific fuel-switching procedures that include or take into account the following:
- To the extent possible, avoiding fuel-switching operations in restricted waters or congested traffic areas.
- Designating sufficient fuel tank capacities.
- Performing fuel-switching calculations for ensuring operation on compliant fuel upon entry into ECA.
- Ensuring a detailed fuel system diagram is available.
- Monitoring the performance of engines, machineries and boilers during fuel-switching.
- Checking the fuel system for leaks, or testing after fuel-switching.
- Testing proper function of the main propulsion machinery and all auxiliary engines after fuel-switching.
- Testing the ship's manoeuvrability.
- Ensuring onboard training of relevant crew and officers.

Consider these additional steps for preventing propulsion losses when performing fuel-switching:
- To the extent possible, control the quality of the bunker delivered.
- Monitor fuel system, engines, machineries and boilers performance on all fuels.
- Monitor lubricating oil consumption.
- Monitor the engine/fuel system components for wear and evaluate maintenance period intervals accordingly.
- Ensure fuel viscosity does not drop below engine manufacturer's specifications.
- Ensure proper heat management of fuel systems to maintain minimum viscosity values.
- Start air supply should be sufficient and fully charged prior to any manoeuvring.

Record keeping and documentation for fuel-switching:
- Ensure that as a minimum, the following information is recorded every time change-over between fuel oil occurs:
  - Tanks used and quantity of fuel oil in each tank at the time of the change-over.
  - Exact time/date of start and end of change-over.
  - Position or location of the ship (start/finish).
  - Name/signature of ship's responsible person.
- It is recommend to not use any of the existing logbooks onboard to record the entire fuel oil change-over operation. Instead, a separate record book (e.g. Marine Fuel Sulphur Change-Over Record Book) should be used to record that the fuel change-over has been carried out properly and in accordance with the ship's change-over procedure.

NOTE: It is not compulsory to record the fuel oil change-over in a separate record book.

Liquefied Natural Gas

Another option for compliance is to change fuel type altogether to a fuel that produces no SO_x and PM emissions – Liquefied Natural Gas (LNG).

The combustion of LNG also results in lower NO_x and carbon dioxide (CO_2) emissions when compared to using residual fuel oils and marine gas oils. When LNG is vaporised and used as a fuel, it reduces PM emissions to near zero, and CO_2 emissions by 70%, by comparison with heavier hydrocarbon fuels. When burned for power generation, the results are even better. SO_2 emissions are virtually eliminated, and CO_2 emissions reduced significantly.

Although still a niche market, LNG production for and use as marine fuel is gaining ground in certain regions. Advocates of LNG claim it is an ideal fuel solution that could enable ship operators to meet sulphur rules in ECAs and other emissions-limiting zones, without the need to carry out fuel-switching or blending, or invest in EGCS.

A challenge with regards to the use of LNG as a ship's primary fuel is that LNG bunker tanks require considerably more space than fuel oil tanks and thus take away space for cargo stowage. The new-build cost of LNG-fuelled ships can be between 10-15% higher than for equivalent diesel-fuelled ships. Although LNG bunkering infrastructure is currently still limited, a significant increase in the number of bunkering terminals is expected in the coming decades, especially at ports within ECAs.

Biofuels

Research and studies that have examined and tested the application of biofuels as an alternative fuel strategy for the shipping industry have shown promising results and some owners and operators are in fact testing the use of biofuels within their fleets through small-scale pilot projects. The most promising biofuels for ship fuel are biodiesel and crude plant oil. Biodiesel is most suitable for replacing marine distillate, and plant oil is suitable for replacing residual fuels. In principle, existing diesel engines can run on biofuel blends.

Most biofuel originates from lignin - CyclOx - and represents a class of molecules which improves the fuel-air mixing process and reduces soot. Research has shown that adding 10% CyclOx to standard diesel fuel reduces soot emissions by up to 50%.

Challenges with biofuels include fuel instability, corrosion, susceptibility to microbial growth, and poor cold flow properties. Although these technical challenges can be resolved, widespread use of biofuel in shipping will depend on price, availability in sufficient volumes, bunkering locations and other incentives.

Furthermore, not all biofuels are environmentally-friendly. The lifecycle carbon savings from biofuels compared to fossil fuels vary widely depending on the material used to produce biofuels, the refining process, and particularly any changes to land-use that are made to grow the fuel (i.e. if rainforest is cleared to plant biofuel crops, this will almost certainly have a negative impact on the climate).

Exhaust Gas Cleaning Systems

EGCS, commonly knowns as 'scrubbers, are considered to be an 'equivalent' means of ensuring compliance within ECAs as they remove the harmful substances directly from the exhaust gas and allow the use of high-sulphur residual fuel oils.

EGCS technology has been used for several decades in land-based industries but the application of the technology is a relatively new concept for the shipping industry where there are a number of significant differences as regards operational factors and the consumables used.

NOTE: EGCS are distinctly different to the inert gas generating systems that have been installed for many years on oil tankers.

However, the application of EGCS is attracting increased attention from operators as a realistic solution that would allow the continued use of cheaper and more readily available fuels.

There are two main types of systems: 'wet' and 'dry' EGCS.

Wet Exhaust Gas Cleaning Systems

A wet EGCS uses seawater or freshwater with the addition of chemicals to 'wash' the harmful components from exhaust gases. Wet systems generally comprise:

- A unit where the exhaust gases come into contact with the water being used.
- A treatment unit that removes pollutants from the washwater.
- Sludge handling capability, to store the waste safely prior to onshore disposal.

A wet EGCS can be either designed as open or closed-loop arrangement, or as hybrids that can be operated in either mode.

In an open-loop system, seawater is pumped from the sea through the scrubber, cleaned and then discharged back to sea. Washwater is not recirculated.

In a closed-loop system, the water, whether freshwater or (more rarely) seawater, is treated with an alkaline chemical, commonly sodium hydroxide, as the scrubbing medium. This results in the removal of SO_x from the exhaust gas stream as sodium sulphate. The bulk of the water recirculates through the system in a closed loop, with a small bleed-off being extracted for processing in the treatment unit with a corresponding make-up of water and dosing chemical. The treated water is disposed of back into the sea or, due to the relatively low flow rates, can be held temporarily in a storage tank.

A hybrid system is one that can be used in open-loop mode while at sea (in order to conserve the use of chemicals), and in closed-loop mode when operating in areas of limited alkalinity or in port, if necessary to comply with any port discharge regulations.

In all cases, the washwater needs to be processed to remove harmful substances and then monitored to ensure that it meets applicable water discharge standards given in the IMO Guidelines for Exhaust Gas Cleaning Systems (see section below for further information).

Washwater And Treatment Residue

Resolution MEPC.184(59)

The IMO 2009 Guidelines for Exhaust Gas Cleaning Systems, contained in resolution MEPC.184(59), specify the discharge water quality criteria and monitoring requirements for a number of parameters.

The condition of any washwater discharged to sea must be continuously monitored and data for the following parameters must be securely logged against time and ship's position:

- pH - a measure of acidity,
- PAH (Polycyclic Aromatic Hydrocarbons) - a measure of the harmful components of oil; and
- turbidity - a measure of washwater clarity, indicating the amount of PM.

The discharge water should comply with the following limits:

- pH of no less than 6.5.
- Depending on the washwater flow rate, the maximum concentration of PAH should be within the following limits:

Flow Rate (t/MWh)	Discharge Concentration Limit (µg/l PAHphe equivalents)
0-1	2,250
2.5	900
5	450
11.25	200
22.5	100
45	50
90	25

- Turbidity not more than 25 formazin nephlometric units or 25 nephlometric turbidity units above inlet turbidity.
- Nitrates not higher than that associated with 12% NO_x removal or 60 mg/l for washwater discharge rate of 45 tons/MWh, whichever is greater.

Any washwater residues generated by the EGCS should not be discharged to sea or incinerated onboard, but instead be delivered ashore to adequate reception facilities. The storage and disposal of such residues should be recorded in the EGC Record Book.

The washwater discharge criteria are intended to act as initial guidance for implementing EGCS designs. The criteria should be revised in the future as more data becomes available on the contents of the discharge and its effects, taking into account any advice given by the Group of Experts on the Scientific Aspects of Marine Environmental Protection (GESAMP).

Dry Exhaust Gas Cleaning Systems

Dry scrubbers do not use water or any liquid to clean the exhaust gas. Instead, the exhaust gas is fed through a container filled with calcium hydroxide granulate. This calcium hydroxide reacts with SO_x to form calcium sulphate (gypsum), thus binding SO_x. The level of sulphur absorption can be regulated to achieve the stipulated limits. After some time, the calcium hydroxide granulate loses its ability to react, so it has to be replaced. The hydrated lime is supplied in a granulated form and as such can be transferred from the supply truck through a pneumatic conveyor system. There is a steady feed into the system of granulate in order to maintain performance with a corresponding removal of used material.

One particular advantage of dry EGCS is that, unlike wet systems, they do not cool the exhaust gas. This allows them to be used in conjunction with selective catalytic reduction (SCR) units (as NO_x reduction devices) which require inlet gas temperatures to be maintained typically above 300-350°C and have only limited tolerance to sulphur in the exhaust gas stream to be positioned downstream of the EGCS. This will be a key point for ships built on or after 1 January 2016 – when all engines falling within the scope of Regulation 13 will need to meet the low NO_x emission levels of Tier III (2.0-3.4 g/kWh depending on rated speed) when operating within ECA-NO_x areas (currently the North American and US Caribbean Sea ECAs).

Differences Between Wet And Dry Exhaust Gas Cleaning Systems

In order to compare EGCS, several parameters should be considered, such as operation in fresh water, weight, power consumption and compatibility with other systems. The table on the following page provides a comparison of the different systems available.

	Wet scrubber			Dry scrubber
	open-loop	closed-loop	hybrid	
Main system components	• Scrubber • Washwater piping • Washwater pumps • Washwater treatent equipment • Sludge handling equipment	• Scrubber • Washwater piping • Washwater pumps • Washwater processing tank • Washwater holding tank • Sodium hydroxide storage tank • Washwater treatment equipment • Sludge handling equipment	• Scrubber • Washwater piping • Washwater pumps • Washwater processing tank • Washwater holding tank • Sodium hydroxide storage tank • Washwater treatment equipment • Sludge handling equipment	• Absorber • Fresh granulate hopper • Used granulate hopper • Granulate transport system • Additional granulate storage (new and used granules)
Operation in fresh water	No	Yes	Yes (only when operating in closed loop mode)	Yes
Operation without discharge to sea	No	For a limited time depending on the size of the washwater holding tank	For a limited time depending on the size of the washwater holding tank	Yes
Weight (typical values for a 20MW SO_x scrubber)	30-55t (excl. washwater system & treatment equipment)	30-55t (excl. washwater system, treatment equipment, washwater processing tank & washwater holding tank)	30-55t (excl. washwater system, treatment equipment, washwater processing tank & washwater holding tank)	≈200t (incl. granules stored adjacent to the absorber but excl. additional granulate storage)
Power consumption (% of max. scrubbed engine power	1-2%	0.5-1%	0.5-2% (depending on whether it is operating in open or closed-loop mode)	0.15-0.2%
Scrubbing chemical consumable	No consumable	Sodium hydroxide solution (≈6 l/MWh·%S)	Sodium hydroxide solution (only when operating in closed-loop mode) (≈6 l/ MWh·%S)	Calcium hydroxide granules (≈10 kg/MWh·%S)
Compatibility with waste heat recovery system	Yes, provided the scrubber is installed after the waste heat recovery system	Yes, provided the scrubber is installed after the waste heat recovery system	Yes, provided the scrubber is installed after the waste heat recovery system	Yes. Can be placed before or after the waste heat recovery system
Compatibility with SCR system	No, unless a reheater is fitted after the wet scrubber to raise the exhaust gas temperature	No, unless a reheater is fitted after the wet scrubber to raise the exhaust gas temperature	No, unless a reheater is fitted after the wet scrubber to raise the exhaust gas temperature	Yes
Compatibility with Exhaust Gas Recirculation system	Yes	Yes	Yes	Yes
PM removal	Yes	Yes	Yes	Yes

Source: Lloyd's Register (2012) Understanding exhaust gas treatment systems: Guidance for shipowners and operators

Approval Procedures For Exhaust Gas Cleaning Systems

For ships using EGCS, detailed documentation requirements are set out in the 2009 IMO Guidelines for Exhaust Gas Cleaning Systems. They distinguish between two statutory approval procedures known as Scheme A (unit approval of the EGCS before installation with ongoing performance checks) and Scheme B (principally based on continuous emission monitoring).

Nearly all EGCS installed so far are approved according to Scheme B.

Regardless of the scheme, all ships using an EGCS must hold:

- SO_x Emissions Compliance Plan;
- Onboard Monitoring Manual;
- EGCS Technical Manual for Scheme A or B (ETM-A or ETM-B); and
- EGC Record Book: A record of the EGC unit in-service operating parameters, component, adjustments, maintenance and service records as appropriate.

In addition, 'Scheme A' ships must hold a SO_x Emissions Compliance Certificate.

These documents and records could be subject to verification by port States, and if the port State considers that a more detailed inspection is necessary, this could extend to the inspector undertaking a check of the EGCS itself and being shown that it is functioning correctly.

For more information on the different documents required, please check the 2009 Guidelines for Exhaust Gas Cleaning Systems, contained in resolution MEPC.184(59).

10.3.4 Monitoring And Reporting Requirements

10.3.4.1 General Requirements: Bunker Delivery Note

NOTE: These reporting requirements are the same for all air pollutants covered by MARPOL Annex VI.

Any fuel oil for combustion purposes delivered to and used onboard ships shall be accompanied by a Bunker Delivery Note (BDN) of defined minimum content. The information to be included in the BDN is outlined in Appendix V to MARPOL Annex VI.

The BDN must be readily available for inspection and be kept onboard for a minimum of three years from the delivery date of the fuel oil to which it relates. In the case where a ship makes scheduled regular port visits, the relevant Administrations may agree to alternative arrangements by which the fuel oil as delivered is documented.

Every BDN must be accompanied by a representative sample of the fuel oil delivered. This sample is to be drawn in accordance with the Guidelines for the Sampling of Fuel Oil for Determination of Compliance with Annex VI of MARPOL 73/78, contained in resolution MEPC.96(47).

The sample is to be sealed, signed for by both the supplier's and receiver's representatives and retained under the ship's control until the fuel oil it represents is substantially consumed, but in any case for a period of not less than 12 months from the date of delivery.

Where the ship's flag State has particular recording requirements, for example the use of a prescribed log book, then those are to be followed.

10.3.5   Surveys And Certification – MARPOL Annex VI

NOTE: These reporting requirements are the same for all air pollutants covered by MARPOL Annex VI.

10.3.5.1   *General Certification Requirements Applicable To All Air Pollutants*

Resolution MEPC.176(58)

Every ship covered by MARPOL Annex VI must carry a valid International Air Pollution Prevention (IAPP) Certificate onboard for inspection by port or flag States. Usually, the IAPP Certificate is valid for five years – provided that no change of flag takes place.

The basic prerequisite to obtain an IAPP Certificate is that the ship complies with the requirements of the applicable regulations of MARPOL Annex VI. This has to be proven through an initial survey.

After the IAPP Certificate has been issued for the first time, each ship has to undergo periodical surveys in order to avoid the Certificate cease to be valid. These are:

- Annual surveys within a time window of ± three months of the anniversary date of the IAPP Certificate.
- One intermediate survey either after 2 or 3 years after issuance of the IAPP Certificate.
- A renewal survey before the end of every five-year period after issuance of the IAPP Certificate.
- An additional survey after a repair following an accident to the ship or when a defect is discovered in a ship, either of which substantially affect the integrity of the ship or the efficiency or completeness of the equipment of the ship. An additional survey is also required after an important repair or renewal is made.

A model IAPP Certificate is included in Appendix I to MARPOL Annex VI. It has been amended by resolution MEPC.194(61). This model certificate is also included in Part Three - The Maritime Environmental & Efficiency Templates provided on the USB memory stick.

Questions to Consider

How can I comply with ECA requirements?
Currently, there are three options to comply with the ECA requirements:

- Fuel-switching.
- LNG.
- EGCS.

Fuel-switching is currently the most common ECA compliance option: changing over to a lower-sulphur fuel, a process which must be complete before entry to an emissions-regulated zone, and changing back to the regular fuel after the ship has left the zone.

Another option is to run a ship on LNG. Using LNG essentially eliminates all SO_x and PM emissions and usually results in lower NO_x and CO_2 emissions.

EGCS – or 'scrubbers' - are an alternate means of satisfying the requirements of the ECA by removing the harmful substances directly from the exhaust gas and allowing the use of regular high-sulphur residual fuel oils.

What are the benefits and challenges of fuel switching?
The table below lists the different benefits and challenges of fuel switching:

Benefits	Challenges
The fuel-switching solution is immediately available with no need for initial investment for existing ships.	Low-sulphur fuels command a much higher premium compared to the price of HFO. Ship owners and operators are predicted to pay a premium of approximately US $300+ per tonne of fuel.
Compliance can be readily demonstrated by providing full fuel change-over records and BDN receipts.	The availability of lower-sulphur fuels is not yet clarified for 2015 and beyond.
Outlay is spread over time and operators can potentially adjust trading routes where applicable to take account of fuel availability and price changes.	Necessary system modifications to provide the required segregated storage, piping and changeover mechanisms.
In the mid- to long-term, fuel-switching allows operators a greater degree of control and flexibility, as the fuel can be changed to meet the requirements in a specific emissions-limiting zone at a given time.	Change-over process management and crew training to minimise operational accidents and fuel spillage.
In the case of MGO, there is no need for fuel treatment and therefore sludge production in ECAs is significantly reduced. Also, there is no need to heat the fuel when using MGO, resulting in a reduction of up to 10% power demand and fuel consumption and a significant reduction of maintenance and repairs.	Suitability of ships' fuel systems, and consequent impacts on performance. Potential for loss of propulsion.
No need for redundancy in terms of carrying low-sulphur fuel in case of a malfunctioning EGCS.	Potential fuel incompatibility.

What do I need to consider when switching to low-sulphur fuel?

Many fuel supply systems are closed-loop systems in which the fuel is continuously circulated. When changing over from residual fuel oil service tanks to low-sulphur fuel service tanks, there will be no immediate change of supply to the engines and boilers, only a dilution of the fuel circulating in the supply system. Consequently, the change-over time will be determined by the fuel oil consumption.

Due to the relatively large quantities of fuel circulating, the time needed to complete the change-over can be relatively long. With only the main engine running, the blending-in ratio may be in the region of 1% per two minutes, and with only one auxiliary boiler or one auxiliary engine in operation the ratio can be much lower. Experience has shown that in some cases fuel change-over from high- to low-sulphur fuel is not complete even after 48 hours. As a result, the sulphur content of the fuel consumed may be in excess of the applicable sulphur content limits. Therefore, you need to allow sufficient time for the fuel change-over before entering an ECA.

Furthermore, sufficient time should be allowed to maintain the temperature gradient recommended by the engine manufacturer, e.g. 2°C/minute, in a controlled manner. In many cases, this will be necessary to avoid a thermal shock to the system, e.g. seizure of fuel injection pumps, and/or other operational problems that may occur due to low viscosity and/or rapid temperature changes.

What can I do in preparation for fuel-switching and operating in an ECA?

The specific issues related to fuel-switching and the modifications and precautions that may be necessary are unique to each ship. However, the following is intended as a guide that is widely, if not universally, applicable:

- Operators should first carry out an extensive evaluation and risk-based analysis of the suitability of ships, either individually or fleet-wide depending on the nature of the fleet, to operate, when appropriate, on low-sulphur fuel.
- From a commercial perspective, this evaluation should take into account a ship's routes, the frequency of entry into an ECA, length of time to be spent in an ECA (or other emissions-limiting zone), and expected fuel consumption.
- Technical analysis should cover all components of a ship's entire fuel system, including the engine, boilers (auxiliary and main), storage capacity and location, fuel system pipes and onboard control systems. Operators should check with engine, boiler and control systems manufacturers as to the suitability for their equipment to operate on distillate fuels as well as on residual fuel oil.
- Consider consultation with other component specialists (i.e. not only the manufacturer) to gain wider understanding of modifications that may be necessary across the ship fuel system, in particular ship's class society.
- If fuel-switching, prepare a detailed fuel-switching procedure, and have it available onboard. This should include inspection and maintenance schedules, which may very well change as a result of the new operating methods. At particular potential risk are flanges, seals and gaskets. These may need enhanced attention to avoid leakage owing to lower-viscosity fuel.
- A written fuel change-over plan is required by MARPOL Annex VI
- Maintenance schedules for system purifiers, filters and strainers should also be checked for possible augmentation.
- Establish a rigorous cylinder lubrication monitoring schedule to help guard against high consumption caused by liner lacquering.
- Have control system alarms and indicators checked.
- Train crew and onshore support personnel in the new procedures and ensure appropriate and regular communication to keep them up to date with new developments. Crew should also be familiarised with all modifications and adjustments made to any of the ship's components. Care must be taken to ensure thorough training of new crew.[5]

What if I am unable to purchase a sufficient quantity of low-sulphur fuel before arriving at an ECA?

Low-sulphur fuel is expected to be available for ships that plan to operate in ECAs and ports which are intending to enforce the low-sulphur regulations will make compliant bunkers available to ensure that ships can quickly restock their low-sulphur fuel requirements.

However, if despite your best efforts, you are unable to procure compliant fuel oil prior to entering an ECA, your ship record should identify all attempts to bunker the required fuel.

The US Environmental Protection Agency (EPA) has issued guidelines on actions to be taken if fuel oil, of a compliant grade, is not available before entering the North American ECA. According to these guidelines, both EPA and the ship's flag State must be notified.

This notification must be made through the email submission of a Fuel Oil Non-Availability Report as soon as possible but no later than 96 hours prior to entering the North American ECA.

How does fuel switching impact on ship design?

The modification of engines and boilers for the use of low-sulphur fuel has implications for ship layout and design, in particular fuel storage, and the ship's piping systems.

Fuel Storage: In determining whether a ship will require modification, the first step is to calculate the required storage capacity for distillate fuels. This will be a function of:

- Which ECAs will be entered during a typical voyage.
- The size of the zone and length of required transit.
- The usual length of time, speed and therefore expected volume of fuel required.
- Possible need to re-route in order to obtain low-sulphur compliant fuel (although suppliers are likely to be concentrated in or near ECAs).
- The extent to which compliant fuel is carried outside the ECA areas (resulting in poor bunker tank utilisation).
- Time in port.
- Possible availability of shore-side power (if ship capable of using).

Most ships which have been regularly trading within ECAs will have designated tanks for low-sulphur fuel (<1.00%). After 1 January 2015, this particular grade of oil will be rendered non-relevant as it will be replaced by a demand for 0.10% MDO or MGO. Thus the low-sulphur fuel tanks could be cleaned and converted into designated MDO or MGO tanks.

To ensure compliance and to reduce the risk of inadvertent admixture, total segregation of ECA compliant fuel oils from other fuel oils is advised, right up to the fuel supply pumps to the engine or boilers. With such an arrangement fuel-switching is both easier and more precise, thus allowing the exact change-over time, as required by the ECA regulations, to be logged. The majority of ships built post-1998 have double service tanks that make segregation possible.

Is LNG a viable fuel option for the future?

The concerns of owners are the issues of price, availability, and safety. They question if LNG is viable as a fuel of the future. But engine manufacturers have committed to R&D which would indicate a belief that LNG will indeed be the main marine fuel for the future. There are already examples of LNG-powered ships that regularly bunker, especially in Scandinavian locations, or large fuel-selling ports which is evidence of the viability of LNG as a ship fuel.

Is new LNG bunkering infrastructure expanding rapidly enough?

An effective LNG infrastructure is crucial when it comes to the feasibility of LNG becoming a common fuel of choice in the shipping industry. With a number of upcoming LNG terminals being considered, one factor for deciding geographical location is the possibility of offering speedy, effective and adapted bunkering solutions to all types of traffic.

Consideration will be needed for container ships which rely on bunker operations whilst offloading their cargo. Existing container terminals may require upgrading of typical container lifting equipment to be aligned with LNG regulations such as Gas Detection Systems.

What are the safety implications of using LNG fuel?

Transfer and storage of LNG is not a new concept. The equipment, systems and procedures associated with LNG that are in place have resulted in a strong safety record. The safe experience of LNG-fuelled bunkering operations on a global scale is good.

Industry professionals have met in numerous organised discussions to provide agreed operational guidelines. These guidelines define the overall philosophies of designs and operations relevant to LNG bunkering.[6]

What are the benefits and challenges of using LNG fuel?

The table below lists the different benefits and challenges of using LNG fuel:

Benefits	Challenges
Automatic compliance with present and future ECA limits except for NO_x Tier III for two-stroke engines.	Higher construction costs for new ships; high retrofit costs
Potential reduction in fuel cost	Supply infrastructure in its infancy
Avoiding fuel oil availability issues	Safety concerns
No engine room fuel treatment system or sludge	Regulatory uncertainty
	Ship out of service during bunkering

What operational issues must be considered when using EGCS?

Space and weight: Some systems can be fitted in an existing or extended funnel or outside the funnel, but the weight of the unit when full and its effect on the ship's stability must be considered. The water treatment plants required for wet systems can be located in the ship's engine room or, dependent on the design, in one of a number of other possible locations on the ship. Manufacturers should be able to advise operators on the best location for individual ships.

Waste: As the sludge from the washwater treatment system cannot be incinerated onboard arrangements must be made for its storage and subsequent discharge ashore. Washwater from scrubbers should be monitored and its discharge should comply with special discharge criteria as set out in resolution MEPC.184(59).

Power: Power requirements for a wet scrubber are estimated to be generally around 10-30kW for each MW of engine power. By contrast, dry scrubber power consumption is given as being as low as 1.5-2kW per MW of engine power.

Reliability: The various monitoring systems required will need to be reliable enough to operate continuously as required without undue maintenance demands. The same applies to the washwater treatment system components. EGCS performance also needs to be guaranteed: operators need to have confidence that Annex VI requirements will be met 100% of the time.

[6] ISO/DTS 18683 Guidelines for systems and installations for supply of LNG as fuel to ships; DNV GL (2013) Recommended Practice on LNG bunkering

What are the benefits and challenges of using EGCS?

The table below lists the different benefits and challenges of using EGCS technology:

Benefits	Challenges
Lower fuel cost	Investment cost
Greater fuel availability	Novel equipment and system to be integrated into the ship's core operating procedures
Single grade of fuel oil onboard simplifying bunker tank distribution and usage	Washwater discharge controls to be met
Good retrofitting possibilities, dependent on ship type	Reliability of required monitoring systems
	Additional space and power requirements
	Unclear interpretation of washwater criteria by various port States and even by individual ports

What guidelines are in place to ensure the certification of EGCS?

EGCS have to comply with the 2009 IMO Guidelines for Exhaust Gas Cleaning Systems. They specify the requirements for the testing, survey, certification and verification of the EGCS.

NOTE: The ship's flag State (the Administration) has to approve of the use of EGCS and is not mandated to accept such proposals automatically. It may furthermore impose additional requirements to those given in the IMO guidelines (MEPC.184(59)). Consequently, before ordering or installing an EGCS, ship owners should check with the Administration whether it accepts such arrangements and whether there are any specific requirements.

What should be considered when selecting a system?

When selecting a system, ship owners must consider the different timescales of ECAs and other emissions-limiting zones and the consequential variations in SO_x limits the ship may encounter globally. Care must be taken to ensure that the system selected and installed is capable of 'cleaning' the quantity of exhaust gas produced to bring eventual emissions down to the lowest level required by the regulations in every zone the ship may enter.

What types of EGCS systems currently exist and what distinguishes them from each other?

Currently there are two main types of EGCS:
- Wet scrubbers that use water (seawater or fresh) as the scrubbing medium.
- Dry scrubbers that use a dry chemical.

Wet systems are further divided into:
- Open-loop systems that use seawater.
- Closed-loop systems that use fresh water with the addition of an alkaline chemical.
- Hybrid systems, which can operate in both open-loop and closed-loop modes.

10.4 Regional Regulation

Besides IMO regulations, there are several regional regulatory requirements governing SO_x and PM emissions.

10.4.1 EU Regulations

10.4.1.1
Directive 2005/33/EC

EU Directive 2005/33/EC

The EU Directive 2005/33/EC, an amendment of the earlier Directive 1999/32/EC, introduced a new limit on the sulphur content of the fuel oil used by ships when 'at berth' in EU ports, which came into effect on 1 January 2010.

This Directive enforces that ships 'at berth' in EU ports must use fuels with maximum 0.1% sulphur content. This applies to any use of the fuel e.g. in auxiliary engines, main engines, boilers. The same requirement also applies to ports in the European Economic Area, i.e. Norway and Iceland and now also Turkey. In this context, 'at berth' includes ships at anchor in a port but not during their arrival and departure transits or when shifting from one 'at berth' position to another.

The Directive also stipulates that:

- Ships must document in their logbooks the change-over times, to and from the 0.1% maximum sulphur fuel.
- These change-overs must take place as soon as possible after arrival 'at berth' and as late as possible before departing.
- Inspections, involving fuel sampling to verify compliance, may take place.

These requirements do not apply:

- To ships which spend less than 2 hours at berth according to published timetables;
- for hybrid sea-river ships while they are at sea; and
- for ships which switch off all engines and use shore-side electricity.

10.4.1.2
Directive 2012/33/EU

EU Directive 2012/33/EU

The EU adopted amendments to the EU Sulphur Directive in order to align the Directive with the 2008 amendments to MARPOL Annex VI, which included more stringent limits of sulphur content in fuels which are to be used in the ECAs and on a global basis.

According to the new Directive, by 2015, the sulphur content of fuel used in shipping is to be lowered from its current 1% to 0.1% in ECAs – the Baltic Sea, the North Sea, and the English Channel. In practice, this means that the ships will either have to switch to fuel with lower sulphur content, or start cleansing their emissions, for example by introducing EGCS or other means of alternatives.

Another important issue which is contained in the Directive is that outside ECAs (i.e. in territorial waters, exclusive economic zones and pollution control zones), the ships will be required to burn fuels with a maximum sulphur content of 0.50% after 2020. This requirement will apply regardless of the results of the forthcoming 2018 IMO availability study which may decide to postpone the entering into force of the 0.50% limit to 2025.

10.4.2	Hong Kong Fuel-Switch Scheme

Hong Kong Fuel-Switch Scheme

In 2014, the Hong Kong Environmental Protection Department adopted a new regulation to limit local air pollution from marine traffic.

As of 1 January 2015, ocean-going vessels (OGVs) have to switch to low-sulphur fuel with a maximum 0.5% sulphur content when at berth in Hong Kong waters.

All OGVs must initiate the fuel switch upon arrival at berth, complete the switch to low-sulphur fuel within one hour, then use low-sulphur fuel throughout the berthing period until one hour before departure unless:

- Using low-sulphur fuel will pose safety risk to the OGV;
- all practicable measures according to the established fuel switch procedures have been followed to ensure the use of low-sulphur fuel as soon as possible after berthing and as late as possible before departure; or
- there is a justified and unexpected event beyond the shipmaster's control causing delay to the departure of the OGV. In that case, the shipmaster must ensure the event be recorded in the logbook.

In line with international practices, exemptions from the fuel switching requirements are provided in the following situations:

- OGVs due to be at berth for less than two hours;
- OGVs adopting alternative fuel (such as LNG) or compliance method with emission reduction performance comparable to that of using low-sulphur fuel;
- OGVs calling Hong Kong under emergency conditions; or
- warships or ships on military services.

Enforcement will in the first instance involve inspection of logbooks detailing the fuel switch, and BDNs. Authorities may also sample the fuel being used while at berth and analyse the collected sample and the sealed bunker sample for sulphur content.

The proposed maximum penalty for non-compliance will be a maximum fine of HK$ 200,000 (approximately US$ 25,800) and up to six months imprisonment.

Another new rule in Hong Kong bans dark smoke emission of shade 2 or darker on the ringelmann chart for three minutes or longer continuously at any one time.

In cases of contravention involving foreign ships, parties would each be liable to a fine of HK$ 25,000 for a first conviction, and to a fine of HK$ 50,000 for any subsequent conviction.

10.4.2.1   Local Bunker Supplies

In addition, since 1 April 2014, a new law requires that local bunker suppliers sell MGO with a maximum sulphur content of 0.05%.

The regulation is primarily aimed at reducing emissions from local ships, but will also mean that OGVs lifting MGO in Hong Kong should get a fuel with maximum 0.05% sulphur.

What do the European regulations mean for ship operations?

Ship owners and operators should be prepared for stricter reporting requirements and a tighter inspection regime. In June 2013, the European Commission issued a tender for development of sampling, analysis and inspection guidelines for marine fuels regulated under recently revised European regulations. The aim is to ensure harmonised and comprehensive reporting on the sulphur content of liquid fuels falling under the scope of the Directive.

What are the different sulphur limits in the various regions?

The table below provides an overview of fuel oil sulphur limits for ships after 1 January 2015.

Description Of Area	Effective Date	Maximum Sulphur Limit
Worldwide		
Outside ECAs	In force	3.50%
	1 January 2020/2025[7]	0.50%
Inside all ECAs (MARPOL): • Baltic Sea ECA. • North Sea ECA. • North American ECA. • US Caribbean Sea ECA.	In force	0.10%
Europe		
All EU ports and anchorage within port limits	In force	0.10%
EU territorial waters (only passenger ships)	Until 1 January 2020	1.50%
EU territorial waters (all ships)	1 January 2020	0.50%
Turkish ports and anchorage within port limits	In force	0.10%
Other Areas		
Hong Kong waters	In force	0.50%

10.5 Going Beyond Compliance

There are several ways to go beyond compliance and further reduce SO_x and PM emissions.

10.5.1 Scoping Current SO_x And PM Emissions

Before embarking on the journey to reduce SO_x and PM emissions, it is recommended to first take stock of emissions. Therefore, you should:

- Record and archive fuel consumption data.
- Record statistics on average SO_x content of fuel for all bunker types.
- Complete an annual inventory of SO_x and PM emissions for all the company's ships.
- Sample PM emissions for one of the fleet's main engine types to validate inventory emissions factors. Sampling should be repeated every 5 years. The company should follow a recognised methodology that is consistent with the fleet and from year to year.

To make sure these measures are adhered to, documenting fuel consumption data should become an integral part of the company's strategy and be required by company policy.

The methodology for estimating SO_x and PM emissions is explained in Section 10.7.

---

[7] The 0.50% limit is subject to a global review of the availability of such fuel oil. The review must be completed by 2018 and may recommend the postponement of the 0.50% limit until 2025.

10.5.2 Monitoring SO$_x$ And PM Emissions

SO$_x$ and PM emissions can be monitored either by inferring the emissions from the amount and type of fuel consumed or by using dedicated equipment.

The first option is explained in Section 10.7.

In terms of equipment, various emissions monitoring systems are available for the analysis of exhaust gases from the engines and boilers of ships. Many of the systems on the market offer proven reliability, and can measure up to six gases including SO$_2$, CO$_2$ and NO$_x$.

Typically, the systems comprise of exhaust mounted analysers. Emissions data from the entire system is managed and displayed at a dedicated panel computer, with outputs to networks, control systems, and reporting facilities offered to ensure that the emissions levels can be easily monitored at all times from the bridge.

10.5.3 Reducing Fuel Consumption

Regardless of the fuel type used, reducing fuel consumption will also reduce SO$_x$ and PM emissions. There are various operational and technological measures available to the industry that can be applied and strategies that can be undertaken to achieve this. These are discussed in more detail in Chapter 9 'Carbon Dioxide' in Section 9.5.2.1.

10.5.4 Using Low-Sulphur Fuels Or Exhaust Gas Cleaning Systems Outside Emission Control Areas And On Port Areas

As explained in Sections 10.3 and 10.4, the use of low-sulphur fuels is already required in ECAs.

In order to increase your environmental performance and move beyond compliance, you should consider switching to low-sulphur fuels or using an approved EGCS when operating outside these areas in addition to doing so when restrictions are in place. For example, you could allocate 25% of the company's global fuel consumption to fuel with a sulphur content equal or less than 1.5%

As SO$_x$ and PM contribute to local air pollution, reducing these emissions when approaching a port and during every port stay is particularly important. Toward this end, you should consider switching to low-sulphur fuels, using an ECGS or using shore-power.

10.5.5 Engine Modifications To Reduce PM Emissions

In addition to the measures mentioned above, there are certain engine modifications you could take to reduce your PM emissions. These are:

- Modified fuel injection valves.
- Electronically controlled main and/or auxiliary engines.
- Adjustable vane turbochargers.

10.6 Business Benefits

At first sight, the benefits for complying or even going beyond SO$_x$ and PM emission regulations may seem non-existent: higher costs for low-sulphur fuels, higher costs for ordering or retrofitting LNG ships, and high upfront investments for EGCS. Nonetheless, there are significant benefits involved in reducing your SO$_x$ and PM emissions.

10.6.1 Compliance Rates And Penalties For Non-Compliance

The penalties imposed in instances of non-compliance range from detention of ship, monetary fines of varying amounts, and/or non-conformity notices issued under the International Management Code for the Safe Operation of Ships and for Pollution Prevention (ISM Code).

It must be expected that sanctions for non-compliance will vary significantly between North Europe and North America. They will presumably also vary between cases where the fuel oil is purchased in good faith, but later proves to be above the allowable sulphur content and cases of deliberate non-compliance, e.g. steaming ahead on HFO where MGO would be required.

If ship owners or operators try to cover up deliberate non-compliance by tampering with the paper work, for example wrong log book entries and falsified BDNs, this will in many countries be considered a criminal act. In the US, in particular, it could result in millions of dollars in fines and year-long imprisonment of the Master and Chief Engineer. In repeated cases, an owner's entire fleet may be banned from entering US waters.

10.6.2 Incentive Schemes And Funding

Some countries and ports, recognising the financial implications of the increased consumption of low-sulphur fuel oil, are 'rewarding' ships to help counter the higher costs.

In Sweden, for example, the Port of Gothenburg reimburses shipping companies that choose to operate their ships on cleaner fuels when in port waters. Similar incentive schemes are also available in other ports. To provide an example, ports participating in the Environmental Ship Index of the World Ports Climate Initiative reward lower SO_x and PM emissions with reduced port dues.

10.7 Measuring Environmental Performance

Estimating SO_x and PM emissions can be attained through the application of this formula:

$$Emission = Fuel\ consumed\ x\ Emission\ factor$$

The emission factors for SO_x and PM are shown in the table below:

Engine Speed/Type	Fuel Type	Main Engine Emission Factor (kg/tonne fuel)	Auxiliary Engine Emission Factor (kg/tonne fuel)
SO_x			
SSD	HFO[8]	52.77	n/a
MSD	HFO	52.79	52.78
HSD	HFO	n/a	52.78
Otto	LNG	0.02	0.02
Gas turbine	HFO	52.79	n/a
Steam boiler	HFO	52.79	n/a
PM			
SSD	HFO	7.28	n/a
MSD	HFO	6.65	6.34
HSD	HFO	n/a	6.34
Otto	LNG	0.18	0.18
Gas turbine	HFO	0.20	n/a
Steam boiler	HFO	3.05	n/a

Source: IMO (2014) Third IMO GHG Study

CHAPTER ELEVEN

CONTENTS

NITROGEN OXIDES

NITROGEN OXIDES

11.1 Introduction

Nitrogen oxides (NO_x) is a generic term for compound oxides of nitrogen - a mixture of nitric oxide and nitrogen dioxide. NO_x are produced as a result of the reaction of nitrogen and oxygen gases in the air during fuel combustion, especially at high temperatures. Only a limited fraction of NO_x emissions formed are attributed to the nitrogen contained in fuel, however, the amount of NO_x formed is very dependent on the fuel type.

Every year, international shipping produces on average 18.6 million tonnes of NO_x emissions which represents approximately 13% of global human-caused NO_x emissions.[1]

11.2 Environmental Impact

The principal environmental impact of NO_x emissions is that they contribute to the ozone layer depletion. NO_x emissions also accelerate acid rain formation.

The human health impacts related to NO_x emissions are of particular concern. NO_x emissions are a leading cause of, or contributing factor to, a range of respiratory diseases such as asthma, emphysema and bronchitis. All these conditions can lead to premature death.

11.3 International Regulation

Resolution MEPC.176(58), as amended by resolution MEPC.251(66)

Regulation 13 of MARPOL Annex VI sets mandatory limits for the emissions of new build engines. These limits (detailed below) apply to all marine diesel engines with a power output of more than 130kW installed on ships constructed on or after 1 January 2000.

However, engines which are solely used for emergency purposes are exempt from this regulation.

11.3.1 NO_x Emission Limits

Resolution MEPC.176(58), as amended by resolution MEPC.251(66)

Under Regulation 13 of MARPOL Annex VI, the International Maritime Organization (IMO) introduced a tiered system to reduce NO_x emissions. Different levels (tiers) of control apply based on the ship construction date, and within any particular Tier, the actual limit value is determined from the engine's rated speed (rpm).

Tier I and Tier II limits are applicable to engines installed on ships constructed on or after 1 January 2000, and 1 January 2011 respectively.

Tier III limits will apply to ships constructed on or after 1 January 2016 when operating in the North American Emission Control Area (ECA) and the US Caribbean Sea ECA - the two NO_x Emission Control Areas (NO_x ECAs) that have been designated so far. Outside NO_x ECAs, Tier II controls apply.

Tier	Ship construction date on or after	Total weighted cycle emisson limit (g/kWh) n = engine's rated speed (rpm)		
		n<130	130≤n<2000	n≥2000
Tier I	1 January 2000	17.0	$45 \cdot n^{-0.2}$	9.8
Tier II	1 January 2011	14.4	$44 \cdot n^{-0.23}$	7.7
Tier III	1 January 2016	3.4	$9 \cdot n^{-0.2}$	2.0

Resolution MEPC.190(60)
Resolution MEPC.202(62)

Resolution MEPC.176(58),
as amended by resolution
MEPC.251(66)

NO$_x$ Emission Control Areas

There are currently two NO$_x$ ECAs:

- North American ECA.
- United States Caribbean Sea ECA.

When operating in these two areas, marine diesel engines installed on a ship constructed[2] on or after 1 January 2016 will be required to comply with the more stringent Tier III NO$_x$ standard.

For future NO$_x$ ECAs, ships will have to comply with NO$_x$ Tier III standards only if they are constructed on or after the date of adoption of the NO$_x$ ECA, or a later date as may be specified when designating a new NO$_x$ ECA, whichever is later.

Some smaller ships are not required to install Tier III engines, i.e.

- Purely recreational ships of less than 24 metres length.
- Ships with less than 750 kW propulsion power where the Administration accepts that a Tier III engine could not be fitted due to the ship's design or construction.
- Purely recreational ships constructed prior to 1 January 2021 of less than 500 gross tonnage (GT) and with a length $\geq$ 24 metres.

Resolution MEPC.176(58),
as amended by resolution
MEPC.251(66)

Major Conversions

The NO$_x$ emission limits also apply to engines of existing ships which undergo a major conversion after 1 January 2000.

Major conversion means any of the following changes to a diesel engine on or after 1 January 2000:

- Installation of a replacement engine which is not a type identical to the one it is replacing, or the installation of an additional engine. (Even if the engine type is the same as the engine being replaced, there are cases where it is considered as 'non-identical', e.g. when ratings are different, see Annex of MEPC.1/Circ.795/Rev.1).
- The maximum continuous rating is increased by more than 10% compared to the original certification.
- A substantial modification is made to the engine:
    - for engines installed onboard ships constructed on or after 1 January 2000, this means any modification that can cause the engine to exceed the applicable emission limit.
    - for engines installed onboard ships constructed before 1 January 2000, this means any modification that increases the existing emission characteristics.

If you currently intend to make any changes to a diesel engine that are covered by the above definition of a 'major conversion', the Tier II requirements apply.

The only exception is if the type of the replacement engine is identical to that of the engine it is replacing, in which case the requirements applicable to the original engine apply.

Resolution MEPC.176(58),
as amended by resolution
MEPC.251(66)

Pre-2000 Engines

Certain marine diesel engines require a retrospective NO$_x$ certification. This is the case for diesel engines:

- With a power output of more than 5,000 kW;
- with a per cylinder displacement at or above 90 litres; and
- installed on ships constructed between 1 January 1990 and 1 January 2000.

Such engines must meet the Tier I standards, provided that an approved method for that engine has been certified by an Administration of a Party to Annex VI.

---

[2] In this context, 'constructed' means the time of keel laying.

What Is An Approved Method?

Resolution MEPC.176(58), as amended by resolution MEPC.251(66)

An Approved Method is a measure defined, normally by the engine manufacturer, to ensure that the engine's NO_x emissions comply with Tier I limits. It only applies to pre-2000 engines.

Approved Methods have to be certified by a Party to MARPOL Annex VI. This does not necessarily have to be the ship's flag State.

Once the Party has notified the IMO about the certification of an Approved Method, then that Approved Method must be applied no later than the first renewal survey which occurs more than 12 months after the Party's notification.

However, if the ship owner can demonstrate that the Approved Method is not commercially available at that time, then it is to be installed no later than the next annual survey after which it has become available.

Resolution MEPC.243(66) contains guidelines on the process of approving an Approved Method.

An overview of Approved Methods certified by a Party to MARPOL Annex VI is provided on the IMO's website.

11.3.2   Meeting NO_x Emission Standards

There are three key options for ship owners looking to reduce NO_x emissions:

- Preventing the formation of NO_x during combustion.
- Treating exhaust gases.
- Using alternative fuels.

These options are described further in the subsequent Sections 11.3.2.1 to 11.3.2.3.

11.3.2.1   *Preventing The Formation Of NO_x During Combustion*

The main factors that influence NO_x formation are the concentrations of oxygen and nitrogen within the air, the local temperatures during the combustion process as well as the fuel type used.

Therefore, primary measures focus on lowering the concentrations, peak temperature and the amount of time in which the combustion gases remain at high temperatures.

Internal Engine Modifications

Internal engine modifications can optimise engine parameters with respect to emissions, i.e. fuel injection, valve timing, charge air and compression ratio.

Examples of such internal engine modifications include the following:

- Decrease of injection duration, delay of start of injection and pre-injection.
- Modification of fuel injectors.
- Modification of the combustion pressure.
- Scavenging air cooling.
- Miller cycle.

Depending on the measure taken, internal engine modifications can reduce NO_x emissions by approximately 20-30%. This means that Tier II limits for NO_x emissions can be achieved by internal engine modifications.

However, these measures have a major disadvantage as they generally increase fuel consumption. This is explained by the fact that they all aim to decrease combustion temperatures which in turn lowers combustion efficiency and increases fuel consumption.

Water Injection

Decreasing the temperature in the combustion chamber, and thus NO_x emissions, can also be achieved by using water or water vapour. Examples are the direct injection of water in the combustion chamber, emulsifying water in the fuel prior to injection and charging cylinder with humidified air.

The actual NO_x reduction is determined by the amount of water used, but as a rule of thumb, 1% of water reduces NO_x by 1%. This explains why emission reduction potential of these technologies varies largely from 10-85%. Tier II and possibly even Tier III NO_x emission limits could thus be partly achieved by using water injection technologies.

On the downside, these 'wet' technologies may increase the specific fuel oil consumption and consume additional energy for water treatment. This may be the reason for the little use of this method within the industry.

Exhaust Gas Recirculation

Another possibility to reduce NO_x emissions is Exhaust Gas Recirculation (EGR). EGR is a mature technology within the automotive market, but new to ships. As the name suggests, a fraction of the exhaust gas is filtered and re-circulated back into the combustion chamber after cooling. This lowers the oxygen content of the mixture and increases its heat capacity, resulting in a reduction of peak combustion temperatures and thus decreased NO_x formation.

Tests carried out on a container ship[3] equipped with a two-stroke MAN EGR main engine since March 2013 show that by recirculating 5-10% exhaust gas, Tier II can be achieved in a very fuel-efficient way. By recirculating 40-45%, Tier III can be achieved with a minimum fuel penalty.

11.3.2.2 Post-Combustion: Selective Catalytic Reduction

Selective catalytic reduction (SCR) is a technique to remove NO_x from exhaust gases. SCR systems use urea – or in certain cases ammonia – with a catalyst to convert NO_x into nitrogen and water.

SCR can reduce NO_x emissions by more than 90% and can thus be used to achieve Tier III limits. Some sources also state that a particulate matter (PM) reduction of 25-40% is possible and that the general noise is reduced due to replacement of the silencer.[4]

SCR systems also offer ship operators a potential fuel-saving benefit when operating outside a NO_x ECA, as the systems can be used to meet Tier II NO_x limits. This would allow the engine settings to be adjusted for optimum efficiency – Tier II engines are typically 4-4.5% less efficient than Tier I engines – resulting in reduced fuel consumption and lower carbon dioxide (CO_2) emissions.

11.3.2.3 Alternative Fuels And Onshore Power Supply

Replacing conventional fuels by alternative fuels or switching to other power sources results in reduction of both NO_x and sulphur oxide (SO_x) emissions. In case of using LNG, NO_x can be reduced by 60% on a two-stroke engine and up to 90% on a four-stroke engine. SO_x can be reduced by 90-100%, depending on the amount and type of pilot fuel, if any.

Another option is to use onshore power supply, also known as cold ironing, at ports where available: connecting to shore-side electrical power in exchange for switching off their main and auxiliary engines whilst in port. Other projects are currently being explored as shown in the Box Out below.

The LNG Hybrid Barge Project

Becker Marine Systems and AIDA Cruises have come together with other partners to develop a forward-looking project for the energy-saving and emissions-reducing supply of power to cruise ships during layovers at the Hamburg port. In this project, LNG will be used to generate energy in combined heat and power units and generators aboard the floating LNG Hybrid Barge. The electricity thus generated will be fed into the cruise ship's power supply as needed.

---

[3] 'Maersk Cardiff', 4500 TEU, Main Engine: 6S80ME-C9-EGR
[4] Clean North Sea Shipping (2011) A review of present technological solutions for clean shipping; Wahlström, J., Karvosenoja, N. and Porvari, P. (2006) Ship emissions and technical emission reduction potential in the Northern Baltic Sea, Reports of Finnish Environment Institute 8

Survey And Certification

General Survey Requirements Applicable To All Air Pollutants

Every ship covered by MARPOL Annex VI must carry a valid International Air Pollution Prevention (IAPP) Certificate onboard for inspection by port or flag States. Usually, the IAPP Certificate is valid for five years – provided that no change of flag takes place.

The basic prerequisite to obtain an IAPP Certificate is that the ship complies with the requirements of the applicable regulations of MARPOL Annex VI. This has to be proven through an initial survey.

After the IAPP Certificate has been issued for the first time, each ship has to undergo periodical surveys in order to avoid the Certificate cease to be valid. These are:

- Annual surveys within a time window of ± three months of the anniversary date of the IAPP Certificate.
- One intermediate survey either after 2 or 3 years after issuance of the IAPP Certificate.
- A renewal survey before the end of every five-year period after issuance of the IAPP Certificate.
- An additional survey after a repair following an accident to the ship or when a defect is discovered in a ship, either of which substantially affect the integrity of the ship or the efficiency or completeness of the equipment of the ship. An additional survey is also required after an important repair or renewal is made.

A model IAPP Certificate is included in Appendix I to MARPOL Annex VI. It has been amended by resolution MEPC.194(61). This model certificate is also included in Part Three - The Maritime Environmental & Efficiency Templates provided on the USB memory stick.

Engine Certification

Engine International Air Pollution Prevention Certificate

All engines required to meet Tier I to Tier III standards must be certified with an Engine International Air Pollution Prevention (EIAPP) Certificate to demonstrate compliance with NO_x emission limits.

The EIAPP Certificate is issued by an authorised organisation for each applicable engine, engine family, or engine group after the engine manufacturer demonstrates that the engine complies with the NO_x limits set out in Regulation 13 of Annex VI.

The EIAPP Certificate is valid throughout the life of the engine subject to correct maintenance or until it undergoes a major conversion.

Technical File And Record Book Of Engine Parameters

In addition to the EIAPP Certificate, each engine must have a Technical File and a Record Book of Engine Parameters.

The Technical File is a record containing all details of parameters, including components and settings of an engine that influence the NO_x emission of the engine. The Technical File is typically prepared by the engine manufacturer, must be approved by the relevant certifying Authority, and has to accompany an engine throughout its life onboard the ship. It must be updated if necessary and maintained in good order and not be subjected to any unauthorised alteration, amendments, omission or deletions.

The Record Book of Engine Parameters is a document for recording all parameter changes, including components and engine settings that may influence NO_x emissions. This information is used during ship surveys and inspections, to make sure the engine has been complying with the NO_x limits. The ship owner must make sure the Record Book is always accurate. If the settings on the engine do not match those in the Record Book, an engine survey may include a more time-consuming investigation and, potentially, onboard measurement of NO_x emissions.

Questions to Consider

Which ships do the NO$_x$ emission limits apply to?
The NO$_x$ emission limits apply to all marine diesel engines with a power output of more than 130kW installed on ships after 1 January 2000.

Under certain circumstances, the NO$_x$ emission limits also apply to pre-2000 engines, i.e. for marine diesel engines:
- With a power output of more than 5,000 kW;
- with a per cylinder displacement at or above 90 litres;
- installed on ships constructed between 1 January 1990 and 1 January 2000; and
- for which an approved method has been certified by an Administration of a Party to Annex VI.

Engines which are solely used for emergency purposes are exempt from this regulation.

Are there other MARPOL Annex VI requirements that apply to engines?
Next to documenting engine compliance by carrying an EIAPP Certificate, there are two other requirements for compliance with Annex VI.

First, each engine must have a Technical File. This document is usually prepared by the engine manufacturer and contains information needed to inspect the engine to verify compliance. A paper copy of this document is required to be available onboard the ship, although in the future an electronic copy may be sufficient.

Second, each engine must have a Record Book of Engine Parameters. This is a document for recording all parameter changes, including components and engine settings that may influence NO$_x$ emissions. This information is used during ship surveys and inspections, to make sure the engine has been complying with the NO$_x$ limits. The ship owner must make sure the Record Book is always accurate. If the settings on the engine do not match those in the Record Book, an engine survey may include a more time-consuming investigation and, potentially, onboard measurement of NO$_x$ emissions.

Which NO$_x$ emission limits do I need to comply with?
The NO$_x$ emission limits are divided into three tiers. The tier you need to comply with depends on the ship's construction date – or the date of installation of additional or non-identical replacement engines -, the engine's rated speed and the area of operation.

Tier I (globally):
- Engines installed on ships constructed on or after 1 January 2000.
- Engines larger than 5,000 kW and with a per cylinder displacement at or above 90 litres, installed on ships constructed on or after 1 January 1990 but prior to 1 January 2000. (This requirement is subject to the availability of an Approved Method).

Tier II (globally):
- Engines installed on ships constructed on or after 1 January 2011.

Tier III (sailing in NO$_x$ ECAs):
- Engines installed on ships constructed on or after 1 January 2016 when operating in the North American ECA and the US Caribbean ECA.
- Engines installed on ships constructed on or after the date of adoption of a new NO$_x$ ECA, or a later date as may be specified in the amendment designating the new NO$_x$ ECA, whichever is later and which are operating in the new ECA.

What is an Approved Method?

An Approved Method is a retrofit for a particular engine, or a range of engines, installed on ships constructed between 1 January 1990 and 1 January 2000, with a power output of more than 5,000kW and a cylinder displacement of above 90 litres. It ensures that an engine which formerly did not comply with MARPOL Annex VI emission limits becomes compliant with emission limit Tier I.

An overview of Approved Methods certified by a Party to MARPOL Annex VI is provided on the IMO's website.

What are the advantages and disadvantages of the different options to reduce NO$_x$ emissions?

The main advantages and disadvantages are summarised in the table below:

Solution	Advantage	Disadvantage
Internal engine modification	• Simple and inexpensive	• Increased fuel consumption • Does not comply with Tier III
Adding water	• Simple and inexpensive	• Increased fuel consumption • Uncertain if it can comply with Tier III
EGR	• Known technology • Requires no addition of chemicals • Proven development to reach Tier III emission level • Works well with a SO$_x$ abatement system (EGCS)	• Requires engine modifications and additional arrangements
SCR	• Effective NO$_x$ reduction	• Complex system and operation • Requires ammonia normally in the form of urea • Challenging to integrate with a SO$_x$ abatement system (EGCS)
LNG	• Right now and in certain places LNG may be cheaper than HFO • Effective NO$_x$ reduction	• Retrofit difficult • Fuel availability uncertain • Infrastructure currently limited

What is an EIAPP Certificate?

An EIAPP Certificate is the abbreviation for 'Engine International Air Pollution Prevention Certificate'. It is a document which shows that an engine complies with emission limits defined in Regulation 13 of MARPOL Annex VI. An EIAPP Certificate is issued for an individual engine (serial-number based). The EIAPP Certificate comes with an approved IMO NO_x Technical File.

What is an approved IMO NO_x Technical File?

An approved IMO NO_x Technical File is a booklet of emission-relevant information about an engine, approved by an Administration or classification society on its behalf. Upon approval of the IMO NO_x Technical File, the Administration or classification society issues an EIAPP Certificate. The IMO NO_x Technical Files generally contains three parts:

- Information about the engine group or engine family.
- Emission test report.
- Information about the onboard verification of the engine.

Who issues an EIAPP certificate and approves of an IMO NO_x Technical File?

The Administration of the flag State the ship is flying assumes full responsibility in every case. However, the Administration may delegate the survey and certification to Recognised Organisations then acting on the Administration's behalf.

Will I need to get a new EIAPP certificate for the Annex VI Tier II and Tier III standards?

No. The new Annex VI Tier II and Tier III standards will apply only to engines installed on ships constructed on or after 1 January 2011 (Tier II) and 1 January 2016 (Tier III), or engines that undergo a major conversion on or after those dates.

What engine features control NO_x formation rates?

The formation of NO_x is mainly dependent on the combustion temperature and the residence time of the combustion gases at high temperatures: the higher the temperature and the longer the residence time at high temperature, the more NO_x will be created. Therefore, engine features that influence these variables will also influence the NO_x formation rate. The most influential engine features are:

- Injection and atomisation equipment.
- Injection timing equipment.
- Compression ratio.
- Combustion chamber geometry.
- Turbocharger type and build.
- Charge air cooler/pre-heater.
- Valve timing.
- Rated engine speed.
- Fuel composition.

11.4 Regional Regulation

11.4.1 Norway: The NO_x Tax

In November 2006, the Norwegian Parliament decided to introduce a tax on NO_x emissions, effective from 1 January 2007.

Since implementation, a fee was charged per kg of NO_x emitted from all engines exceeding 750kW, boilers over 10MW and flaring. In 2007, the NO_x tax amounted to NOK 15/kg, in 2011, it was NOK 16.43/kg and in 2013, the tax was raised to NOK 17.01/kg.[5]

NO_x tax applies to Norwegian registered ships within 250 nautical miles (nm) from Norway's coast. It also applies to ships under foreign flag operating in the territorial waters, which mean within the 12 nm. Innocent passage for ships in transit are exempted from the Norwegian tax rule.

Norway allows for three methods to calculate the total amount of emissions:

- A pre-defined NO_x Tax Calculations Table or 'rate card'.
- A source-specific Manual Onboard Measurement.
- Continuous Onboard Monitoring.

11.5 Going Beyond Compliance

There are several ways to reduce NO_x emissions beyond the levels required by international regulations.

11.5.1 Understanding NO_x Emissions

Understanding how much NO_x is emitted by your ships can provide you with guidance on how to reduce your environmental impact and what to focus your efforts on. Taking stock of NO_x emissions can be achieved by taking the following steps:

- Record and archive fuel consumption data.
- Complete an annual inventory of NO_x emissions for all the company's ships.
- Sample NO_x emissions for one or several of the fleet's main engine types to validate inventory emissions factors. Improve your NO_x inventory according to the sampling results. Sampling should be repeated every 5 years. The company should follow a recognised methodology that is consistent with the fleet and from year to year.

To make sure these measures are adhered to, documenting fuel consumption data should become an integral part of the company's strategy and be required by company policy.

The methodology for estimating NO_x emissions is explained in Section 11.7.

11.5.2 Reducing Fuel Consumption

As a rule of thumb, reducing fuel consumption will also reduce NO_x emissions. This rule applies to most technical and operational measures which increase fuel efficiency, except for measures taken to improve combustion efficiency. The latter increase combustion temperatures which lead to higher NO_x emissions.

11.5.3 Technical Measures To Reduce NO_x Emissions

As explained in Section 11.3.2, there are several technological measures which can be taken to reduce NO_x emissions. The emission reduction potential for these technologies differs significantly.

Some of these technologies are already being used to achieve the required IMO NO_x emission limits, i.e. Tier I or Tier II. Going beyond regulatory requirements thus means reducing NO_x emissions below the applicable Tier.

This can be done by fitting one technology which reduces NO_x emissions below regulatory requirements on one or two ships, analysing their performance and consequently deciding about a further roll-out or trialling other technologies.

---

[5] Åsen, E.M. (2013) Norway: The NOx tax scheme, Norwegian Ministry of the Environment; Norwegian Maritime Authority (2012) Guideline on the NOx tax

11.6   Business Benefits

There are several benefits for you to reap if you reduce your NO_x emissions.

11.6.1   Incentive Schemes And Other Financial Support

There are various schemes that provide financial incentives for the reduction of NO_x emissions.

In Norway, for example, the NO_x Fund offers financial support to enterprises that implement NO_x emission abatement measures and for measurements in order to define source-specific emission factors. The Box Out below presents more information on the NO_x Fund. Please also refer to Section 11.4 for information about the corresponding Norwegian NO_x Tax Scheme.

The NO_x Fund

After the introduction of the NO_x tax in 2007, a number of Norwegian business organisations have entered into an agreement with the Ministry of the Environment to establish the Business Sector's NO_x Fund. This agreement allows participating organisations to pay a fee to the Fund per kg of NO_x emitted. This fee amounts to NOK 4 per kg of NO_x emitted and is thus significantly lower than the fees charged under the NO_x tax.

This agreement generates an annual income to the Fund of about NOK 0.6 billion. The Fund offers financial support to enterprises that implement NO_x emission abatement measures and for measurements in order to define source-specific emission factors.[6]

Ports participating in the Environmental Ship Index, part of the World Ports Climate Initiative, reward reductions of NO_x emissions beyond regulatory requirements with reduced port dues. For example, ships calling at the Port of Los Angeles are eligible for an incentive grant of US$ 3,250 per port call if their main engine meets IMO Tier III requirements.[7]

[6] Åsen, E.M. (2013) Norway: The NOx tax scheme, Norwegian Ministry of the Environment.
[7] Port of Los Angeles (n.d.) Environmental Ship Index Incentive Program: Ocean-Going Vessel Incentives

11.7 Measuring Environmental Performance

Estimating NO$_x$ emissions can be achieved through the application of this formula:

$$Emission = Fuel\ consumed\ x\ Emission\ factor$$

Multiply the fuel consumption data in tonnes by the NO$_x$ emission factors to obtain an emission estimate.

11.7.1 NO$_x$ Emission Factors

NO$_x$ emissions are highly dependent on the conditions under which the fuel is burned in the engine. NO$_x$ emissions are therefore specific to engine type, conditions and settings. This also explains why there is not one universally applicable emission factor for NO$_x$, but rather several, depending on the type of engine used.

For the purpose of establishing emissions inventories, it is common to distinguish between slow, medium, and high-speed diesel engines as well as engines using LNG as fuel. Furthermore and if applicable, you need to know under which IMO Tier the engine falls.

The different NO$_x$ emission factors are shown in the table below:

IMO Tier	Engine Speed/ Type	Fuel Type	SFOC Main/ auxiliary engine	Main Engine Emission Factor (kg/ tonne fuel)	Auxiliary Engine Emission Factor (kg/tonne fuel)
0	SSD	HFO	195/ n/a	92.82	n/a
	MSD	HFO	215/227	65.12	64.76
	HSD	HFO	n/a /227	n/a	51.10
I	SSD	HFO	195/ n/a	87.18	n/a
	MSD	HFO	215/227	60.47	57.27
	HSD	HFO	n/a /227	n/a	45.81
II	SSD	HFO	195/ n/a	78.46	n/a
	MSD	HFO	215/227	52.09	49.34
	HSD	MDO	n/a /227	n/a	36.12
all	Otto	LNG	166	7.83	7.83
n/a	Gas turbine	HFO	305	20.00	n/a
n/a	Steam boiler	HFO	305	6.89	n/a

Source: IMO (2014) Third IMO GHG Study

Using the fuel consumption data and emission factors, emissions of exhaust gases can now be calculated by multiplication.

CHAPTER TWELVE

CONTENTS

OZONE - DEPLETING SUBSTANCES

OZONE-DEPLETING SUBSTANCES

12.1 Introduction

Ozone-depleting substances (ODS) are used in cooling and freezing systems onboard all ships, for refrigeration of cargo and provisions as well as in air conditioning systems.

The most common ODS refrigerant used onboard ships is difluorochloromethane (HCFC-22). It is used onboard approximately 80% of the current fleet. Non-ozone-depleting HFC refrigerants have been replacing HCFC-22 in new-built ships.

A typical refrigerant charge for ships above 100 gross tonnage (GT) is between 100 and 500 kg for direct systems, and between 10 and 100kg for indirect systems. In addition, there are about 1.7 million refrigerated containers used for the transport of perishable goods, each of which carries approximately 6 kg of refrigerant.[1]

12.2 Environmental Impact

ODS are man-made substances that cause damage to the stratospheric ozone layer. Most ODS are potent greenhouse gases.

The principal environmental impact that is associated with ODS use across the shipping industry is leakage into the environment. The leakage rate of refrigerants from ships is estimated to be between 20-40%.[2]

Once released into the atmosphere, ODS emitted by ships contribute to the depletion of the ozone layer. Ozone depletion can not only cause severe problems to humans, but also to plants and animals through the acceleration of climate change.

12.3 International Regulation

Resolution MEPC.176(58)

The use of ODS is governed under Regulation 12 of MARPOL Annex VI. Regulation 12 applies to all ships, to fixed and floating drilling rigs and other platforms. It explicitly does not apply to permanently sealed equipment without charging connections or removable components, such as domestic refrigerators or freezers, ice makers, water coolers and self-contained air-conditioners.

12.3.1 Refrigeration Equipment And Systems

Resolution MEPC.176(58)

According to MARPOL Annex VI, Regulation 12.3.1, no system or equipment containing chlorofluorocarbon (CFC) or halon is permitted to be installed on ships constructed on or after 19 May 2005 and no new installation of the same is permitted on or after that date on existing ships.

Similarly, no system or equipment containing hydrochlorofluorocarbon (HCFC) is permitted to be installed on ships constructed on or after 1 January 2020 and no new installation of the same is permitted on or after that date on existing ships in line with Regulation 12.3.2.

Existing systems and equipment using HCFCs are permitted to continue in service and may be recharged as necessary.

However, a ship is required to comply with any stricter legislation applied in its flag State.

---

[1] IMO (2014) Third IMO GHG Study; UNEP (2011) 2010 TOC Refrigeration, A/C and Heat Pumps Assessment Report
[2] UNEP (2011) 2010 TOC Refrigeration, A/C and Heat Pumps Assessment Report

163

Resolution MEPC.176(58)

Discharge Of ODS Emissions

While the use of certain ODS are still allowed in refrigeration equipment and systems, the deliberate discharge of ODS to the atmosphere is wholly prohibited. This includes emissions occurring in the course of maintaining, servicing, repairing or disposing of systems or equipment.

When servicing or decommissioning systems or equipment containing ODS, the gases must be collected in a controlled manner and, if they are not reused onboard, discharged to appropriate reception facilities.

Any redundant equipment or material containing ODS is to be landed ashore for appropriate decommissioning or disposal. The latter also applies when a ship is dismantled at the end of its service life.

12.3.3

Resolution MEPC.176(58)

Monitoring And Recording Requirements

Ships of and above 400 GT that have ODS containing systems or equipment are required to maintain a list of these systems and equipment. This list has to correspond to the Supplement to the IAPP Certificate (see MARPOL Annex VI, Appendix I, Section 2.1).

The same ships must also keep and maintain an ODS Record Book onboard. On each of the following occasions, an entry into the ODS Record Book must be made:

- Recharge, full or partial, of equipment containing ODS.
- Repair or maintenance of equipment containing ODS.
- Deliberate and non-deliberate discharge of ODS to the atmosphere.
- Discharge of ODS to land-based reception facilities.
- Supply of ODS to the ship.

These entries must be made in terms of mass (kg) of the ODS in question.

The record book may form part of an existing record book or electronic recording system as approved by the Administration.

12.4 Regional Regulation

12.4.1 European Union

In addition to regulations by the International Maritime Organization (IMO), the European Commission has imposed requirements on the use of ODS in shipping.

Regulation EC 1005/2009

According to Regulation EC 2037/2000 – now recast as Regulation EC 1005/2009 -, producers and importers are not allowed to place HCFCs on the market. This means that virgin HCFCs are not available anymore within the EU. However, the refrigerant system can utilise reclaimed HCFCs until 31 December 2014, after this date all HCFCs are prohibited.

Furthermore, servicing and maintenance of HCFC based systems within the EU or onboard EU-flagged ships will only be possible until 31 December 2014. However, systems using HCFCs may continue to be used provided their refrigerant circuits are not accessed for either service or maintenance.

Questions to Consider

Do I have to remove ODS from my ships?

No, not necessarily. With regards to MARPOL Annex VI, existing installations may remain in use. Restrictions only apply to new installations: new installations which contain ODS are not allowed on ships anymore, except that new installations containing HCFCs are permitted until 1 January 2020.

If ODS are used onboard, and if the ships has an IAPP Certificate, record keeping of ODS is mandatory. A record book has to be kept onboard, together with a list of equipment of ODS. The form of the record book is not prescribed, but the entries to be made are: Entries must be made in kgs upon each recharge and discharge of ODS, and upon maintenance and repair of the system.

Can I get HCFC in European ports?

Yes. Reclaimed HCFC for servicing can be obtained from any supplier in the EU until 31 December 2014. Containers with reclaimed HCFC must be labelled accordingly and thus can be identified easily.

Virgin HCFC for the supply of non-EU-flagged ships can be obtained only from producers or re-packagers until 31 December 2019.

Can I get halon fire extinguishers for ships in European ports?

No. The use of halon and equipment containing or relying on halons onboard of non-military ships is prohibited in the European Union. The placing on the market or export for these purposes is also prohibited. Thus, in EU ports, you will not be able to purchase any halon, halon-based fire extinguishers or spare parts for such uses for use onboard non-military ships.

Can I service or supply an EU-flagged ship?

Servicing is only permitted until 31 December 2014 and only non-virgin HCFC may be used. Import or export licenses are not required.

If an EU-flagged ship is serviced in a non-EU port, no import license is required because servicing is considered as consumption by the country in which the port is located. However, only non-virgin HCFC may be used and the servicing is only permitted until 31 December 2014.

The supply (without servicing) of HCFC to an EU-flagged ship in a non-EU port is prohibited because this would constitute an import into the EU. Imports of HCFC for servicing are prohibited under the Regulation.

Can I service a non-EU-flagged ship in an EU port?

Non-EU-flagged ships can be serviced until 31 December 2014. The same rules apply as for servicing any fixed installation within the EU. Only non-virgin HCFC may be used.

If the servicing involves the recovery of an ODS refrigerant that is removed off board, an import license for destruction will be required.

Can I supply HCFC to a non-EU-flagged ship in an EU port?

HCFC can be exported until 31 December 2019. The same rules apply as for any other export of HCFC.

12.5 Going Beyond Compliance

Moving beyond regulatory requirements can be achieved by:

- Reducing leakage rates of ODS.
- Replacing ODS with ozone-friendly refrigerants.

12.5.1 Reducing Leakage Rates Of ODS

Monitoring the consumption of refrigerants can not only help detect, but also prevent leaks.

It is estimated that the installation of leak detectors in machinery and processing rooms combined with a visual inspection routine every 2 weeks with a portable leak detector could reduce emission rates to as low as 20% of the current level. Refrigeration equipment and systems should always be maintained and controlled by trained personnel.

Minimising the impact of leaks can be achieved by reducing the refrigerant charge (i.e. by indirect cooling) and compartmentalising the piping system so that a leakage may be isolated. It is also important that facilities are available to allow safe and easy recovery of refrigerants during maintenance.

Furthermore, designs that are more resistant to corrosion, vibration and other stresses reduce refrigerants leaks.

12.5.2 Replacing ODS With Ozone-Friendly Chemicals

The reduction of ODS leaks is more of a short-term solution. While it is good for the environment, ODS are still being used and thus continue to pose an environmental threat. In addition, they have to be phased out in the future.

Therefore, in order to solve the ozone depletion problem, alternative refrigerants must be applied in the systems onboard the ships. Many alternatives to ODS exist, including ozone-friendly HFCs, ammonia and carbon dioxide (CO_2).

Carbon Dioxide As A Refrigerant

In the beginnings of mechanical refrigeration, at the end of the 19th century, CO_2 was one of the first refrigerants to be used in compression type refrigerating machines. Later, it gained widespread application onboard refrigerated ships, but became common in other sectors of refrigeration too. It was only immediately after World War II that CO_2 was rapidly eclipsed as a refrigerant, due to the advent of synthesised halogenated working fluids, that were considered as safe and ideal refrigerants at that time.

With the phasing out of HCFC, CO_2 could become an attractive refrigerant again. In 2013, the heating and air conditioning company Carrier launched their CO_2-based refrigerant system. According to the company, the system reduces the carbon footprint by 28% compared to previous units using synthetic refrigerants. The system recycles CO_2 that has been pulled out of the environment which makes it carbon neutral.

Questions to Consider

Which refrigerant is suitable for my operations?

Although no perfect refrigerant is known, there are certain factors which determine a refrigerant's desirability for a particular duty. The one selected should possess as many as possible of the following characteristics:

- Moderate condensing pressure, obviating the need for heavily constructed compressors, condensers and high pressure piping.
- High critical temperature, as it is impossible to condense at a temperature above the critical, no matter how much the pressure is increased.
- Low specific heat of the liquid because throttling at the expansion valve causes liquid refrigerant to be cooled at the expense of partial evaporation.
- High latent heat of vaporisation, so that less refrigerant may be circulated to perform a given duty.
- The refrigerant should be non-corrosive to all materials used in the construction of the refrigerating machinery and systems.
- It should be chemically stable, non-flammable and non-explosive.
- Worldwide availability, low cost and ease of handling are desirable.
- The problem of oil return to the compressor crankcase is simplified when an oil-miscible refrigerant is used, by the admixture of the oil and the refrigerant in the system. With non-miscible refrigerants, once oil has passed to the system, its return to the crankcase can only be effected with difficulty.
- Finally the refrigerant should be non-toxic, have satisfactory heat transfer characteristics, and leakages should be easy to detect either by odour or by the use of suitable indicators. Not all known refrigerants should be listed or dealt with, only those likely to be encountered onboard. These refrigerants are referred to by their trade name, chemical name or their internationally recognised numbers.

Furthermore, you need to consider that all refrigerants have an ideal operating temperature, below which they will go into vacuum. It is not desirable to run a unit in vacuum conditions due to the possible ingress of air and moisture. The operating temperature will become a limiting factor in the choice of refrigerant.

For example, R-134a goes into vacuum at temperatures below minus 26.1°C. This means that it is only suitable for operating temperatures above this level. R-22 goes into vacuum at minus 40.8°C, so it is suitable for applications only above this temperature. However, R- 504a and R-507a remain under positive pressure at minus 45.6°C.

How can I prevent ODS from being emitted into the air?

You can take the following steps to reduce your ODS emissions:

- Do not vent CFCs and HCFCs out into the atmosphere.
- Convert existing equipment to using non-ODS refrigerants.
- Ensure any new equipment/machinery ordered for refrigeration and air conditioning uses an HFC refrigerant (however, be cautious with HFCs as their inclusion in the Montreal Protocol is currently under discussion).
- Educate and train the staff onboard regarding the importance of these steps.

How can I monitor refrigerant leaks?

You could take regular readings of refrigerants (e.g. level or pressure gauges) and maintain a record of how much refrigerant is used to top-up the system. If the maintenance of refrigeration systems is undertaken by the staff onboard your ships, you should make sure a recovery unit is provided. It will include a specialised container or external cylinder for each type of refrigerant to enable the recovered substance to be stored. Such recovery cylinders will be marked clearly e.g. 'CFC R-12 – Recovered'.

12.6 Business Benefits

Reducing leakage of ODS is not only environmentally beneficial, it also good financially as reduced leak rates mean that less ODS have to be replaced.

A study by TemaNord (2000) estimated that approx. 15-20% of the total HDCFC-22 charge or 150,000kg is lost from leakages every year. Average recharging cost amount to approximately DKK 15,000-25,000 per ship.[3]

The installation of refrigeration systems and equipment containing ODS is already restricted and regulatory requirements are tightening in the next few years. Even though ODS may still be used in already installed systems and equipment, it is possible that the use of ODS will be prohibited in the longer term. In this case, ship owners and – operators taking action now would be one step ahead and not have to worry about the matter anymore.

12.7 Measuring Environmental Performance

The amount of ODS (in kg) supplied, added or discharged has to be recorded in the ODS Record Book. Comparing this data allows estimating leakage rates and gives a good indication of environmental performance.

In addition, leak detection devices with alarm function are available and should be installed in the machine room, direct refrigerated areas and in safety valve discharge lines.

[3] TemaNord (2000) Alternatives to HCFC as refrigerant in shipping vessels.

CHAPTER THIRTEEN

CONTENTS

VOLATILE ORGANIC COMPOUNDS

VOLATILE ORGANIC COMPOUNDS

Please note: Only applicable to tankers.

13.1 Introduction

Volatile organic compounds (VOCs) are a large group of carbon-based chemicals that evaporate easily at ambient temperature.

They are formed through evaporation of crude oil and its products and are a mixture of hydrocarbons, mainly methane, propane, and butane, and several other gases. VOCs are frequently divided into non-methane (NMVOC) and methane.

During loading, storage and transportation of crude oil on ships, a significant amount of VOCs may be emitted to the atmosphere.

VOC emissions from shipping mainly depend on the following factors:

- Characteristics of current and previous cargo.
- Temperature and diurnal variation.
- Loading rate.
- Turbulence in the vapour space.
- Sea and swell conditions (for offshore loading).
- Time since unloading of previous cargo.
- Design of ship.

13.2 Environmental Impact

In the presence of sunlight and nitrogen oxides (NO_x, generated during combustion processes), VOCs react to form ground-level ozone. Ground-level ozone has a detrimental effect on vegetation and human health.

Furthermore, methane, a component of the VOC emissions, acts as greenhouse gas and contributes to climate change.

13.3 International Regulation

Resolution MEPC.176(58)

VOC emissions are addressed in Regulation 15 of MARPOL Annex VI.

In general, this regulation only applies to tankers. However, it also applies to gas carriers in case the types of loading and containment system allow safe retention of non-methane VOCs onboard or their safe return ashore.

The regulation can be split into two main requirements:

- Utilisation of a vapour emission control system (VECS) in certain ports or terminals.
- Establishment and implementation of a VOC Management Plan.

13.3.1   Vapour Emission Control System

Parties to MARPOL Annex VI can designate ports and terminals where VOC emissions from tankers must be regulated.

IMO MEPC.1/Circ.774 contains a list of designated ports intending to regulate VOC emissions. These ports are in the Netherlands and the Republic of Korea. There are, however, other ports and terminals where vapour recovery systems are available, although they are not specifically designated for VOC emissions and thus they do not appear in the IMO MEPC circular.

Resolution MEPC.176(58)

At these designated ports and terminals, VOC emissions from tankers must be controlled by VECS. The VECS must be in accordance with MSC/Circ.585 Standards for vapour emission control systems. Tankers not fitted with VECS may be accepted at designated ports and terminals for up to three years from the effective date of the controls.

13.3.2   VOC Management Plan

Resolution MEPC.176(58)

All tankers carrying crude oil are required to have an approved ship-specific VOC Management Plan onboard and must implement it.

The plan is to be prepared according to the guidelines contained in resolution MEPC.185(59). An example is contained within the Maritime Environmental & Efficiency Templates on the USB memory stick.

As a minimum, the VOC Management Plan must:

- Provide written procedures for minimising VOC emissions during the loading, sea passage and discharge of cargo.
- Give consideration to the additional VOC generated by crude oil washing (COW).
- Identify a person responsible for implementing the plan.
- For ships on international voyages, be written in English, French or Spanish or include a translation into one of these languages if the working language is not English, French, or Spanish.

The VOC Management Plan also requires the recording and estimation of the extent of VOC emissions during a voyage.

Section 13.7 on 'Measuring Environmental Performance' explains how to estimate your VOC emissions. In addition, technical information to assist the development of VOC Management Plans is provided in MEPC.1/Circ.680 and in MEPC.1/Circ.719.

13.3.3   Reducing VOC Emissions

The purpose of the VOC Management Plan is to ensure that during the operation phase of a tanker voyage, VOC emissions are managed, minimised or prevented as much as possible.

This can be achieved by the following operational procedures:

- Reducing the content of light ends in the cargo before loading.
- Reducing the temperature of the cargo.
- Filling cargo tanks sequentially instead of in parallel.
- Increasing the cargo tank pressure.
- Reducing the amount of COW.
- Reducing the roll and pitch of the ship in the seaway.

Under which circumstances do my ships need a VECS?

The requirement to install a VECS only applies to tankers that call at certain ports and terminals. IMO MEPC.1/Circ.774 contains a list of designated ports intending to regulate VOC emissions. These ports are in the Netherlands and the Republic of Korea.

Tankers not fitted with VECS may be accepted at designated ports and terminals for up to three years from the effective date of the controls.

Under certain conditions, the requirement to install a VECS also applies to gas carriers. This is the case if the types of loading and containment systems allow safe retention of non-methane VOC's onboard or their safe return ashore. For more information, see the International Code for the Construction and Equipment of Ships Carrying Liquefied Gases in Bulk (IGC Code), Chapter 5.9 and MSC.30(61).

Does the requirement for VOC Management Plans apply to my fleet?

All tankers carrying crude oil are required to carry an approved ship-specific VOC Management Plan and effectively implement it.

How do I get a VOC Management Plan?

Contact your technical consultant to produce a VOC Management Plan for each of your ships that have crude oil on their cargo list.

How do I make sure all the relevant information is contained in the VOC Management Plan?

Many classification societies have produced templates that can be used as a basis for a ship's VOC Management Plan. These templates will help you make sure that your plan includes all items required.

Further guidance on the development of the VOC Management Plan can be obtained from resolution MEPC.185(59). Circular MEPC.1/Circ.680 contains technical information on systems and operations to assist in developing such a plan.

13.4 Regional Regulation

13.4.1 Norway

Measured per capita, the Norwegian VOC emissions are among the highest in Europe. These VOC emissions originate mainly from offshore loading of crude oil.

In order to reduce VOC emissions during the loading operations for crude oil, both offshore and onshore, regulatory measures have increasingly been required by the Norwegian Pollution Control Authority and also form part of international environmental agreements.

The current Norwegian emission regulations for crude oil loading operations require a minimum recovery efficiency of not less than 78% of NMVOC. This particular recovery efficiency requirement is applicable to shuttle tankers operating in the Norwegian sector of the North Sea. The laws and regulations for onshore sites require facilities to apply for their own independent concession under which to operate.

The same shuttle tanker is normally used by several oil companies lifting crude from different fields. To comply with the regulation, the oil companies therefore decided to jointly make the efforts needed and the Norwegian VOC Industry Co-operation was established in June 2002.

13.4.2 United States Of America

The Clean Air Act Amendments of 1990 (CAA 90) issued national standards for control of VOCs and other pollutants emitted during ship loading operations. CAA 90 also authorises individual States to set vapour emission standards and to require that marine terminals and tank ships be equipped with a vapour control system (VCS). The national requirements can be found in 40 CFR 63 Subpart Y and 40 CFR 61 Subpart BB.

Today, VCS design and technology are more advanced than they were in 1990, and VCSs control more types of vapour than the crude oil, gasoline blend, or benzene vapours to which they were limited in 1990. Furthermore, the US Environmental Protection Agency (EPA) and US States now permit or require the control of vapour emissions from many other cargoes, e.g. chemicals.

In light of these changes, the US Coast Guard (USCG) revised its safety regulations for ship and facility VCS to promote safe operation in an expanded range of activities. These revised regulations were made to improve operational safety by regulating VCS design, installation, and use, however they do not require anyone to install or use them.

The majority of ship VCS regulations can be found in 46 CFR Part 39. Important areas addressed by these regulations include:

- Cargo gauging system (§39.20-3).
- Tankship liquid overfill protection (§39.20-7).
- Vapour overpressure and vacuum protection (§39.20-11).
- High and low vapour pressure protection for tankships (§39.20-13).
- Operational requirements (§39.30-1).
- Lightering and topping-off operations with vapour balancing (§39.40).
- Personnel training (§39.10-11).

Other applicable regulations for ship VCS and loading operations are contained in 33 CFR section 155.750 (Oil transfer procedures), 33 CFR section 156.120 (Requirements for transfer), 33 CFR section 165.170 (Equipment tests and inspections), and 46 CFR section 35.35-30 (c) (Declaration of inspection).

Although the regulations permit vapour to be processed onboard a tank vessel, in most cases the collected vapours are sent ashore to the facility VCS for processing. If the vapour processing unit is located onboard a tank vessel, it must meet the requirements of 33 CFR part 154, subpart E to the satisfaction of the Commandant of the USCG in addition to complying with the requirements of 46 CFR part 39.

In case the VOC will be processed onboard the tank vessel, the system shall fulfil the following to address the safe design and operational aspects:

- Liquid overfill protection (§154.812).
- Overpressure and vacuum protection (§154.814).
- Fire, explosion and detonation protection (§154.820).
- Requirements for inerting, enriching and diluting systems (§154.824).
- Vapour compressors and blowers (§154.826).
- Vapour recovery and vapour destruction systems (§154.828).
- Personnel training and operating requirements (§154.840 and §154.850).
- Design, performance, and testing standards for detonation and flame arresters (§154 Appendix A and B).

The VCS requirements found in 33 and 46 CFR specifically address facilities and ships transferring cargoes of crude oil, gasoline blends or benzene. At the time the regulations were written, these were the only cargoes that States were targeting for vapour control. Since that time, an increasing number of facilities have been required to collect the vapours of other hazardous cargoes. Over 70% of certified facility VCSs are certified to collect vapours from cargoes other than crude oil, gasoline blends, or benzene.

13.5 Going Beyond Compliance

Current regulation only requires the use of VECS in certain ports and terminals as well as the implementation of operational procedures to reduce VOC emissions (in the context of the VOC Management Plan). However, it is neither specified which operational procedures should be taken, nor how much VOC emission a tanker is allowed to emit. This gives a lot of freedom to ship owners and operators to decide which action to take in reducing VOC emissions.

Besides improving processes, technical equipment or design changes can help reduce VOC emissions.

While there are a multitude of different systems, they can be broken down into the following three categories:

- Installations onboard the ship to reduce the formation of VOCs.
- The installation of equipment onboard to recover VOCs inside the tanks:
    - Recovery of excess VOC and tank absorption (Venturi system);
    - Direct Absorption of VOC in the Crude Oil (CVOC system);
    - Vapour recovery system: condensation, absorption and adsorption.
- Cargo tanks designed and built to cope with increased tank pressure:
    - Vapour Pressure Release Control Valve (VOCON valve);
    - Cargo Pipeline Partial Pressure control system (KVOC).

13.5.1 Improving The VOC Management Regime

The following presents specific procedures that can contribute to improving the VOC management regime:

1. Consider requirements for periodical maintenance and pressure testing/verification of set-pressure of Pressure/Vacuum (P/V) valves (to avoid leaks and the reduction of opening pressure).

2. Consider requiring loading to be started with a loading rate which is conducive to reduced VOC generation until loading outlets in tanks are well submerged (e.g. filling to 1m) to avoid agitation of the layer of saturated vapour at the bottom of the tank.

3. Consider actively managing the pressure of the cargo tank atmosphere in the ullage space to reduce vapour release from the cargo during loading. A procedure where the initial slow loading takes place with the mast riser valve, if fitted, open (to release mainly inert gas) followed by closing the riser valve and let the P/V valves on the tanks or in-line in way of the mast riser take care of the release of excess vapour/inert gas during the subsequent loading.

4. Consider carefully managing manual pressure relief/blow-down of ullage (vapour space) pressure. The inert gas pressure is required to be continuously recorded and enforcement of such a requirement is possible. It is recommended that pressure relief should be handled automatically by P/V valves, by in-line P/V breather valves or by in-line pressure control systems. Most VOC manuals specify that manual pressure relief is to be conducted at the mast riser, despite the fact that all ships have P/V valves that can do this automatically. Furthermore, a number of ships are equipped with in-line P/V breather valves (in way of mast riser) for the specific purpose of automatic pressure relief. It has been indicated that the reason for this is to concentrate the release to mast riser and avoid multiple VOC releases from P/V valves in the cargo deck area as a measure of crew safety, especially when the cargo being carried has a high hydrogen sulphide content. It has also been indicated that some consider the P/V valves to be an emergency device only, although this is not the case as per SOLAS. It should also be noted that for onboard chemical tankers as well as some older oil tankers, automatic pressure relief through P/V valves is the only means of full flow tank venting. In many cases, the manual pressure relief at the mast riser is specified to be carried out at a pressure significantly below the P/V valve opening pressure.

5. Consider requiring the supply pressure to be kept below opening pressure of the P/V valves in the event of inerting during voyage; this can be achieved by careful selection of the inert gas output pressure setting apparatus.

6. Consider requiring that, in connection with COW, the ship shall not wash more tanks than required by MARPOL Annex I (1/4 of the tanks), unless circumstances make it necessary (dependent on crude quality). Currently, it is understood that some major oil companies specify that tankers are to do a complete COW of all cargo tanks after discharge.

7. Notwithstanding the requirements outlined within MARPOL, consider requiring that during COW, a full cycle (top-bottom-top for single nozzle machines) is to be avoided (dependent on crude quality). Washing that covers lower stringers and tank bottom will in most cases be enough for sediment control.

8. Consider using closed cycle COW, i.e. recirculate crude oil used for washing to/ from the slop tanks which are filled with fresh dry crude oil. This reduces vapour release from the crude oil compared to using 'fresh' oil bleed from discharge lines. Note that the solvent effect of the crude may be jeopardised when 'spent' crude is used for COW.

9. Consider requiring that tanks intended to be crude oil washed should be discharged first if the ship's trim/bending moment permits. Vapour released to atmosphere may be mitigated when these tanks are washed whilst other tanks are being consecutively discharged.

10. Consider operating fully in the closed condition. With requirements specifying that all tank connections that may be opened during normal operations are to be designed to prevent emissions of VOC. Typically all tankers today have so called 'vapour-locks' which are pipes at top of tanks provided with ball valves with threads for connection of instruments, e.g. for manual sounding, temperature measurements and cargo sampling.

13.6 Business Benefits

The release of VOC emissions from loaded fuel represents an economic cost as the amount of loaded fuel is reduced. This economic cost can be considerable.

A MARINTEK report has measured variations in emissions from 0.1 kg VOCs per tonne of cargo (terminal loading) to 2.8 kg VOCs per tonne (offshore loading in bad weather). For a typical Aframax tanker load of 100,000 tonnes, the latter represents around 1,761 barrels of oil. With US$ 100 per barrel, this amounts to a monetary value of US$ 176,100.[1]

Therefore, reducing VOC emissions can result in cost savings.

13.7 Measuring Environmental Performance

Estimating the extent of VOC emissions during a voyage – as required in the VOC Management Plan – can be done by:

- Recording the time and pressure within the tank/gas vapour system before the release takes place.
- Recording the time and pressure within the tank/gas vapour system after the release has been completed.

Based on this data, the VOC emissions can be calculated. Please refer to the NMVOC spreadsheet included in Part Three - The Maritime Environmental & Efficiency Templates provided on the USB memory stick. The equations used in the spreadsheet and their derivation follow from extensive research published in 'Volatile Hydrocarbon Emissions from Crude Oil carried by Sea in Tankers'.

NOTE: The spreadsheet only applies directly to crude oil cargoes. The applicability to product or chemical cargoes, however, is doubtful given the variance of the correlation of the cargoes True Vapour Pressure to the equivalent Reid Vapour Pressure.

CHAPTER FOURTEEN

CONTENTS

BALLAST WATER

BALLAST WATER

14.1 Introduction

The intake and discharge of ballast water was first introduced as a method of stabilising steel hulled ships over 120 years ago. It is the practise of pumping water (usually seawater) into a ship to keep the trim, draught, stability and structural loading within safe operating conditions, improve propulsion and manoeuvrability and compensate for any weight loss over the voyage.

Volumes of ballast carried vary drastically from a few hundred litres to over 100,000 tonnes depending on the ship size and purpose.

14.2 Environmental Impact

Ballast water is often taken onboard in one part of the world and discharged in another, an operation that usually takes place in or near port areas, where marine biological diversity is richest.

Inevitably, aquatic organisms are transported from one environment to another through the discharge of ballast in different ports along the voyage. As a result, some transported species become invasive, disrupting the ecology of the area where they are discharged. This explains why the discharge of ballast water can pose some serious ecological, economical, and health risks. It is estimated that 4,500 different species are carried around the world at any one time in ballast tanks.

For some examples of invasive species that are transported around the globe in ballast water, see the Box Out below.

Examples Of Invasive Species

The Zebra Mussel - is native to the Black Sea, but has been introduced to parts of Europe and North America. The adult zebra mussel fouls all available hard surface in mass numbers (including infrastructure and ships), blocks water intake pipes, sluices and irrigation ditches, displaces native aquatic life and alters habitat, ecosystems and food webs.

The North Pacific Seastar - is native to the Northern Pacific, but has been introduced to Southern Australia. It reproduces in large numbers and rapidly reaches 'plague' proportions in invaded environments. It feeds on shellfish, including commercially valuable scallop, oyster and clam species.

Toxic Algae – there are various species of toxic algae, but they all may form harmful algae blooms. Depending on the species, toxic algae can cause massive kills of marine life through oxygen depletion, release of toxins and/or mucus. They can also foul beaches and impact on tourism and recreation. Some species may contaminate filter-feeding shellfish and cause fisheries to be closed.

14.3 International Regulations

In order to avoid the negative environmental and economic impacts caused by marine invasive species carried in ballast water, the International Maritime Organization (IMO) adopted the International Convention for the Control and Management of Ships' Ballast Water and Sediments (BWM Convention) in 2004. The BWM Convention, once ratified, will introduce new standards for both ballast water exchange (BWE) and treatment, impose reporting requirements, and requirements to carry out ballast water management (BWM) procedures to a given standard.

At the time of writing (*December 2014*) the BWM Convention had not yet entered into force. It will enter into force 12 months after its ratification by 30 Member States representing at least 35% of the world's tonnage.

14.3.1 Scope Of The BWM Convention

The BWM Convention applies to all ships that are designed to carry dischargeable ballast water; this includes submersibles and floating craft and platforms. It applies to ships flying the flag of Parties to the Convention, and also ships operating under the authority of Parties (i.e. in Party territorial waters). A Party has discretion whether to enforce the Convention for a ship operating only in its territorial waters (or only in its territorial waters and the high seas). BWM is not required in certain exceptional circumstances, such as where it would endanger the ship.

In addition, discharge to approved onshore reception facilities or mobile BWM system can be used as an alternative to BWM.

14.3.2 Standard For Ballast Water Management

The BWM Convention defines two basic methods of managing ballast water:

- BWE (Regulation D-1): Specifications of volume of water to be replaced.
- BWM systems (Regulation D-2).

14.3.2.1 Ballast Water Exchange (D-1)

BWE means replacing the water that was taken up while in port or near the coast at the beginning of the voyage with water taken from the open ocean. The basis for this procedure is that aquatic organisms transported from coastal environments are unlikely to become established when discharged in deep water. Conversely, those aquatic organisms taken onboard when drawing ballast water from the deep ocean are far fewer in number and unlikely to become established if discharged in a coastal environment.

D-1 standard specifies that:

- A 95% volumetric exchange of ballast water must be achieved.
- If the exchange involves pump-through of ballast tanks, at least three times the volume should be pumped through each tank.
- Exchange should be conducted at least 200 nautical miles (nm) from the nearest land and in water of at least 200 metres in depth. (If a ship cannot comply with these distances, the exchange is to be conducted as far from the nearest land possible, but at least 50 nm from the nearest land and in depth of at least 200 metres).

The location, volume and depth of the water where the exchange is conducted must be recorded in the Ballast Water Record Book (see Section 14.3.4.2).

Ballast Water Exchange Methods

The IMO have recognised three methods of BWE:

- **Sequential method** - A process by which a ballast tank is first emptied and then refilled with replacement ballast water to achieve at least a 95% volumetric exchange.
- **Flow-through method** - a process by which replacement ballast water is pumped into a ballast tank intended for the carriage of ballast water, allowing water to flow through overflow or other arrangements. At least three times the tank volume is to be pumped through the tank.
- **Dilution method** - a process by which replacement ballast water is filled through the top of the ballast tank intended for the carriage of ballast water with simultaneous discharge from the bottom at the same flow rate and maintaining a constant level in the tank throughout the ballast exchange operation. At least three times the tank volume is to be pumped through the tank.

NOTE: BWE is intended to be phased out when all relevant ships are required to have installed onboard a BWM system compliant with the D-2 standard.

14.3.2.2 Ballast Water Management (D-2)

Regulation D-2 requires ships to treat ballast water prior to discharge so that it meets specified criteria for the maximum content of organisms.

It sets maximum limits for the number of generic organisms (split into two size categories) and the concentrations of three indicator microbes (as a human health standard) in a given volume of ballast water. Therefore, BWM systems must treat water for discharge to the following standard:

- Organisms ≥ 50 μ in minimum dimension: less than 10 viable organisms per m^3.
- Organisms < 50 μ but ≥ 10 μ in minimum dimension: less than 10 viable organisms per ml.
- Toxicogenic Vibrio cholera: less than 1 colony forming unit (cfu) per 100 ml or less than 1 cfu per 1 gram zooplankton samples.
- Escherichia coli: less than 250 cfu per 100 ml.
- Intestinal Enterococci: less than 100 cfu per 100 ml.

Ballast Water Management Methods

BWM and treatment methods have been ferociously developed over the last decade in preparation for the ratification of the BWM Convention, to replace the practice of BWE at sea.

Options to consider include:

- Mechanical treatment methods such as filtration and separation.
- Physical treatment methods such as sterilisation by ozone, ultraviolet light, electric currents and heat treatment.
- Chemical treatment methods.
- Various combinations of the above.

The technology options and the considerations for each are detailed below.

Mechanical

Filtration or other forms of mechanical separation are often used as the first element of a combination BWM system, as a precursor to chemical or physical disinfection. The filtration removes the larger organisms and increases the effectiveness of the secondary treatment.

- **Filtration:** Sediment and particles are removed with disk and screen filters during ballast intake. They are often self-cleaning with a back-flushing cycle. This backwashing is required to maintain a flow with minimum pressure drops. The waste stream is directed overboard back to the water source. These filtration systems create pressure drops and a reduced flow rate due to resistance in the filter elements and the self-cleaning procedures.
- **Magnetic Separation:** Seawater taken in is treated by adding a coagulant and magnetic powder. Coagulants are chemicals which, when added to water, bring the suspended particles together into larger, heavier masses of solids. These are called floc. The magnetic powder makes the floc magnetic, so it can be collected with magnetic discs in a magnetic separator.
- **Hydrocyclone:** Solid particles are separated from the water due to centrifugal forces. Only those particles with a specific gravity greater than that of water can be separated.

Physical Disinfection
- **Thermal:** Thermal treatment within ballast water treatment applications is similar to that of processes that use high temperatures to sterilise water. The idea of thermal treatment is to heat the ballast water to a high temperature to kill any unwanted organisms before the water is discharged.
- **Ultraviolet Irradiation:** Ultraviolet radiation is used to break down the cell membrane of the organism, killing the organism outright or destroying its ability to reproduce.
- **Cavitation and Ultrasound:** Venturi pipes or slit plates are used to generate cavitation bubbles and this high energy bubble creation and collapse results in hydrodynamic forces and ultrasonic oscillations, or high frequency noise, which disrupts the cell walls of organisms, effectively killing them. Ultrasonic treatment systems use transducers to generate alternating compressions and rarefactions in water to be treated. The removal of an undesirable organism is influenced by the frequency, power density, time of exposure, and the physical and chemical properties of the ballast water being treated.
- **Inert Gas De-Oxygenation:** Most aquatic organisms require oxygen for survival. Therefore the deprivation of oxygen within the substrate that supports the existence of the organisms can be used as an effective mechanism to remove unwanted organisms from ballast water. Various methods are used to remove the dissolved oxygen in the ballast water and replace it with inactive gases, such as nitrogen or other inert gas. Lowering the level of oxygen to less than 3 mg/l will result in effective kill rates.

Chemical Treatment
- **Disinfectants:** Pre-prepared or packaged disinfectants designed to be dosed into the ballast flow and kill the living organisms by chemical poisoning or oxidation. A number of different chemicals or chemical processes have been employed in the ballast water treatment systems including:

  - Chlorination.
  - Electrochlorination.
  - Ozonation.
  - Chlorine dioxide.
  - Peracetic acid.
  - Hydrogen peroxide.
  - Menadione/Vitamin K.

  The efficacy of these processes depends on the conditions of the water, e.g. pH, temperature and the type of organism. Chemical treatments are dosed into the existing ballast piping during intake or directly into the ballast tanks.

- **Electrolysis/Electro-Chlorination:** Electrical current is applied directly to the ballast water flow in an electrolytic chamber, generating free chlorine, sodium hypochlorite and hydroxyl radicals, causing electrochemical oxidation through the creation of ozone and hydrogen peroxide.

Type Approval Of Ballast Water Management Systems

Each BWM system must be type-approved by the Administration, taking into account the Guidelines for Approval of BWM systems. The type approval demonstrates that the system is in compliance with the standards set out in Regulation D-2.

The approval process differs according to whether the system uses an active substance.

An active substance is defined within the Convention as:

> *"a substance or organism, including a virus or a fungus that has a general or specific action on or against harmful aquatic organisms and pathogens".*

Ultraviolet light is not classed as an active substance.

Resolution MEPC.174(58)

Systems without active substances can receive type approval from a flag State (or organisation approved by the flag State), following both land-based and shipboard testing procedures. See IMO G8 Guidelines for further details. These guidelines are currently under review aiming at introducing a more robust type approval scheme.

Resolution MEPC.169(57)

Systems using an active substance, in addition to the above, must first receive Basic Approval from the GESAMP Ballast Water Working Group (BWWG), which examines whether the discharged ballast water has a harmful effect on the aquatic environment. Following Basic Approval, the system can then proceed to testing similar systems without active substances under the auspices of the Administration, then back to GESAMP BWWG for Final Approval once testing is complete. Following Final Approval, the Administration can issue type approval. See IMO G9 Guidelines for further details.

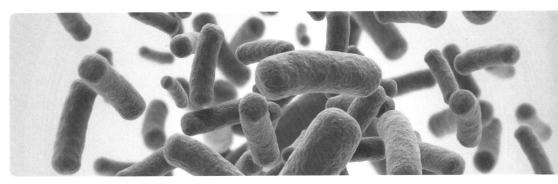

Sampling & In-Service Testing

Port State Control (PSC) and other authorised regulatory officers may, at any time for the purpose of determining whether the ship is in compliance with the discharge requirements, come onboard and take samples of the ballast water. That is why the BWM system should be designed with adequate sampling and testing facilities. The IMO G2 'Guidelines for Ballast Water Sampling' call for the sampling to be:

- Safe to the ship, inspectors, crew and operators; and
- simple, feasible, rapid and applicable at the point of ballast discharge.

In-tank samples may be taken via sounding or air pipes and manholes by using pumps, sampling bottles or other water containers. Samples may also be taken from the discharge line.

14.3.2.3 Implementation Timeline

The BWM standards will be phased in over a period of time. As an intermediate solution, ships should exchange ballast water mid-ocean (D-1). However, eventually most ships will have to install an onboard BWM system.

The BWM Convention defines three size classes of ships according to their total ballast water capacity. For each size class, the Convention determines the date from which BWM is required according to the date the ship was built.

The table below shows the new implementation schedule.

Ballast Water Capacity (m³)	Keel Laid	Date From Which BWM Compliance With D-2 Is Required
1,500 or more, but less than 5,000	2009	By the first renewal survey for IOPP Certificate following the date of entry into force of the Convention.
Less than 1,500, or more than 5,000	2009	By the first renewal survey for IOPP Certificate following the anniversary date of delivery of the ship in 2016.
Less than 5,000	During 2009, or after 2009, but before 2012	By the first renewal survey for IOPP Certificate following the date of entry into force of the Convention.
5,000 or more	During 2009, or after 2009, but before 2012	By the first renewal survey for IOPP Certificate following the anniversary date of delivery of the ship in 2016.
All ships	During 2012, or after 2012, but before the date of entry into force of the Convention	By the first renewal survey for IOPP Certificate following the date of entry into force of the Convention.
All ships	On or after the date of entry into force of the Convention	By the completion date of the ship construction.

The above applies if the BWM Convention enters into force on or after 2015 but not later than 31 December 2016.

14.3.3 Monitoring And Reporting

The Convention requires all ships to carry:

- A BWM Plan (Regulation B-1), detailing the procedures for safe compliance with BWM Convention requirements.
- A Ballast Water Record Book (Regulation B-2), recording when ballast water is taken onboard, circulated or treated, or discharged into the sea.

14.3.3.1 *Ballast Water Management Plan*

The BWM Convention requires every ship to carry a ship-specific BWM Plan that has been approved by its flag State or a Recognised Organisation.

Regulation B-1 sets out the minimum requirements. It states that a BWM Plan shall:

- Detail safety procedures for the ship and the crew associated with BWM.
- Provide a detailed description of the actions to be taken to implement the BWM requirements and supplemental BWM practices.
- Detail the procedures for the disposal of sediments at sea and to shore.
- Include the procedures for the coordination of shipboard BWM that involves discharge to the sea with the authorities of the State into whose waters such discharge will take place.
- Designate the officer onboard in charge of ensuring that the plan is properly implemented.
- Contain the reporting requirements for ships provided for under the BWM Convention.
- Be written in the working language of the ship. If the language used is not English, French or Spanish a translation into one of these languages shall be included.

Associated guidelines were adopted in 2005 as resolution MEPC.127(53), (the G4 Guidelines). There are seven mandatory aspects of the BWM Plan and the G4 Guidelines provide greater detail in addition to providing a standard format BWM Plan.

A standard format BWM Plan is included in Part Three - The Maritime Environmental & Efficiency Templates provided on the USB memory stick.

14.3.3.2 Ballast Water Record Book

The Convention (Regulation B-2) specifies that all ships must carry a Ballast Water Record Book, which must be completed after each ballast water operation and:

- May be paper, electronic, stand-alone or be integrated into another record book or system.
- Must record all ballasting operations in the working language of the ship (and in English, French or Spanish if one of these is not the working language of the ship).
- Must record circumstances and reasons for any accidental or exceptional discharge of ballast water.
- Must be signed by the officer in charge of the operation with each completed page signed by the Master.
- Must be readily available for inspection.
- May be inspected and copied by Officers duly authorised by Parties to the Convention.
- Must be kept onboard for at least two years after the last entry has been made, and retained by the ship operator for possible inspection for a further three years.

A model Ballast Water Record Book is included in Part Three - The Maritime Environmental & Efficiency Templates provided on the USB memory stick.

14.3.4 Certification Requirements

The Convention requires that all ships over 400 gross tonnage (GT) carry an International Ballast Water Management Certificate, awarded subject to survey by the flag State or a duly authorised organisation.

In order to obtain an International Ballast Water Management Certificate or Certificate of Compliance, the following must be done:

- The BWM Plan must be approved or examined and available onboard.
- A Ballast Water Record Book must be available onboard.
- An initial survey must be conducted.

The Certificate is valid for five years subject to annual, intermediate and renewal surveys.

An additional survey will be required to maintain a valid International Ballast Water Management Certificate if any part of the BWM system is changed, or the BWM system replaced or significantly repaired, or if the ship changes flag.

Ships below 400 GT could be subject to national survey and certification regimes.

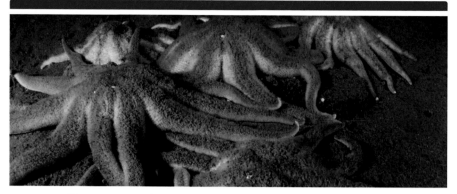

Questions to Consider

What types of ships are covered by the BWM Convention?
The BWM Convention applies to all sea-going ships greater than 400 GT that use ballast water. Ships below 400 GT could be subject to national legislation. In the US the regulations apply to all ships greater than 300 GT.

Can I be issued with a BWM Certificate for my ship before the BWM Convention enters into force?
Yes, classification societies can issue on request a certificate of compliance or statement of compliance with the Convention at any time before entry into force of the BWM Convention.

IMO has agreed that once the date of entry into force of the BWM Convention is known, Administrations and Recognised Organisations may issue International Ballast Water Management Certificates endorsed to state they are valid from the entry into force date.

What happens when the BWM Convention comes into force?
Ships must comply with the IMO Regulation D-1 or operate an approved BWM system as defined in the implementation schedule contained within the BWM Convention or any alternative implementation schedule agreed by the IMO.

How will the BWM Convention be enforced?
Enforcement of the BWM Convention in terms of sampling and testing is still under discussion by the IMO. However, an enforcement methodology has been outlined including:
- Proof of equipment certification (type approval).
- Verification of the BWM system condition and maintenance records.
- Crew ability to operate the BWM system and carry out ballast water operations in accordance with the BWM Plan.
- Inspection of the ship's BWM Plan and associated logs and record book

Ballast water discharge sampling to prove compliance with Regulation D-2 is only expected in cases where PSC is unable to verify the above information and/or have cause to invoke verification sampling.

What do I need to do to comply with the BWM Convention?
The BWM Convention requires that a ship has:
- A ship-specific BWM Plan that is approved by the Administration.
- A Ballast Water Record Book.
- An approved BWM system (Regulation D-2), or BWE (Regulation D-1) if specified in the BWM Plan.
- An International Ballast Water Management Certificate.

In order to comply with the Convention, the ship operator must ensure that:

- All ballast discharges are in accordance with regulation D-1 or D-2.
- All ballast water operations are carried out in accordance with the ship's BWM Plan.
- The Ballast Water Record Book is maintained and kept up to date according to regulations.
- The BWM system is operated and maintained strictly in accordance with the manufacturer's instructions.

Will PSC authorities sample and test ballast?

Yes. PSC will have the right to sample and analyse the ballast being discharged to ensure that it has been exchanged (a salinity test) or treated to meet the regulation D-2 standard.

IMO Guidelines for PSC provide basic guidance for PSC inspection to verify compliance with the BWM Convention. Under the guidelines, the PSC procedures are divided into the following four stages:

1. To check documentation.
2. To check the operation of the BWM system.
3. To conduct indicative analysis of ballast water.
4. To conduct detailed analysis of ballast water.

What if I want to exchange ballast water if the treatment system malfunctions?

In principle, the Convention does not allow for the use of exchange methods when the requirement is to treat the water according to the D-2 standard. Exchange under the D-1 standard will not be mentioned as a management method in the International Ballast Water Management Certificate. Such malfunction of a BWM system has to be reported to the appropriate authorities' and seek their advice on how to proceed.

NOTE: It will be illegal to discharge under D-1 when D-2 is applicable to your ship.

What documentation is required to be submitted when a treatment system is intended to be retrofitted onboard a ship?

For installations of BWM systems onboard ships in operation (retrofit installation), classification societies will request documentation for all ship systems affected by the installation of the BWM system. This includes documentation for piping systems, electrical systems and control systems. In case the installation requires changes to the ship arrangement, the classification society may also request documentation regarding fire safety, stability and structure.

Where can I get more information on how to plan the implementation of a BWM system?

In Part Three - The Maritime Environmental & Efficiency Templates provided on the USB memory stick, you will find an overview of key considerations that will help you plan the implementation of a BWM system.

14.4   Regional Regulations

Regulation C-1 of the Convention allows Parties to take additional measures to limit the spread of organisms and pathogens in ballast water, and IMO's G13 Guidelines offer some guidance to States in this regard. In practice, however, many non-Parties have simply developed ballast water regulations under national legislation. Some apply to all territorial waters, some only to particular ports or ecologically sensitive areas, and some to both, with more stringent standards for particular areas.

The most important national ballast water regulations are the United States requirements[1] which are detailed below.

14.4.1 United States Requirements

US Coast Guard (USCG) Regulations 33 CFR Part 151 and 46 CFR Part 162 entered into force on 21 June 2012 and are applicable to new ships constructed on or after 1 December 2013, as well as to existing ships from 2014 onwards.

All ships that call at US ports intending to discharge ballast water must either carry out exchange or treatment, in addition to fouling and sediment management. The exchange of ballast water will be allowed until the reach of the applicable implementation deadline for BWM systems, after which all discharges must be treated.

Table: Implementation schedule for the USCG ballast water treatment standard.

	Ship's ballast water capacity	Date constructed	Ship's compliance date
New ships	All	On or after 1 December 2013	On delivery
Existing ships	Less than 1,500m³	Before 1 December 2013	First scheduled drydocking after 1 January 2016
	1,500 - 5,000m³	Before 1 December 2013	First scheduled drydocking after 1 January 2014
	Greater than 5,000m³	Before 1 December 2013	First scheduled drydocking after 1 January 2016

BWM must be carried out using either a USCG type-approved system or a system type-approved by another Administration that the USCG has accepted – an Alternate Management System (AMS). As a USCG type-approved BWM system is not available at the time of writing *(December 2014)*, the USCG is providing extensions to ships which had to comply in 2014 and 2015. These extension dates are 'hard dates'.

An AMS is an already IMO type-approved system that meets the interim USCG requirements and has been assigned AMS acceptance status by USCG. An AMS acceptance is intended as an interim measure to allow foreign type-approved BWM systems to be used on a ship for up to 5 years after the ship is required to comply with the Ballast Water Discharge Standard, provided this has been installed prior to the compliance date of that ship. It allows the BWM system vendor or manufacturer time to obtain final US type approval.

NOTE: AMS acceptance is not related to the process of achieving type approval under the US regulations (33 CFR Part 151 and 46 CFR Part 162).

The USCG's type approval process includes the following steps:

- Manufacturers of BWM systems must apply to the USCG for approval.
- Manufacturers of BWM systems have to ensure that the equipment is tested by an independent laboratory, approved by the USCG.
- BWM equipment has to be constructed in accordance with 46 CFR Part 162.
- BWM equipment must be tested according to the requirements of the Environmental Technology Verification Protocol.

These requirements are all in excess of the IMO guidelines' requirements for type approval by a Member State.

Difference Between USCG Discharge Requirements And IMO Discharge Performance Standard

The major difference between the IMO BWM Convention discharge performance standard and the US Ballast Water Discharge Standard is the terms used as follows:

- The IMO BWM Convention uses the term 'viable organism', meaning that the organisms allowed in the regulated sizes and numbers after treatment are in a non-reproductive state.
- The US Ballast Water Discharge Standard stipulates 'living organism', meaning that the organisms allowed in the regulated sizes and numbers after treatment are dead.

Therefore, even if the number of organisms that can be present post-treatment is the same across both the US and IMO regulations, a BWM system that has been type-approved in accordance with IMO regulations may not be able to achieve type approval for use in US waters.

Vessel General Permit Requirements

The National Pollutant Discharge Elimination System is a system under the US environmental protection rules (Clean Water Act) to minimise pollution within US territorial waters (i.e. 3 nm off the US coast).

For ships greater than 79 feet (24.079 metres) in length, all the requirements are laid out in the US Environmental Protection Agency's (EPA) Vessel General Permit (VGP). These requirements are additional to international regulations such as the International Convention for the Prevention of Pollution from Ships - MARPOL. The VGP establishes technology-based effluent discharge limits for all ships and for specific discharges arising from the normal operation of a ship.

The revised VGP, effective since 19 December 2013, includes elements related to BWM such as:

- Monitoring equipment performance to ensure that the system is fully functional.
- Monitoring all ballast water systems for selected biological indicators.
- Monitoring the ballast water discharge itself for biocides and residuals to assure compliance with the effluent limitation.

Specific US State certification and discharge standard requirements beyond the federal VGP requirements have to be investigated taking into account the applicable US trading areas.

14.5 Going Beyond Regulatory Compliance

BWM has a baseline compliance with the IMO, however to exceed this level owners must upgrade their systems to comply with USCG. It is widely accepted that complying at this level enables the ship to sail in all waters.

Type approval by the USCG is not expected to be any more difficult to obtain than it would be in other jurisdictions but until USCG approval is given, operators should understand that the certificates on their ship are effectively worthless if the operator intends to trade in US waters.

14.6 Business Benefits

Good BWM practices demonstrate environmental leadership which can not only enhance the ship owner's good reputation, respond to stakeholder pressure for better environmental performance but also provide great PR opportunities.

14.7 Measuring Performance

Resolution MEPC.173(58)

Environmental performance is measured during the sampling of the ballast water. Towards this end, the IMO MEPC has adopted Guidelines for Ballast Water Sampling (G2).

The objectives of these guidelines are to provide Parties, including PSC officers, with practical and technical guidance on ballast water sampling and analysis for the purpose of determining whether the ship is in compliance with the BWM Convention. The guidelines are still under review.

CHAPTER FIFTEEN

CONTENTS

BIOFOULING

BIOFOULING

15.1 Introduction

Biofouling, or biological fouling, is the colonisation of microorganisms, plants, algae, or animals on surfaces exposed to sea (and fresh) water.

On a ship, the hull is the largest surface area that is susceptible to biofouling. However, other areas of the ship can succumb to the accumulation of biofouling including: heat exchangers, water-cooling pipes, propellers, sea-chests, sea-chest grids and ballast water tanks. The biofouling process begins within the first few hours of a ship's immersion in water.

The accumulation of biofouling on the hull reduces the ship's hydrodynamic performance, increases fuel consumption and decreases top speed and range.

Biofouling is influenced by a range of factors, including:

- Design and construction, particularly the number, location and design of niche areas.
- Specific operating profile, including factors such as operating speeds, ratio of time underway compared with time alongside, moored or at anchor, and where the ship is located when not in use (e.g. open anchorage or estuarine port).
- Trading routes (sea- versus fresh water).
- Maintenance history, including the type/technology, age and condition of any anti-fouling coating system, installation and operation of anti-fouling systems and dry-docking/slipping and hull cleaning practices.

In order to moderate the process of biofouling, the shipping industry has seen vast developments around the practice of anti-fouling. For a ship's hull the principal anti-fouling practice is the application of paint coatings. The practice of applying an anti-fouling paint coating to the ship's hull can not only greatly reduce or prevent the accumulation of biofouling but also, as with all paint applications, contribute to the protection of the ship's hull from the corrosive effects of saltwater.

The search for ways to protect hulls while eliminating or reducing the effects of biofouling has gone on for centuries. Many solutions have been used, from covering the hull with copper sheeting, to using arsenic, lead, organotin or a variety of other toxic materials in paints. Modern anti-foulings typically combine copper with environmentally acceptable organic biocides (co-biocides) or try to make the surface so slippery that nothing can attach.

Four different types of fouling control technologies are currently available:

- Biocidal anti-fouling coatings.
- Foul release coatings.
- Hard coatings.
- Alternative coatings.

15.1.1 Biocidal Anti-Fouling Coatings

Biocidal anti-fouling coatings are by far the most commonly used paint today (97-98% of all anti-fouling volume globally). They release active ingredients (or biocides) which prevent or slow the settlement of marine fouling organisms. Copper-based biocides are the most commonly used, often in combination with co-biocides in order to achieve a wider spectrum of activity.

The three main categories of biocidal anti-fouling coating technologies are:

- Self-polishing copolymer.
- Contact leaching systems.
- Controlled depletion polymer.

Self-polishing copolymers are the dominant technology today - there are several sub-divisions within this category and a number of innovations are brought to market every year.

15.1.2 Foul Release Coatings

Foul release coatings work on a different principle than biocidal coatings. They create a smooth, slippery, low-friction surface onto which fouling organisms have difficulty attaching. In theory, any organisms which do attach, do so only weakly and can easily be removed.

Silicone polymer represents the foundation on which all modern fouling release coatings are built. Fouling release coatings can perform reasonably well under favourable conditions – e.g. high speed and activity, low water temperatures and low severity fouling environments.

There are several sub-divisions within this category and a number of innovations are brought to market every year. Still, foul release coatings remain a niche technology with limited uptake in the market (they account for <3% of the global market).

15.1.3 Hard Coatings

A third general set of hull coating systems can be categorised as hard coatings. They are generally either epoxies, polyesters or vinyl esters, some are reinforced with glass flakes. In general, they are intended to be used in conjunction with a high frequency of cleaning, either using high pressure washing in drydock, or underwater cleaning with the ship still afloat.

15.1.4 Alternative Coatings

Finally, a number of alternative and innovative approaches to hull fouling prevention have come onto the market or are currently in development. They prevent the attachment of biofouling by, for example, using microfiber foils, water encapsulation, natural product anti-foulants. Others employ nanotechnology or are based on biomimetics.

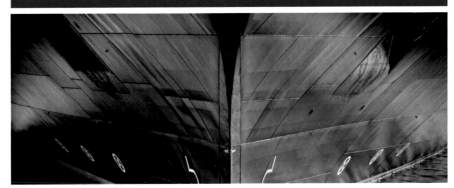

Questions to Consider

Why do my ships need anti-fouling coatings?
Just a minimal amount of biofouling can lead to an increase of fuel consumption, since the resistance to movement will be increased. A clean ship can sail faster and with less energy.

What makes a good biocide in an anti-fouling system?
A good biocide for use in an anti-fouling system has the following characteristics:
- Broad spectrum activity (in preventing slime, algae and barnacles).
- Low mammalian toxicity.
- No bioaccumulation in the food chain.
- Not persistent in the environment.

In some important markets, regulatory approval of biocides in anti-fouling paints is subject to a comprehensive risk assessment process covering all of the above (e.g. EU's Biocidal Products Regulation). In order to be approved, the biocide must be proven not to have a negative environmental impact. Globally available anti-fouling products must comply with the sum of all regulatory requirements in all underlying markets.

What are the advantages and disadvantages of foul release systems?
Advantages:
- Less time in drydock required.
- Less paint required.
- Lower application costs at future dockings.
- Similar costs to some biocidal products.

Disadvantages:
- Higher initial cost of application.
- Masking and dedicated equipment (as foul release products are not compatible with other paint types) required.
- As product is biocide-free, silicone foul release systems are less resistant to slime than many biocidal anti-fouling coatings.

What are the key points that should be considered when looking to save fuel through selection of anti-fouling paint?
- What is the expected fuel cost saving on average over the lifetime of the anti-fouling paint solution (compared to what)?
- Will it be possible to reliably measure and document the actual fuel cost saving on the ship in question?
- If the expected fuel cost saving is delivered, what is the return on investment?
- What happens if the expected fuel cost saving is not delivered?
- How does the return and risk profile of this investment compare with other potential fuel saving investments?

15.2 Environmental Impact

The environmental impact of hull maintenance, including anti-fouling selection, is of high importance for both cost-efficient operations and for lowering a ship's overall environmental impact. In general, three main environmental impacts are associated with biofouling and anti-fouling practices:

1. High fuel consumption.
2. Transmigration of invasive species.
3. Pulse of biocides into the marine environment.

15.2.1 High Fuel Consumption

Biofouling reduces the ship's hydrodynamic performance and increases fuel consumption and cost. This means that the ship will emit more greenhouse gases (GHG) and other air pollutants. Biofouling and mechanical damage on underwater hulls and propellers currently account for around 1/10 of world fleet energy cost and GHG emissions.[1]

15.2.2 Transmigration Of Invasive Species

The attachment of biofouling to ship's hulls and cavities is a principal vector of invasive species across the globe. Organisms that colonise the hull 'hitch a ride' from one port or region to the next. When these organisms come in contact with structures in a new port or release their larvae into its waters, they can establish themselves in the new area and spread to other nearby areas. Here they can cause disruption to the local ecosystem, the local environment, industry and commerce.

15.2.3 Pulse Of Biocides Into The Marine Environment

Biocidal anti-fouling paints work on the principle of leaching or gradually emitting poisonous substances into the water to kill off the marine organisms attached to the hull of the ship. These substances can persist in the water where they continue to kill sea life, harm the environment and possibly enter the food chain.

Biocidal anti-fouling paints containing the organotin compound tributyltin (TBT) are particularly harmful. In fact, TBT has been described as the most toxic substance ever deliberately introduced into the marine environment. However, when it was first introduced into anti-fouling paints, it was considered less harmful than biocides used in anti-fouling systems at the time. As TBT began to be widely used in anti-fouling paints, scientists began to understand its negative consequences for the marine environment. Specifically, TBT was shown to cause shell deformations in oysters, sex changes (imposex) in whelks, and immune response, neurotoxic and genetic affects in other marine species. The use of TBT in anti-fouling pain products has therefore been banned by the adoption of the International Convention on the Control of Harmful Anti-Fouling Systems on Ships (AFS Convention).

In modern biocidal anti-fouling coatings, biocides have been more rigorously examined by regulatory bodies and are non-persistent in the environment and do not have the same impact on the environment that those using TBT had. On the downside, many of them do not have the same ability to prevent fouling than TBT had – so in comparison causing higher fuel consumption and GHG emission.

15.3 International Regulation

15.3.1 Biofouling

There are currently no international regulatory requirements concerning the control of biofouling. However, in July 2011, the International Maritime Organization (IMO) adopted voluntary Guidelines for the Control and Management of Ships' Biofouling to Minimise the Transfer of Invasive Aquatic Species.

Resolution MEPC.207(62)

These guidelines were put in place to provide a globally consistent approach to the management of biofouling. They recommend that every ship has onboard a:

- Biofouling Management Plan; and
- Biofouling Record Book.

---

[1] Clean Shipping Coalition (2011) A transparent and reliable hull and propeller performance standard, MEPC 63/4/8

15.3.1.1 Biofouling Management Plan

Resolution MEPC.207(62)

The Biofouling Management Plan should be specific to each ship and be included in the ship's operational documentation. It may be a stand-alone document, or be integrated into the existing ships' operational and procedural manuals and/or planned maintenance system.

It should describe the biofouling management strategy for a ship with sufficient details to allow a ship's Master, the designated ship's officer, or crew members to understand and implement the biofouling management strategy.

The Biofouling Management Plan should include the following aspects:

- Description of the ship's anti-fouling system.
- Description of the ship's operating profile.
- Description of areas on the ship susceptible to biofouling.
- Operation and maintenance of the anti-fouling system.
- Safety procedures associated with biofouling management measures.
- Disposal of biological waste.
- Recording requirements.
- Crew training and familiarisation.

As the Biofouling Management Plan is dependent on the aspects mentioned above, it will have to be updated on a regular basis.

A template of a ship's Biofouling Management Plan can be found in Appendix 1 of resolution MEPC.207(62) as well as in Part Three - The Maritime Environmental & Efficiency Templates provided on the USB memory stick.

15.3.1.2 Biofouling Record Book

Resolution MEPC.207(62)

In line with IMO guidelines, a Biofouling Record Book should be maintained for each ship and record details of all inspections and biofouling management measures undertaken on the ship.

This serves two purposes:

- It makes it easier for the ship owner and operator to evaluate the efficacy of the overall Biofouling Management Plan and the specific anti-fouling systems and operational practices on the ship.
- It helps State authorities to quickly and efficiently assess the potential biofouling risk of the ship, and thus minimise delays to ship operations.

The Biofouling Record Book may be a stand-alone document, or be integrated into the existing ships' operational and procedural manuals and/or planned maintenance system. It is recommended that the Biofouling Record Book is kept onboard for the life of the ship.

Information that should be recorded in a Biofouling Record Book includes the following:

- Details of the anti-fouling systems and operational practices used (where appropriate as recorded in the Anti-fouling System Certificate), where and when installed, areas of the ship coated, its maintenance and, where applicable, its operation.
- Dates and location of drydockings, including the date the ship was re-floated, and any measures taken to remove biofouling or to renew or repair the anti-fouling system.
- The date and location of in-water inspections, the results of that inspection and any corrective action taken to deal with observed biofouling.
- The dates and details of inspection and maintenance of internal seawater cooling systems, the results of these inspections, and any corrective action taken to deal with observed biofouling and any reported blockages.
- Details of when the ship has been operating outside its normal operating profile including any details of when the ship was laid-up or inactive for extended periods of time.

An example of a Biofouling Record Book and information to be recorded is included as appendix 2 to resolution MEPC.207(62), as well as in Part Three - The Maritime Environmental & Efficiency Templates provided on the USB memory stick.

15.3.2   Anti-Fouling Practices

In order to prevent the very harmful effects of the organotin compound TBT on marine life, the use of TBT in anti-fouling paint products was banned by the adoption of the AFS Convention. The AFS Convention was adopted at the IMO in October 2001 and entered into force in September 2008.

In response to the AFS Convention, the major hull coating manufacturers voluntarily decided to withdraw tin-containing anti-fouling hull coatings from the market before the IMO Convention entered into force.

15.3.2.1   *General Requirements*

The total phase-out of organotin anti-fouling coatings should have been completed by 1 January 2008.

AFS Convention, Annex 1

This means that ships either:

- Do not bear organotin compounds which act as biocides on their hulls or external parts or surfaces; or
- have a coating that forms a barrier to such compounds leaching from the underlying non-compliant anti-fouling systems.

15.3.2.2   *Survey, Certification And Control*
International Anti-Fouling System Certificate

AFS Convention, Annex 4

Ships of and above 400 gross tonnage (GT) engaged in international voyages (excluding fixed or floating platforms, floating storage units and floating production storage and off-loading units) have to obtain an International Anti-fouling System Certificate.

To this end, they are required to undergo an initial survey before the ship is put into service or before the International Anti-fouling System Certificate is issued for the first time; and a survey when the anti-fouling systems are changed or replaced.

A Model Form of International Anti-Fouling System Certificate is contained in Appendix 1 to Annex 4 of the AFS Convention. It is also included in Part Three - The Maritime Environmental & Efficiency Templates provided on the USB memory stick.

To support the survey and certification of anti-fouling systems, the IMO has adopted guidelines which are contained in resolution MEPC.102(48).

Declaration On Anti-Fouling System Measures Beyond Regulation

Ships of 24 metres or more in length but less than 400 GT engaged in international voyages (excluding fixed or floating platforms, floating storage units and floating production storage and off-loading units) have to carry a Declaration on Anti-fouling Systems signed by the owner or authorised agent. The Declaration will have to be accompanied by appropriate documentation such as a paint receipt or contractor invoice.

A Model Form of Declaration on Anti-fouling System is contained in Appendix 2 to Annex 4 of the AFS Convention and is also included in Part Three - The Maritime Environmental & Efficiency Templates provided on the USB memory stick.

Inspection

In order to determine whether a ship is in compliance with the AFS Convention, Port State Control (PSC) can inspect the ship in ports, shipyards, or offshore terminals of a Party to this Convention.

These inspections must be limited to:

- Verifying that the ship carries a valid International Anti-fouling System Certificate or a Declaration on Anti-fouling System onboard; and/or
- a brief sampling of the ship's anti-fouling system. The IMO has developed Guidelines for Brief Sampling of Anti-Fouling Systems on Ships which are contained in resolution MEPC.104(49).

If there are clear grounds to believe that the ship is in violation of the AFS Convention, a thorough inspection can be carried out. This has to take account of the IMO guidelines contained in resolution MEPC.208(62).

15.4 Regional Regulation

15.4.1 Regional Biofouling Regulations

In order to prevent the spread of invasive species via biofouling, the US Coast Guard (USCG), the State of California and New Zealand have adopted regulations to control and manage biofouling.

In many parts of the world, in-water hull cleaning is prohibited or there are certain restrictions on how this can take place.

Such restrictions may involve written permission by local authorities. The cleaning of sea chests, sea suction grids, propeller etc. may be permitted provided that any debris is collected. Normally the containment method to collect and dispose of debris will have to be described. A number of countries have adopted unilateral regulation on hull husbandry prohibition thus making hull cleaning very difficult or impossible.

Please clarify with the Port Authority if there are any restrictions or bans on hull cleaning.

15.4.1.1 United States Requirements

In the US, the prevention of biofouling is an important component of the Ballast Water Management (BWM) Plan which is outlined in 33 CFR 151.2050.

Accordingly, every ship equipped with ballast tanks operating in US Waters is required:

- To rinse anchors and anchor chains when the anchor is retrieved to remove organisms and sediments at their places of origin; and
- to remove fouling organisms from the ship's hull, piping, and tanks on a regular basis and dispose of any removed substance in accordance with local, State and federal regulations.

In addition, a specific BWM Plan is required for each ship. Amongst other things, this plan must include procedures for detailed fouling maintenance and sediment removal.

These procedures can either be incorporated into the ship's existing BWM Plan or be in a separate Biofouling Management Plan that is referenced in the BWM Plan.

While the regulations do not detail which items to include in the fouling maintenance procedures, the USCG has advised that the guidelines contained in IMO resolution MEPC.207(62) and the latest draft of the California State Lands Commission (specifically Section 2298.4 entitled 'Biofouling Management Plan') provide a basis for developing a ship-specific Biofouling Management Plan.

Currently, BWM Plans do not have to be approved.

15.4.1.2 California

California's biofouling requirements apply to ships of and above 300 GT operating in California waters and capable of carrying ballast water. The requirements fall into two categories: biofouling removal and reporting form submission.

Biofouling Removal

Biofouling organisms from the hull, piping, propellers, sea chests, and other wetted portions of a ship must be removed regularly, defined as any one of the following:

- No longer than by the expiration date (or extension) of the ship's full-term Safety Construction Certificate.
- No longer than by the expiration date (or extension) of the ship's USCG Certificate of Inspection.
- No longer than 60 months (5 years) since the ship's most recent out-of-water drydocking.

Hull Husbandry Reporting Form Submission

Ships must submit the Hull Husbandry Reporting Form once each calendar year, if operating in Californian waters during that year. The Hull Husbandry Reporting Form can be found on the website of the California State Lands Commission but is also included in Part Three - The Maritime Environmental & Efficiency Templates provided on the USB memory stick.

15.4.1.3 New Zealand

In 2014, the New Zealand Ministry for Primary Industries has issued the Craft Risk Management Standard (CRMS) for Biofouling on Vessels Arriving to New Zealand. This Standard comes into force on 15 May 2018 and applies to all types of sea-craft that have come from or recently visited coastal waters of another country.

The CRMS requires ships to arrive with 'clean hulls'. 'Clean hull' is defined for two categories of ship, with 'short-stay' ships allowed more light biofouling than 'long-stay' ships which are allowed a slime layer and goose barnacles only.

There are a number of measures given in the new CRMS that ships can use to comply with the Standard, and during the lead-in period, the Ministry will work with ship operators to help them decide which measures are most suitable for them.

In addition, hull inspection and cleaning services, both in New Zealand and offshore, will be encouraged to become approved by the Ministry during this period.

NOTE: The CRMS is aligned with the 2011 IMO Guidelines for Biofouling Management, and following best practice according to these guidelines is deemed to meet the requirements of the CRMS. This means that much commercial shipping is already compliant. Other options for compliance will ensure that ships should be able to become compliant with minimal disruption.

15.4.2 Regional Anti-Fouling Practices

15.4.2.1 *United States Requirements*

2013 VGP Part 2.2.4

The 2013 Vessel General Permit (VGP) addresses the issue of copper in the paragraph on anti-fouling hull coatings. Accordingly, ship owners and operators shall consider refraining from copper-based anti-fouling paints when they spend considerable time in ports and harbours which are impaired by copper. Considerable time means when they spend more than 30 days per year in that port or harbour.

Ports and harbours impaired by copper include Shelter Island Yacht Basin in San Diego, California, and waters in and around the ports of Los Angeles/Long Beach. A complete list of such waters may be found at www.epa.gov/npdes/vessels.

If after consideration of alternative biocides, ship operators continue to use copper-based anti-fouling paints, they must document the reasons for this decision in their record keeping documentation.

2013 VGP Part 2.2.23

In addition, ships using copper-based anti-fouling paints are not allowed to clean their hull in copper-impaired waters within the first 365 days after the paint has been applied, unless there is a significant visible indication of hull fouling.

15.5 Measures Beyond Compliance

With regards to biofouling, there are currently no regulatory requirements related to how 'un-fouled' a hull should to be. However, it is recommended to develop a Biofouling Management Plan. This plan should include measures to prevent and control biofouling. Resolution MEPC.207(62) lists and describes the measures which can be taken towards this end.

However, there are many ways to move beyond regulatory compliance with regards to the anti-fouling practices that can be undertaken.

15.5.1 Anti-Fouling System Installation

Anti-fouling coatings are the primary means of biofouling prevention and control for existing ships' submerged surfaces, including the hull and niche areas.

While the IMO has banned the use of organotin in anti-fouling paints, it has not imposed any requirements as to which anti-fouling system should be used. Any anti-fouling system not containing organotin thus meets IMO regulations.

However, certain anti-fouling coatings are more environmentally-friendly than others and should thus be the preferred option when it comes to going beyond compliance. In addition, the effectiveness of the coating in preventing fouling is crucial to reduce fuel consumption and thus GHG emissions.

15.5.2 Management Measures For Sea Chests And Niche Areas

Before installing, re-installing or repairing the anti-fouling system, all biofouling residues, flaking paint, or other surface contamination should be completely removed, particularly in sea chests and niche areas. This facilitates good adhesion and durability of the anti-fouling system. Niche areas include sea chests, bow thrusters, propeller shafts, inlet gratings, drydock support strips, etc.

Inlet grates and the internal surfaces of sea chests should be protected by an anti-fouling coating system that is suitable for the flow conditions of seawater over the grate and through the sea chest. Foul-release anti-fouling may be the most suitable option for these places, but it is technically more difficult to apply on the grids.

15.5.3   Condition-Based Hull And Propeller Maintenance

Knowing when to clean the hull and the propeller is the goal of condition-based hull and propeller maintenance. This can be done in two ways: observe and inspect actual hull and propeller fouling, or use performance-based systems that track changes in ship speed and required power (or using fuel consumed as a proxy for required power) to identify degrading surface conditions.

15.5.3.1   *In-Water Inspection*

In-water inspection can be a useful and flexible means to inspect the condition of anti-fouling systems and the biofouling status of a ship. Divers assess the actual surface condition while the ship is in port. By correlating the roughness and degree of fouling to losses in efficiency and increases in fuel consumption, an economic decision can be made on when hull cleaning and/or propeller polishing should be done.

In-water inspections should be undertaken regularly as part of routine surveillance or in accordance with the performance management readings.

They are especially important:

- Before and after any planned period of inactivity or significant or unforeseen change to the ship's operating profile;
- prior to undertaking in-water cleaning to determine the presence of known or suspected invasive aquatic species or other species of concern on the ship;
- after a known or suspected marine pest or other species of concern is discovered in a ship's internal seawater cooling systems; and
- following damage to, or premature failure of, the anti-fouling system.

15.5.3.2   *Performance Monitoring Systems*

Ship performance monitoring systems that offer condition-based hull and propeller maintenance track engine power and changes in fuel consumption to identify degrading surface conditions. In order to understand the impact of hull and propeller surface conditions on fuel consumption, it is necessary to isolate the effects on fuel consumption of the parameters being studied. This can be done by collecting records of ship speed and required power (or using fuel consumed as a proxy for required power) under controlled or repeatable conditions.

As engine power requirements (and fuel consumption as a proxy) for a given ship depend on numerous effects (operational conditions, loading conditions, environmental conditions, hull and propeller surface condition), the performance monitoring system has to isolate the impact of hull and propeller from the other effects. To this end, power and fuel data is either collected when operational, loading and environmental conditions are comparable or the data is normalised and/or filtered to remove the effects of operational variation (e.g. speed, pitch angle, etc.), of loading variations (draft, trim, list) and of environmental variations (wind, waves, water depth, water temperature, etc.). The details how this is done differ in different approaches available from performance monitoring companies. ISO 19030 (under development) will present a standard methodology for how to measure changes in hull and propeller performance and calculate a basic set of performance indices for hull and propeller performance.

Performance monitoring can be used in calculations against drydock and out-of-service costs to advise on optimum maintenance procedures and schedule.

Questions to Consider

How much anti-fouling paint do I need?
This is dependent on the type of anti-fouling, the size of the area to be painted, the required life of the anti-fouling paint, the operating area and operational characteristics.

It is normal practice to apply thicker self-polishing anti-fouling paint on vertical sides, than on flat bottom. This, however, only applies to biocidal anti-fouling.

How can I check the compatibility of anti-fouling paint?
As a rule of thumb, the same type of anti-fouling coating can be applied directly on one another as long as the existing anti-foul is in good condition. Alternatively a sealing coat can be applied. Paint manufacturers should be consulted if unsure.

The same type of anti-fouling can be applied directly on top of anti-fouling of the same type applied at last drydocking. This is provided that there is no leach layer. If there is a leach layer and no blasting is done, then a sealer coat has to be applied.

How long will the coating last?
Varying systems have a varying lifespan. Some systems are designed to last 3 - 5 years. Some will aim to last the lifetime of the ship. This will vary on product type chosen. Check for product specific lifespan information and case studies of longevity form manufacturer, as well as reliability of and liability under lifetime performance guarantees.

How can I check that the coating is still active?
If your coating is not active any more, you will see a lot more fouling. So the first thing to check is the condition of the hull. If your fuel consumption has been going up as well and you can exclude other factors being responsible for this, your anti-fouling coating is probably not working properly anymore and should be replaced.

In addition, the ISO 19030 standard (currently under development) will present a standard methodology on how to measure changes in hull and propeller performance and calculate a basic set of performance indices for hull and propeller performance.

Will the coating system suit the needs of a particular ship or fleet?
Different ships, fleets, routes, activities operate under different conditions. The sailing conditions of the ship have bearing on the optimal coating product for the hull.

Check for the ship's trade route or voyage path, frequency of port calls, lay up periods. Ask for specific evidence that the product is suitable for that type of route.

Alternatively, ask for a reliable performance guarantee whereupon it is in the paint maker's own best interest to ensure the product is the right given the specifics of the situation.

How frequently must the hull be cleaned to maintain coating performance?

It is important to ascertain how often the hull will require maintenance and what impact this will have on the coating.

Even though regular drydockings (every 7.5, 5 or 3 years depending on type and age of ship) are required by class, in-water cleaning may be necessary to run a ship at optimum performance.

The following points need to be considered:
- Will underwater hull cleanings be necessary?
- Does routine underwater cleaning damage the coating?
- Can the coating be cleaned without damage to it?
- Will in-water cleaning of the hull pose and environmental hazard, such as a pulse release of biocides, silicone oils or other substances? How can this be mitigated?
- Is in-water cleaning prohibited on the planned routes of the ship or ships for which the coating system is being chosen?

How much time do I need to plan in should my coating system require major repair or reapplication?

Surface preparation plus application of paint can vary from five or six days for some coatings to as much as 17 or 18 days for others.

Does the manufacturer reliably guarantee performance?

The type of hull coating system chosen can make a big difference to the ship's fuel efficiency.

Great care must be taken to understand exactly HOW any fuel savings are calculated.

NOTE: It is actually 'reduced loss in performance' that claims are made on not active savings themselves i.e. a paint will degrade in performance less than another.

Check the reliability of, and the liability under, the performance guarantees. Is there any third party verification and is a reliable monitoring solution offered with the product?

How much does the paint cost?

Cost is a vital consideration in choosing a hull coating system for a new ship or for repainting a ship. However, prices per litre of paint can be misleading, as can cost of surface preparation.

There are a number of factors which contribute to the real cost of a hull coating system and they must all be taken into account for a total ownership cost assessment. One of these considerations would be the total costs of materials for coating the entire hull. Some hull coating systems require five or more coats with lengthy curing times in between, stretching a full painting job out to as much as 17 days or more. Others can be applied in just two coats with a few hours between coats and can be fully prepared and painted in under a week, ready for launching or re-launching. The costs involved include labour, drydock time and off-hire time.

15.6   Business Benefits

Anti-fouling coatings can provide great cost savings to ship owners and operators as they prevent the formation of biofouling. Biofouling reduces the ship's hydrodynamic performance and increases fuel consumption.

Application of anti-fouling coatings can be seen as an investment. The cost of maintaining the underwater hull (including pre-treatment, application, paint and any in-service maintenance) typically accounts for approximately 0.5% of the total cost of owning (depreciation and interest) and operating the ship. Fuel cost, on the other hand, typically amounts to more than 50-60% of total cost. An anti-fouling coating that delivers even a moderate saving, if this saving can be reliably documented, will therefore typically yield a very attractive return on investment.

In-water cleaning between drydockings may boost the ship's performance when using anti-fouling coatings that result in the accumulation of marine growth. In particular in heavy fouling areas in-water cleaning may be required. In-water cleaning is, however, not always possible due to local or regional regulations or health and safety concerns.

While anti-fouling coatings containing TBT proved to be very effective at keeping a ship's hull smooth and clean, they have been completely banned under the IMO's AFS Convention due to their devastating effects on marine life. Ships that are found to be in violation of this Convention may be detained, dismissed or excluded from all ports in the inspecting Party's jurisdiction. Non-compliance with relevant regulations can also result in criminal prosecution and fines.

15.7   Measuring Environmental Performance

The most straightforward way of measuring hull coating performance is to measure how easily a ship moves through the water. A commonly used proxy for this is the resistance of the hull.

However, ship resistance is difficult to measure directly, and there are a wide range of environmental and ship-specific factors which influence it.

One commonly used approach to teasing out these individual effects is to create theoretical or empirical models for each single factor and then use those models to make resistance corrections to a standard baseline of performance. Separate models are commonly developed for each component of resistance by using tank tests of small-scale models.

Another approach is based on applying advanced mathematical modelling tools on automatically collected sensor data from onboard the ship in order to identify the effect of different factors on the ship resistance. The so-developed model is then used to track deviations over time and to identify hull and propeller performance losses. Furthermore, continuously collected sensor data from onboard measurement devices can be filtered for comparable conditions. Over time trends in the speed to power relation under comparable conditions (operational, loading, and environmental) is used to quantify the effect of hull and propeller surface degradation.

The advantages and disadvantages of each measuring approach are presented in the table below:

Approach	Advantage	Disadvantage
Dedicated speed trials	• Most accurate method • Results easily understood	• Only for performance decay over time • Interesting effects may be missed due to time between trials • Dedicated manoeuvres needed • Limited volume of data
Noon reports	• Easy to implement • Data is already there	• Changing weather conditions over 24hrs • Must account for acceleration and deceleration • Manual input from crew limits accuracy • Time between measurement points very large (even though nothing prevents you from sending 'noon reports' at the end of each watch)
Continuous monitoring	• Big volumes of data • Can detect short-term changes in performance	• Requires sophisticated analysis

The best method will depend on the purpose of the monitoring. This will again depend on factors such as the person in charge, the available resources, the operational profile of the ship, ship type as well as the commercial setup of the ship (owned-operated, time chartered, voyage charted, managed).

CHAPTER SIXTEEN

CONTENTS

UNDERWATER NOISE

UNDERWATER NOISE

16.1 Introduction

Underwater noise from human activities and man-made structures arises from a number of sources including seismic surveys for oil and gas exploration and scientific research; and sonar systems for military purposes, fishing, and research. Another major source is commercial shipping.

In recent years, the issue of underwater noise has been highlighted by government bodies and conservation groups, urging the industry to examine and address the negative effects on marine fauna. Underwater noise generated by shipping are a major contributor to the ambient noise levels in ocean, particularly at low (<300 Hz) frequencies. Scientific data, while not conclusive, suggest that commercial shipping may be causing significant increases in the overall underwater noise environment in many ocean areas, particularly coastal zones.

Underwater noised produced by ships can be classified by the following:

- Noise generated by dynamically active devices, placed inside and on the surface of the hull, mainly by engines, propulsion, and auxiliary, and system of transport of mechanical energy – shafting;
- noise produced by the ship propellers, and;
- acoustic effects connected with cavitation of the propellers and flow around the underwater part of the hull.

16.2 Environmental Impact

Sound is for marine mammals what sight is for humans. Marine mammals use sound for communication, navigation, individual recognition, predator avoidance, prey capture, orientation and many other functions.

The diagram below shows that the frequency ranges of shipping noise fall within those of marine mammals' sounds, highlighting that shipping noise has an impact on marine mammal communication.

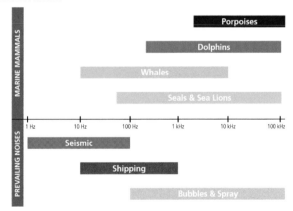

Potential effects of anthropogenic sounds on marine mammals include physical injury, physiological dysfunction (e.g. temporary or permanent loss of hearing sensitivity), behavioural modification (e.g. changes in foraging or habitat-use patterns, separation of mother-calf pairs), and masking (i.e. inability to detect important sounds due to increased background noise).

Though some of these impacts are not easily detected, they all can have adverse effects on marine mammals, with worst case scenarios being mortality, threatening their survival or reproductive success.

MEPC.1/Circ.833

16.3 International Regulation

There is no international governance on the generation of underwater noise by commercial shipping. Guidelines and regulations are up to individual countries. Explicit guidelines have only been issued for certain operations, mostly pile driving and seismic surveying (both impulsive sound sources), primarily with regards to impacts on marine mammals - predominately cetaceans.

The International Maritime Organization (IMO) approved non-mandatory Guidelines for the Reduction of Underwater Noise from Commercial Shipping to Address Adverse Impacts on Marine Life.

The new guidelines:

- Recognise that shipping noise can have short-term and long-term impacts on marine life;
- call for measurement of shipping noise according to objective ISO standards, which are themselves on the verge of adoption;
- identify computational models for determining effective quieting measures;
- provide guidance for designing quieter ships and for reducing noise from existing ships, especially from propeller cavitation; and
- advise owners and operators on how to minimise noise through ship operations and maintenance, such as by polishing ship propellers to remove fouling and surface roughness.

16.4 Regional Regulation

16.4.1 European Union

Directive 2008/56/EC

In 2008, the European Union adopted the Marine Strategy Framework Directive 2008/56/EC which aims to achieve good environmental status of the European marine environment by 2020.

GES is defined according to a set of 11 broad indicators or 'descriptors', the 11th of which refers to underwater noise.

Under the Directive, Members States are required to define potentially harmful levels of underwater noise, put in place a monitoring system and develop a programme of measures (by 2015) to reduce underwater noise if needed. Such measures should enter into force by 2016 at the latest in order to achieve good environmental status by 2020.

This means that the Directive provides a baseline for regulating underwater noise from shipping.

United States Of America

The Marine Mammal Protection Act specifically protects marine mammals from anthropogenic noise. This is administered by the National Marine Fisheries Service (NMFS) who has jurisdiction over species such as manatees, polar bears, walrus and sea otters. NMFS has lately taken a more active role in issues related to underwater noise.

Though NMFS has issued 'soft regulation', the US currently does not enforce any domestic or regional legislation on the matter of underwater noise. There has been some push on this subject at State level, the push has been particularly strong from those States on the west coast such as Washington, California and Alaska.

The National Oceanic and Atmospheric Administration has established voluntary vessel speed restriction zones (Dynamic Management Areas) in the vicinity of Portsmouth (NH) to protect aggregations of the right whales. Though a voluntary requirement, mariners are requested to route around these areas or transit through them at 10 knots or less. Not only will this protect right whales from ship strikes, but also reduce the level of underwater noise generated by ships in these areas.

For more information about Dynamic Management Areas, their specific requirements and geographical coordinates, please visit the website of the National Oceanic and Atmospheric Administration (http://www.nmfs.noaa.gov/pr/shipstrike/).

16.5 Going Beyond Compliance

The IMO's non-mandatory guidelines to reduce underwater noise from commercial shipping, contained in resolution MEPC.1/Circ.833, provide guidance on designing quieter ships and advise ship owners and operators on how to minimise underwater noise through operational measures.

The largest opportunities for reducing underwater noise are during the initial design of the ship, when designing the hull form and selecting the propeller.

16.5.1 Propellers

Propellers should be designed and selected in order to reduce cavitation. Cavitation is the formation and then implosion of water vapour pockets which are caused by pressure changes across the propeller blade. Under normal operating conditions, cavitation can be reduced through good design, such as optimising propeller load, ensuring a smooth wake flow (which can be influenced by hull design), and careful selection of the propeller characteristics including diameter, blade number, pitch, skew and sections.

Advances in propeller design have allowed owners to modify existing propellers, or fit new ones with noise reducing technology. Both methods have the potential to reduce underwater noise for the noisiest merchant ships, and increase propulsive efficiency.

Improving the wake flow into the propeller by fitting appropriately designed appendages such as wake equalising ducts, vortex generators or spoilers can also have a positive effect on noise reduction. Although there is some understanding of the improvement that these devices will have on propulsive efficiency, there is little knowledge about how they will reduce the underwater noise – however, available data suggests that they will do so.

16.5.2 Hull Design

The hull form has a considerable influence not only on the power required to propel the ship, but also on the underwater noise generated by its propeller. A well-designed hull form requires less power for a given speed, which is likely to result in less noise being transmitted into the water.

In addition, a well-designed hull form will provide a more uniform water inflow to the propeller, thereby increasing the propeller's efficiency, and reducing noise and vibration caused by the uneven wake flow. This will further reduce the level of underwater noise generated.

16.5.3 Onboard Machinery

The engines and thrusters are also contributors to underwater noise generation. The main path is structure borne noise/vibration transmitted through engine foundations into the hull 'violin box' and radiated from the shell into the water. Resilient mounting (or even double resilient mounting) is the key practical measure for diesel engine underwater noise. While the large two-stroke diesel engines used for most ships' main propulsion are not suitable for resilient mounting, four-stroke engines are and should be considered for resilient mounting and flexible couplings.

Other sources creating underwater noise are, for example gears, propulsion e-motors (AC–DC to various levels), thrusters, pumps, chillers, sewage plants, switchboards, transformers.

16.5.4 Operational And Maintenance Considerations

There are a few operational modifications and maintenance measures that can be taken to reduce the generation of underwater noise. These include:

- Propeller cleaning reduces surface roughness and helps to reduce propeller cavitation.
- Making sure that the underwater hull surface is smooth reduces the ship's resistance and propeller load and hence improves the ship's energy efficiency while reducing underwater noise.
- Reducing ship speed can be an effective operational measure for reducing underwater noise, especially when it is lower than the cavitation inception speed.
- Speed reductions or re-routing to avoid sensitive marine areas including well-known habitats or migratory pathways when in transit will help to reduce adverse impacts on marine life.

16.6 Business Benefits

By addressing the cavitation around the hull and propeller/s, the propulsive efficiency may be improved and energy consumption reduced.

Furthermore, reducing underwater noise directly contributes to reduced noise and vibration levels on board, which improves crew and passenger comfort.

16.7 Measuring Environmental Performance

Even though it is difficult to isolate the source, the underwater noise level can be measured by using either fixed or moving hydrophones.

Two committees of the International Organization for Standardization (ISO) are working on standards for measuring underwater acoustics from ships. They have already developed the standards known as ISO 16554.2 and ISO/PAS 17208-1:2012.

In addition, the American National Standards Institute has developed and published its final procedures for measuring underwater noise from shipping in 2009 known as S12.64-2009 American National Standard, Quantities and Procedures for Description and Measurement of Underwater Sound from Ships - Part 1: General Requirements.

NOTES

The Guide to
Maritime Environmental &
Efficiency Management

Part Three - The Templates

Summer *in* Mayfair

SUSANNAH CONSTANTINE

ONE PLACE. MANY STORIES

HQ
An imprint of HarperCollins*Publishers* Ltd
1 London Bridge Street
London SE1 9GF

This paperback edition 2020

1
First published in Great Britain by
HQ, an imprint of HarperCollins*Publishers* Ltd 2020

ISBN: 978-0-00-821972-7

MIX
Paper from
responsible sources
FSC™ C007454

This book is produced from independently certified FSC™ paper to ensure responsible forest management.

For more information visit: www.harpercollins.co.uk/green

This book is set in 11.5/15.5 pt. Bembo

Printed and bound in Great Britain by
CPI Group (UK) Ltd, Croydon, CR0 4YY

For Prue and Peder

Chapter One

Culcairn station was tiny, barely the length of a carriage. The platform was deserted and a light veil of summer drizzle fell, cobweb-fine yet saturating. The mist of tiny droplets crept into the creases of her collar and settled everywhere. Esme Munroe felt her skin was weeping. It ought to be. She was going. Her parents and sister had already gone so she had been left no option but to do the same and it broke her heart. She was leaving home and her beloved Mrs Bee for the next chapter in her life. London. A place teeming with strangers, lives and loves and languages she knew nothing about as yet. She told herself that boarding this train had to be about more than the sorrow that wreathed her family home. It had to be about her future and whatever lay ahead, a voyage of discovery of the city and herself.

In the end, the decision to go to London had been a quick one. Esme knew that once she had accepted she must leave The Lodge – her childhood home, where all her yesteryears were buried deep – it had to be a swift uprooting. The move had filled her past with a rose-tinted glow, nostalgia papering over any bad memories and turning the years gone by into a safe but unreachable land, while her future seemed hazy and unknowable from up here in the Highlands.

As she'd shut her bedroom door that morning, she'd known she was leaving something of herself behind, ready for her to find again when she returned. She reasoned that everybody had to leave home at some point and when she came back she would see The Lodge with fresh eyes and love it again for new reasons. But it was time for her to go. Time to change and time to leave.

Leave. She rolled the word around her tongue for a bit. A beautiful and definite word; strong and forceful, the way she had always wanted to be.

The process of packing had been simple for her and frustrating for Mrs Bee. The woman who had devoted her life to the Munroe family as beloved housekeeper wouldn't let her youngest charge leave home without enough luggage to last a lifetime. There were two suitcases on her bed. One with the bare necessities and the other piled high with the entire contents of an airing cupboard and a supermarket aisle's worth of toiletries and cleaning supplies.

'You'll need sheets and a hot-water bottle, at least. Things to make you feel at home.'

Esme had told Mrs Bee not to worry about her as she packed her bag of basic belongings. The housekeeper kept trying to add more things. But Esme insisted that the less she took the easier it would be to move around.

'Don't be so dramatic, love. You're not going to be sleeping on the streets.'

Indeed, Esme had her sister Sophia's godfather to thank

for that. Bill Cartwright had come to her rescue. Having no qualifications in anything that might lead directly to a job, Esme had slowly realized it was assumed that she would follow the example of her mother and marry well. When she left school, her father had patted her hand and humoured her when she expressed a desire to follow her passion and study art. But now Bill Cartwright had given her a chance, offering temporary lodging and a job in his London gallery. It had become a standing joke that she wanted a job, so she felt slightly vindicated that she had done her history of art course and now deserved her position at the gallery. She was to be that lowest rung of the art-world ladder: a receptionist sitting prettily front-of-house filing her nails in between making tea and coffee. No matter. Perfectly shaped nails would pay just enough for her to survive on for a while, especially since the job came with the bedsit above the gallery. She had allowed her father to pay for her train ticket but refused his offer of a weekly allowance. It would have been too easy to rely on family funds, and if she was going to become independent she would have to be frugal and spend her salary wisely. And anyway, the money her parents had gained from selling their London residence had now been mostly eaten up by overdue bill payments, or her father's addiction to antiques meant it was hanging on walls or lying unworn in her mother's jewellery box. But there was no need to worry about money until she had to move out of the gallery and pay proper rent, and that wouldn't be for a few weeks. Instead, her first priority was to find and make friends, to live the real London life and frequent the niteries she *hadn't* read about in social columns, while spending her salary on essentials. She didn't want so much to become a better person but a cooler, more independent one. Someone who had the courage of her convictions, once she had discovered what those were.

'Don't worry, love. Everything will be here when you get back. Just the same. It will be you who will have changed,' Mrs Bee had said as they drove to the station.

Esme opened the carriage door now. Mrs Bee was right. The Tuesday sleeper was almost empty. Just a few scattered passengers inhabited the berths in second class. The housekeeper helped Esme board with her small bag and one extremely large wooden crate.

'Och. Where on earth are we to put this thing?'

The cubicle was a womb of tartan and plastic wood panelling, and contained everything a passenger required for an overnight stay. Leather straps ran from the top bunk base to the ceiling so it could be flipped up for day travel when it became a regular compartment for first-class customers. The beds had been turned down and gifted with a packet of shortbread. It was compact to the point of being claustrophobic, especially with a socking great wooden packing case crammed in.

'You're the one who insisted I bring it, Mrs Bee.'

Esme was still reeling from the death of the Earl of Culcairn, and the fact that he had left her a painting in his will. The Earl and his family lived at the castle – and as neighbours to the Munroes at The Lodge, it was natural the families became friends. But the Earl and her mother, Diana, had become much more than friends. News of their affair had been discovered when Esme was too young to understand what infidelity was. Her father had yelled for a couple of hours and then like anything that would crack the façade of respectability, it was swept under the carpet and never spoken of again. And now the Earl was gone, and her mother might as well as have been too, her body nearly as fragile as her spirit.

Esme's eyes felt heavy with unshed tears but she'd walked out the door without putting a handkerchief in her pocket again. The letters the Earl had written to her at boarding school and his words of advice and encouragement still resonated today: 'Fear is just a feeling and when it comes, ask for more.' It took her many years to understand that. 'Hate is a weakness that can be used against you' and the most pertinent, 'never believe you are better than anyone else'. When her mother was ill, with her father holding vigil, it was the Earl who had come to cheer her on at sports day. He who taken her for Welsh rarebit at the local tearoom to celebrate her winning the swimming cup.

She hadn't wanted to expose the painting, let alone bring it with her. She felt that once the packing crate had been opened, her last physical contact with the Earl would be gone, the final essence of him escaping the container for good. Now he was dead, his wife, the Contessa, had made it very clear that she was no longer welcome at Culcairn Castle. Her loathing of Esme went beyond being simply the daughter of the woman her husband had loved illicitly. It was a cancerous hatred that mutated towards anyone who was fond of Esme, including the Contessa's own children. Growing up, their friendship had been intense but the secrets and lies had pulled them apart over the years.

Esme ended her reverie, aware that Mrs Bee had offered a response.

'Well, you don't want your father getting his hands on it. It could be worth a wee fortune.'

Esme knew Mrs Bee meant this kindly but art was her father's drug of choice and he wouldn't think twice about commandeering it as his own.

'Or not. I can't imagine the Bitch would let something valuable slip through her bony hands. Especially if she knew that the Earl was leaving it to me.'

Esme knew Mrs Bee wouldn't react to her name-calling of the Earl's wife. The housekeeper had tried to temper her resentment of the woman but it was a waste of time and quite frankly, given half a chance, Esme would call her something far, far worse.

'I guess we can shove it on the bottom bunk and pray no one gets on at Edinburgh,' suggested Esme.

The two women lifted the crate and pushed it back against the compartment wall but the overhang jutted out leaving barely enough room to squeeze by. Unfortunately, it was Mrs Bee who got hemmed in.

'I'm stuck!' she laughed. 'Looks like I'm coming to London with you. We're going to have to try again, darling.'

Esme took the window side this time and they repeated the manoeuvre.

'Ah, look at you, you wee thing. Slim as cotton thread. It's been a few years since I could have wheedled through that gap.'

Esme used to hate being as skinny as she was. She loathed her stick-thin legs to the point of padding them out with two pairs of thick tights under her jeans. Since leaving school, her pins had garnered enough compliments for her to believe they were good enough to show off without the extra layers.

'Right, love, I'd better skedaddle or I really will be coming with you and you don't want your old Mrs Bee cramping your style.'

The whistle blew – a staccato accompaniment to Mrs Bee's soft-shoe shuffle along the narrow corridor. Standing on tiptoes she reached up from the platform and gave Esme a hug.

'I love you, darling. Look after yourself and *be careful*. There are all kinds of strange folk in London.'

This was exactly what Esme hoped but she said, laughing, 'Don't worry, Mrs Bee, it's not like I'm heading off to war or exploring sub-Sahara.'

Esme had lived in the capital until she was four years old when her parents relocated to Scotland. They had kept the South Kensington house she was born in and continued to use it on a regular basis for some years. School holidays had kicked off with a few days in the city before journeying back up to the Highlands until their crumbling finances had forced them to sell. Esme's knowledge of London was hazy, thinking back to those childhood years, but she knew how the buses and Tube worked. She'd find her way, she was sure.

As the train heaved out of Culcairn station, Mrs Bee stood alone and silhouetted against the platform lamp like some Eastern bloc infiltrator. Esme pushed away the lump of sadness rising in her throat, as she continued to wave until the old lady melted into the darkness. She would miss the one person who had been a constant source of love. Her dear Mrs Bee. Time for her to put her feet up but Esme worried that she would be lonely now both her parents had vacated The Lodge and her sister Sophia was living in New York.

Esme closed the window and she leant against the berth wall eyeing the painting in its crate. She tried to visualize the Earl adding her name to his last will and testament and sticking on the label with her name written in his hand. Part of her wanted the picture with her more than anything else in the world; it represented all the truths he had taught that she considered valuable and professed he really cared about her. It was a piece of him. A talisman for a safe passage. The rest of her screamed to throw it onto the tracks, be rid of anything from her past that could reach out to hold her back.

She climbed up onto her bunk without bothering to change into her nightclothes and listened to the wheels on the track. The noise was deep and secure. Metal grinding on metal in perpetual, rhythmic motion. The train was in no rush to reach its destination given its twelve-hour journey. But sleep was miles away, back in her bedroom at The Lodge. A combination of excited anticipation and abject fear churned in her stomach confusing pangs of hunger for nausea, the kind she felt before riding a new horse. Mrs Bee's chiding tapped at her brain. 'I've made you a wee picnic. You must eat. Keep your strength up. You don't want to start this new life of yours on an empty stomach.'

Esme rifled through her bag to find her supper. When she looked at the contents of the Tupperware box – the kind Mrs Bee stacked and hoarded – she was touched by how some things never changed. Marmite sandwiches, crusts off, quartered apple, Wagon Wheel and a packet of roast chicken flavoured crisps all wrapped in grease-proof paper. Exactly the same as the packed lunches Mrs Bee made for her as a child.

She remembered an occasion when Mrs Bee had gone on holiday to Skegness. It was bad timing as her mother was just emerging from an extended period of depression and the beast of mania was awakening. Her 'reward', as her mother put it, was in some ways even more torturous than her depressive state, for those living under the same roof. Wildly erratic and unpredictable, she was at once an innocent child and all-knowing demon. Vicious in parts and helpless in others, Esme preferred the pitiable mute to the volatile moods of the upswing. She was easier to ignore. Riding up the crest towards full-blown delusion, her mother had made a packed lunch for her youngest daughter's journey back to boarding school down south. Comprising an uncooked chicken thigh, a teabag in a thermos of cold water and baked beans still in their tin, Esme was too ashamed to show it on the school bus or ask the teacher for a sandwich and went hungry instead.

Esme felt her father had sentenced his wife to a colourless existence compared to the homeliness of The Lodge and grandeur of the castle. An affordable care home was never going to have the luxuries of The Savoy. But it did have the advantage of being close to The Lodge and Mrs Bee promised she would visit regularly: 'Don't you worry, love, she'll be well taken care of and I'll make sure she always has a wee slice of cake to nibble on.'

It had been left to Mrs Bee and Esme to drop her off. The nurses had been kind and the place was pristine but the accommodation was basic, to say the least. A bare room with wood-chip walls and a pine furniture. It had an en-suite shower room with a red emergency cord.

Esme and Mrs Bee had done their best to cheer the place up by hanging some of her father's paintings and replacing the plywood furniture with antique pieces from home. Mrs Bee had made up her bed in linen sheets and goose-down pillows. Nothing was too small and easy to steal and once they had finished the mini makeover, her mother's room was quite cosy.

Not that Diana noticed. Most of the time she was too sedated to even recognize Mrs Bee.

Esme was sure her soul had already flown with the Earl's and that they were finally united in heaven. Looking back, Esme realized that her mother's heart, the only piece that had remained unaffected by her depression, had broken that horrible Christmas of 1969. Esme remembered overhearing her mother pleading with the Earl not to leave her, when they thought they were hidden from view in one of the many rooms at Culcairn Castle. Just like that, her mother disappeared into herself never to return. Esme never again felt her unconditional love and the abrupt shock of emotional abandonment had wreaked havoc on Esme over the years. She still had morning terrors but had come to accept them as a kind of haunting that would pass as soon as she got out of bed. Now that she was older, she was grateful to the Earl for giving her mother some happiness and the kind of love her father had never shown her, beyond an obsessive admiration of her beauty.

She could have blamed the Earl and her mother for so much – not least the emotional bullying inflicted on her by the Contessa, when she had had to stay at Culcairn Castle. Maybe this was why the Earl had left her a painting. By way of apology. A guilty conscience placating itself before death. The Culcairns had three children, one boy, Rollo and two girls, Bella and Lexi, who was the same age as Esme and had been her best friend throughout her childhood. Often when her mother was sent away to a mental facility, sometimes for weeks at a time, Esme was sent to stay with Lexi. There she was a target for the Contessa's bitterness, using Esme to vent her spleen. She did it subtly, bullying Esme with silence and instructing staff to ignore her, too. There was never a place laid for her at meals and the Contessa acted as if she was invisible during her incarceration at the castle. Frankly, she understood why the Earl had strayed from the Bitch, as Sophia referred to her. Who would want to be tied to a woman so filled with hatred and poison? But even when the Contessa had finally physically attacked Esme and the Earl promised his wife he was leaving her, he'd only got as far as moving out of their marital bed and into the adjoining dressing room. Esme wondered whether the Earl had been more afraid of his wife than he'd ever admitted.

Esme was woken by a knock on the compartment door and realized that she must have fallen asleep.

'Rise and shine. We're coming into Euston,' said the guard cheerfully, through the opaque glass.

She looked at her watch: six thirty. The train hissed and spluttered to a halt and Esme tugged at the blind which snapped open to reveal a landscape of grey. Bin bags banked against metal girders and the weak rays from the rising sun trickled through the grubby roof of Euston station, illuminating the grime. It occurred to Esme that unlike rural dirt, which was a working layer of earth, suburban dirt was nothing to be respected. The farmers liked dirt whilst city dwellers got rid of it, or at least they did in residential areas. Here in a grand public gateway to the city decades of grease and soot coated the glass roof and clung to its beams. Sparrows and pigeons pecked at crumbs of bread and flies caught in abandoned spiders' webs that wafted in high corners.

Gathering her belongings, Esme wondered how the hell she was going to get the crate off the train. She looked down the platform to see if there was a porter but aside from her few fellow passengers and early male commuters with big hair and sideburns, Euston station was quiet. She had readied herself for the onslaught of mass human bedlam, pushing and shoving to begin their day but the city still slept. A homeless man with a shopping trolley was checking pieces of litter strewn across the platform. He picked up a beer can and drained what was left, wiping his mouth with a dirty sleeve. Sensing Esme's gaze, he turned to look at her and she blinked, turning away and embarrassed by her luck of the draw in life. Mrs Bee never let her forget that life was a lottery and, despite her mother's mental health, she was fortunate in so many ways.

With no choice, she dragged and tugged the crate out of her compartment and pushed it onto the platform. It clattered to the ground causing the wood to split down one side. She felt her throat thicken signalling the onset of tears. Telling herself to get a grip, she grabbed an abandoned trolley and heaved the picture aboard, smiled at the homeless man and headed for the taxi rank.

Compared to the nostalgic romance of Culcairn station, Euston appeared vast and hostile; even more so given its lack of people at this time in the morning. She felt tiny and insignificant and clutched at the bar of the trolley as a couple of early commuters charged past. A wave of longing for The Lodge made her want to get back on the train and she dragged her feet as she forced her way forward through the cloying urban air, pretending to feel confident and grown up. The last thing she wanted was to be pitied.

There was no queue and a line of taxis sat idly waiting for custom. Esme double-checked the address of the gallery, scribbled on a piece of paper that she unfolded from deep within her pocket.

'Jermyn Street in St James's, please, sir.'

The taxi driver was generous and didn't turn his meter on until they had managed, after multiple attempts, to get the giant crate at the right angle to fit inside.

She sat down on the leather seat, wedged between the crate and the door, and closed her eyes for a moment.

'Oh gosh. Thank you so much.'

'Happy to help, love. Don't know how you managed this far.'

The man's kindness caught her heart and if there hadn't been the glass screen dividing them, she would have leant over and hugged him.

The traffic was slow but not yet nose to tail so it didn't take long to get to Mayfair. Even so, the expensive fare left her with little remaining cash, which she knew she should use to tip the friendly driver.

'Don't worry, love. You can tip me next time.'

'Thank you so much, sir. Are you sure? I will be able to because I'm starting a new job. Here. At this gallery. It's my first day,' she said.

'I'm sure, sweets. Looks very fancy,' said the cabby.

Getting the painting out of the taxi was less difficult but left splinters of wood all over the interior. Esme went to sweep them out.

'Oh don't you worry about that. It's the end of my shift, anyway.'

'But it's made so much mess,' said Esme. 'I don't mind. Really.'

'Not a problem. I'm ready to go home to a nice hot breakfast from the missus,' he said. 'I haven't slept for eighteen hours.'

'Oh, well if you're sure then, thank you. I hope you get home soon,' she said, then waved him off.

The gallery hadn't opened up yet. It was too early and she didn't have enough money for a cup of tea, let alone breakfast. Mayfair and St James's wasn't an area she knew well, apart from the Ritz hotel. Her grandfather had moved into a suite there when he retired and only left in a coffin. She had joined him for tea once; an ostentatiously English cliché down to potted shrimps and a tea menu longer than the wine list. Nowhere else in this part of town would be open this early and anyway, she couldn't exactly lug her bags and the blasted painting around town. She would have to wait for nearly two hours on the step.

The pangs of nerves in her stomach had now been overthrown by a gnawing hunger. She felt uncomfortably empty as she parked herself on the gallery step using the pallet to protect her bum from the cold. Stretching her legs out, she leant back against the door. Thankfully it wasn't raining and the street was still deserted apart from the dustbin men.

All around her the shop windows were so clean, catching the light of the sun as it rose over the rooftops. St James's was surely the most salubrious borough in London. Everything displayed in the gleaming windows was of the highest quality and had a price tag to match. By comparison she felt shoddy and out of place. As a teenager, Esme had immersed herself in the Regency world of Georgette Heyer and she felt the author's vision come alive as she looked up and down the street. It was nearly 300 years since Jermyn Street had been built by the Earl of St Albans but it had not lost its quintessentially British character: wealth and extravagance.

Many of the gentlemen's shops had been there for decades as had their private members' clubs, most notably, White's. She knew this section of St James's had always been very much a male domain, where a woman's reputation could be ruined in minutes if she so much as set foot on a flagstone of the street at the wrong hour or in the wrong company. Tucking herself further into the doorway, she hoped times had changed, on that front at least.

The noise of emptying rubbish bins reverberated down the street. Esme heard the clash of glass and thud of paper being chewed by a truck. The bins at home were at the end of the drive and their gardener took the bags down on the tractor for collection. She was going to have to get used to city living. The sheer density of people, the sky reduced to a strip of blue above the street, still felt alien to her. People drank a hell of a lot of wine in this part of town, she thought, as she caught sight of a flash of green emptying out of the bins, followed by the crunch of breaking glass. Mind you, she knew selling art was all about networking and networking involved oiling prospective art buyers with alcohol. Despite the early hour, her mouth watered at the thought of a large glass of burgundy. Things were looking up.

Up at the Piccadilly end of the road, she saw a man walking with purpose. A fellow early riser? But as he approached, his attire came into view. Black tie suit, sans bow tie. He looked bleary and dishevelled. Bit old to have partied all night, she thought. As he passed, he dropped a fistful of coins at her feet without even looking at her. The gesture was deliberate and unquestionable. Shame flamed into her reddening face.

'No... I'm not...' Esme called but the man had already turned the corner. He clearly thought she was homeless and taking refuge in a posh doorway. Did she really look so incongruous against the opulent surroundings? she wondered, looking down at her jeans and a Fair Isle sweater. She stood up and leant against the doorframe to avoid any further confusion but still slightly guiltily pocketed the four pounds the man had tossed at her feet.

'Hello? You must be Esme,' said a crisp voice out of nowhere.

'Er, yes. Hello?' said Esme, turning around and quickly taking in the young woman standing in front of her.

Navy court shoes, matching fifteen-denier tights, navy pinstripe skirt, pale-pink frilled shirt and minimal make-up on an incredibly pretty face that looked at her with a huge grin.

'I'm Serena but everyone calls me Suki. Come on, let's get you in. Looks like you could do with a cup of coffee.'

'I'm dying for one.'

Suki bent down. 'Help me move this wood thing. We can put it by the bins for collection.'

'Oh no! That's mine.'

'Really? You came all the way from Scotty with that? What is it?'

'A painting. I think. It was left to me by someone who died and Mrs Bee insisted I bring it.'

'What do you mean, you *think* it's a painting?'

'I haven't opened it yet.'

Suki looked surprised.

'Well, you're at the best place to get it looked at if it is a painting. Bill will be excited. He loves an unexpected treasure turning up.' Suki unlocked the door and rushed inside to a loud beeping noise. 'Just turning the alarm off,' she shouted over her shoulder.

'There we go,' she said, coming back and bending down by the crate. 'Here, you take the other side.'

They lifted the crate into the gallery and leant it up against a wall. Esme looked around the room. It was small and decorated like a Napoleonic salon. Ormolu wall sconces, ice blue silk covered the walls and a three-piece set of Empire sofa and chairs. A fine pair of neo-classic candelabra embraced the fire surround. Suki switched the lights on and four paintings sprang to life, the bright colours revitalized from their slumber.

'Oh, wow,' sighed Esme. 'Who are these by? They are beautiful.'

'Someone French, I think,' replied Suki, without bothering to look.

'You don't know?'

'No idea. To be frank, I know nothing about art but I can type sixty words a minute. And cook a super avocado mousse. Learnt both at finishing school in Switzerland. Both equally useful, I'd say.'

'So why did you choose to work in an art gallery?'

'I'm here because Daddy knows Bill and begged him to give me a job. Old boy network and all that jazz. I'm just passing time until I get married and have a stately home full of children. A duke would be ideal but a lord will do. As long as he's tall, rich and handsome I don't mind if he's one of those fake European aristos. I have a boyfriend who's stinking but its new money. At least he's got a posh name. Johnny. And he's in the army.' She blew a strand of hair from her face. 'Must get my hair cut. I want a Heather Locklear flick. I'd love to get it done by Leonard but Mummy says it's common.'

Esme knew nothing of Leonard or Heather what's-her-face or a flicky hairdo. She felt dowdy and provincial. Suki pushed her hair back with a velvet headband and twizzled one of her pearl earrings.

'Have you got your ears pierced?' she asked, lifting Esme's long hair from her ear. 'No. That's something we can do one lunch hour. But first, coffee.'

Esme followed her into a kitchenette at the back of the showroom. Dirty mugs piled up in the sink. Suki rinsed two, leaving a brown ring in both.

'Sugar? Oh yes. Three, I think. We want to fatten you up. Like the Christmas turkey.' Suki laughed, a deep gurgle coming from her core.

Over a weak brew, Esme gave Suki a potted history of her life – leaving out some of the parts she felt she barely understood herself, or which hurt her too much to admit. There was an odd liberation in telling her version of her story to someone new – someone who didn't already know her family or was just keen to get juicy gossip on the notorious Munroes. Yet it made her realize that while she could talk about where she came from, she didn't yet really know where she wanted to go or who she wanted to become.

'Well, now you have given me your life story, I feel we are already friends.' Suki smiled.

'Sorry,' said Esme, feeling flustered. She found it hard meeting new people and shyness brought on verbal diarrhoea.

'Don't be silly. It's good to get to know you. But you'll find

I like to cut to the chase,' said Suki, laughing. 'Are you looking for a husband? Is that why you have come to London? Apart from having nowhere else to go.'

'I haven't given that much thought, really,' said Esme. 'One day, maybe. But certainly not in the imminent future. I'm happy being single. And it's not that I have nowhere...'

'Well, you'll meet someone soon enough. Our kind of London is a small place. Once you've met one person, you'll meet everyone. And you now know me. So, there we go.'

But Esme wasn't sure she wanted to meet Suki's kind of everyone. She'd had enough of privilege and the lies stitching high society together at the seams. She wanted to meet people who had worked hard to get somewhere, not just been born with the right surname. One thing she was sure of, for her this job at Cartwright Fine Art wasn't just to pass the time – or simply because Sophia was Bill's goddaughter. She loved art – and while everyone always told her she shared her father's eye, art meant more than just the Munroe family business to her. Growing up in a world where everyone seemed to speak in double meanings, paintings seemed to speak a language she felt she could understand. And now she hoped it would give her a career. She knew she wanted to make her own money, not just marry it. Ever since she could remember she was coming up with ideas and schemes, but in her father's eyes she'd always been labelled as the 'pretty one' and Sophia the 'clever one'. Both sisters had been furious. But Esme was determined to prove him wrong even if she had no idea how to do so yet. But swimming purely in the sea of silver spoons was going to get her nowhere.

'Thanks, Suki,' said Esme, draining her coffee and going to wash her mug.

'Oh, don't do that. We have a cleaner for that. The bloody woman didn't come in yesterday. Fake flu.'

Esme ignored her, rinsed out the mug and put it back in the cupboard.

'Right. I had better show you the ropes. Bill will be in soon.'

Taking Esme by the arm, she led her to a fine mahogany table with turned legs and gilt finish.

'This is your desk. Pride of place in the window. Lucky you're pretty as here you basically double up as the shop mannequin. Passersby might be lured in by your looks. Not stupid, our Bill. He knows how to attract the big fish.'

Suki picked up the telephone receiver.

'You press nine for an outside line and push whichever of these buttons are flashing when the phone rings.' She picked up a notepad – 'This is for messages' – as her eyes swept the table. 'Yikes. No pen! God, I'm thick. I'll get you one.'

'What do you do here, Suki?'

'Oh, you know, typical secretarial stuff: paying invoices, typing letters, arranging meetings,' she said. 'Then the slave jobs like taking Bill's dry cleaning and parking his car. He's always telling me I'm useless but I know he wouldn't survive without me,' she laughed.

'Do you have your own office?'

'In the room at the back. Held prisoner by filing cabinets and a typewriter. And of course, stacks of paintings. The less valuable ones, anyway. The priceless ones are in a strong room along with the treasure.'

'Treasure?'

'Yes, you know. Booty. Bundles of cash, small sculptures and jewels of every description and carat. There's probably literally millions worth of stuff in there. Perhaps your painting will join it.'

Esme had forgotten all about the picture. She wasn't sure she was ready to open it just yet, for fear of what lay inside. All the notable paintings at Culcairn were catalogued and had mostly hung on the castle walls for centuries. She knew that hers must have been one gathering dust in a distant tower, and despite her curiosity opening it would still symbolize a kind of farewell to the Earl. She swallowed as she remembered her other fear – the thought that the Contessa might have found out and switched the painting for something terrible.

'Esme. Darling!'

Esme swivelled around.

It was Bill, just as she remembered him, a bird of paradise, resplendent in a plum suit and turquoise shirt, polished loafers and no socks. Time had thickened his waistline and thinned his hair, which was slicked back in a pomaded cap. His bottle-thick glasses were as round as he was.

'Hello, Bill!' Esme went over to him, unsure how to greet him. A peck? Or a hug. The last time she'd seen him a decade ago, he had just been Godfather Bill. Now he was her boss.

Before she had time to decide, she was swept into the solid bulk of the man, his thick arms encircling and squeezing the very breath from her. He released her and waved his hand in front of his nose.

'I can tell you have had a coffee! Oh, my. Here. Have a Polo. Still, there are those far greater than either of us who have worse than coffee-breath. My father's halitosis? Urgh. Smells like a badger shat in his mouth. And there's a principal Royal

Ballet dancer... Well, you wouldn't understand the source of his foul breath.'

Suki burst out laughing, 'Bill! That's no way to greet a lady. Poor Esme, you have embarrassed her.'

Esme crunched the mint. Forcing aside her awkwardness, she lifted her arm and sniffed her sweater 'At least I don't have BO.'

'Ha! We are going to get on famously. We always did, when you and Sophia were girls. Do you recall the time we hid your hamster in the laundry basket? Poor Mrs Bee nearly had a heart attack.' He pressed a fist against his wide grin and stood back. 'How are you, my darling girl? Let me look at you.'

He spun her around, patting her down like a champion breed at Crufts.

'My, how you have grown. What's it been? Eight years?'

'Probably.'

'How do you like the gallery? Has Suki Su been looking after you? When did you get in?'

'Seven thirty,' she said. 'And yes, the gallery is beautiful.'

'Goodness, you've been loitering for hours. Have you seen your lodgings?'

She shook her head.

'They're not much, I'm afraid, but you can stay until the next waif blows in. I'm sure it won't take long for you to find something more permanent, once you've sorted that death breath.'

Esme laughed. She could see why her father loved this man. And why Sophia worshipped the shag-pile carpet he walked on. Everything about him was over the top. Flamboyant, fabulous and warm. She was instantly in love.

'So, where are your things? I'll show you upstairs as Suki has clearly been too busy deciding if you are going to be competition for my affections.'

Suki looked at Esme and rolled her eyes. 'You're an evil queen, Bill.'

'And that, my dear, is why I rule supreme on Jermyn Street. The gayest, and most expert eye in the art world.'

'I've hardly brought a thing. Just a few changes of clothes. And my toothbrush, you'll be happy to hear,' said Esme.

'Want to start afresh eh? I completely understand, my darling. All those useless toffs. Time for you to be introduced to the real world. My Javier is longing to meet you. He wants to take you on as a "project", whatever that means. You will come for dinner with us tonight. We can catch up. The house is walking distance from here. Come at six thirty, we can have drinkies whilst Javier slaves over the hot stove.'

'Sounds lovely. Thank you.'

'Suki, was that delivered this morning?' asked Bill, pointing at Esme's wooden pallet.

'It's Esme's.'

'Yours? You brought that huge fucking thing all the way down from Scotland? I'm impressed by your tenacity. What is it?'

'She doesn't know,' answered Suki.

'Darling Suki, you wouldn't know the *Mona Lisa* if it slapped you in the face.'

'True,' she said, no offence taken.

Esme realized you'd soon grow a thick skin working for Bill – and that his astonishing rudeness was matched by an equal warmth and *joie de vivre*. She felt instantly accepted and suddenly the thought of opening the painting didn't send a chill through her. Still, she wondered how much Bill knew of the depth of the relationship between her family and the Culcairns. Her father might have been too ashamed to tell him of her mother's affair with the Earl or the subsequent fall-out. She also knew Bill had curated an exhibition which included some of the castle's equestrian paintings a few years back and that he and the Earl had a shared interest in eighteenth- and nineteenth-century portraiture. They had become friends in their own right so he might have heard a different story to her father's.

'Well, we better open it up and take a look,' said Bill. 'Your room can wait.'

Bill disappeared into the office and came back with a crowbar. Contrary to his camp demeanour, he attacked the wooden shell with the force and expertise of a lumberjack.

'Your testosterone is off the chart today, Bill,' said Suki.

Clearly, she and Bill had a thriving understanding and appreciation of each other which allowed them to get away with personal verbal assassinations. Esme chuckled.

Bill dropped his voice several octaves and growled.

'C'mon, ladies. Don't just stand there. Help me lever this thing open. You too, Esme, my honeypot.'

The three of them pulled and forced the planks to break apart.

'There she is. Now careful. We don't want to damage the canvas.'

They eased the picture out.

'Deliver it like a baby. Forceps please, nurse,' said Bill, taking hold of the crowbar that Suki handed to him.

Gently, he slid the picture from its protection. Esme held her breath. Bill lifted the painting up.

'Christ alive,' he breathed.

Chapter Two

No one spoke. The painting Bill held up was barely recognizable as a painting. Were it not for the frame, it might as well have been a piece of blackened chipboard.

'This looks like a set piece from *The Towering Inferno*,' Bill said, eventually.

Although Esme's expectation had been low, her hopes had rested on something she could at least hang and admire. This made no sense. Why would the Earl bequeath a picture so damaged? One thing she knew for certain was that there was more to this picture than the charred wreck in Bill's hands. There had to be. She hadn't expected to get anything when he died but she was certain he wouldn't have left this mess unless there was meaning to it. It wasn't in his nature to play games. Unless this was all a cruel joke by the Contessa. Esme stood by Bill who was looking closely at the picture through a magnifying glass.

'You see here?' he said, pointing to a spot at the top of the canvas.

Esme could just make out the vague relief of brushstrokes.

'It's not beyond repair. The actual canvas is still intact. Looks more like smoke damage than anything sinister. Wait…'

Now inspecting the bottom right corner, he said in a whisper, 'It's been cut. Look.'

He stood back and gave Esme the glass. 'Is that a signature?'

'Could be, but whoever did this – and believe me it was deliberate sabotage – wanted to ruin the picture's most obvious sign of authenticity. Very amateur. There are more subtle ways of ruining a work of art. And look at how fine and precise the cut is.'

Esme looked and said, 'The edges are clean.'

'Exactly. This was done after the fire damage discoloured it. My reckoning would be a Stanley knife. They didn't have those in the eighteenth century.'

'How do you know it's eighteenth-century?' asked Suki.

'The frame. Classic French but still, that doesn't mean the picture is by a French artist or indeed of the same date.'

Suki sighed. 'Well, at least you won't have to lug the thing around London anymore. There's a skip in St James's Square.'

'Oh, for God's sake, Suki. Have you learnt nothing since you've been here? Of course, it's not going to the junkyard. Esme, you are going to take this painting to my dear friend, Max Bliss.'

'The restorer?' said Suki.

'Well, I'm not suggesting Esme take it to the bloody fishmonger,' said Bill and turned to Esme.

'Max is the most talented picture restorer working today. Rescued paintings by you name it – Leonardo, Gainsborough, Corot. He's a genius and frightfully nice with it. A bit scatty but brilliant. He owes me a favour. If anyone can save your painting, it's him.'

'But what if it's a dud underneath all that smoke? I'll just be wasting his time,' said Esme.

'Anything with the Culcairn provenance won't be a dud. As you know, that gloomy place holds one of the best private collections in the world.'

Esme had studied the castle's paintings at all hours of the day and night, padding down the long corridors in the moonlight, the eyes of Culcairn ancestors watching over her. There was a painting to reflect and deflect every emotion. Where there was rage, Madonna gazed peacefully down at her newborn. Where there was sadness, Turner's strokes frothed a sunlit sea into joyous life. Ugliness could be brushed away with the delicacy of Tiepolo's luminous execution of form with colour. In the paintings, Esme was able to escape from the muddle of her family life and the toxicity doled out by the Contessa. In them she found calm. Some of the sitters had become friends to whom she could express herself without fear of judgement or reprisal. Forget about the famous 'Munroe eye', it was the collection at Culcairn which had instilled the love of art that ran in her blood.

Bill handed her the painting.

'Keep it upstairs for now. I don't want clients being put off.'

Bill flicked a flashy watch from his shirtsleeve.

'Unfortunately, I have a meeting now that will most likely take all day. Suki, help Esme take her things up to the garret. Don't expect too much. It has that dank, unlived-in feel but it's cosy; barely big enough to swing a cat. And remember, you're coming for supper with Javier and me this evening. See you tonight.'

★

Suki took Esme to her room. They climbed a narrow staircase, past a small landing with a closed door and red-wine stains and cigarette burns on the threadbare carpet outside.

'Some people have no bloody respect. Uncouth guests come up here to smoke when there are too many people in the gallery.'

In sharp contrast to the spotless showroom, paint cracked and peeled away from the walls leaving the stairwell moth-eaten and derelict, so the faded charm of her top-floor room was a relief.

After giving her a one-second tour of the amenities, Suki left Esme to unpack. A Louis Vuitton trunk that had seen better days doubled up as a bedside table. She would put her clothes in it. Added to that she had a total of two plug sockets, a rickety bed and a hook on the back of the door with three coat hangers. At least she had a bathroom to herself. It was bigger than the bedroom with a panelled tub and skylight. Ancient bottles of Floris bath oils lined the edge of the bath. She picked one up. It was sticky with age and smelt more of cooking oil than the Rose Geranium printed on its label. But since there was no room for the painting in her bedroom, she set it down next to the loo. Appropriate place for the wretched thing, since it was now likely to be worth nothing more than the loo paper next to it.

She opened the window. There was no view, just a redbrick wall that looked like it needed repointing. Pockets of moss grew from cracks in the brickwork. Subsidence maybe, given Jermyn Street was built on an incline. The curtains were dated but she recognized them as classic David Hicks, a geometric design in varying shades of brown and orange. Not what Esme

28

would have chosen but they were lined and thick enough for total blackout.

The bedcover was in the same fabric and reminded her of a ploughed field. Lying down, the mattress felt like it looked; a lumpy, unyielding pad of knotted horsehair that was more like sleeping in a ditch than on a divan. The springs no longer sprung but screeched like a crying baby. Oh well, she wouldn't be in it much.

'All settled?' Suki came back in carrying a desk lamp. 'Thought you could use this. Save you getting out of bed to turn the light out.'

The thing she held resembled no lamp she had seen before. It had a spaceship sphere aboard a reedy little stem which bent according to the desired angle.

Esme plugged into the wall. 'Well, it works.'

'It's horrid, I know, but I thought we could nip out and buy a few things to brighten the place up.'

'There's not much point. I'm going to be sleeping here for such a short time and I'll bring more stuff from Scotland once I've found somewhere permanent to live.'

Esme began the sentence to cover for having no money and then realized it was in fact true. And if she did end up staying here longer than planned, she may not have cash to splash but she knew she could 'borrow' some bits and pieces from her father's business. Surplus furniture and objects from her parents' former London home sat in profuse quantity at a warehouse in Peckham along with the countless shelves of antiques and collectables he was supposed to be selling on. Their London house in Pelham Place was the only one of her parents' assets that her father had been willing to relinquish to pay for the school fees, domestic bills at The Lodge and his continued antique collecting. He had more than enough furniture and artwork to stock ten houses but flatly refused to put any of them up for auction saying they would always increase in value. He was a hoarder not through necessity but possessiveness and not a little pride. He liked being known for his brilliant eye and had to continue his charade with dealers that he was still flush with cash.

Esme had been 'Christmas shopping' at the warehouse a few times with her mother, who filched presents for her sisters and godchildren. 'Daddy won't notice, darling. He bought one chandelier only to buy an identical one a week later. He doesn't care what he buys, just so long as he is spending. Far better to give these pretty things a happy home.' Esme had seen the sad look in her mother's eyes and realized she too was one of the pretty things left to linger unseen and unloved – little wonder she'd sought solace with the Earl.

Norman the warehouse manager was, like so many men, half in love with her mother. He had worked in the storage depot – part of the Munroe family business – for years. The warehouse and affiliated fine art transportation company housed and moved works all over the world. Her father joked that the humidity- and temperature-controlled Munroe lorries would keep a body in perfect condition for decades. If Diana decided she wanted a Raphael in holding for the National Gallery, Norman would have turned a blind eye as she popped it into the boot of her car. He adored Esme too, so surely having a few bits on loan would be no problem.

When she'd finished unpacking, she went back downstairs to set to work. The phone didn't stop ringing from the moment she sat down. Unfamiliar with the flashing extension buttons she'd cut the first caller off.

'Cartwright,' she said as she'd tried again.

'What happened?' said a strong accent. 'Is Bill there?'

'I'm so sorry,' apologized Esme, grateful the caller couldn't see her blush. 'I'm afraid not. May I take a message?'

'It's Serge. I've got news on the Claude.'

Esme scribbled his name and the time. It was ten thirty and a stack of messages had already built up.

'May I take a surname?'

'*Très amusant*, Suki…'

'It's not Suki. My Name is Esme. I've just stated working here.'

'Ah. OK. If you could ask Bill to ring. Etienne is my surname.'

Esme reckoned she spoke to six different accents from around the world that first morning. Each individual must have been a multi-millionaire, considering the easy way they spoke about snapping up masterpieces and artists that commanded hundreds of thousands of pounds on their price tags. At one point there were three customers holding on the line and she felt like queen bee of a hive she had no control over. It wasn't till noon that things calmed down and she was able to leave her desk.

'Esme?' shouted Suki.

'Hang on, I'm just on the loo. Haven't been since I arrived,' she yelled back.

'I'm coming up. It's nearly one o'clock. Shall we grab some lunch?' said Suki, a little breathless after the stairs.

'Yes. I feel faint with hunger,' said Esme, hanging a dress behind the door.

'Let's see that.'

Suki held up a floral printed frock.

'Oh my God, Esme. You can't possibly wear that. It's so dated. Fine for tea with the vicar's wife but not for London. Bill will have a coronary if he sees you in this sack. Fire you on the spot. We better go shopping at the weekend. I'll bring some things of mine in until then. We're about the same size.'

'What's wrong with it? I got it from Laura Ashley.'

'Exactly,' said Suki, tossing it on the bed. 'Come on. We better go out now as we have to be back by two. You can wear my coat.'

Suki set the gallery alarm and locked the door.

Jermyn Street had filled up. A mass lunchtime exodus of office workers and gallery owners. They looked like pupils leaving school all in a uniform similar to Suki's. A gaggle of big hair and navy blue. Esme was grateful for Suki's mac.

The restaurant was a small Italian cliché, like the ones Esme had seen in films. Red-and-white check tablecloths and hurricane lanterns burning moodily despite it being the middle of the day. They were shown to a tiny table above which lopsided photographs littered the walls. A smell of thyme and wine wafted through the air. The Italian owner posed with friends in all of them. Esme recognized Francis Bacon in one and Michael Caine in another.

'Do these people really come here?' she asked Suki, pointing to another photo where the owner stood grinning next to Bill Wyman.

'Not so much at lunchtime but during Wimbledon all the tennis players come here. Look. There's Vitas Gerulaitis and I saw Roscoe Tanner in here once. Did you know his serves reach over 150 mph, 153 actually?'

'Wow,' said Esme, having no idea who the girl was talking about.

'He's divine too. So, handsome in a preppy kind of way,' she dug her grissini in the butter.

Esme did the same. If there was one thing she would never be able to give up, it was butter.

'I love it, don't you? Specially this cheap salty stuff.'

'What do you mean cheap?' said a deep Italian voice.

'Lorenzo!' shrieked Suki.

It was the man in the photographs.

'*Ciao, bella!*' bellowed Lorenzo giving Suki a double kiss. 'And who is this?' The grey hedgehog–haired man with a matching beard looked at her with kind eyes and a big smile.

'Lorenzo, this is Esme. It's her first day at the gallery. She's Bill's goddaughter.'

'Well, my sister is. Nice to meet you, Lorenzo.'

The proprietor took her hand, kissed it then stroked her face in a paternal way.

'*Bellisima signorina.* Welcome to my humble ristorante. I am at your service.' Esme flushed.

'What's the special today?' asked Suki.

'Lasagne, *amore*. It's always LASAGNE! Food of the working man… and woman.'

Lorenzo winked at Esme. 'You like?'

'That would be lovely.'

'I'll have tomato, mozzarella and avocado, please, Lorenzo. With extra basil.'

'*Perfezionare*. And to drink I'll bring you peach bellini. On the house, to celebrate Esme.'

'Are the white peaches in yet?' Turning to Esme, Suki was

33

almost dribbling as she described the pale fruit with a pink blush that Lorenzo got sent from his farm in Calabria. 'It's hotter there so they ripen earlier.'

Lorenzo reappeared with the said fruit cut into slices, then proceeded to mash them up with a fork. Juice seeped from the flesh. Using his hand to dam the pulp, he poured the nectar into two champagne glasses and topped them up with sparkling wine. It was a far cry from the Buck's Fizz concoctions Esme had tasted before.

'Oh my God! This is literally the best thing I have ever tasted.'

'Isn't it?'

The sweetness of the peaches coated her tongue as the alcohol hit her empty stomach with a tide of reassurance.

'So,' said Suki. 'Tell me more. Which school did you go to?'

Esme wiped the froth from her upper lip. 'St Anne's in Glamorgan. A convent run by sadistic nuns. I hated it.'

'Oh, I loved mine.'

You would, thought Esme. She imagined Suki was the kind of jolly hockey sticks Hooray Henrietta who had been sent away at six years old and developed the stoicism of a Land Girl. Had this been the nineteenth century, she would have had skin thick enough to thrive in some far-flung British colony. But Esme admired her forthright approach. And she was kind and not only interested in herself.

'How old are you? Actually, let me guess. Twenty? I'm twenty-four and you look way younger than me but maybe it's the bumpkin clothes you are wearing.'

'Oi! I'm twenty-two and I'll thank you to know that my jeans are from Fiorucci. My sister will kill me when she realizes I've *borrowed* them.'

34

'The jeans are OK. It's the sweater that lets you down. I've kept mine for my children.'

Esme knew her sweater was dated and regretted wearing it. She desperately wanted a new image, one that was cooler and less Highlands or Home Counties, the two categories all her clothes currently fell into.

'I know and as soon as I get my first paycheque I am going shopping.'

'And I'm coming with you,' said Suki.

The kitchen doors swung open as Lorenzo came through them backwards carrying a double draw of plates.

'There you go, my ladies. Your lunch.'

Esme had to ask three people directions to Bill's road that evening. Tucked away near the American Embassy, the little mews house had a chic exterior with glossy black door standing stark against the white façade. A pair of box trees flanked the entrance. She rang the bell. From inside she heard a high-pitched, 'I'm coming, Esmeee.' Must be Javier, she thought. Then an equally shrill bark followed.

The door flung open and out rushed a squeaking, clipped Shih Tzu. Framed in the doorway was a man standing barefoot and in what appeared to be nothing more an apron with the words 'Choke n Puke' printed on the front. His olive skin gleamed and smelt of sandalwood and citrus.

'At last. The famous Esme. I'm Javier. But you probably worked that out. Come in. Come in.' He looked her up and down, making a not altogether positive evaluation, judging by his arched eyebrows.

35

'Let me take your… um… coat,' he said, pulling it off her shoulders and discarding it on a chair with two fingers, like it was contaminated. So much for Suki's taste in clothes, thought Esme.

Javier had an American accent, with musical undertones. Spanish or Portuguese, she guessed. His slick black hair was salted with grey flecks that grew in density on his unshaven chin. The deep furrows on his forehead served as guttering to prevent sweat running into his eyes and his rugged good looks gave him a kind of sexual magnetism that she imagined all ages and genders would find hard to resist. Her parents had never mentioned Bill's boyfriend but clearly he knew all about her.

'It's divine to meet you finally. Bill isn't back from his meeting yet. Work, work, work. That's all he does while little Javier cooks, cleans and fucks. A whore in the bedroom and goddess in the kitchen. That's what all men want, darling Esme.'

Esme laughed. She liked him at once.

Music blared, an echo that was trapped and condensed by the marble hallway. Unlike his gallery, Bill's house was monochrome and modern. Black, white and grey created a cool atmosphere that was masculine and immaculate. Not a thing was out of place. Everything was perfectly arranged with precise symmetry and unpretentious good taste. A huge black-and-white image of an orchid hung above the hall table. Powerful in its stark simplicity, it was one of the most beautiful photographs Esme had seen.

'Wow. This is stunning,' she said.

'My friend, Robert Mapplethorpe. Bill collects him. He's photographed both your parents, you know. I met Diane the Divine and your handsome father many times. Adore them both…'

The sentence was interrupted by the ecstatic barking.

'Bill is here. Tinky recognizes the engine, don't you, clever girl?' said Javier, giving her a pat. Tinky was hypnotized by the door, too focused on keys in the lock to react. She sat ears cocked, whining, her little body shivering.

'Sorry I'm late, darling.' Bill said, pecking Javier on the cheek and gently kicking Tinky out of his path before hugging Esme.

'You found us no problem?'

'I got a bit lost. I never knew this street existed nor did my *A-Z*. It's not on the map.'

'Don't you love that? It's like we don't exist. Our hidden gem.'

Bill put his arm around Javier.

'I see you have put some underpants on in honour of Esme's arrival.' And then to Esme, 'You are lucky. Or unlucky. Depending on your broadmindedness, he normally wanders the house starkers.'

'Oh, don't worry. I've seen it all before,' lied Esme.

She wasn't accustomed to such open displays of emotion and she didn't want to appear gauche.

'Toots, do you need any help?'

'No. Give the girl a drink, *please*. I've made pisco sour. Ice in the bucket. I couldn't find limes, I'm afraid so it's lemons.'

'Delicious. Have you had pisco before, Esme, darling?'

'Is it a cocktail?'

'Yes, from South America. Like Javier. He whooshed into New York from Puerto Rico. Sit down, darling.'

Esme did as bid and sat on a stylish but uncomfortable sofa. The west-facing windows captured the evening sun, stealing the contrast from her vision. She shaded her eyes from the light to get a better look at the first-floor drawing room; a highly polished oak floor and an Aubusson rug in almost pristine condition. A low glass table was stacked with coffee table books and three ashtrays, although neither Bill nor Javier appeared to smoke. An enormous arrangement of freshly cut flowers filled a Chinese vase confusing a fat bumblebee collecting pollen from one of the blooms. Another photograph hung above the fireplace, a portrait of a messy-haired woman with a big nose and intense stare.

'Patti Smith. Beautifully ugly,' Bill said.

'The singer?'

'Yes. Amazing woman. Super bright and with a highly evolved sense of rebellious creativity.'

'Do you know her?'

'I do. Give me a writer, singer, artist any day over the upper classes. Don't get me wrong, there are − like everything − exceptions to the rule but most of them are bores and their offspring messed-up wastrels. Look at your friend, Lexi. Did you see the way she threw herself on Henry's coffin?'

The hideous scene was one no one would forget. As the Earl was being lowered into his grave, Lexi, sobbing hysterically, tried to join her father. It would have been heart-wrenching were it not so melodramatic. This attention-seeking drama had astonished Esme, but she went to comfort her friend, nonethe-less. As had been the case ever since they had gone to different boarding schools, her kindness was rejected. As children, they had been more than friends and closer than sisters, pledging eternal love and comfort through thick and thin. Their bond had seemed unbreakable but returning from her first term away, Lexi had changed. She was cold and snipey − like an ex-girlfriend. Esme was confused and hurt but Sophia told her to move on. 'She's jealous of you, Es,' she had said. But Esme, grieving for the friendship, was unable to imagine a single reason for that jealousy.

'I know she adored her father to the point of obsession, but really it was beyond the pale. We are all devastated and no one more than your dear mother. Now she really loved Henry, unlike that ghastly wife of his.'

It had been the perfect day for a funeral. Cold, grey and drizzly. Hundreds of people had turned up to the service at Sellington Church, from the great and the royal to tenant farmers whose families had worked on the estate for genera-tions. It was probably why she hadn't spotted Bill among the mourners. That and the fact she'd been too busy keeping an eye on her mother. Diana, composed but withdrawn, stood regally like a head of state. It had been a long time since Esme had witnessed the kind of self-possession her mother held that day. Almost as if she wanted the Earl to be proud of her. A quiet 'Goodbye, my love,' heard only by Esme, were the last articulate words she said.

All through her childhood, covering for her mother had been second nature to Esme, and only now, finally an adult herself, did she see how much it had cost her in tears, loneliness and confusion. Whilst it upset Esme that her mother was now in an institution, and that she couldn't visit as often as she would like, she knew that she was in the best place and cared for in the way she had needed for a long, long time.

Her mother's decline had been rapid after the Earl's death. Whilst she still possessed a ghostly beauty, it was now like a sapped peach deprived of sun. Esme's father could no longer cope and despite Mrs Bee and Esme and to a lesser degree Sophia's objection, he had elected to send her to a local care home. Esme had wanted her to stay at home and hire a carer but the Munroe funds didn't stretch to that, thanks to her father's continued extravagant antique collecting. Esme often felt like her mother had been one of his greatest acquisitions. Beautiful, brilliant and funny, she'd shone brighter than any of her father's ornate vases or diamond brooches. But, as time went by, her cracks had begun to show.

'You know Mum is…' she faltered over the words, fearing Bill would judge her '…in a home now?'

'No, I didn't but it doesn't surprise me, darling. She has been ill for so long and your poor father has been on the end of it. To be honest I think he was quite relieved that Henry took her off his hands and now he can enjoy himself without the guilt.'

'But to send her away like a retired greyhound? Talk about death in the fast lane. He might as well have put a bullet in her head.'

The words just tumbled out – she'd barely even acknowledged to herself that that was how she felt. She'd been too busy putting on a brave face. But now, here on her own in London, she could let rip. She felt a wave of gratitude for Bill – he knew all the people in her family and their circle, yet somehow had escaped their rules and suffocating expectations. After so many years of hidden meanings and things unsaid, his directness was wonderfully refreshing.

'I imagine she doesn't know where she is, dear girl. Most of the time, anyway. Terrible thing, manic depression when it's as severe as hers. Nigh on impossible to manage at that level, and it really took its toll on your father, and you and your sister, I imagine.'

Esme was grateful that she remembered her mother before the illness took got a real grip when she was ten or so; before that she was up or down but never in between.

'In truth, I feel like Mum died years ago but I've never lost hope that she might return. In her mind, I mean.'

'It is so sad but you must remember she would be happy to know you are here making your own way in life. You were her favourite, you know.'

She did. And her sister's jealousy had been made blatantly clear by years of persecution when they were young. Once Sophia got her first boyfriend, everything changed, though. They were now great friends and each other's main source of support. With both parents notoriously unreliable, the girls had come to rely on each other.

'And Sophia is Dad's favourite. By the way, do you know who he's staying with in France?'

'Yes. Francis Burn.'

Of course it was Francis, thought Esme, the kaftan-wearing extrovert who loved antiques as much as her father.

'He has an exquisite house near St Remy. Colin has always maintained the best light is to be found in the Alpilles... He and Cezanne both. Lovely place to spend the summer. I know your father needs to get away sometimes, take solace in his painting.'

Bill looked at the clock on the mantelpiece. 'Let's go down for dinner. We don't want a tantrum.'

The house had a formal dining room, but they were to eat in the kitchen, being just the three of them. Javier had replaced the apron with a flamingo-pink shirt and pale-blue trousers. He was a beautiful man. There was a clarity about him. The sharp relief of his features and the brilliance of his eyes made him cry out to be put on show and admired.

The kitchen table was set for three courses. Esme sat between the two men. She shook her napkin and laid it on her lap.

'It maybe a kitchen supper but we never drop standards here,' laughed Bill. 'I only write thank you letters to a hostess who uses real napkins that need to be washed and ironed. It is the surest sign of respect for their guests.'

Esme made a mental note.

The first course was a fishy mousse with diced tomato and cucumber dressed in oil and lemon juice with buttered brown bread cut into triangles. Javier sprinkled a bright red sauce over his starter. 'Careful, it's very spicy,' he warned. 'Like me—'

'Like you,' Bill and Javier said in unison, taking each other's hand.

The affectionate bickering and bitching that ping-ponged between the two was a refreshing relief to the stony silence she was used to at the dining table at home. Esme couldn't remember the last time she had laughed so much. There was no sense the couple were putting on a show by being on best behaviour for public eyes. This relationship was genuine and made her feel completely at home. Warming to their outrageous indiscretions, Esme found herself matching their gossip with stories of her own. She told of the time the Contessa had tried to kill her dog by locking him out on the castle terrace in the sub-zero winter of 1969. And how Princess Margaret had asked her to collect a knife when they had gone to powder their noses at the Culcairn Hunt Ball.

'A knife?' said Bill.

'Yes. She put it in the loo and started chopping. "It simply won't go down," she said.'

The two men – or the Boys as she now thought of them – howled with laughter. 'That is the funniest thing I have ever heard!' said Javier. 'They always say think of the Queen on the toilet—'

'Loo, Toots—' Bill gently corrected Javier.

'—on the *loo* when you're nervous. But *this*! I will never get stage fright again.'

'She's amazing,' said Esme. 'Incredibly dignified when she wants to be – but she knows all the best stories too.'

'Indeed, she does. You must invite her to the gallery. If she's anything like her mother, she will love us queens,' Bill replied.

'I grew up knowing her but I don't feel I could invite her to anything. I mean she's not my *friend* as such. More of a fairy godmother. Like you are to Sophia.'

'And now to you too, my darling girl.'

In the end, the Boys had insisted she spend the night. 'Far too late for you to walk back to the gallery. Our ladies of the night begin their shift around now.'

They put her in the guest bedroom which was no bigger than a broom cupboard but decorated in a splendour worthy of Versailles. It was like walking into a womb of pink-and-white toile de jouy. The floor, walls, ceiling and bed cover were all illustrated pastoral scenes of the Orient. She got undressed to her bra and pants and listened out for the Boys to finish up in the bathroom. Their hushed voices were punctuated by screams of laugher. Eventually, Javier poked his head around her door and told her they were done.

'I've left a toothbrush out for you. And a flannel.'

'Thanks, Javier. Sleep well.' She gave him a kiss. 'That was a delicious dinner. You are an incredible cook.'

'I know. You will probably have left before I get up but I will be in touch. We will go out. Bill is too old and fat...'

'I heard that! And I would never, even if my life depended on it, go to the cesspits you like to frequent. Horrible homosexual dives!' shouted Bill from his bed. Esme caught sight of naked belly rising from the sheets like a molehill in snow, a chubby leg slung over the white linen.

'He exaggerates. Just jealous. They are so entertaining – wild and crazy,' giggled Javier.

'Sounds fun,' said Esme – feeling that at last, the life she'd dreamed of was in touching distance.

Eventually, Esme climbed into bed, the cool sheets coating her body in luxurious softness. She was exhausted having barely slept on the train. Despite being in a strange bed she fell asleep happily, surrounded by the kind of high spirits and affection so long absent from her life.

Chapter Three

Esme woke, bewildered by the pink glow that enveloped her bedroom. Where the hell was she? A smell of coffee and burnt toast reminded her, she had spent her first night in London. A thrill of the new zipped through her replacing the gnawing anxiety that usually startled her awake. No threat of domestic bombshells unless they were of her own making and, as the mistress of her own destiny, what made her uncomfortable was now in her power to change.

There was a knock on the door and an arm reached around to put a mug on the bedside table.

'Morning, blossom. Tea. Milk and two sugars. We'll head off in half an hour. Time for a quick shower and slice of charred Hovis first, though.'

'Thanks, Bill. Can I borrow your shampoo?'

'Of course. Clean towels are on the rail.'

Apart from boarding school, Esme could count the number of times she had taken a shower on one hand. The Lodge had none and neither did the castle. Hair rinsing was done with a detachable head hose forced to fit enormous taps that were no longer in production. Despite this, she always would prefer having a bath. Standing naked in a glass cubicle made her feel vulnerable, whereas a bath was a warm embrace.

Bill's walk-in shower took up half the bathroom. The showerhead was the size of a dinner plate and drenched her in freezing water. She shot out, slipping on the tiled floor.

'Shit.'

Reaching in, she put her hand under the spray waiting for it to warm up before re-entering.

Esme held her face up to the showerhead and allowed the water to wash over her. There was no sense of vulnerability today and despite feeling like a taxidermy creature in a display cabinet, her exposed nakedness was liberating. She squeezed shampoo into her palm and stood back from the downpour, lathering it through her hair. A razor lay next to the conditioner. Did the Boys rid themselves of stubble in the shower, like she was about to do? Javier was very smooth. Surely he wouldn't mind her borrowing it. She still felt like a country mouse, and figured she needed all the help she could get fitting in with London life.

The razorblade cut a pathway through the rampant wilderness that had grown on her calves over the winter months. She never shaved in the winter, unless she had a boyfriend, which she hadn't now for several years. Even that hadn't lasted long. A few months that she had had to cut short when she started to fall in love. She didn't want that. She'd seen enough of the twisted relationships at home not to share her friends' dreams of love and fairy-tale weddings.

It was better not to become too attached; safer to keep things casual. A brief and unsatisfactory union with a Flemish aristo from a family of vast wealth accumulated from growing coffee

46

in South Africa followed. He had dumped her upon discovering her own pedigree didn't match his own. Snob. She'd then fallen headlong for a DJ who was the antithesis – considered a lascivious predator by the low-hanging female fruit growing in the affluent suburbs. Esme was thrilled by his knowledge of music and ability to create at an atmosphere at the endless round of eighteenth birthday balls she attended. He was the rock star standing in his booth manipulating the crowd of beautiful young things to dance to his tune. A pied piper that all the girls fancied but were too scared to approach. Esme's parents would have disapproved, which was a major part of his attraction. It had only been a one-night stand but it had felt like rebellion.

Esme towel-dried her hair and dressed, turning yesterday's pants inside out (Mrs Bee would be horrified, she thought) and went to join Bill in the kitchen.

Breakfast was the polar opposite of dinner and had all the hallmarks of someone who quite literally couldn't boil an egg. She bypassed the burnt toast and said she would grab something from a café on the way to the gallery.

'I drive to work.'

'It's…' started Esme.

'I know it's only a five-minute walk and takes longer in the car but I have a severe aversion to exercise of any kind. Besides, it's a beautiful day and we can go topless.' He winked. 'Are you ready?'

★

47

Bill's pale-aqua Bristol was parked outside, its two nearside wheels mounting the pavement. A parking ticket was held in place on the windscreen by one of its wipers.

'Fuckers,' he said, tossing the fine into the road.

At the press of a button the canvas roof glided back and down, tucking itself into the boot. Petals drifted over them from a nearby tree. How different this was from the luxe but dull top-of-the-range Rolls or standard-issue Land Rover favoured by the landed gentry. This was Monte Carlo glamorous, Grace Kelly classy and only suitable for a driver keen to be noticed. Heads turned as they coasted through Mayfair. When they approached the traffic lights Bill pumped the brake like he was riding a bicycle. It made Esme feel sick.

'You drive like an old woman, Bill,' laughed Esme.

'And you would know, having been on the road for what? Two years?'

'I've driven since I was eight which is why it took three goes to pass my test. Got into bad habits.'

'I'll wager you have never driven in London? Takes skill.'

'This is like driving a go-kart. No gears, just brake and accelerator.'

'But I drive to be seen not to get from A to B.'

Bill was certainly visible today. He had adopted Javier's colour palette from last night but the blues and pinks were deeper, presumably to harmonize with the paintwork of the Bristol. He wasn't the most handsome of men but he certainly made the best of what little he had, thought Esme. He fed the steering wheel through chubby fingers with the grace of a concert pianist.

'Do you play the piano, Bill?'

'I wish. The cello is my instrument of choice. I started with the violin and when the fat started to stick I went on to its big brother to make myself look smaller. It's all about visual deception, my darling.'

Rotund or not, there was an essential grace to the man. He floated. Nothing about him jarred. He appeared to roll through life like a smooth pebble too weighty to be pushed around by the sea.

'We have a busy day today, Esme. Well, you and Suki do. There will be paintings delivered throughout the day. I'll need you to inspect each one to ensure no damage has been caused in transportation. Bit like hiring a car when the rental company walks around it and notes the condition before and after you have used it. If you are anything like your father, you will spot imperfection. Flaws will leap out at you.'

'Are you having an exhibition?'

'Yes. The kind that will make or break my business. I need something to alleviate the scandal last year when I inadvertently sold a forged Watteau. The asshole who I bought it from had doctored its papers of authentication and even to me it looked like the real thing. It taught me a lesson. Never deal with those who have nothing to lose. This bullshitter walked in off the street with no prior appointment or connection to me in any way. My fault for being greedy and rash.'

Esme felt the weight of responsibility. What would happen if she failed to notice a blemish?

As if reading her thoughts, Bill said, 'Don't worry, angel, you are not looking for forgeries – just scratched paint or an obvious dent. I found all these works through my network of ambulance chasers so I know their pedigree. People die and their children have to pay for the funeral or need the cash to split between

49

siblings. I ferret these families out. Rather grubby, if you think about it, but by helping others sell, I make my own money in taking a hefty percentage. Sometimes I have a private individual who is looking for a particular work. I'll find it and sell directly. My gallery is my shop window but essentially I am a common dealer like the lizard who brought the supposed Watteau to me.'

They arrived at the gallery, just as Suki was opening up.

'Suki the Sloane is late. Would have fired her months ago but her parents are good friends and I've grown fond of her. And anyway, I have you now to whip things into shape.'

Esme wished his confidence had been in her and what she'd studied rather than his faith in an instinct he supposed she had inherited from her father. But still she felt a rush of adrenaline at the thought of adding value to Bill's make-or-break show.

'Morning,' said Suki, handing Bill a Styrofoam cup. 'I would have got you one, Esme, had I known you weren't sleeping here.' There was a slight edge to her voice.

'Put your talons away, Suki. She only stayed because Toots and I want to adopt her and I plan to sack you so she can take your place.'

Suki laughed, seemingly put at ease by this insult.

'You see, Esme? She's too thick-skinned to take umbrage.'

There were three locks on the door and as the door opened, a high beep startled a group of pigeons waddling aimlessly hoping for non-existent scraps. Bill swung his briefcase at them.

'As bad as rats.'

They flapped lazily into the air only to land back where they had set off.

Suki sprinted in to turn the alarm off and returned exclaiming, 'I remembered the code!'

'Incredible, Suki Su. And after three years of doing that every day. You'll be given a scholarship in higher maths at Imperial soon,' said Bill. 'I did offer to pay for the number to be tattooed on her hand but she declined saying "tattoos are for sailors".'

'Tattoos are common. Imagine what Daddy would say if I turned up with one. Be almost as bad as bringing home the wrong type of boyfriend.'

'Nothing wrong with a bit of variety, I can assure you. Your father, much as I love him, is from the stone age. He is a racist pig. And a homophobic one. He's the only person who isn't aware of my sexual persuasion – his brain is simply incapable of even imagining let alone acknowledging such a thing, despite going to an all-boys school.

'Right girls. Enough chatter, there is work to be done. Suki, I need to switch off the alarm in the strong room. Most of the paintings are arriving today. You can take delivery of them and make sure all have the correct paperwork. Esme will inspect them for damage.'

'Have I got time to change?' she asked.

'Quickly, and I suggest you stick to trousers as you will be on your hands and knees for most of the day.'

Esme bounded up the stairs and threw on a fresh shirt. It was an old one that had belonged to her mother; faded navy blue with frayed cuffs and patch pockets on the front. All but two strategic buttons were missing but it still held a faded glamour; St Tropez, circa 1958. It could have been a man's shirt but for the hint of a tailored waist and narrow shoulders. The collar was small, the fabric soft and still intact at the seams. Her mother would have worn it in her twenties too.

In the bathroom, she tied her hair back in a ponytail, splashed some water on her face and swiped a film of moisturizer over her skin. No time for make-up. But then she rarely wore any except going out in the evenings.

Bill did a double-take when she reappeared.

'My God, I thought you were Diana for a second. I remember that shirt – I never forget an outfit. I was staying with the Guinnesses in Gassin. There was a fabulous shop called Chose. Brigitte Bardot and Roger Vadim made it famous. St Tropez was just a fishing village then. We always bought things there, your pa too. It had the best ice creams next door. Pistachio and chocolate combo was your ma's favourite.'

Esme had seen the photo albums of those days. Her parents had had a tiny dolls' house in Gassin, which sat in the hills behind St Tropez. Apparently, they'd spent the whole month of August going to the beach, catching sardines from the side of their little fishing boat called the *Pistou*. Her mother was film-star stunning back then. Every photograph showed her smiling or laughing. Hard to imagine today.

The first of the day's deliveries had arrived. A Munroe truck was double-parked on the street and a familiar figure was climbing out of the back. Of course, she should have known her father's delivery firm would be along sooner or later. The art world was a small community, and even in his absence, his firm was the gold standard for dealers and their best customers. Her father might summer in the south of France but the Munroe business never stopped.

'Norman! What are you doing here?' said Esme, delighted to see her father's warehouse manager.

'Miss Esme, hello! I wanted to come and see how you are getting on. Thought I'd surprise you. A familiar face in the big old city. Don't tell Mr Munroe.'

'It's so lovely to see you.' And it was. She adored this man with his sing-song Caribbean lilt and freckly nose. 'I was going to get in touch with you – I hoped I could come and collect some stuff for my new flat.'

'Have you found somewhere to live already?'

'Not yet. I'm staying here at the moment, but as soon as I do I'll come along for a raid.'

'You do that, choonkoloonks. Norman is always there to pick the best pieces for his Esme.'

Esme laughed. 'I don't want anything *too* good,' she said, and felt an arm around her shoulder.

'Surprised to see our Norm?' said Bill. 'He insisted on bringing the Poussin I needed collecting himself. How was the drive from Paris?'

'Not a problem, Mr Cartwright. I drove through the night. You might have warned the mistress of the house I was collecting. She thought I'd come to burgle her. The lorry saved the day. Nothing like putting these rich lolos at ease.'

Bill burst out laughing.

'Good for you, Norman. Right, we better take this painting off your hands so you can get some well-deserved rest.'

Norman went inside the mouth of the vast lorry holding its solitary cargo. The painting was cloaked in a rough fire-proof blanket and lay some six feet along one side tied in place with fabric tape. Nothing had been left to chance. Everything transported by Esme's father's company was insured to the full and guaranteed to arrive as it had left.

The heavy artwork was placed on a trolley and wheeled into the gallery.

'I'll take it out of its crate, Mr Cartwright.'

'That would be marvellous, Norman. And if you wouldn't mind removing the wood.'

'Might be wise to do this on the pavement,' said Norman, holding a cleaver. He then proceeded to loosen the nails that held the crate together. With tender strength, he drew out each nail with surgical care.

The contents told a different story to Esme's painting. Colour shone from the canvas.

'Crying shame the family have to sell this,' said Norman, propping the painting like a cricket player holding his bat at the crease.

'That's death duties for you,' said Bill. 'Collections get broken up all over the country. Let's hope our new prime minister shows favour towards our national treasures. Did you vote for her?'

'Did indeed. True blue to the core, I am, Mr Cartwright.'

Esme was surprised. She knew a little of Thatcher's views on immigration and her brand of Britishness didn't always include the likes of Norman. Maggie Thatcher spoke for the majority, people like her father included. But unlike lots of her parents' generation, Esme felt no hostility towards 'foreigners' – after all, some of the best times of her life had been when *she* was the foreigner, at art school in Brussels, but like Norman, Esme had still voted Tory because it seemed the better option – and to be honest, because that was what everyone around her did. She swore to herself next time she'd try to make sure she was making up her own mind, not just ticking the same box on the ballot her family always had.

'Esme, why don't you show Norman your painting?'

'I'm not sure you'll want to see it when you find out the state it's in. It's in my bathroom.'

'You oughtn't to be keeping it in the bathroom, lovely, damp is no good for pictures. You know that.'

'It can't get any more wrecked than it is already.'

Norman followed Esme through the gallery to the stairs and Esme caught Suki's expression: surprise at letting 'the help' up to her rooms, she supposed.

Upstairs, in front of the canvas, Norman bent down and took a closer look. There probably wasn't a single major artist's work he hadn't handled before.

'I think there's a fine picture under there. Don't be worried by its discolouration. A good restorer can easily fix that.'

Esme felt a frisson of excitement. If Norman said it was a fine picture, then it most probably was.

'I'm taking it to Max Bliss.'

'I don't know him well, but if Mr Cartwright has recommended him then he will be your man.'

'I'm so glad you've seen it. Once it's repaired I'll bring it to the warehouse and show you.'

'I'll be happy to collect it. Just give me the nod.'

As Norman headed downstairs, Esme glanced back at the blackened canvas. For the first time she could look at it as a mystery, a riddle to solve – rather than a threat or the cold hand of the past trying to clamp itself around her. Norman's optimism was infectious. Maybe this Max Bliss really could reveal the colours beneath the soot. And, she realized, she was ready to go in search of them.

Chapter Four

Esme had left her wallet at Bill's house and returned to collect it at the end of the day. He was off to some function and said Javier would be at home.

The front door was wide open and Esme could see right through to the back of the house to the garden. She tiptoed through and found Javier sitting outside with a sweating glass of rosé. He was in a tiny pair of Speedos and slippery with oil. He kissed the air either side of her face, his arms behind him like he was about to dive into a pool. He smelt of Earl Grey tea.

'Piz Buin tanning oil. Not for an English peach like you but perfect for a cactus like me.'

'You are lucky. I never go brown. I get heat rash if I get too much sun.'

'Then I hope you're being careful, it's so scorchy hot today. Mind you don't get it on that pretty face.'

Esme's skin prickled at the thought of it and she held out one pale arm against Javier's burnished skin. 'Look at you after just one tanning day!'

'Oh, but think what beautiful skin you will keep. You'll never become a cracked leather sandal like me.'

'You are gorgeous, Javier.'

Javier's modesty was false but with the confidence of one born beautiful, he made light of it and regularly put himself down with great humour.

'I've come to get my wallet. I left it in the guest room.'

'Stop and have a glass of wine with me. I bet the gallery is like a sweat shop today. And your attic room! Unbearable. Stay until it cools down.'

He was right. Her room was stifling and it would take the darkness of night to blot the sticky heat.

'That would be lovely.'

Javier padded off to collect her a glass and poured the pale-pink liquid into it. It was delicious. Ice cold over her tongue, warming nicely down her throat and emitting a different, welcome kind of heat as it hit her stomach. Her parents had always chosen the drinks at home. When it was hot, the Pimm's had always come out, which she found sickly. But this was more refreshing; strong and clean. She felt the flush of alcohol spread to her skin in little beads of sweat.

'How was day two at the gallery?'

'Oh, you know, a bit of a whirlwind! Deliveries all day. The running of such an amazing place is all new to me and I feel a bit out of my depth. But Suki is sweet and while she shows me the ropes, I can help her out with the art history side of things. For once, I actually feel like I know something useful. I just want to drink it all in and earn my keep.'

'As I have learnt, *carina*, you will only truly succeed in this game if you are born with an artistic parasite in your gut, one that feeds off beauty. Your father has one so I'm sure it's found a host inside you, too.'

'Javier, that's disgusting! But it's true – between my father's business and the treasures at Culcairn, I have been surrounded by art since I was born. Sometimes so much so I felt like I was drowning in it – but I look back and see it was the opposite. It's probably what saved me and I love it for that. I feel a state of grace when I see something really beautiful.'

Javier clapped his hands.

'See? You have the instinct. You can't buy that at a fancy school.'

Esme thought of what she had learnt in Brussels. She had found the endless lists of names and dates dull and dry, compared to the analysis and comparisons of paintings, but now she saw that all aspects of her formal qualification had helped her get the job she so wanted. She might not be able to answer the phones properly yet or find her way around the files like Suki, but she was familiar with the artists whose works were to be on display at the gallery, opening each delivery had been like a piece of a puzzle she could slot together.

'Bill knew what he was doing when he hired you. I knew it from the moment he told me about you. He is never wrong about people.' Javier smiled.

'How long have you and Bill been together?' Esme asked.

'A long time.'

'Was it love at first sight?'

'No. Truth be told, he was my ticket out of my sleazy life in New York. There I had many men wanting me. Beautiful, rich and famous ones. But Bill was the only who wanted more than sex. He was prepared to invest his time – and money – bringing me to London, building a home together. He said he knew we would be a perfect fit, and what did I tell you? Bill is never wrong about these things. He was patient, he was funny, he was honest. My gratitude eventually turned into love. Now I can't imagine life without him. And of course, he is generous. He knows I get my sex elsewhere.'

Like my mother, thought Esme.

'Doesn't he get jealous?'

Javier laughed.

'No! We have loyalty of mind and heart. Our bodies have a will and life of their own, though. Anyway, Bill likes to watch.'

'Oh.' Not wanting to appear prudish, Esme quickly changed the subject.

'Did Bill tell you about my painting?'

'Briefly. Henry Culcairn left it to you, no?'

She nodded.

'I never met him but I know all about that deliciously poisonous wife of his.'

'Lucia? How do you know about her?'

'Only her reputation and the legend of her background.' He made a face of gleeful revulsion. She is no more Italian than I am Scandinavian. You British are too stupid and insular to distinguish one accent from another. In London, we all know she is Uruguayan. An air hostess who helped a Scottish earl join the Mile-High Club.'

'She's South American? I thought she was from a noble Spanish family.'

'You look surprised, Esme. Didn't you know she's a gold-digging hustler?'

Esme found it hard to imagine the Contessa – that tall column of granite devoid of empathy – coming from poverty.

But it was new information she relished. How had her parents not known? Or maybe they did and because of her acquired title chose to ignore it. She couldn't wait to tell Sophia.

'That's amazing. She comes across as being grander than royalty.'

Javier shrugged, stroking his bare chest then stretching his arms up, arching his back until his spine gave a satisfying crack.

'Just an act that has now become her reality. I know many people like her. Very few remain true to themselves,' he said.

Esme thought about this. How could she be true to herself when she had yet to become the person she wanted to be? Or was that the point? To remain the same inside and adapt by decorating the façade to fit in. She definitely didn't want to put herself in a position to be judged too quickly. She was used to people having decided who Esme Munroe was before they even met her. It was easy to make assumptions that turned out to be false – she'd done it herself, after all.

Javier shared the last of the wine between them and said, 'I'm going out tonight. Why don't you come with? Do you have any plans?'

'Um…'

'You are trying to think of some excuse because you look a mess and have nothing else to wear.'

Esme laughed. It was true. She didn't want her first night out on the town to be ruined by scruffy jeans.

'Can I go like this?'

'Absolutely not. Sure, it's chic in a retro way but the gays like glitz. What have you got underneath that shirt? Anything?'

She looked down her cleavage.

'Just a camisole.'

'Perfect! Let's see.'

Esme slipped her shirt off to reveal a pretty antique lace and satin vest.

'Heaven – but the bra has to go. I'll lend you my Gucci belt and we'll ransack the safe for some of Bill's mother's jewellery. She's too tight to pay for the insurance herself, so she keeps it here, luckily for you.' He stepped back and appraised Esme. 'Earrings, I think.'

Javier bounded upstairs and returned with a box. She recognized it from the kind her own mother had, navy leather with a gold crest embossed in the centre. Inside were a pair of fabulous pearl and diamond clips.

'I can't wear those,' she said. 'They're far too good.'

'Not for my friends they're not, and anyway they're insured for being worn as well as just cluttering up our safe. Just don't take them off, even if they pinch like witch's fingers.' He handed them to her. 'Wonderful! All a girl needs is some diamonds and fewer clothes. My friends are going to be dazzled by you.'

'By the earrings.'

As she put them on and looked at her reflection in the glass of the window, she realized she felt cool for the first time ever. Expensively casual. Then she wrapped her arms around herself in embarrassment – her nipples were visible through the fine satin.

'Don't worry about that. It's testicles not tits the boys there want,' Javier said as he went to dress.

Still, Esme felt extremely exposed and draped her shirt over her shoulders – 'In case I get cold,' she said, although with

London baking in a heat wave, her excuse was as transparent as her top.

When Javier reappeared, he was wearing a matching outfit but with a white vest in place of her camisole. Esme took a deep breath and followed him out into the summer night.

They took a taxi to Soho. The club was hidden away down a cobbled cul-de-sac. The street was dimly lit by lamps that flickered as moths divebombed the glow in constant frenzy. She had hated moths ever since one had got caught in her hair as a child. The memory made her skin crawl. She shivered.

'I thought you'd be immune to the cold coming from Scotland. It's not exactly Arctic tonight,' said Javier.

'I'm not cold, just revolted by all those moths.'

Javier followed her gaze. 'You should see the ones we have in Puerto Rico. The size of eagles and bloodthirsty too.'

'I am *never* going there,' she laughed.

The stairwell into the basement was steep and drab. It smelt of beer and yesterday's cigarette butts. But it was exactly what Esme was after; the underbelly of a London her peers would never see. At the bottom two men were kissing. They parted to let Javier and Esme through the door.

'Javs!' said the blond of the two. 'Great to see you, girlina. Where have you been hiding?'

'Chained to the stove.'

'Lucky you. I have to go to Charing Cross for that,' said the other, smart in his expensively cut pinstripe suit. They both lit a cigarette.

'Want one?' said Blondie, proffering his packet to Esme.

She extracted an elegant gold-tipped Sobrani from the packet. She didn't smoke often but didn't want to seem inexperienced.

'Let me present Esme Munroe. The new hottie in town,' said Javier, pushing her forward like he was introducing her to a dance partner.

'Lovely to meet you, lovely Esme,' said City Boy. 'I'm Ben. You should go in and grab a table. It's filling up fast. We'll come and join you after I've found Gary's tonsils.'

Gary was the younger of the two and undoubtedly from what Esme's father would call 'the underclass'. She smiled at him. He was incredibly handsome and looked closer to her age than City Boy.

'He'll be searching for hours. Had them taken out when I was a kid.' Gary laughed as he returned his attention to Ben's mouth.

Esme was delighted by their sense of fun and acceptance. It was the same warmth that emanated from Javier. This was who he was, what he was and he wore his sexuality with pride.

The club bore little resemblance to its exterior. As a private members' bar there was a faded splendour to the small space. Large ornate mirrors dominated the walls. The banquette seating was buttoned leather with low glass tables straining under crowded bottles and glasses. Cigarette smoke curled around an overbearing chandelier, its weak fingered glow casting shadows in recessed booths.

The company was eclectic and predominantly male. Men of all ages were coupled up dancing to Barry White, chatting or locked in intimate embrace. Not so different to any other club Esme had been to but there was definitely more emotional freedom here. No one was judging.

Javier led her to a bench. The carpet was sticky underfoot and she placed her shirt under her bum to stop sliding about on the shiny upholstery.

'Easy to clean. Things get a bit heated in here later,' said Javier.

'It's already boiling,' thought Esme.

A tall waiter appeared with a notepad in his hand and a biro behind his ear.

'Javier!'

It took Esme a second to realize he was in fact a she. The waitress was striking with cropped auburn hair and pale skin. A large dragoon tattoo breathed fire across her shoulder, emerging from the man's vest she wore. Esme was surprised to hear an Australian accent.

'Where the hell have you been, you old bugger? It's been, what, two months?'

'Work, work, work, Cece.'

'Oh fuck off, Javs. You're a kept woman. All play and no work for you,' she laughed and turned to Esme. 'Hi, I'm Cecelia. Cece to my friends.'

'This is Esme. She's just arrived from Scotland. A country girl and new to London,' said Javier putting an arm around her.

'Throwing her in at the deep end, eh, Javs?' Cece put out her hand. 'Great to meet you, Esme. Now, what will I be getting you two lovebirds to drink? Your usual, hon?'

'*Si*. And Esme will have the same. They make the most divine champagne cocktails here.'

'Lovely. Thanks,' said Esme.

She watched Cece navigate her way across the small dance floor to the bar, giving and receiving kisses along the way.

'She's a great girl, Cece. Balls of steel and a heart of gold. And funny. So funny. She doesn't care who she offends.'

'She's very pretty,' said Esme, watching the Australian lean over the bar and give their order to the bartender. She turned to wave at them and rolled her eyes as a short fat man came to talk to her.

'The only girl who could turn me straight,' Javier said, 'and now you too, *carina*.' And kissed her on the cheek.

Cece returned with the drinks tray expertly balanced on one hand. She put their champagne down, along with two small bowls of nuts. She sat herself next to them.

'That dag Clement is giving me grief tonight. Someone's been dipping their fingers in the till and he accused me. It's bullshit. And you know, it's not like it's much that's missing. Just a few pounds. I make more than that in tips.'

'Ignore him, silly old queen,' said Javier, rising. 'Just nipping to the little boys' room. Save my place and look out for Gary and Ben.'

Esme took a sip of her cocktail. Bubbles fizzed from a sugar cube resting on the bed of the glass. It was sweet and bitter at the same time with a hint of something much stronger than champagne.

'So, Esme. What brought you to London?'

Esme paused. She badly wanted to impress this girl who was so cool and at ease with herself.

'I've got a job and I'm looking for somewhere to live. Where do you come from in Australia?' she tried shifting the focus back to Cece.

'A Hicksville town called Maryborough. Close to the Gold Coast. Noosa and all that. I miss it, the beaches and outdoor life. But I don't miss the claustrophobia of the place. Nothing to do but drink, fuck and surf. Gets boring after twenty-five years of it.'

Esme would have put her as being older. She felt like a schoolgirl who'd sneaked out for the night compared to her.

'Don't you miss your family?'

Her question was automatic, and now she dreaded being asked it in return. Any mention of her family still sent her emotions into overload – a whirling mix of anger, guilt and grief – everything she was trying to escape in her new life.

'Shit, yeah, but it's not forever and Mum's sister lives Cardiff. She's old now and on her last legs, so I expect Mum and Dad will be over for the funeral when she cops it.'

Esme drained her drink and reached for Javier's. 'I'd buy him another one but…'

'No need. He gets them on the house, courtesy of Clement. Must have something on him because he's a tight bastard. What about you? Where's your family?'

Was she going to lie or tell this girl the truth? It seemed not much would shock her and perhaps her dysfunctional parents would seem glamorous.

'Well, my mother's in a nuthouse and my father has pissed off to France. Sophia, my sister, is living in New York. She got on a plane as soon as she could afford to escape.'

Esme immediately felt disloyal.

'Crikey. That sounds very aristocratic. Are you from a posh family? Are those heirlooms?' she said, fondling one of Bill's earrings.

66

'The jewellery's borrowed! And in answer to your other question: no, or rather, sort of. My mother had a long affair with an earl and I had to live in his castle with his horrid wife, the Contessa, when my mum had her "episodes". All in all, I've had enough of the upper classes; they're not as glamorous as you might think.'

'Hang on, hang on. You actually know an earl and a contessa and lived in an actual castle?' Cece let out a slow whistle.

'It sounds more exciting than it was, trust me.'

With a wave of embarrassment, it occurred to Esme that she had never really thought what her life at Culcairn must seem like to those on the outside. Until now, practically everyone she met knew her family's background and took it for granted. Now she was having to explain it out loud, she heard how eccentric it sounded.

'Have you been to Scotland?' she asked Cece.

'Nah. The furthest north I've got is Camden Lock.'

'I don't even know where that is.'

'You don't? Christ, Esme, it has the best market in the world.'

'I don't really know London well. Just Kensington and Chelsea. My parents used to have a house in South Ken. I'd be living there if my father hadn't spent all his money.'

'How about this: you can take me to Scotland and show me your fancy pants castle and friends and I'll show you Camden?' Cece's grin was infectious.

'I'd love that. It's a date.' Esme smiled back.

A sudden commotion erupted from behind the bar. Everyone sat at it turned to look in their direction.

'Oh God, Clement is flapping his hands at me. Better get back to work. I'll call you.'

Cece gave Esme a quick hug and sauntered back to an irate Clement.

The champagne cocktail was doing its work. Esme had an urge to dance and before Javier had a chance to sit back down, she pulled him onto the dance floor. Whether it was the music, the drink or the fact that she might actually just have made a friend, she felt something she'd missed for a long while. She felt joy.

Chapter Five

Esme looked at the address for Max Bliss's studio again. She was in Fulham and on the right street, outside the correct number. She rang the bell for a second time and stood back to see if there was any movement in the windows. Her painting clattered to the ground.

'Fucking hell.'

All the curtains were drawn. Maybe Bill had forgotten to tell him she was coming? She started to count the seconds before she rang the bell again, waiting then counting her heartbeats so that she felt like she had power over her nerves. There were two choices: to leave or persist even though she felt out of her depth. All her earlier curiosity about the painting's real identity had changed to anxiety. She chewed the inside of her cheek and told herself to stop being pathetic.

Hellooooooo?' she yelled, head upturned like a she-wolf howling at the moon.

'Yes? Are you Esme?'

Esme looked around to see where the voice was coming from.

'Here. To your left,' said a deep voice filled with mirth.

A tall blond man in his forties, wearing ragged clothes and a broad grin was standing outside some garage doors.

'Are you Max?'

'No, I'm the fucking Queen of Denmark. Of course, you nit. Come in.'

The door which swung shut behind him had a heavy padlock dangling from a metal arm. Grabbing her painting, Max held the door open for her to enter the great man's grotto.

An overpowering smell of turpentine and glue stung her eyes.

In her mind's eye, Esme had envisaged the studio to be lofty, light and airy. A restorer was the custodian of works worth millions and his place of business would surely reflect that. As would the man himself. But neither Max nor his chaotic studio matched what she'd imagined. Thinking at first that Max was wearing leather trousers, she saw that they were in fact jeans lacquered with spilt oil and varnish. His shirt and jumper were more gamekeeper than art historian. The checked collar was dirty and frayed and his pullover was pelleted by moth holes and crumbs of God knows what. Although it was only eleven o'clock, he held a smeared goblet of red wine in one hand and picked up a chipped mug of tea with the other. His hair was deeply parted to one side and he had the bluest eyes that glinted with merriment.

'Builders' or vino?'

'Just some water, please.'

He cut a path through the clutter to a cracked Butler sink stockpiled with an assembly of crockery and congealed cutlery. Taking a cup that dislodged the heap – which he ignored as it mostly clattered to the ground – he filled it from the tap.

The studio was a barely converted garage stuffed with frames and canvases stacked against exposed brick walls. Dust and long-abandoned cobwebs capped the rough blocks like forgotten tombstones. The space was long and narrow with scarcely enough room to move. Every surface – be it the trestle table, water pipes or shelves – was littered with pots, brushes, bottles and old tins. Dirty rags were strewn across the paint-splattered floor. Strip-lighting and a tree-like lamp made up of bare light bulbs illuminated the only clean thing in this pigsty. Gleaming upon a battered easel was an exquisite still life. It rose like Venus from a polluted sea, proud, commanding and spotless.

'There you go.'

The water was warm and the mug had a tide line of curdled milk. It still smelt strongly of coffee.

'She's a beauty, isn't she?' he continued.

Esme didn't know what to say. The painting moved her in a way that made her feel euphoric and overwhelmed with emotion. At once she was both close to tears and yet also consoled. It was extraordinary how a painting could summon such feelings instantly, could bring the past alive in such a tangible way. The flowers were more vibrant and alive than the real thing.

'Who is it by?'

'Simon Verelst. A Dutch painter.'

'Sixteen hundreds?'

Max nodded.

The Dutch Golden Age. Esme had studied it in Brussels.

'Bullseye. He was known for his flowers but painted marvellous portraits, too.'

Max handed her a Polaroid. It was a photograph of shadowed colour and indistinguishable form.

'Is this the same painting?' she asked, thinking it impossible.

'Yes, poor love. She arrived a month ago. It beggars belief how people are capable of such abuse. Of course, the muck had built up over centuries but it's a crime to allow a painting to suffer like this. The owners should be shot. The only reason they are having her cleaned now is because they want to sell her and they wouldn't have bothered had the dealer not told them a sale was inconceivable in this state. Greed has saved her from a life of grime.'

Esme held her painting more tightly. When he saw the state of it, would Max consider her a criminal inoculated against culture and the responsibility that comes with owning fine art?

'Is this what Bill wants me to collect?' She almost had to pinch herself at the fact she was trusted with such treasures.

'Yes, but it's not quite dry yet,' he said, dabbing his finger on the paint.

'Where's the frame?'

'That'll take two seconds. Just got to find the bloody thing.'

Fat chance, thought Esme. She'd be here for hours whilst he rifled through the hundreds of mounts that all looked the same.

As Max rooted through frames, a grey blur of a dog rushed into the studio and practically assaulted Esme.

'Leave her alone, Flea, for fuck sake.'

Max pushed the hound's nose away from Esme's crotch.

'Don't worry, I'm used to dogs,' she laughed.

She knelt down and took the dog's face in her hands, kissing it on the forehead.

'Boy or girl?' she asked.

'A boy. Dirty old bastard. Like his owner.'

'He's lovely.'

Flea was more wolfhound than lurcher, with a rough, steel-grey coat, shaggy face and kind eyes. Bred to course hares, they were as fast as greyhounds and notoriously lazy. He grunted with pleasure as Esme scratched him behind the ears, trying to lick her wrist without moving his head away from her fingers. He smelt of paint and turpentine. It can't be good for him being surrounded by these fumes, she thought. Satisfied Esme was friend not foe, Flea finally loped back to a battered wicker basket under the sink.

'How old is he?'

Flea had the same wise eyes as her old dog, Digger. Esme often thought that the only reason she was vaguely sane, aside from having Mrs Bee, was because of Digger's unwavering loyalty and love. He had instinctively known when she was upset or lonely, was always there when she'd needed something to cry into.

'I have no idea. Rescued him from some yobs who were torturing the poor bastard. That was six years ago and he was fully grown then.'

'He was lucky.'

'That's debatable, but he's certainly better off than being kicked around like a football,' said Max, turning to Esme's painting. 'So this is the picture Bill wanted me to have a look at?'

There was no point in trying to hide anything from this man, Esme decided. She sensed he had the kind of emotional intellect that could sniff out everything you tried to hide. He was direct, with no bullshit. She gave him a look she hoped said, 'Let me introduce you to your nemesis.'

Without so much as a glance at the front of her painting,

Max swiped clean the trestle table. Tubes, paint, boxes of nails were all sent flying before he placed the picture face down on the surface. He then got a piece of chalk, drew two double lines that bridged from frame to panel and wrote, CART.

'Now I know who the dealer is and which frame and where to put it back. Like a puzzle. Simple but effective.'

It seemed the restoration was beginning without the restorer having inspected the actual painting or asking anything about it. Clearly, he and Bill had spoken and Max had been instructed to clean it, regardless. Did he know it was actually hers or a perhaps he thought it was a work to be cleaned for the Culcairns?

'Pass me those, will you?' said Max, pointing to a wall covered in tools nailed to chipboard.

He could have been pointing to one of a hundred instruments of torture. Screwdrivers, hammers of every size, carving chisels and gouges. Esme took a lucky dip and lifted a pair of pliers.

'Perfect.'

He pulled out the rusty nails holding the canvas to the frame. Each came out with surprising ease, like rotten teeth from an old man's jaw. There was nothing delicate or careful in his method. The pincers nicked the wood leaving splintered scars.

'Does it matter that you have damaged the frame?'

'No. Shows the age of the picture.'

He then lifted the frame off the canvas and added it to stack behind him.

'Right. The moment of truth,' he said, turning it over.

Esme tried to lift her heart that was sinking to the floor.

'Oh God, I'm so embarrassed.' She covered her eyes.

The responding silence spoke a language she didn't understand. In the distance, she heard the siren of an ambulance or fire engine. She ought to know the difference, having had both turn up at The Lodge on multiple occasions. Both emergency services were appropriate for this corpse of a painting laid naked on the slab, though. But as they passed and the silence returned, she peeked through her fingers and saw Max inspecting the canvas through a magnifying glass. He tore a piece of cotton wool off its roll and tipped purple liquid onto it. Swabbing gently in the centre, the alcohol uncovered a rosebud pink that with soft swipes became a shy smile. The wad turned a brownish-yellow within seconds and was deposited into an old petrol drum brimming with fellow clumps of cotton wool turned the same ugly colour. Taking what looked like a skewer, he wrapped the tip in more wool and gently rubbed it over the thulium oil paint.

Still mute, he lifted the Verelst off the easel and replaced it with Esme's painting.

A piece of fresh cotton wool – larger this time – was doused in more alcohol and wiped in broad circles across the canvas. The rhythmic movement made a quiet comforting sound, like a breeze through trees. Once again, the varnish – yellow with age – readily came away and with each sweep it was as if someone had flicked a switch on. The dirt cleared to briefly reveal the portrait of a woman before evaporating and clouding the image back under the soot that had blanketed but not destroyed the image. But already a shadow of the portrait was visible. It looked like a young woman. For a fleeting moment, the image reminded Esme of her mother. But unlike the Verelst,

Esme could see there was less precision in the paintwork and the brushstrokes seemed to be bigger and less photographic.

'Can you tell if it's any good?' asked Esme, relieved there was at least recognizable form.

'The composition is very pretty. Lots of movement,' he said.

All Esme could see was a ghostly figure draped in material. A kind of spirit bride that was impossible to date by what she was wearing. As far as Esme was concerned this could have been painted any time in the last two hundred years.

'You see how the artist has created a figure of eight – well, more of a question mark, with the veil?'

Peering again, she could see Max was right. The fabric almost floated around the sitter's head, falling loosely over her breasts and shoulders. If it was her mother, at least she wasn't naked.

Max rubbed another section then pointed at the bottom right side, next to the slash.

'You see this bubbling?'

'You mean the cut?'

'No. We'll get to that.'

He reached for a paintbrush and pointed at a small gathering of pimpled oil, like nettle rash or goosebumps.

'That's from heat. Most likely a fire, given the soot coming off. It's interesting that the frame wasn't scorched.'

It did seem strange that the frame was intact. Perhaps the damage happened before the frame was put on. Having no clue as to the age of the picture it was impossible to say whether the frame was original.

'Can you tell who the artist might be?'

'Christ, no. But what I can say is that I have never restored a painting by this artist before. I've restored so many that I can recognize an artist's hand instantly. I'm never wrong.'

Esme looked at him, deflated that Max had ruled out it being by one of the big-name artists in the Culcairn collection. Only when it was ruled out did she realize a part of her had been hoping some precious treasure had been lurking under the soot.

'Don't look so crestfallen, Esme,' he laughed. 'I could lie and say you've brought me a Renoir but it certainly isn't French' – he studied it briefly again – 'or even Italian.'

'And you're *never* wrong?'

Max laughed, 'It's simply a fact, Esme. I may be many things but a bullshitter, I'm not. The problem comes when I try and get my own treasures authenticated. The so-called experts don't like that one bit. They hate to be caught out.'

As much as she adored Bill, she could easily imagine him casually turning his nose up at a Rococo masterpiece he hadn't snuffled out himself. But his insides would be an enraged, boiling vat of envy. She chuckled thinking of him desperately trying not to show it. There was nothing subtle about Bill.

'Why are you laughing?'

'Just thinking of Bill as one of your "experts". He would rather boil his balls than admit you had beaten him to a long-lost gem.'

Max filled his wine glass, with white this time, from a bottle that looked lifted from one of his paintings. It poured more like honey than wine.

'Sure?'

Esme shook her head.

'The thing about Bill is that, for all his hysteria, he is one of

77

the most loyal men I know. He authenticated a painting I knew to be by Pontormo. I picked it up at Christie's for a pittance. Bill was the only dealer who had a) the eye and b) the imagination to see what I did before I had cleaned it. Some owners have no artistic vision, no patience. That's where I step in and get to buy up overlooked gems.'

Bearing in mind Max's words, Esme was reluctant to state outright that the painting was hers and that Bill had pulled rank to get it looked at. The last thing she wanted was for him to think her to be a spoilt brat who would use contacts to get what she wanted – or worse, that it was somehow her fault that the thing got damaged.

'I mean, look at what's lying in wait behind the soot and dirt. This has been painted by someone very accomplished. I just don't know who yet because I suspect it's later than my area of expertise. Whatever is revealed will be beautiful. As to its value, I have no idea. But that's not the point, is it?'

Esme wasn't sure. She had begun to hope the painting would be of some value, perhaps something that she could sell to reinvest in a work of her own choosing. But to air this thought to Max would be like force-feeding Darwinism to the Pope. He would be deeply insulted and she was in no position to do that.

'D'you think the Verelst flowers are dry yet? I should get back to the gallery. Bill will be pacing and unable to do a thing until he gets it. You know what he's like.'

'When he sees how beautifully she has polished up, he won't care if you are a month late. He will be thrilled and deservedly so. Leave it with me a while longer and you can collect it when you come to check on how our soot-covered lady is coming along.'

Esme knew her painting was in safe hands but it still pained her to leave it. Not because she would miss it – she would be glad of not tripping over it in her bathroom every day. No, it was more a question of finality, of confronting her own history. And along with the dirt, would her past be washed away – and then what?

Chapter Six

The week that followed was a baptism of fire. Planning for Bill's upcoming exhibition was an unrelenting frenzy. Bill – dear old Bill, her knight in kaleidoscopic colour – transformed into a carping tyrant, sniping and finding fault with the tiniest of details and drowning her in a slew of trivial tasks. His eye kept veering from the critical parts of the exhibition to trivialities that bore no relevance to its success or failure – or for that matter anything at all. Silly little things like the angle of the desk diary (which he straightened on Esme's desk with a sharp sigh) and emptying a practically empty wastepaper basket. When he wasn't in the running to become Irritating Boss of the Year, he was winning an Oscar as Best Despot in a Leading Role. The gallery was his territory and he governed it in a constant state of panic, with no clear directive or consideration for its people. Suki and Esme were issued tasks that had already been done, or in Esme's case were far beyond her realm of experience. The two girls worked tirelessly, Suki motivated by obedience and Esme, fear. The stakes were higher for her. She couldn't afford to lose this job.

Her first encounter with a photocopier, something she

had never seen let alone used before, was a nightmare. Not daring to admit ignorance, she fed price lists into every orifice until in frustration, she recruited Suki's help. How was she supposed to know that the built-in stapler was a vicious little thing? It clamped its teeth before piercing the copied sheets together. A pile of squashed staples grew until she gave in and used paperclips.

The stationery cupboard became her refuge as well as her operations centre. Once she had mastered the workings of the office paraphernalia, if she needed to escape an outburst, she could retreat to her bunker. She took pride in organizing the blocks of A3 and A4 paper, alphabetically ordering the reference books and tidying the spare biros. Pencils of varying softness lined a tray with the precision of an army on parade. The red petty-cash box had its key left conveniently in the lock for anyone needing to dip in. There wasn't an inch of that room she didn't know intimately so was able to find anything at a moment's notice if Bill had a fit of temper.

The exhibition had diverted her from the paintings themselves but she still desperately wanted to succeed and was willing do whatever was required, however menial. She took great pleasure in being organized and hoped Bill would see how hard she was trying after the opening night was over. Meanwhile, she kept out of his way and increasingly worked from the back rooms rather than front-of-house as she got more done. She addressed the invitations on her knee, using a stepladder as a stool, pausing to take in some of the grand names and fine addresses. Bill had said the guest list was select and focused, only collectors interested in seventeenth-century landscapes rather than anyone just chasing a night out and some fizz. Suki pointed out that none of his famous friends were coming.

'I'm not interested in getting into Nigel Dempster's column.'

'Bullshit, Bill. You thrive on gossip pages,' said Suki.

'Not when it comes to my work. I can be omnipresent on the social scene but I don't want my work to be cheapened by café society.'

Fair enough, thought Esme, although there must be some famous people who liked this kind of art, surely?

'My father told me you know lots of rock stars. Don't any of them collect art?' she ventured.

'They are generally too busy shovelling powder up their noses or injecting opioids into their veins. A good habit doesn't come cheap.'

'Well, whoever comes, I've bought loads of champagne. It's the good stuff, as you realized after you'd calmed down,' said Suki.

Bill had initially berated Suki for ordering the wrong label. 'We can't serve that shit,' he had said.

Rather than arguing, Suki – in her usual apathy – was unwilling to rise to the bait and waited for her boss to discover there were ten cases of Bollinger in the back, the very one he normally served at all his gallery opening nights.

'I'm not awash with money but need to give the impression I am. Money makes money.'

It certainly didn't seem to Esme as though he was cutting any corners. Searcy's was doing the food. Probably the most expensive caterers in London had been instructed to provide bite-sized blinis and smoked salmon topped with sour cream and Beluga, foie gras on mini brioche with a caramelized onion

82

marmalade and cocktail sausages from Suffolk. Esme had been surprised when Suki had balked at such indulgence.

'Jesus, Bill, this is going to cost a bomb! What's wrong with cheese and pineapple or mini quiches?'

Bill looked like she had lobbed fish guts at him. He physically heaved.

'Revolting, repellent and vile. That might suffice for your bourgeois friends in the Home Counties but I am catering to a different class of people. The kind that would use your home as a garden shed.'

Here we go, thought Esme, quickly busying herself with some non-existent paperwork. She put a guest list in the desk drawer and waited for Suki's counterblast. After all, Suki's family home was hardly a hovel. Suki had told Esme the eight-bedroom house sat in 130 acres of Surrey countryside complete with tennis court and swimming pool. A Home County with lots of brogue- and sports jacket-wearers, Bill said, but having seen a photograph, it looked rather pretty. It had less majesty than The Lodge, but Esme suspected its four walls also contained less drama and heartache than her own home.

While Esme admired the way Bill's barbs bounced off Suki, she found it more difficult to remain detached because most of the time she was flying by the seat of her pants, learning as she recoiled from one bollocking to the next. When he accused her one morning, of being 'a pathetic waste of space', despite working late for four consecutive nights her self-doubt believed him. She wished she was more relaxed, like Suki, who knew this job was only a stopgap. But Esme was only one paycheque away from having to return to Scotland. If she didn't find her way in the art world, she knew her father would expect her to become a tame society wife. Even though her first taste of independence had been brief, Esme knew she could never go back, never follow her mother's unhappy path.

But her pent-up anxiety risked turning to hysteria. One moment she was terrified to put a foot wrong, paralysed with fear of the next outburst and then the next moment, she'd be suffocated by suppressed giggles when Bill bounced around like a temperamental bald baby. She thought he would erupt when getting her pen to work one morning she accidentally flicked ink on his white jeans. She tried to gag her laughter but it was that irrepressible, inappropriately timed laughter – the kind that out of nowhere turned into tears of mirth – which sprayed from her eyes like a sprinkler.

'It is not fucking funny, Esme. I got these jeans in Capri. Takes me two hours to get the zip up with a coat hanger and now I have to change. After all that effort.'

Suki was looking at Esme when she said, 'They look cool now, Bill. Tie dye.'

Esme spat her coffee over her desk.

'Go... and... get... a... cloth,' said Suki like a mother to her child.

'Christ!' shrieked Bill. 'Look what you have done!'

He hopped around like he had walked through a hornets' nest, his sunglasses falling from his head and landing askew on his nose.

'Calm down, Bill, you're going to have a coronary!' said Suki, in hysterics.

Bill spun around and stood stock still, as if the music had

stopped. Hand on hip, right foot pointed forward in second position, sunglasses now on his chin. Esme braced herself for a storm. She picked up a bottle of Tippex with an expression that said, 'Shall we give it a try?'

'Give that to me,' he said, snatching it from her.

'I'll do it for you, Bill. You can't see the bits on your bum,' said Esme.

Bill bent over and offered his backside, tight as a drum in the white denim.

'I can see you have done that before,' said Suki, suggestively.

'Shut up, Suki,' said Bill, still enraged.

Esme dabbed on the white paste, which worked a treat.

'I think we've invented a new way of dry cleaning. Look, Suki, you wouldn't even know Bill's bum had been spat on by an octopus,' said Esme, trying to make light of the situation, while internally praying this wasn't the last straw that might get her fired.

Suki came close and inspected Esme's handiwork. She grimaced at Esme as the ink began to bleed through, the chalky paste being no match for the density of the ink.

'Perhaps add another layer when this one has dried. Just to be sure,' said Suki.

Esme took a catalogue and began to fan Bill's bottom.

'Jesus. If Javier could see me now...' said Bill, beginning to see the funny side.

After the second coat, the stains were gone and the atmosphere went from red to amber alert.

Feeling guilty that she was the cause of Bill's raised blood pressure, Esme asked if he would like her to deliver the invitations.

'How good are you with a map?' he asked, handing her an *A-Z*.

Although most of London wasn't her stomping ground, she knew the majority of his clients lived in Kensington and Chelsea.

'I'll be fine. It will be good for me to learn my way around – for the next time,' she grinned, hopeful that Bill had forgiven her.

Bill returned her smile.

'If there is a next time, missy.'

'I really am sorry, Bill. I'd be furious if someone stained my favourite trousers,' she said, scooping up the pile of invites and putting them in a carrier bag. Giving him her most contrite look, she pecked him on the cheek.

'Maybe it was meant to be.' Bill said. 'If I'm honest, I was much smaller when I bought them. Perhaps you have done Javier a favour. He can have them.'

Esme didn't think Javier was the kind of man to be happy in cast-offs.

'Lucky Javier,' she said. 'His will be the first invite I drop off. Want me to take the jeans too?'

'Away with you, young lady. Make sure you get them all delivered today.'

Esme walked to Green Park Tube station, not looking forward to being swallowed underground on such a glorious day. The air was hot and in short supply as she bought her ticket with money she'd borrowed from the red petty-cash box. She felt sweat spring at the back of her neck and trickle down her spine. It was cool to the touch but warm on her skin. She could have taken enough money for a taxi – it wasn't like Bill or Suki ever even considered taking public transport – but her conscience wouldn't allow for such extravagance when this was meant to be a peace offering to Bill. Anyway, it would be quicker by Tube.

She had hated escalators ever since her laces had caught in one when she was a child. Her mother had pulled her shoe off just in time. It was the first step that was the worst and made her feel drunk going from inert concrete to moving metal with teeth. A man pushed past her, making her cling a little tighter to the handrail. She felt the wind of passing trains whip at her hair. It was filled with recycled grime and other people's breath. Holding her own until the air was still, she gingerly stepped off, her feet sticking to the ground. Like coming off the ice wearing skates, the transition was abrupt. Esme had always been clumsy and uncoordinated; Mrs Bee claimed it was because her legs were too long to control, 'like saplings,' she said. At least they weren't tree trunks, she supposed, but they had sustained multiple injuries, a series of twisted ankles and a litany of grazed knees and elbows.

Looking along the platform, advertisements lined the walls. There was one that stood out to her – announcing an exhibition at the Wallace Collection, *The Laughing Cavalier* by Frans Hals prominent in its layout. Her father said the gallery was the best-kept secret in London. She had always wanted to go and if the preview went well, perhaps she would treat herself to a visit. She made a mental note to ask Bill more about it.

She moved towards the tracks holding the invitations close, wanting to feel relevant but knowing that she had a long way to go before she felt a true part of this city. She knew her first task was to become a useful, if not vital cog in Bill's business. But what then? Among the five or so people waiting for the train she felt as though she floated in the emptiness, loose and boundary-less, waiting for a kind of certainty to kick in. It didn't. Instead, she was suddenly more unsure than ever, stuck between this new life and the one she'd left behind. She stared at the Tube map next to her, and spotting Camden further north, she remembered Cece and wished she'd called her. She needed all the friends she could get.

The rumble of an oncoming train was magnified in sunken confinement. It felt deafening. An assault on her senses, pushing all available air into the dark chasm ahead like a syringe being prepped for use. It was eleven o'clock, the rush hour was over and Esme stepped into an all but empty carriage. A lone old man looked at her as if she had trespassed onto his property. He shook his newspaper in protest, peering over the pages at her with furious eyes. This was the kind of passive-aggressive behaviour she recognized in her father, typical of the old guard who believed they had automatic ownership of everything, even public transport. Esme could see this man was part of that tribe by his shoes. They were polished hand-made leather. Esme could tell a lot by a man's shoes. Pointy toes belonged the cocksure. Brown shoes in the city, new money. Boots not to be trusted at all. Newspaper man was grumpy but harmless.

She sat down and checked the map. She'd be at South Kensington in three stops. The plastic bag was heavy and sweated on her knee. Hand-printed and embossed with the gallery logo, the invites were made up in thick gold-edged card; 'stiffies' nearly capable of cracking flagstones upon delivery. Bill spared no expense when it came to first impressions, and for all his flare-ups and stress, he knew exactly what was needed to satisfy his highfaluting clientele.

Back at ground level, she pulled out her *A-Z* and mapped her delivery route. Most of the addresses were in three pockets: SW1, SW7 and W8. If she was organized she could get the drop done in a couple of hours. Deciding where to go first, she chose to face her ghosts and picked the most familiar of all the addresses.

Upon entering Pelham Place, she was sorry that the cherry blossom was over. In spring, the street floated in a cloud of softest pink. It was strange walking down a street that her family was no longer a part of. She hadn't been back there since the house had been sold some eight years ago but it was so familiar that she still knew every crack in each paving stone and remembered how she used to skip over them to avoid bad luck.

The stucco houses were three-storey with low ceilings. Unostentatious compared to some in the borough, relatively small but very pretty with their sash windows and polished doorknobs gleaming against black lacquered doors. There were no rogue residents in Pelham Place. No dusty net curtains or dirty windows. Everyone who lived here had a primary home in the countryside. The houses weren't big enough for full-time occupation by the kind of families that picked Pelham Place as their London address. There was no competitive planting in the front garden and most instead had tamed roses, lavender and box in lead urns. Subtle colour schemes and architectural shapes were ideally suited to the formality of this moneyed borough – restrained yet expensive.

Number 6 sat next to Cecil Beaton's old house. When she was a child, he would doff his fedora at her and ask after her teddy bear, Gelatin, when she was playing in the front garden. Once, a very beautiful guest put a copy of *The Tale of Peter Rabbit* in her pram. Inside she had written, 'To a sweet cherub. With my love. Vivien Leigh.' One day Esme hoped she would give it to her own children.

She was suddenly consumed by nostalgia for that lost little girl, whose mother could be seen cooking through the window, who spent winter days home sick from school reading Enid Blyton and sucking menthol cough drops. There was a trace of herself in this street, where she had felt comfortable and secure; where her mother had been the verdant version of her now-withered self. An aching familiarity made her feel she was still nine. Sweeties, splinters, bikes and buttered toast. Tangled hair, dirty feet, Simon and Garfunkel and bed by seven thirty. But with the bittersweet wave of sentiment came frustration, too. She was in London now to create new memories. Yet she couldn't escape the pull of the past, her memory dwelling on the happy times, making it harder to move on.

Two people living on the street had been invited to the opening and Esme put invites through their respective doors. Unable to restrain her nostalgia, she peered through the last letterbox, belonging to the parents of a girl who was at school with her. She'd often spend happy days there. As she peered through, her narrow view of black-and-white tiles was the perfect study for painting in perspective. Then a pair of chunky calves in sturdy shoes came into sight and a duster brushed against pink-and-white stripes and a starched apron. A housekeeper never wore a uniform in the countryside, even at Culcairn, but it was acceptable and indeed expected in townhouses for your maid to don a work outfit that screamed 'servitude'. Esme thought this was fine in a hotel but pretentious and demeaning in a home. Embarrassed, she stood up and rang the doorbell.

'Rosa!' said Esme, giving the woman who opened the door a hug before she had time to get over her surprise.

'Esme! I didn't expect to see you again.'

At the start of school holidays when she spent a few days in London en-route to the Highlands, Esme often popped into number 11. At first she'd come to see her friend, but soon she visited even when the family wasn't there. *Especially* when the family wasn't there. To see Rosa and taste her halo-halo, an exotic concoction of shaved rice and purple yam ice-cream.

'What are you doing here?'

Esme held up the envelope addressed to 'J Richardson Esq'.

'Are you having a ball for your twenty-first?'

Trust Rosa and her good taste. She immediately knew that the envelope held an invitation to an event worth attending.

'I wish! I'm twenty-two now. It's for a gallery opening,' said Esme, placing the invite on the hall table. 'Is Anna home?'

'Sadly not. She would have loved to have seen you.'

'Shame. Would you mind if I grabbed some water? It's so hot out there.'

'Come. Come,' said the maid, closing the door behind Esme. 'And I've just made some spring rolls. You look like you need some flesh on your bones.'

Esme sat at the kitchen table and allowed Rosa to fuss over

her. As she bit into the crisp pastry skin, she remembered she hadn't eaten properly for twenty-four hours.

'Oh my goodness, these are delicious, Rosa,' she said, wiping flakes from her mouth and reaching to pick up a second.

'May I have another one? But I don't want to scoff all your lunch.'

Rosa laughed and piled another batch onto the plate.

'No problem! Mr and Mrs Richardson are having fish pie for dinner. No one likes my spicy food. Too scared,' she said, rolling her eyes.

'They don't know what they are missing.'

After she'd finished her exotic titbits, Esme took a gulp of water, and rose and said, 'I don't want to be rude, Rosa, but I have to get going. Got lots of these things to deliver by the end of the day, but at least I won't faint from hunger now. It was lovely to see you again.'

'I'll be sure Mr and Mrs get the letter. Come see me again when you want some proper food. Anytime, Esme.' She pronounced Esme's name with an elongated 'e' at the end.

'I'll definitely take you up on that, Rosa. Thank you.'

As she stepped out onto the street, for a moment it was like she was back in her old life. Her childhood rhythms of town and country houses, maids and balls, felt reassuring and familiar. But she knew the door had closed on that carefree world. The money that had paid for the lavish addresses and parties had been poured into care home bills and her father's locked-down warehouse of untouched treasures. The home she still had, The Lodge, was filled now with little more than memories of loss and infidelity. The house of cards might have fallen, but she realized she was luckier than most. She had a chance to build a new life. She just had to not blow it. She reopened her *A-Z* with new resolve.

With the bulk of the invitations left to drop off around Eaton Square, Esme took a short-cut down Pavilion Road to get onto Sloane Street. The cobbles made a passing car sound like it had a puncture, rubber flapping on stone. The uneven stones were an accident waiting to happen with her uncoordinated gait. Although her shoes were flat, she felt her ankle go on two or three occasions, the last time painful enough to make her stop. She put her bag on the ground and rubbed her leg. She was outside a shop and she realized she recognized the dresses that adorned the mannequins in the window. The designer was familiar from her mother's wardrobe. Many of the shops had sales on at this time of year but not this one. Their clientele had no need for cut prices.

Too young and too scruffy to be a customer, she went in anyway – partly to escape the heat momentarily but more because the dresses took her back to the days when her mother would let her play in her wardrobe while she dressed, when she would transform herself into the belle of any ball. The saleswoman immediately gave her a look that said, 'You're wasting my time.' She had a tape measure draped around her shoulders and a spray of pins clamped in her teeth. Seeing that Esme was going nowhere, she took the pins out and asked, 'Can I help you?' like she was talking to a tradesman.

'Not really. I just wanted to have a look,' said Esme, putting the last of the invites on the counter so she could feel the delicate fabric of the dresses, artfully arranged around the hushed interior of the shop.

'We are Belleville Sassoon. We are not open to the public, dear,' said the woman coldly.

Esme was already running her hands through the rails of silk.

'This is a shop, isn't it?'

The woman huffed which Esme translated as 'not for people like you'.

'Well… but if one of our customers comes in…'

'I'll have to leave?' finished Esme. 'I only want to look. My mother shops here.' She held up a bold paisley-patterned gown with blouson sleeves.

The woman came forward to retrieve the dress but not before glancing and raising an eyebrow at the stack of envelopes that had slid out from Esme's bag. Most of the invitations had titled names above their Westminster addresses.

'Oh? And who is your mama? I know all our lovely customers,' she said, her voice softening now.

'Diana Munroe.'

Instantly, the assistant went from suspicious to charm personified. 'How silly of me! You look just like her! I haven't seen her in an age. Is she well?'

'Yes, she is, thank you.' The fib rolled all too easily off her tongue.

'I haven't seen her in here for over a year now. I hope she hasn't forgotten about us. I have some gorgeous pieces that would look divine on her.'

'Ah, yes. She's been travelling. With my father.'

'Lucky girl. Tell her Miriam says hello,' said Miriam.

The shop was more of a showroom than a retail store. Esme saw now that all the clothes were samples that could

94

be made to measure. There was one of each design. Quality not quantity.

'What do you do if a lady isn't a sample size and can't fit into these?'

She wanted Miriam to know that she wasn't unaccustomed to expensive shopping.

'Our ladies have a toile that can be adapted to any style. If they are new we take their measurements and make one up for them in calico. Our most faithful customers have their own dressmaker dummy in their exact size.' She gave Esme the once over. 'You could fit into the samples, though.'

'I could?'

Miriam looked furtively around the shop. 'Seeing as we are having a bit of a lull, why don't we try something on?'

Nepotism talks and tempers change. Esme was no longer a face without provenance.

'I can't afford to buy anything,' she said, strangely proud of being broke. There was a liberation in coming right out with it rather than covering and blustering – though had she confirmed the obvious a few minutes ago, she knew Miriam would have thrown her out. Instead, she was clearly still thinking of the vast sums her mother must have spent here on account.

'Don't be silly. It will be fun and Monsieur Sassoon will be delighted to see one of his creations on such a stunning young lady. Such a talented man.'

Her large bosom swelled under her grey cashmere twinset that matched her chignon. She was elegant in a stylish governess kind of way. North of fifty-five and in good shape, her pencil skirt showed a firm bum and great calves. Lifting her horn-winged spectacles on her head she took a dress off the rail

95

and walked it across the minimalist expanse of the showroom floor and hung it in a changing room.

'Size 8,' she said, holding the door open for Esme. 'I'll be right outside if you need anything.'

The changing room wasn't your usual abattoir with a skimpy modesty curtain and strip-lighting. Belleville Sassoon boasted an opulent chamber with a door that locked from the inside; more opium den than sartorial slaughterhouse. A chaise longue was pushed up against one wall, its aged red velvet glowed rather than shone like the cheap stuff used for modern upholstery. The mirror was framed in carved, gilded wood and two sultry fringed lanterns hung either side, their low voltage making the old look young and the young look old enough to be considering high-end fashion. A chiffon square was provided to protect the clothes from heavily made-up faces and a selection of nude heels in various sizes lined the skirting.

'Do you need help with the zip, dear?' Miriam said through the keyhole. Was she peeping?

Esme had slipped the dress on but was struggling to do it up. Even undone Esme could tell it was expertly cut. It was as soft as butterfly wings with the colours of peacock feathers. She put on a pair of shoes and floated out of the changing room feeling like mutton dressed as lamb.

Miriam gave a staged look of one who had seen a spirit and was having an attack of the vapours, fanning herself with a notebook.

'Who is this vision of loveliness?' she quizzed, her voice breathy as if in awe of what she was witnessing. In her hands, the zip slid up, smooth as molten wax.

Esme was sure this was a reaction Miriam had practised over many years with hundreds of gullible patrons and would have been exactly the same had she been a seventy-year-old hunchback in a boiler suit.

'A heavenly princess from paradise,' said Esme, deciding to play along.

Whilst it was gossamer soft and beautifully made, the dress was too long, and too old. She had disappeared beneath the overpowering pattern and become a walking waterfall of silk georgette.

'I must summon Monsieur Sassoon from his atelier,' squealed Miriam, suddenly a Frenchwoman speaking pidgin English. '*Quelle surprise*, he will have!' She was now on tiptoes in her excitement.

'Oh, please don't bother him, Miriam. A maestro must not be distracted from his art. I'm sure he is far too busy creating his wondrous designs.'

Lowering her heels, Miriam looked a little deflated.

I've hurt her feelings, thought Esme. The poor woman clearly lives for her job, and worships the water Mr Sassoon walked on.

'You can tell him all about it and thank him from me for making the world a more beautiful place with his creations.'

Miriam rallied, 'That's exactly what I will tell him. He will be gracious as always when he receives such compliments.' She smiled as if the compliment was for her. 'But perhaps I might take a picture of you?'

She was already pointing the camera at Esme with her finger poised and ready above the shutter-release button.

'Pull your shoulders back, stomach in and put your weight on your back leg.'

Draw, suck, step, click, clunk, whir.

The Polaroid camera idly extricated its photograph and Miriam pinned it under her cashmere-clad armpit.

'It processes more quickly if you warm it up. One of the many things I have learnt from Monsieur.'

I'm sure, thought Esme. Bet he shits gold too – the woman's sycophantic idolization now wearing thin. But she was anxious to see the photo. To see herself as others might; how she looked glammed up – albeit in the wrong dress. Had she changed since arriving in London? Would her budding confidence be evident? Would she look more cultivated? Even if she hadn't changed on the outside yet, she could tell things were shifting within. She just hoped this was self-awareness and not self-obsession.

Miriam checked the photograph, slowly peeling back the processing paper. Holding it at arm's length, she let out a contented sigh.

'Very lovely, Miss Munroe. I think we should take some more.'

'May I have a look?'

She hardly recognized herself; a skinny, self-assured blonde wearing an extortionately priced dress like she owned it. Before she had time to respond, Miriam had wheeled out a demi-rail with five or six more dresses for her to try on. More posing, more clicking, more Polaroids each as sophisticated as the last, more exclamations of approval from Monsieur's disciple.

When Esme finally emerged from the changing room back in her own clothes – which now felt shabbier than ever – Miriam was pulling down the grilles on the windows.

'Goodness,' said Esme, 'is it five thirty already?'

'Indeed it is. And I believe these are still yours?' Miriam held up the bag of invites.

'Shit.'

The manageress's eyebrow rose.

'I have to run but thank you so much. It's been such fun.'

But Miriam was already putting on her coat and didn't give her a second glance.

Esme closed the door behind her, deflated that her vanity had allowed her to be distracted from the task Bill had given her. He had said he wanted all the invites delivered before dinner and she had no idea how she was going to manage in time. She looked in the bag and tried to count how many were left, panic rising.

'Twice in one day. What are the chances of that?'

A grinning Rosa stood before her laden with shopping bags from Partridge's, the exclusive delicatessen on Sloane Street.

'Are you all right? You look like you've had a shock,' she said.

'Oh, Rosa, I don't know where the time went and I've got all these invitations to deliver but I'm not sure where any of the houses are.' She felt embarrassed – like she was a schoolgirl again, panicking about being late with her homework.

'Let me have a look.' Rosa put down her shopping and pushed her hands into the small of her back, stretching before rifling through the envelopes. 'Quite a few of these addresses are on my way home. I can take most of them for you.'

'Oh Rosa, would you?' Something about Rosa's offer made her feel less of a failure and her embarrassment turned to gratitude.

'Of course. Just make sure you come and visit me again soon.'

Esme hugged her. 'I will, I promise I'll come very soon.'

She hugged her again and helped to load her up with the

carrier bags including her own and watched the small woman set off at a brisk pace.

'Thank you, Rosa. You've saved my life,' she shouted after her. In reply Rosa lifted the bags in her right hand.

It was people like Rosa and Mrs Bee that kept the world turning, thought Esme. Not people like her getting stuck on posting a few invitations, or Miriam and her frocks that probably cost more than Rosa's annual salary. Thinking of Mrs Bee, she suddenly longed for her mothering ways. Deciding that if she couldn't have Mrs Bee with her, the next best thing would be to make her proud, and not get fired. She picked up the few remaining invitations that hadn't been on Rosa's route home. If she could either be like Miriam or like Rosa, she knew who she'd choose. She set off into the summer's evening.

Chapter Seven

Art had always been Esme's escape – paintings took her to a place where she didn't feel lonely. At Cartwright Fine Art, she was living and breathing art on a daily basis but her loneliness still seemed to taint everything. Work, eat (sometimes), sleep, repeat. The days played out with little variety. She knew she was fortunate on many counts with a job and place to live, but she felt alone. Suki was yet to ask her out and to be fair, Esme hadn't exactly encouraged an invitation. But if things carried on like this, she would have to park her ambitions for an alternative social life, get over her fear of rejection and make the most of the one person – Sloane Ranger or not – with whom she was able to pursue a friendship.

Esme didn't want to admit that she was lonely. She could make jokes about it, of course. She had written to her sister and told Sophia that she was spending all of her days and nights working and that she hadn't left the office in days because she was chained to her desk because Bill was a hysterical slave driver. It all sounded very funny on paper. But she didn't want to divulge the true depths of her loneliness, or admit that she felt more and more alienated each passing day and she wasn't sure how to fix it.

She wanted to be less scared, less anxious, and be the best she could at her job but still have a social life. Right now, she felt like she was vanishing into the madness of pre-preview nerves. She longed to meet all kinds of different people, perhaps even to wake up in a stranger's bed once or twice just to see if it felt good to feel nothing. More than anything she wanted a group of friends that felt like a tribe, a bona fide family. She wanted to go from one place to the next constantly and have her weekends feel like one long epic day.

When Javier popped by the gallery at lunchtime, he told her to stop complaining and call Cece.

'But she said she would call *me*.'

'Are you still a little girl, Esme?'

No, she wasn't and she knew she sounded like a petulant child.

'I'm too embarrassed,' she admitted.

It was true. She had thought about asking him for Cece's number but didn't want to appear desperate, to make the first move. She knew she was being pathetic and behaving like a teenager with a crush but building friendships didn't come naturally to her. She often felt intimidated by new people, especially if they were cool like Cece.

'She really liked you, Esme. Said you seemed like you had a story to tell,' he said and wrote on a bit of paper which he handed to her. 'Call her. She'll still be at home.'

The office was empty and, taking a deep breath, Esme dialled the number. It answered immediately.

'Hello?'

'Hi, Cece. It's Esme. We met the other night with Javier.'

'Esme! So pleased you rang. I lost your number and haven't got around to asking Javs for it again. How you doing?'

'Oh, you know. Busy.' Shit. Why did she say that?

'Don't I know it.' Cece laughed. 'Listen. What are you up to tomorrow arvo? I'm going to Camden Market. Why don't you come?'

There was no way Bill would let her off early unless he was going away for the weekend and wanted to miss the Friday rush hour. But she couldn't say no.

'That sounds great. I'd love to.'

She'd work it out and surely Bill owed her a favour after all the overtime she'd done.

'Fantastic. Shall we meet at the Tube station at, say, one?'

'Sure. See you tomorrow.'

Esme replaced the receiver, realizing she had no idea how long it would take her to get to Camden Market. She hadn't asked, not wanting to sound like a total idiot. Suki might know. Bill definitely would but she was too scared to ask him. But she was excited. She had been saved from eternal isolation.

'Suki?'

Suki was at her desk shovelling what smelt like a tuna and sweetcorn sandwich in her mouth.

'That smells foul.'

Suki smiled, her mouth full. She raised a hand, sped up her chewing and swallowed.

'You have no idea how delicious this is,' she said, wiping her mouth. 'Want a bite?'

'No, Suki, it reeks.'

'Your loss,' she said, taking another huge bite.

Esme spotted a tube of Smarties on Suki's desk and reached for one but Suki slapped her hand on the packet.

'No pudding until you've eaten your main course,' said Suki, between mouthfuls.

'You're so mean,' said Esme, ignoring her and sliding her finger into the packet of sweets. She prayed for an orange one.

'How far is Camden Market?'

'It's North London somewhere. Not my scene. A sort of hippy dippy place,' said Suki, giving a peace sign. 'Bill will know.'

She shouted to Bill, who was somewhere out back. Esme wasn't ready to have her Friday truancy revealed yet. She needed to plan a strategy.

'Bill! Esme wants to know about Camden Market,' Suki yelled.

Bill appeared looking flustered. 'Why on earth do you want to know about Camden?'

'I was thinking of going.'

Not wanting to let on about Cece, that was all she could think of to say.

'Dirty, full of stoners and punk rockers. Not the kind of place your parents would want you to go.'

Perfect, thought Esme, but she would have to think of a plausible lie to get off at lunchtime the next day.

'Sounds awful,' she said. 'I think I'll give it a miss. Just as well I asked you.' She turned back to her work hoping an excuse would come to her.

With diplomatic handling and a long day of intense servitude, the girls had calmed Bill down to Gale Force 3 by the time five o'clock came. Esme was used to walking on eggshells at home, but she was exhausted and gratefully accepted Suki's offer to go for a drink. She tried to be casual, but inside she was fizzing. Two invitations to go out places. To see people and finally get to know London beyond Bill's domain.

'A bunch of us are meeting at The Antelope, you should come too. We need it after all those histrionics,' Suki said, putting on her lipstick. 'I love Bill but sometimes I want to murder him. All that fuss over nothing yesterday.'

'He's probably nervous. And at least we're organized,' reasoned Esme. 'But yes. A vat of wine would go down well.'

Esme was particularly pleased by Suki's invitation, as she'd wondered if she resented her being at the gallery. Suki had managed perfectly well before her arrival and could easily be put out by Bill treating Esme as his new protégée. She hoped this invitation meant Suki had decided they were a team rather than rivals.

The pub was in Chelsea and just round the corner from one of the invitations Esme had dropped off. She could hear the braying voices of the drinkers from the street and a crowd of pinstripe and pearls greeted her inside. Suki took her by the hand and introduced her to a few of her friends then disappeared to the bar.

'Wine?' she shouted over her shoulder.

Esme gave the thumbs up.

'How d'you know Suks?' asked a small girl with round eyes and pageboy haircut. 'Were you in Verbier with her?'

'Er, no. I work with her at the gallery,' replied Esme.

'I must ask Suki if she's doing next season. Nice to meet you.'

And with that the girl turned away to talk to someone else. Esme found a patch of wall and leant against it, making an effort to look purposefully stranded. The couple next to her were talking about weekend plans and she tried to introduce herself but lost her nerve when they didn't even pause for breath. Suki hadn't left the bar and was laughing with a bunch of friends. Any normal person would barge over and gatecrash the jolly assembly, she supposed, but Esme was too shy. She had always found it easier to get along with the older generation; felt less judged. These people came from the same family background as her, she guessed, but she couldn't have felt more out of place than if she had been on Mars. Trying to blend in to the background, she couldn't wait to get away. When Suki finally returned and thrust a glass of wine into her hand, Esme didn't even have a chance to say a thing before she turned back to the bar and the crowd of friends gathered there.

Esme necked her wine as quickly as she could then, not wanting to embarrass Suki, caught her eye and cheerily waved goodbye.

'See you tomorrow,' mouthed Suki, blowing her a kiss.

Once again, Esme gave the thumbs up and left.

Chapter Eight

The smell caught and coalesced in Esme's nostrils. Unidentifiable spices, exotic scents mixed with the mundane. Tarmac and sweat, garlic and ginger with musky overtones. A far cry from The Lodge kitchen that smelt of her childhood, all Delia Smith recipes, coal tar soap and the occasional whiff of dog blankets.

A clock stuck on the side of a graffiti-covered building told her she had time to kill before meeting Cece.

It wasn't wholly a lie that had got her here. The words 'wealthy' and 'art collector' had been fibs, but 'Australian' and her meeting location were accurate. Securing a prospective buyer in the art world was never guaranteed but as she knew from dealers who contacted her father when they had something to his taste, it was always worth the punt. But although Bill didn't know that what lay beneath her request for the afternoon off was a lie, she did and she felt guilty. He had been so generous to her, not least with his friendship, but he was more her parents' generation than her own and she was desperate to make friends her own age. And, she reminded herself, she had been working her tits off.

All her senses told her she was entering a hub of integration and multi-culturalism. Foreign languages crossed swords in the air, their tone urgent and purposeful. This was the sound of commerce, tradesmen making what money they could from people who, by the looks of them, had precious little. All genres of music were playing, the beats clashing, representing the variety of mods, rockers and punks loitering with no intent other than to pose. Pink Floyd and Peter Tosh boomed from stalls manned by hippies and Rastafarians hawking mysterious ingredients.

To Esme, it was a heady, eye-opening place. She knew Bill and Suki would shudder at the fast-food containers that spilt out of rubbish bags yet to be collected. The putrid waste boiling in the heat and discarded boxes from the stalls were punctuated by small groups of punks sitting on the pavement, rolling cigarettes. It was a far cry from St James's. But she didn't see the dilapidation, rather the opportunity. It was a new side of life to experience. The boys wore as much black eyeliner edging their lips and eyes as the girls. Their Mohicans stood rigid as weapons. It occurred to Esme that they were dressed for the battlefield of social alienation. Were they really as angry as they looked or just making an empty assertion to get noticed?

Esme felt completely out of place. A foreigner in her city of birth. It was at once intimidating and exciting. Dressed in her conservative clothes, it was she who stood out as the minority. Everyone around her was cool, a cacophony of fashion statements defined by music. Everyone was part of a clique and she worried that she would be held up as some kind of fraud. She was beginning to feel a sense of rising panic. Looking around she wondered which clique she could join and what one garment might transform her? There were stalls selling hippy flares, leather jackets, ripped T-shirts, slogan T-shirts, platform boots and battered Dr Martens. A cheesecloth dress looked like the best option and easiest to slip over what she was wearing. She could put her dated jeans in a bag and pray no one noticed her stubbled legs.

She rifled through a rail capped by dust and chose a frock in a small floral print with a smocked bodice. It had balloon sleeves and tiny buttons down the front.

'How much is this, please?' she asked a young man bare-chested beneath an open waistcoat which revealed multiple bead necklaces and a peace sign pendant. He flicked his long hair and looked at her as if she was an audience member in a crowd of adoring fans.

'Two quid, man,' he replied, holding out a ring-encrusted hand.

With diminishing resources and her salary yet to be paid, every coin that left her purse brought Esme closer to the shame of having to ask her father for a loan. Although even if she had known exactly where in France he was, she was determined not to turn to him for help – she didn't want him to think she'd failed at her bid to stand on her own two feet. Esme counted coins and handed the stallholder the money, which he in turn totted up.

'Need another penny.'

Surly git, thought Esme. And as she looked in vain for somewhere to get changed, she realized she was about as far away from the luxe changing rooms of Belleville Sassoon as she could get. She ducked behind a rail of clothes but it gave her precious little cover.

She put the dress on over her T-shirt and reaching underneath, she undid her zip and slithered out of the trousers, careful not to reveal any more flesh than was absolutely necessary. It was a bold move, but worthwhile. Dressed as she had been, she'd felt more exposed than she did now.

'Jerry'll buy those jeans off you if you wanna sell them. His stall is two down. Karma boutique.'

With her jeans around her ankles, she looked at the stallholder, embarrassed that he had seen her undress. She quickly kicked the trousers off over her shoes, grateful for their wide legs.

'Oh?' She felt herself redden.

'You're not from here, are you?' He'd clearly marked her as a tourist.

'Is it that obvious?' Esme replied, relieved to have the attention diverted from her fumbling attempt to get changed.

'Yeah. Your skin is too clear to be a London girl.'

Well, at least it wasn't her gauche demeanour or unfashionable get-up that gave her away. But as he sized her up his attention now seemed slightly sleazy.

'I live in London, actually,' she said, gathering herself to move on.

'If ever you want to do some modelling, here's my card.'

He handed her a flyer saying 'Models Wanted', above a photograph of two girls sucking lollipops. It was clearly suggestive and not a fast track to *Vogue*. Esme didn't know what to say or how to rebuke the offer. Given her awkward semi-striptease to get into the dress, she felt like she had asked for this. The man obviously assumed she would be more than willing to get her kit off for money. Shame flooded her. She gave the flyer back.

'I'll take that, thank you, asshole.'

The paper was swiped from her hand and torn in two. It was Cece.

'This guy, Esme, is a sordid pig-fuck' – she leant over the trestle table laden with clothes, her face inches from his – 'get lost, loser.' Then she turned back to Esme. 'Come on, let's get out of here.'

Wow. How did Cece have the balls to do that? She looked like a woman not to be messed with. Esme hadn't recognized her at first because her hair had changed colour. She had dyed it black and worn it gelled at the sides and swirled into a Mr Whippy quiff. Her pale skin glowed in contrast. The bib of her denim dungarees worked hard to cover her bare breasts partially on display through a string vest. Dressed in her smock – which a moment ago seemed like her ticket to blending in – Esme felt dowdy. She looked back at the 'sordid pig-fuck' and was given a wink and lick of his lips. Revolting man.

'How have you been, hon? It's great to see you,' said Cece giving her a hug.

'Busy. Had to lie to leave work early. But I'm so glad I did. This place is wild!'

Her enthusiasm seemed make little impression on the worldly Australian. This was clearly Cece's natural habitat – rebellion was in her DNA. Esme wondered how long it had taken for Camden to become Cece's normal and if there would ever be a time for her when London would feel as familiar as the Scottish Highlands.

'Christ, me too. Haven't had a day off since I saw you. But last night I went to bed before the sun came up, so all is good.'

The two girls continued down the high street. The people,

the beats, the dirt, the pulsating vibe made Esme feel alive. But more than anything, she got a kick out of sharing it with someone.

The sun was blistering and heat rose from the pavement, which despite the lack of rain still had puddles of God-knows-what collecting in small potholes. It was either water from cracked pipes or the juice of rotting fruit and veg seeping from bin liners. The artery of residential streets that fed off left and right looked derelict at first glance but she soon saw signs that they were densely packed. How could this be the same city that provided upmarket townhouses for her friends and manicured mews cottages with clip-hedged window boxes for Bill and his crowd?

She looked at the houses – pretty but in need of repair – with bicycles fighting for space outside and discarded shopping trolleys propped up against railings. Most of the cars looked like they had seen better days with many of their windscreens wallpapered with parking tickets. There were few people on the street but the noise of cohabitation clattered out of windows.

It occurred to her that money silenced a neighbourhood. Kensington and Chelsea were so quiet. Camden was so loud. Sirens blaring, people shouting, car doors slamming, stereos thumping. There was someone, somewhere, making noise at all times.

'Who lives here?' said Esme when her eye was caught by a wheel-less van propped up on bricks.

'Squatters and smack addicts mainly. But also musicians and poets. We'll go to Dingwalls one night.'

Esme had heard of Dingwalls, the infamous music venue

where fights broke out as often as bands played. Whilst The Clash and The Sex Pistols' music wasn't her thing, she would have loved to have seen Debbie Harry.

They stopped at a stall selling more clothes.

'Gotta be honest with you, Es. You need some new pieces. Have you been paid yet? This place sells some great stuff.'

'Oi. What about this?' she replied looking down at the new purchase.

'It's fine… but hardly cool.'

Esme ran her hands down the rough fabric of her smock. She wanted to be more like Cece but was her world too different from hers? How could she combine the two? On the one hand she was working in a job that required respectable conformity but on the other, she desperately wanted to break from her stuffy society roots. Could she be two people rolled into one? Was it possible to pull off two sides to her story? The country girl felt like her authentic self and had taken a lifetime to crystallize. But the life she had had in the country had disintegrated. It was time to work out who the adult version of her was to be. Could she fast-track the urbanite version of her in a genuine way? Could she pull off 'girl about town'?

The quickest way to do this was through clothes, she decided. They were the most effective conduit to project your desired image for the day. With expert speed, Cece gathered a selection of pieces that Esme had no time to identify. They could have been dishcloths or couture. But instinctively she trusted this girl to choose the right thing for her, to take her out of her comfort zone. Despite Cece taking control, Esme didn't feel she was judging her. Far from it. Cece seemed to be enjoying her role as stylist.

'I'll give you two quid for this lot,' she told the stall owner.

'You on drugs?'

'No. Two quid. Take it or leave it. That's two quid more than you had twenty seconds ago. Doubt you'll sell any more of this shit today.'

'Come on, love. You've got at least ten quids' worth there. Call it a fiver.'

'Three quid, and I'll buy you a drink at the Palace,' Cece said, pulling a Tesco bag from a patchwork sack hanging across her body and stuffing the clothes into it.

She handed the money over and told the guy she would see him soon, before he had time to protest. Instead he rolled his eyes and smiled.

'Tequila shot, Cece.'

Cece laughed and gave the man a hug.

'Thanks, Trev. I'll buy you three.'

They knew each other? What was all that bartering about? The haggling must have been for Esme's benefit and she felt bemused that Cece had put on this show. Was this how business was done? Would guests at Bill's show try to beat down the cost? She doubted it as they'd frown upon haggling, too embarrassed it might give the impression of a dwindling trust fund. She would never have had the nerve to pay anything other than the asking price. Especially here where people were on the economic backfoot.

'Don't look so shocked, Esme!' Cece said. 'It's how we do things here. Trevor knew perfectly well I wasn't going cough up more than a few notes. But he is always going to try to get the best price and I will always beat him down. I got a boxful of bootleg tapes last week for 50p. Same price as a cup of tea.'

Esme wasn't shocked, just cross that earlier she had parted with two pounds without complaint. Determined to show Cece there was metal in her bones, she went up to the next stall and swooped with a magpie's eye for a shocking pink sequined jacket.

She gave the bearded vendor a crumpled note.

'Four pounds back, please,' she said with gravel in her voice.

Cece looked at her with one brow arched and a smirk. She folded her arms, clearly enjoying Esme putting her example into practice.

'One fifty.'

Esme glanced at Cece who gave subtle nod.

'Thanks.'

'Fuck, Esme! That was amazing. Let me look at that,' she said, taking the bolero from her to look at the label.

'You do realize this is Biba. Good as new too. Bargain!'

She may have straw coming from her ears but just for a moment Esme felt like she had won the Pools. Using her mother's account card at Harrods had never given her the same rush, even though the clothes at Way In on the top floor were selected for girls her age. There was no victory, no bargain in buying clothes from London's premier department store and anyway, she doubted that anyone with an ounce of street style had ever set foot in Harrods.

'Have you been to Biba?' she asked Cece.

'Yes, its super-cool but I prefer Kensington Market, it's cheaper and has great make-up. I got my tattoo there. Its next door to Biba where I'll go for a coffee. The café is like a psychedelic garden and you sit on giant toadstools.'

'Really? Sounds fun.'

'We'll have to go sometime. It's great for people-watching too. Do you have a boyfriend, by the way?'

'Not at the moment. Had one but he dumped me a while back. You?'

'Yes and no. I'm working on it.'

Esme was certain Cece would have boys queuing up to go out with her – and, she imagined she'd mix with the kind of men she herself hoped to meet. A singer/songwriter or fashion photographer. That was the kind of boyfriend she wanted. Someone her parents would disapprove of. There was no way she wanted to end up as a customer-service wife. She didn't want to play second fiddle to a man. He'd have to be supportive of her career and not just want to get hitched in order to produce an heir. To be honest, it didn't matter if he was a toff but she was too young to worry about getting married. For now, she wanted to have fun – she'd make it clear she wasn't after her parents' idea of an eligible bachelor, and the fastest way of doing this was surely to have a provocative boyfriend on her arm. Long hair, leather trousers and called Jim Morrison, that would be ideal. Him or David Bowie. Although even her father held a grudging appreciation for The Doors and had declared its lead singer 'worthy of being sculpted by Michelangelo'.

Cece's flat was on the first floor of white stucco house in Mornington Crescent. She had suggested Esme come back to try on her new clothes and have a play with make-up. If anyone else had suggested it, it might have sounded childish – like rummaging in a dressing-up box, but there was nothing backward-looking about Cece. Her Antipodean attitude was one of living for the day and making the best of every second. Esme found it easy to get swept up in her enthusiasm.

Her rented home had high ceilings and the faded grandeur of bygone times. Many of the original features remained. Tall windows opened onto a small balcony that looked over the crescent. It must have been salubrious once upon a time but the overground train line had tainted the paintwork grey. The whole place shook as the trains went by. Cece had made the most of what was essentially a studio, with a kitchenette, minuscule shower and a living room that doubled as her bedroom. Much of the contents had clearly been picked up at the market. Ethnic cushions, joss sticks held by a bronze Buddha and twinkly lampshades. In one corner, a mannequin wearing a top hat and feather boa teetered at an angle alongside a rail of clothes. Esme was struck by the myriad textures in Cece's wardrobe: silk, satin, nylon, corduroy, velvet, tweed, knits chunky and fine. Fur, voile and sequins. She wished she'd had the money to buy more at the market.

'Can I use your loo?'

'Sure, hon. I'm just going to nip to the bottle shop. What do you like to drink?'

'How about vodka and lime juice? You know, the cordial stuff?' suggested Esme.

'A gimlet. Remember you are talking to a waitress.'

'Wasn't sure if you had that in Australia.'

'It's not a feral outpost, love. We have moved with the times.'

Esme felt embarrassed, 'I didn't mean…'

'I'm teasing you, silly moo. Anyway, you're a Pom from the back of beyond and I'm an immigrant from the penal colonies.

Guess that makes us quits,' said Cece, wrapping a light scarf around her neck as she headed for the door, calling out, 'Won't be long,' as she slammed it behind her.

Esme still felt like she'd put her foot in it. Cece was way more worldly than she. The way she conducted herself with such confidence was won only through experience and having to stand on her own two feet. Esme had a way to go. She tried to picture Cece at Culcairn. It was not an obvious match. Cece was at home on the fringes. They both had what the other didn't.

Esme went to the bathroom. Cece's open make-up bag was a mess of shimmer and glitter in colours Esme wouldn't have thought to paint on a wall let alone her face. A half-used packet of contraceptive pills sat on the edge of the sink. She squeezed a blob of toothpaste onto her finger, still a little paranoid after Bill's remarks. It tasted old and chalky. She rubbed it into her teeth and rinsed, slooshing her face and back of her neck at the same time. It was hot and sticky. Her cheekbones had a cap of sunburn, as did the tip of her nose.

The minuscule kitchen area was stuffed with crockery and bags of spices. Three terracotta pots grew herbs on the window sill. She opened the window and jumped when a skewbald cat slunk into view and carefully tiptoed around the herbs and into the sink. It lapped at the water that dripped from a mixer tap. Esme hadn't noticed the opened tin of Whiskas next to the chives. She didn't like cats. Found them untrustworthy and sly. Mrs Bee had one, a serial bird-killer called Shifty. When it wasn't out murdering, it cleaned every inch of its body with its rough tongue. He still looked like a renegade. Mrs Bee adored him which was probably why Esme resented him. Ridiculous to be jealous of a cat. But she stroked the new arrival out of duty to Cece.

'I see you've met Dingo.'

Cece put two carrier bags down on the counter. One clanked and the other rustled.

'Yes. He seems very friendly.'

'He's not. Horrible thing. Real bastard. He humps all the females and gets them pregnant. Last year I had two litters in my garden.'

'You have a garden?'

Esme looked out of the window. She hadn't noticed the small patch of uncut grass and weeds out back. It was fenced by wooden slats topped with razor wire. The latch on the gate dangled from its hinges and was wedged open just wide enough to slither through from the mews that ran behind.

'More of a needle park. Keep meaning to do something with it or rather hoping that my neighbours will. If it looked nice, maybe smack-heads wouldn't use it to jack up.'

Whatever Cece was talking about sounded hardcore. Esme realized she had a lot to learn about this side of London life – not least the language.

'Why do you feed Dingo if you don't like him?'

'He's a good mouse-trap. Haven't seen one since he's started to hang out here.'

Cece pushed Dingo off the counter and took a bag of ice out.

'Grab two glasses,' she said, opening a cupboard.

Esme chose two tumblers and opened the Smirnoff. She poured a couple of fingers into both and topped them up with Rose's lime juice. Cece added the ice and stirred the drinks with her finger. The cordial swam in waves as it diluted the alcohol.

'I got some cheese and crackers too. And olives. Come on, let's sit on the balcony and watch the world go by.'

She took out two folding chairs and moved a side table between them for their drinks and 'nibbles'.

'Not much to see but nice to get the sun on our faces. I can't believe how hot it's been.'

She pulled up her skirt and stretched out her already tanned legs. Esme hoiked up her smock.

'Just take it off. No one will care and anyway all the opposite windows are too dirty to see through.'

It was true – and upon looking more closely it seemed that London's pollution had staked an indelible claim on all the glass and everything white, staining everything a dusty grey, including a washing line below, straining under the weight of five pairs of large pants and one enormous bra. Next to it, a woman balancing on her Zimmer frame struggled up the steps to her front door. She wore a floral print skirt with thick tights and slippers. Her cardigan fell off one shoulder. It was hard to see her face behind a mop of oily grey hair.

'Hi, Mabel!' shouted Cece.

'Evening, Cece,' Mabel shouted back gruffly.

'This is Esme. She's very posh and has never seen knickers as big as yours before.'

'*Cece!*' whispered Esme, quickly looking away.

'Need any help, Mabeline?'

'Fuck off, yer bleeding Aussie. I'm not dead yet,' she shouted.

Mabel struggled to find the lock with her key and kept dropping it.

'Urgh, it's painful to watch. I'm just going to let the old bat in. She'll hate me for it but will pass out if I don't, then we'll have to take her to A&E.' Cece crawled back inside and Esme heard her trotting down the stairs.

Esme watched as Cece took the keys from Mabel and helped her inside. As predicted, she shuffled on without so much as a thank you. Cece closed her knocker-less door by pulling the letterbox. But her return to the flat was interrupted by the arrival of a dented Ford Cortina.

The car pulled over and a cloud of smoke escaped the window, as a dark-haired man leant out with a cigarette hanging from his lips. It jiggled up and down as he spoke. Esme couldn't make out his features clearly but she could tell he was attractive. He looked like he owned the road – obviously not caring that a truck was honking at him to move on. Cece took the cigarette from his mouth, took a quick drag and dropped it on the road. Embers glinted on the tarmac before Cece stubbed it out with her heavy boot. She leant into the car and kissed him hard.

Beaming, Cece burst into the flat for the second time and sat down and sipped her now-watery gimlet. She lit a cigarette and exhaled quick words behind the billowing smoke.

'Guess what?'

'What? Who was that in the car?'

'Dan. The guy. My soon-to-be boyfriend. We've only snogged so far but…'

'How long have you known him?'

'Not long. He's a journalist. Reports for the local paper but he's a gifted writer. He's working on a novel. It's an incredible story and beautifully written. He showed me some of his poetry too.'

'A poet? Can't get more romantic than that, although I'd rather a musician. In a band.'

'Dan is very cool. Dreamy good-looking. He came by to say he wanted to go to Heaven tonight. I told him about you and said we can all go together. You have to come.'

'Heaven?'

'Yes. It's the coolest club in town.'

Esme reached for the packet of Silk Cut. 'Can I have one?'

'Sure. It doesn't get going there till at least eleven.' Cece took hold of Esme's hand and looked at her watch. 'That gives us hours to get ready.'

Esme's heart sank. She was in the same predicament as she had been with Javier. A tempting invitation but the sense that she'd be in at the deep end – with no idea about the place they were going to or what she should wear. Maybe she could try the sequined bolero she'd bought.

'Dan is going to meet us there.'

The idea of going out with a guy Cece fancied wasn't ideal. She'd be playing gooseberry as her partner in crime. Nerves curdled her hopes of conquering London's nightlife with her new friend but she swallowed them along with the last sip of her gimlet.

'Jump in the shower and I'll pick an outfit.'

When Esme returned, Cece had laid a selection of clothes on the sofa bed.

'Try this on,' she said, handing her a stretchy tube.

Esme headed towards the bathroom.

'You are a right prude, Esme. Change in here, I've got tits too, you know.'

Standing in her bra and pants, she pulled the tube over her

head, unsure if it was a top or a skirt. As she rolled it down her body she worked out it was a skin-clinging, off-the-shoulder dress. Esme felt as good as naked.

'Wow,' sighed Cece and passed her a pair of fishnets. 'What size feet do you have?'

'Five and a half.'

'Lucky... same as me. Try these for size.'

Esme put on the gold T-bar sandals and went to the mirror.

'No! Don't look yet. I want to do your make-up and hair first. Sit down.'

She did as bid and Cece set to work on her face. First came the foundation which Cece smeared and dabbed on her skin. Next, she pulled an alarming shade of turquoise from the make-up bag.

'Close your eyes.'

Esme felt slow careful brushstrokes colouring her lids.

'Keep them closed.'

The crease of her eye was lovingly tended by a smaller, softer brush that blended the eyeshadow.

'Half open your eyes.'

A mascara wand painted her lashes in thick sweeps. They felt wet and clumpy.

'Blink,' Cece ordered.

At first her lashes stuck together but they soon dried and she felt the tips prickle her skin.

'Pretend to kiss.'

Esme pouted as Cece applied blusher on her cheekbones and around her hairline.

'This sculpts the face.'

'How come you know how to do this, Cece?'

'I'm obsessed with make-up. See that board?'

It was the first time Esme noticed the cut-out magazine pages. A wall of photographs showing portraits of girls modelling all manner of make-up. Heavy, light, glowing, shimmering. Each was a mask of disguise. There was one shot which showed a before and after. The girl looked nothing like her natural self. Esme hoped for the same outcome.

'And now the lips. Smile.'

Esme stretched her lips over her teeth, not daring to breathe. Cece wielded a slippery wand of bright pink over her mouth, then smacked her lips together, beckoning Esme to do the same. She stood back and looked at her work.

'Oh my God, Esme, you are going to die!' she said, waving the lip-gloss like a baton.

'Can I look now?' Esme was dying to see the transformation.

'Not before I've done your hair. Just needs to be fucked up a bit. Won't take a sec.'

Grabbing a large can of Elnett, she told Esme to tip her head forward, and sprayed. And sprayed and sprayed until her hair became candy-floss stiff.

'Flick back.'

There was no gentle swoosh. Esme's hair flew back in one clump, like a trapdoor. She gulped a fresh breath and gently stroked her tresses. Rigid. This was not going so well. Everything felt gloopy, gluey and stiff. The dress had ridden up her thighs and the tights were digging into her toes. She felt trapped.

'Stand up.'

Esme rose and pulled the dress down as far as it would stretch.

'Don't do that. Be more relaxed. You are a woman in control of your sexuality. Confidence is what men find attractive. OK. Are you ready? Close your eyes until I say.'

Cece guided Esme in front of the mirror. She prayed she didn't look like she felt.

'Open!'

Esme took an involuntary step back and trapped a gasp with her hand. She didn't recognize herself. At all. The creature before her would have been swept past the ropes at Studio 54. Never, in her life, had she ever thought she would look like this. Tall, slim and stunning. But it wasn't her. She had been possessed by Jerry Hall.

'Fucking hell, Cece! What have you done?' The words mixed with nervous laughter.

'It was all there, hon. Just needed to be brought out by a bit of magic. And how long did it take? Fifteen minutes? You look fucking unbelievable. I've got my work cut out now to match up to you.'

Esme put her hands on her thighs and turned from side to side looking at her reflection. Her body was entirely on display but no cleavage was showing. This prevented the look from being slutty. She couldn't stop staring at herself.

'Thank you so much, Cece. I love it!'

'Go and celebrate with another drink whilst I get myself ready. Cigs are on the table.'

Esme floated out onto the balcony and posed for a non-existent audience. She lit a cigarette and held it with exaggerated elegance, like she had seen Princess Margaret do when she was a child. She poured another drink and it went down in a few gulps. She took off her watch, remembering what the

Princess said about wearing one in the evening – 'Makes you look like you are waiting for time to pass so you can leave at the earliest opportunity. And no watch has ever added elegance, however fine.'

Music came on from inside. And then there she stood. Cece the ring-mistress. Esme had never seen anything like it. The vision before her wore gold sequined hotpants, a red boob tube, a man's tail-coat and her top hat. Her heavily kohled eyes sparkled with a top layer of glitter which dusted down and over her cheekbones. Her lips were a vivid red. She burst into laughter.

'That's exactly the reaction I hoped for. Close your mouth, love, it's only clothes and camouflage. The real me is still somewhere here underneath all this crap. Come over here.'

The two girls looked in the mirror grinning with excited anticipation. Esme felt as fabulous as Cece looked. They were a team of two and she was thrilled.

'The night awaits…' said Cece.

Chapter Nine

Around the corner from the club Esme pulled her heels from her handbag and swapped her ballet pumps. The Tube had been empty but she was glad to have been in flats going up the escalators and along the echoing tunnels. Heels weren't her natural footwear and she felt her calves cramp up.

'I can't walk in these bloody things, Cece.'

'Just keep them on getting in then put those daggy flats back on to dance. No one will notice and I won't tell. But it's surprising how quickly you get used to them.'

There were hundreds of people queuing and loitering outside the club. Boys wearing make-up. Girls in disco Lycra, T-shirts with offensive slogans, piercings. A gang of skin-headed oafs lurked yelling 'Freaks and faggots!' at the glittering, defiant crowd. Esme felt like an amateur despite fitting in on the surface. She was no more than a heavily disguised pretender infiltrating a defiant minority. Each and every one of these people was making a statement, be it sexual or railing against convention.

Cece barged through the crowd shouting, 'Excuse me. Sorry. Make way. Move over, fuckwit.'

Moments later they were by the entrance and Cece was hugging a drag queen holding a clipboard. She towered over them in six-inch stilettos and a Dusty Springfield wig that added another foot to her height. She wore a full mask of make-up with false lashes that brushed her skin when she looked at her list. The tight sequined sheath left nothing to the imagination. Esme thought her magnificent, like some unworldly creature from Andy Warhol's Factory.

'Cecebella, you look D.I.V.I.N.E.'

'Thanks, Tammy. So do *you*.'

'And who is this sweet little thing?' said Tammy, arching a heavily drawn eyebrow.

Any remaining magic cast by her outfit vanished through Esme's fishnets. She felt like a twelve-year-old dressed as Siouxsie Sioux.

'This is my friend Esme. Isn't she stunning?' said Cece persuasively.

'Low-hanging fruit, Cece. Look after her,' said Tammy, and then in a voice pitched high, 'Have a fabulous time, girls.'

She gave a flamboyant wave and moved on to the next hopeful in line, smile vanishing and becoming once more the clipboard Nazi. Multiple personalities, thought Esme. Everyone seemed to have different versions of themselves that they were trying on for size. Would Tammy still be this hyper-drag queen when she was eighty? Did it matter? She felt no different to Tammy, dressed as a spangled rendering of herself for a few hours before the glitter would vanish come morning time.

Some people were trying to bribe Tammy but it seemed it took more than money to get you in. It was all about attitude and having the right look. Esme overheard Tammy saying, 'Your hair is wrong. Change your hair and I might let you in.' The offending hair in question looked nothing out of the ordinary to Esme, but she guessed that was the problem. An ordinary cut had to be compensated by extraordinary clothes and a 'fuck you' swagger. The guy was pedestrian and dull, suited and booted more for a club like Annabel's than Heaven. The kind of young man her father would approve of. He caught Esme's eye with a beseeching 'Help me?' look, clearly recognizing her as one of his 'kind', which pissed her off.

She blanked him and walked into the club.

A full blast of sound came over her in a big wave. Heavy bass from floor-to-ceiling speakers punched the air, powerful and insistent. Esme felt pinned to the wall by the sheer force of it reverberating through her body, as physical as it was loud. Gay energy was bigger than life. Inside the 'freaks and faggots' were included, accepted, celebrated. It seemed you could be anyone you wanted; steel worker by day, sugar plum fairy by night. Everyone was ready to have a good time with absolute freedom. The diversity created a combustible energy.

Cece shouted something in her ear but she couldn't hear. She grabbed Esme's hand and pulled her forward through the crush. They squeezed by semi-naked bodies dripping in sweat. The air was wet with perspiration and the anticipation of sex. Men moved with balletic grace, their torsos arching back as they lifted arms like wings, hips swinging in rhythm to the music. They didn't miss a beat as the two girls passed. Esme bumped into one gyrating creature wearing a cap and a leopard G-string, making him lose his balance and spill his drink, but he just laughed off her shouted apology and kept on bumping and grinding.

Already sticky, flushed and reeling from the overpowering atmosphere, they found a corner with two gold bean bags by a low table saying 'Reserved'. It was quieter.

'Tammy saved this for us. She's such a darling,' said Cece, who pulled out the vodka bottle bought earlier and two shot glasses from her bag. 'Not supposed to do this but BYO, if you know what I mean.'

Esme didn't.

'Bring your own,' Cece explained.

Cece poured the spirit and knocked her shot back in one gulp. Esme followed suit and sat back, nestling her bum into the dip of the bean bag. She took a lit cigarette from Cece and dragged deeply.

Donna Summer felt love and the dance floor filled, spilling out and into the seating areas. There was an unbridled energy where everyone seemed to feel like a star. People didn't couple up. They danced alone or in groups. Everyone was equal in joyous abandon. So, this was people-watching, thought Esme. It was soon impossible to single out an individual as the crowd became one writhing mass of flesh and limbs. That was when she saw him.

There was nothing gaudy or flashy about him, which is why he stood out. Dark brown curls and a big smile. He wore a creased T-shirt and a velvet jacket with an old pair of jeans. There was something in the way he moved that made both sexes part to let him through. An easy grace that was fundamentally masculine. Esme felt her tummy gallop as he hugged Cece. This must be Dan. He turned and gave her a perfunctory nod and joined Cece on her bean bag. Cece waved for Esme to join them and she pulled her bag nearer to theirs.

'Hi, I'm Dan.' He smiled.

'Esme.' But her name dissolved into a collective whoop, as metallic confetti flew from a cannon-like cylinder above the dance floor. Thousands of gold and silver flakes fluttered down, blanketing the club in glistening dreams.

Esme tipped her face to the ceiling, and tried to catch pieces as they fell around her. Before she knew it, she was swept onto the dance floor by the disco boy in his posing pouch from earlier and they disappeared into the throng. Anonymous hands groped, caressed and twirled her. Every few minutes she had a new dance partner. At first self-conscious, she felt herself liquefy into the music, not caring who, what or where she was. Although she'd never been promiscuous, right then, Esme felt she could be. The sexual atmosphere touched pretty much each of her senses. All that mattered was the moment, the feeling of being present right there and then. She felt part of something epochal. By the end she was dancing with the entire club. She was euphoric.

'Look at you go, Miss Independent,' said Cece, as Esme peeled herself away from a Diana Ross look-a-like and made her way back to the bean bags.

'Oh Jesus, give me a drink!'

'Have mine,' said Dan, passing her something cloudy on the rocks. It tasted of coffee and cream. This was a cocktail of character.

'Delicious. Oh Cece, that was so much fun. These people know how to dance.'

'They are all frustrated cheerleaders,' said Dan.

'Not everyone here is gay, Dan. You're not, for starters.'

'Don't get me wrong. I am eternally grateful for the

welcome,' said Dan. 'And grateful especially to all the hair-dressers here – they bring the models for straight guys to feast upon. And the music in gay clubs is the best.'

'Cece is much more fun than any brainless model – and sexier,' Esme said, in a burst of loyalty.

Dan looked at Cece.

'*Much* sexier,' he said, nuzzling his face in her neck.

She kissed Dan on the mouth, taking in his probing tongue. Esme admired her nerve. She would never have the guts to kiss a guy first. She remembered Charles-Antoine. He'd called her 'concrete knickers', not because they fell down easily but because it had taken him three months to get them off. What a waste of her virginity, that was. He dumped her when he found out she wasn't the heiress he assumed she was. To be fair she talked about Culcairn Castle as if it was her home. It had been, to a degree. She had told Charles-Antoine he was her first but he didn't believe her after the deed was done.

'Why is there no blood? You have no blood.'

She explained that it wasn't unusual in girls who had ridden since they could walk.

He said, 'My first girlfriend was a rider and she had blood.'

'Maybe she didn't have a fat pony like mine. It was like doing the splits every time I got on his back.'

The Belgian boy had laughed at that and the ice was broken, even if her hymen had long since been torn.

'I need a wee,' announced Cece bluntly, bringing Esme back to the present. 'Look after Dan for me.'

As she left, Dan joined Esme on her bean bag. Although she had already drunk more than she normally would, she went to pour herself another vodka from their secret stash.

More Dutch courage was needed now she was alone with this man who would probably be bored by her company. She felt she hadn't experienced enough of London life to have anything interesting to say. What could she talk about? Ponies and sponge cakes at the Highland show wouldn't cut it with a writer probably used to reporting the darker side of the city. Reaching for the bottle, her bag slipped to the floor, depositing its entire contents. Dan looked like she had deliberately tipped out a set of garden tools.

'Shit,' she muttered, trying to scoop up her scattered keys, make-up, money and shoes.

'Here,' said Dan. 'Let me help you.' He picked up a small lamp from the table and shone it on the floor. 'These yours?' he asked, picking up a packet of condoms.

'No!'

Esme was mortified.

'I'm only joking, Esme.'

He remembered her name.

'I can tell you're not that kind of girl,' he said and discreetly put them in Cece's jacket pocket.

He didn't look at her, allowing Esme free access to analyse his features. Individually they were quite heavy; meaty nose roofing a deep groove to a mouth that was full-lipped and languid. It was unusual for someone so dark to have freckles, she thought and wanted to touch a mole on his right cheek. His rich curls framed his face and olive skin. She had never liked sideburns but on Dan they added to his virility. His hands were the most perfect Esme had seen on a man. From wide knuckle bones grew unexpectedly elongated fingers, capped by porcelain-fine nail beds. Languid and expressive yet capable of violence.

'Cece tells me you are a journalist,' she said, not knowing what else to say.

'If you can call writing for the *Camden Echo* journalism. I'm still waiting for that big story. The one that will make my name. Then I can write my novel without being yet another faceless wannabe.'

'It must be exciting.'

'Once you've written about one missing cat, you've reported on them all. Or dogs, in my case. I'm being sent off my patch to write a piece on Battersea Dogs' Home soon.'

'Poor things,' said Esme. 'I'd love to go there – except I'd want to adopt every waif and stray.'

'Well, I'm sure I could smuggle you in as my assistant,' laughed Dan. 'I'll be there on the last Friday of the month. But don't expect Pulitzer Prize material from a visit to a dog refuge. I mean, I love writing – but fiction is my real thing. It's like meditation; a safe place where I feel free to be myself,' he said, looking out into the flashing darkness. 'Do you have a safe place?'

Esme could tell him about the old summerhouse between The Lodge and the castle she used to escape to when she wanted to be alone, but the words dried up in her mouth as she decided it sounded like a child's den rather than the refuge she'd truly found it to be.

'Not really,' she said. 'I'd love to be able to write but I've always felt more at home with pictures rather than words. They seem to say what I can never manage.'

'You can if you want to. Think of an emotional memory. Something that made you feel scared, sad or excited. It's a good place to start.'

'What's your memory? Your starting point?' Esme wanted to keep the conversation off her – she didn't want to go delving into her emotional memories – they were too painful.

'Nothing and everything. Many of my memories are brought back through music.'

Now they were on safe ground.

'I'm music mad. Have been since I was a little girl. My nanny let me watch *Top of the Pops*. She was so cool – until my parents discovered she was moonlighting as a prostitute.'

'You're kidding?'

'No. I remember a stream of men coming and going from our house when my parents were away. She said they were her brothers and cousins. I ought to have clicked because none of them looked anything like her, but I was only six at the time.'

That got his attention. His liquid brown eyes held hers.

'What music do you like?'

'David Bowie. The Stones. Never got The Beatles.'

She had grown up listening to country music. Her father loved Willy Nelson. Her mother, Patsy Cline.

'They are all pretty mainstream. I review emerging bands. You find raw talent that way. Actually, I discovered The Clash.'

'The Clash?'

Dan put two fingers under her chin to close her mouth.

'I understand life better lyrically, musically,' he laughed clearly pleased he had impressed her. 'I'm thirsty for the amazing. Anything I can't transform into something marvellous, I let go.'

Esme hoped she was marvellous or at least someone he could transform.

'I find that kind of music a bit scary. Punk and everything.'

'Try Yellow Magic Orchestra. Japanese band. Electro-pop.'

He was showing off, she knew, but she was still spellbound.

'I'll check them out.'

Dan sipped his drink.

'Did your parents travel much?' he asked.

'Kind of. My mother was away a lot and my father went with her.' She thought that was enough detail to sound convincing but not so much as to invite further questions. She wanted this evening to be about the present, not the past.

'Thought so. You have that rare combination of strength that's born from vulnerability.'

Esme had never thought that about herself but felt it was true. How did this virtual stranger read her so well?

She nodded.

'Was it a terribly difficult childhood you had?'

This conversation had gone from zero to furtive psycho-analysis in minutes. She was unused to gentle probing. No one had been concerned or interested in who she was – to most of her set, she already came with enough labels and preconceptions. This curiosity was unfamiliar to her and she felt someone was 'seeing' her for the first time. But she still didn't know if she wanted the 'real her' to be seen. She'd enjoyed playing the glamorous party girl for a night.

'My mother has been ill for a long time.'

'Cancer?'

Esme was disappointed that he drew an obvious conclusion. People were always so quick to make assumptions.

'Kind of. She'll never get better.' She didn't want his pity by going into details.

'Tragic,' he said, his thick brows bowing under the weight of apparent concern. He sat back and lit a cigarette and regarded her indolently, his eyes crinkling through the smoke.

'Sorry, guys.'

Thank God. Cece was back.

'Hope you don't want to go to piss. The queue is horrendous. Went outside in the end. Behind a car. Not yours, Dan, don't worry. Wouldn't cock my leg on your Cortina.'

Dan pulled her down next to him and rummaged for the condoms in her pocket.

'Naughty,' he said, holding them up to her.

Having shone under the spotlight of Dan's attention, Esme was suddenly an outsider in their foreplay. She felt guilty and decided it was time to leave them to it. Cece was on track to consummate her liking for this man and she didn't want to tread on her toes. She had got there first and Esme wanted to respect that.

Not wanting to cause a fuss, she said she was going to the loo and didn't come back, instead returning to the welcome anonymity of the dance floor.

Chapter Ten

The morning came around too quickly. Esme felt her head was clamped in a flower press. Every time she tried to move it, the grip tightened. Her mouth was parched as an oyster abandoned by the tide and her eyes were filled with grit. An invisible weight pushed her into the mattress. What had happened last night? She couldn't remember getting home. Her arm made an agonizing sweep of the floor by her bed. She felt inside her bag. Nothing was missing.

She carefully levered open one eyelid and shut it fast to block a sunbeam slicing through a gap in the curtains which made her brain bleed. Her head felt like it was being squeezed and pushed out, wailing in protest. She groaned and turned to face the wall. If only sleep would soak up the remaining alcohol trying to escape her shrivelled veins, but its residual sugar rush made her twitchy.

'Urgh.'

She kicked her bedcovers off and curled up into a ball. Nausea made an unwelcome arrival in her throat. She stumbled to the loo, dizzy and disorientated, and chucked up. She put her head under the tap and rinsed her mouth before gulping the tepid water. It did nothing to quench her thirst because it was too warm but she knew her dried-out stomach would appreciate the hydration. When she was sure she wouldn't throw up again, she tossed two Disprin into a tooth mug with a splash of water. The pills dissolved with a 'sigh', creating a chalky froth that hurried up the sides of the cup. Esme knocked it back knowing the medicine wouldn't take long to work. Until it did, she lay on the bathroom floor next to the bin, just in case.

The cold tiles felt good and drew the heat out of her like a compress. She allowed her body to relax into the hard floor and thought back to last night. While she couldn't remember details, the legacy of Dan's attentiveness made her hopeful. She knew *he* was out of bounds, but it had been her first real step towards cultivating a worldly persona – even considering that she could be of interest to that kind of man made a smile flash across her face. She wanted to get as far away as possible from the battery-blonde expectations of her to marry into the right kind of family by the age of twenty-five. Bugger that. She had shown herself that she could fit in where she wasn't meant to; in a culture beyond the fringe of what was deemed by her parents as 'acceptable'.

Looking at the plasterwork surround of her bedroom ceiling, simple and elegant, she wondered what the house had been like before it became a gallery. Had this always been a bathroom? Her bedroom had perhaps been servants' quarters or a child's room holding a cot and bed for its nursemaid. The round skylight had spokes like a wheel. Perhaps this had once been a staircase? Peering up, she could make out blue sky punctuated by fat, lazy clouds floating towards a rainy day somewhere else in the country.

Like the clouds, the day sprawled out ahead of her, empty of plans. Suki had gone to see 'Mummy and Daddy' rather than staying in her little London *pied à terre*, and Cece, was, no doubt, spooning with Dan. Yet Esme didn't feel lonely because she was alone through choice. There was a difference. At boarding school, she had been lonely. Sleeping in a dorm of twelve girls, she had never felt more isolated. At The Lodge when her mother mentally took flight, she felt abandoned. Today being on her own was a gift to do exactly as she pleased with. Where most people of her age wanted constant social interaction, there were times when Esme actively sought solitude.

The aspirin was starting to do the trick. Her headache had gone from sledgehammer pain to a dull ache and the nausea had been replaced by hunger. Time for food and a walk, where she would allow her feet to dictate the route.

She threw on a linen skirt and a T-shirt. It was too hot for jeans. If she had been in Scotland she wouldn't have bothered with shoes so espadrilles were the next best thing. Any attempt to keep her room tidy had passed. Her minimal wardrobe was strewn all over the floor. She hadn't done any washing for a week and if she didn't sort it out she would be down to wearing used pants inside out. 'Dirty linen, disorganized mind,' Mrs Bee always said. She felt a piercing homesickness and longed for the cool comfort of The Lodge. Well, there was no Mrs Bee in Mayfair, not even a washing machine. And it wasn't like Jermyn Street was full of launderettes. Still, convenience was an urban bonus and M&S sold an affordable line in plain white bikini briefs. They would do for now.

She washed her face and moisturized. Since she had turned

twenty, she had taken slightly better care of her skin. Her mother's bottle of Clinique was old and, some might say a bit rancid, but made it feel less dry. Unscrewing the cap, she wiped the bottle neck clean. She tipped the yellow cream onto the palm of her hand and wiped it over her face leaving a greasy sheen. It will soak in, she thought, aware that she had no powder. Cece had opened her eyes to the power of make-up and how war paint gave confidence. No matter. At least it would be nice to get some colour on her pallid body. It hadn't occurred to her to bring a swimsuit when she packed for London, but if she found a quiet spot in the park her baby-blue bra and knickers could be mistaken for a bikini at a distance, she decided.

Saturday was a good day to make a packed lunch and wander the streets of London. Anyone she knew had fled town for the weekend. Tourists of all nationalities hijacked the city for themselves and they didn't care that she was alone.

Jermyn Street was empty of everything. A light breeze blew down the street and Esme half expected a ball of tumbleweed to bowl along the pavement but instead the pages of a lone newspaper took flight, its printed wings curling and twisting up and down like an agitated bird. There was nothing refreshing to the wind, its breathy consistency hot as a hairdryer and smelling of tarmac. A vacant taxi slowed down hoping she might want a ride. Esme smiled and shook her head, following it on foot down the road towards Christie's. Turning right onto King Street she passed the imposing entrance to the auction house, its immense doors shut and alarm winking, alert and watchful. Esme knew no treasures were left on site, the majority being housed securely under the vigilant eye of Norman over at her father's warehouse.

On St James's Street she turned left towards the park, stopping to look through the window of Lock & Co Hatters. It was the oldest hat shop in world and held a double royal warrant. It had furnished the likes of Winston Churchill and Lord Nelson with his bicorn which he wore into the Battle of Trafalgar. But she also knew that only the uninformed, dazzled by its reputation, bought their hunting caps here. Peerless but overpriced, it was Patey's where those in the know sought their made-to-measure riding hats. The quality was just as good and there was no waiting list. It had been her heart's desire as a young girl to get her own Patey's hat. But the visitors on the street were too busy to stop, instead they were all drawn to the most impressive of landmarks in the Queen's borough. All the tourists hurried towards the splendour of Buckingham Palace and the Life Guards standing on watch for hours in their little huts. There was a bunch of holidaymakers circling a young soldier holding sentry under the weight of his bearskin outside Clarence House. Must be hell in this heat, thought Esme.

Like so many Brits – unless they had been on a school trip – Esme had visited precious few of London's landmarks. She had never been to the Tower of London, never seen the Royal Mews, despite her passion for horses. She had taken her city of birth for granted and while she'd always assumed she'd go and see them all 'one day', that day had never arrived. Looking at the throngs of sightseers who had flown thousands of miles to experience London's history, to walk the paths of kings and queens, Esme knew how unusual her childhood had been. Growing up next door to a castle, and socializing with the royalty that visited there in the great walls of Culcairn, made for a funny kind of normal – she could see that now.

She continued down The Mall towards Buck House. The flag was down, indicating Her Majesty wasn't in residence. It was a magnificent building but austere. No wonder Princess Margaret, always Esme's favourite, preferred communal living at Kensington Palace. Her state apartment was said to be enormous, as befitting the queen's sister, but at least there she had neighbours. The Waleses, Kents, the Gloucesters and a household of personnel and staff inhabited the sprawling two-storey stronghold. And it wasn't open to the public so she and Lord Snowdon could live at least part of their lives without scrutiny. Even more necessary since they had divorced, she imagined.

St James's Park was sparsely populated. It wasn't that she didn't like children but, in her hungover state, one of the benefits of St James's was the lack of a playground to attract young families. The pelicans were still a draw however, and she saw a small boy chucking bits of bread into the eagerly waiting beaks. Couples lay, soaking up the sun, flirting and in various stages of intimacy. Clothes had been removed. There was a mildly erotic undercurrent to the lazy heat; people sunbathing but sneaking glances at their companions. Boyfriends and girlfriends meeting in quiet corners. She wondered how many first kisses took place in parks? How often the first intimations of adultery occurred? Then there were scattered groups of picnickers with their potato salad and sliced ham sitting on tartan rugs in dappled shade. One group had managed to pull together a jug of Pimm's. Sitting near a group like that would make her feel awkward for being alone, though she knew in all likelihood they'd be too busy having fun to notice her, still she would feel self-conscious.

The clearing she chose instead was surrounded by shrubs and hidden from prying eyes – but not dogs, it seemed. A red setter trotted by and she wished dear old Digger was still here to provide a foil for her solitude. Making sure she couldn't be seen, she stripped to her underwear, using her skirt as a blanket. Feeling queasy again, she put her lunch in the shade and lay down. The sun was strong and the grass dry and prickly. A draught of wind wafted across her body bringing with it the sweet smell of lime trees. The ground beneath her hands was sticky with their sap. She closed her eyes and listened to the hum of traffic and distant laughter. Her mind emptied and sunspots floated across her vision and disappeared when she followed them from left to right. An insect crawled up her leg. She shook it off and turned onto her stomach.

A pair of sandals came into view. Men's sandals on a pair of tufted feet with yellowing toenails.

She faced the other way hoping the man would disappear. She remembered she was next to naked.

'Do you mind if I join you?'

How dare he? she thought, the brief moment of peace gone.

The accent was Northern. Newcastle maybe. A nice enough voice but she thought it was fairly clear she wasn't looking for company. Esme pretended to be asleep and inwardly told him to fuck off.

'Y'right? Do you mind if…'

She grunted angrily what she hoped he would take for a 'Yes, I do mind.'

She felt the flick of a towel or something being laid next to her and then a groan as he lay or sat down. A waft of body odour and garlic came and went in waves as he got comfortable. This was not what her hangover needed.

'Ahhhh,' he sighed. 'Nice here, don't you think?'

It was a statement rather than a question, indicating this badly washed lump intended staying put. Couldn't he see she was asleep – or at least, trying to maintain the pretence of it?

'Funny how you like the same spot as me.'

Esme tried to make her wall of silence as high as possible. Suddenly the calm of the glade felt like threatening rather than peaceful.

'Didn't know anyone else knew about it. You must like to get away from the crowds too.'

Crowds? What bloody crowds? The park was hardly Brighton beach. What little breeze there was suddenly stopped, like her breathing, as she felt him shuffle closer. Something landed on her back, a leaf or catkin. Esme flicked her shoulder.

'Here, let me.'

A clammy finger lingered a fraction too long on her skin.

This was too much. She jumped up, pulling her skirt over her underwear.

'What is your fucking problem? You've got the whole park to lie in. Piss off.'

Stunned, the man lying on his side raised his hands in mock defeat.

'OK, OK.'

She looked at him properly for the first time. Boiled rice white skin, six o'clock shadow and an enormous Adam's apple that was dotted by stubble and in-grown hairs. Even with wash and a shave, she wouldn't have bought into his clumsy charm offensive.

'It's actually not OK. Go and find someone else to pester.'

Vanquished but unperturbed, the stranger saw that Esme was a waste of time. Gathering his belongings, he moved without further protestation. Esme monitored his departure, watching him scramble through a bush, his hairy back getting scratched by branches. He slouched across the grass in a pair of low-slung football shorts, T-shirt in hand. She waited until he was out of sight then unpacked her lunch, pleased with her boldness. She had probably been unnecessarily rude but it felt good. Like a small victory won only with words and a lot of attitude. Cece would have been proud of her.

Esme woke from a deep sleep. The sun had lost its sting and bled through the trees in the dying twilight. She still felt its heat on the skin of her arms and shoulders where she'd burned. It was tight and prickled like it had shrunk and stretched across her bones. A pleasant feeling, symbolic of the freedom summer offered. Winter was so much more effort. Laying and lighting fires. Heating on or off? Umbrella? Dark afternoons that trapped people indoors. Her mother's bad days were relentless in winter, stretching into weeks and months. It was winter when her mother had first attempted suicide. A winter which felt like it never ended. From then on winter became the season of alcohol, pills and despair. When her mother was prone to torpor, hysteria and suicide. Once her mother had thoughts of suicide in her mind, they were there to stay, slowly corrupting and draining her of hope, until she found her way back to life or gave in and tried again, usually in January.

Distance relieved Esme from constant gnawing guilt and

midnight vigils at her mother's bedroom to check she was sleeping soundly. The kindly nurses and round-the-clock carers shouldered the responsibility for her welfare now. What a relief to know she could rely on their specialist attention. And it was June. Her mother had never attempted suicide in the summer months, being predisposed to finding joy in the bloom of spring and onwards until the world folded into the cold of autumn.

The ambient noise of park life had shifted up a gear and her mood dropped. Laughter, yelps of flirtatious protestation and an acoustic guitar. It was definitely not the time to be seen alone now as friends hooked up to begin their night of revelry.

She slipped on her clothes and wandered back home with no purpose other than more sleep. As she drew nearer the gallery, the hum of urban life reduced to a whisper of activity. The calm before the storm of Saturday night partying when the suburbs descended for a piece of the city's sophistication. Clubs that were closed to bridge and tunnel revellers during the week gratefully accepted the suburban pound. Every now and then an empty bus would pass or the diesel engine of a black cab would amplify her feeling of melancholy. No one would be waiting at the gallery, save her ragged teddy bear Gelatin, the one who had bought comfort at school. He still held the ghost of the scent of her mother's perfume after she'd ritually drenched him before sending her away to school, in the hope it would have the same effect as a 'whelping blanket for pups weaned from their mum'. It hadn't. He had made the journey to London more out of habit than necessity but still, in damp weather, smelt of orange blossom and rose.

She turned into Jermyn Street carrying the weight of the night before. She was hot, sunburnt and dead tired. There was still no wind to circulate the monotonous heat from the concrete jungle. It was hard to breathe in its density and Esme longed for the open wilds of Scotland, a heather bed and to swim in the briny pools of the river that ran through Culcairn. But she didn't feel homesick. It was a physical yearning not an emotional one. Tomorrow she was going to Max's studio and who knew what revelations might turn up. Buoyed by the anticipation of discovery, there was no need to wallow in the past. She turned her key in the lock and climbed the stairs with a smile on her face.

Chapter Eleven

'I've bought some croissants,' she said, handing Max a brown paper bag, spotted by grease.

Esme had at first been surprised that Max had suggested a Sunday to meet up and then she remembered he was doing her a favour and reserved his better-paid work for weekdays.

'Thank you. I'm ravenous.'

There was no sign of her picture. The easel was bare and from Max's appearance it was clear he had just woken up. He looked tired. A hollow-eyed, scruffy inhabitant in his dingy, cramped little room. But he seemed happy enough in solitude (notwithstanding a snoozing Flea in his basket). Bill had told her Max cared for none of the trappings of his work, not money or status or recognition. The nature of restoration meant he worked behind the scenes, allowing the client to benefit from the glory of his expertise. Max was a man without ego who was totally at ease in his own skin. She envied him for the absolute gratification his work bought. Bringing paintings back to life was his vocation and his life's work hung in galleries and private homes all over the world.

'Where's the picture?' she asked anxiously.

'Let's get some coffee on.'

Alarm bells went off. Was he delaying bad news with a drink? She said nothing. He seemed calm as he went about packing ground coffee into a cafétière, the kind you put directly onto a naked flame. Filling the base with water, he screwed on the top and lit a Calor gas stove. It wasn't long until the noxious air had overtones of fresh coffee. The coffee pot soon bubbled and spat with a deep gurgle. He picked it up with a stained towel and poured the coffee into two espresso cups.

'Sugar?'

'Yes, please.'

Esme took a croissant and dunked it in her coffee, the liquid dribbling down her chin. She wiped it with her hand.

'Amazing coffee.'

'Italian. I always bring it back with me.'

Bill had mentioned Max had a studio flat in Porto Ercole where he would disappear in the spring and early summer. It was his base when he trawled local flea markets and houses of newly widowed ladies in search of undiscovered masterpieces. His lanky good looks were no doubt welcomed by lonely women lacking a man about the house.

'How's the cleaning coming along?' she tried again.

'See for yourself.'

He reached behind an enormous canvas facing the wall and placed her picture on his easel.

'*Voila!*' He was clearly pleased with his progress.

Esme choked on her coffee. The portrait in front of her was uncannily like her mother. Her expression held a cunning naïveté that was both self-possessed and needy. She was erotic in her innocence, otherworldly yet so present that her gaze looked right into Esme's heart. It was a ravishing yet unsettling portrait, full of contradiction and nuanced emotions.

'She's stunning, isn't she?'

'Yes,' breathed Esme. But her breath caught in her chest. All the longing, all the turmoil and disappointment – her entire childhood came flooding back. It was as if her mother was revealing herself through this ethereal nineteenth-century beauty and for the first time Esme saw who she was. A shrew inside an angel and an angel inside a vixen. And now she was nothing, just an empty carcass with a beating heart existing because she wasn't allowed to die.

'Are you all right, Esme? You look like you've seen a ghost.'

'Yes… No… I don't know.'

Sensing her distress, Flea padded over to her and put his head on her lap. She stroked him.

'I think you've been burning the candle at both ends, gorgeous. You look terrible. I remember being your age, shagging everything that moved and drinking myself stupid every night. Party, party, party. But it catches up with you.'

If only, thought Esme.

'Who do you think is the artist?'

'I don't think. I know. It's a Romney and I suspect the sitter is Emma Hamilton.'

'Nelson's mistress?'

'The very one.'

There's a coincidence, thought Esme. Beautiful enough to bag a hero but destined to end her life as it began, in poverty. Whilst her mother wasn't a pauper, her life had descended into no life at all. Esme knew Lady Hamilton had been – among other things – an actress, and in this painting she had clearly taken the role of Greco-Roman servant girl. She wondered if the painting had been in the Culcairn collection for years or whether the Earl had bought it after meeting her mother. That Emma Hamilton fell for the great Lord Nelson, a man well above her humble beginnings, would not have passed him by. He would have seen the correlation.

'She's brushing up well. Literally!' she said, trying to regain her composure.

'Most paintings I get have been retouched at some point. Some have had fingers or fig leaves added, or animals blotted out. There is less scope for change in a portrait. Although the paint is very thin in places.'

'Does this mean you have to repaint?'

'More of a touch-up.'

He showed her a patch where the colour had worn thin and was broken up, like a scab. Dabbing his brush in a dot of paint and with the precision of a surgeon he filled a minuscule section of the balding area. There must have been half a dozen shades of blue that could only be differentiated if you looked closely. It was painstaking work.

'I wasn't sure who it was by until I could see the relaxed brushstrokes. There is a feeling of freshness. It's effortless.'

Esme saw that compared to someone like Reynolds, the picture had an instinctive informality. The pose was so natural and the palette exquisite. The artist infused the grand manner of eighteenth-century portraiture with a feeling of freshness and ease. The colours were clear, clean, bright and strong, the pigment freely applied with a loose brush.

When Esme told Max her thoughts, he was impressed.

'Did you learn this on your course?'

'Some. But it's clear, isn't it?'

Max said he wasn't going to restore her fully. Emma Hamilton had led a complicated life. She was a complex character and he felt the painting ought to reflect that.

'Sometimes it's the cracks and imperfections that make a painting more beautiful. Same with women,' said Max. 'What lies beneath is what's important to the restorer. Surface perfection is dull and too easy to manufacture.'

'Do you mean perfect imperfection?'

'Exactly!' Max chinked his mug to hers. 'Any woman can get their nails painted and hair dyed, apply a mask of make-up – but that's bullshit if she's rotten to the core. I have no time for women who try too hard.'

He rubbed the sleep from his eyes.

'I find them disingenuous. I mistrust all women who plaster themselves in make-up. What are they trying to hide?'

'Maybe they are just insecure.' Esme thought of what he'd have said if he'd seen her on Friday dressed for Heaven.

Insecurity is charming, he told her. Vulnerability is what men find attractive in women. If they have the strength to wear uncertainties on their sleeve, then that was a sign of them being open-hearted, he claimed. Esme wasn't sure it was just women who had to make peace with their vulnerability. She didn't buy the whole white-knight-on-a-steed-rescuing-a-fragile-woman idea.

'I want to see a woman, warts and all. Baggy pants and sagging tits. That's a woman I'll to take to bed.' Max grinned and Esme's ire vanished.

'Is Emma wearing baggy knickers?' Esme laughed.

'If she was alive today, I suspect they would be crotchless.'

As Max worked, Esme sat quietly, Flea at her feet. He wore a miner's torch on his head and thick glasses. In profile his hawkish face became even more like a bird of prey devouring its kill with voracious concentration. With no distractions, not even a radio, it was easier for him to shut the world out and focus; much like the peace of mind her father seemed to find when he was painting. If only she had a skill to block negative feelings when they threatened to overwhelm her. She thought again about Max's take on women. She understood it to a certain degree. But as far as she saw it, women dressed to impress each other more than they did to bag a man. Except for on a night out. She had felt liberated from herself by her transformation on Friday but that was, like Max said, because she was hiding behind a disguise.

'What do you think about women dressing up for an occasion? A ball, let's say. She can hardly go in her bra and knickers.' Surely Max couldn't argue against that.

'Obviously not.' Max leant back from the painting and turned to Esme. 'To be honest I hate socializing, for that very reason, unless it's in my own home. Women in their finery are impossible to read. And the occasion lends itself to superficial behaviour. The men are no better. Everyone is trying to outdo the other.' He turned back to the canvas.

Esme considered this. Max wasn't a chauvinist but he was old school in his views. He spent too much time locked away with two-dimensional women who couldn't answer back, she guessed. Though she also suspected he was not the faithful kind, spreading love as thinly as his varnish.

'Are you married?'

'I was. Twice,' he said automatically, without taking his

brush from the canvas, seemingly bored of being asked and answering this question.

'Children?'

Silence.

Apparently, this was not up for discussion and for a man who appeared to be an open book, it led Esme to believe there was more to Max than he was willing to share. He wore his easy-going charm like a mask, too, it would seem. Make-up comes in all guises, thought Esme.

'Are you going to come to Bill's opening?'

Her invitation delivery route hadn't reached the wilds of Fulham but she was sure Bill would have invited him.

'I should. Events like that are rich pickings for folk like me who make beautiful things more beautiful for people who can afford it.'

An inconclusive answer and knowing his focus was on the Romney, not her conversation, she offered to take Flea for a walk.

'Good idea. Never gets out, poor thing.'

A recluse, just like his owner, she thought.

Hearing the word 'walk', Flea had risen and had his muzzle pressed up against a mouse-sized hole at the bottom of the door. He sniffed and scratched with his paw. Glad that someone was keen on her company, Esme and Flea set off.

When they got back to the studio, all the lights were off save the beam of Max's head torch which was trained on the slash on the bottom of the canvas. He was cleaning it with a soft cloth, like a wound before being stitched up. Esme winced as she approached. She could almost feel the pain.

'Bad, isn't it?' she said.

'Bad that it's been done deliberately but not irreparable. I can patch that up. Paintings get re-lined, often more than once in a lifetime.'

'Why would anyone do that? Bill thought it was a Stanley knife.'

'Could have been, or it could have been done with a cut-throat or razorblade. I thought it might have been done to sabotage the artist's signature but I'm pretty sure that's been painted over in the opposite corner.'

He gently pulled the wound apart and went in deeper with his torch and magnifying glasses.

'It's very difficult to tell when this was done. But I suspect within the last twenty years or so.'

Finally dragging his attention from the picture, he looked at her. The sparkle was back in his eyes and a look of determined excitement.

'Are you sure you don't know anything else about the painting?' he asked.

Esme knotted her fingers in her lap. She couldn't bear to tell Max that it lay at the centre of a web of questions about her family and the Earl.

'Nothing more than what you see' – she decided that she had to come clean and tell Max that the painting was hers – 'and the fact that Henry Culcairn left it to me in his will.'

'Hmm. Didn't think it was the kind of thing Bill usually sends me.'

Esme had expected more of a reaction, but saw that Max was only thinking of the painting, not her own family tumult. She could see his mind computing information he garnered from the restoration process and what he wanted to find out. A hunter on the trail of its quarry.

'The damage intrigues me more than the picture itself. We know it's a Romney and we know it's Nelson's love. What I want to find out is who and why they wanted to vandalize something so pretty.'

Esme crossed her arms and held onto her shoulders, hugging a wave of sadness close to her chest. The vandalism was wanton and premeditated, and while she wasn't quite ready to admit her suspicions about who'd done it, Esme was relieved that the painting wasn't beyond repair. If only the same could be said for her mother.

Chapter Twelve

As was common, Bill was away from the gallery on Monday. He had gone to secure the purchase of 'an important work' as the supplier was flying out of London later in the day. He had said it was too good an opportunity to miss and didn't want his rival getting 'his grubby little mitts on it'. Fair enough. So, Esme was left to man the gallery until Suki came back from her dentist appointment. With only two days till the opening she thought Bill would have wanted to be all over the preparations. But this was what he did at least four times a year, Suki said, and all the paintings were hung and lit by a specialist who made the canvases come alive. Esme had already learnt there was more to lighting than a bulb suspended above the frame. The gallery lights themselves were already top of the range, but the bulbs had been changed and casings turned to spotlight each work with the precision of a sniper's rifle.

Esme had been told to expect a prospective buyer coming in for a preview as he wasn't able to make the private view. Bill had told her that the man wouldn't stay long and that she must shut up shop whilst he was there.

It was unusual for random people to walk in off the street.

Most came by prior arrangement and for the most part Bill was there to greet them. With the prices that most of the paintings sold for, he only had to sell one or two every few months to stay afloat. Everything else funded his wardrobe and provided cash to invest in new pieces of art.

'When the client arrives, put a note on the door saying, "Back in an hour." I like all my best customers to feel they have an exclusive on the gallery,' Bill had explained.

He refused to have an OPEN/CLOSED sign hanging on the door. 'Those are for corner shops, my dear.' She would write a note prior to the gentleman's arrival and have it ready to put up, Esme decided.

'What's the man's name?' she had asked.

'Don't worry, you'll recognize him.'

Intriguing. Excited at the thought of the kind of client for whom money was no object, Esme resolved that she would make damn sure that whoever it was wouldn't leave the gallery empty-handed. She was desperate to get her first sale in the bag and prove her worth to Bill.

Esme scanned the gallery to make sure everything was tidy and in order. It was. Immaculate. There was a whiff of Ajax, but at least it was a clean smell. When Peggy, the cleaner, deigned to come in, she did a job worthy of five-star hotel housekeeping. Even the kitchenette was spotless. Filling the kettle and fishing out the teapot and cups from a cupboard marked 'Visitors Only' Esme poured milk into the jug. It came out as yoghurt.

'Shit.'

There had been half a lemon knocking about yesterday, perhaps she could make the tea the French way. But it was neither in the fridge nor in the empty fruit bowl, Peggy must have chucked it out. Snatching keys from her desk, she flew down the street to the corner shop (complete with its sign saying 'Open'), grabbed a pint and dumped 15p on the counter.

'No Tooty Frooties today, Esme?' The owner smiled.

'Not today, Mr Leghari. No time. Got a special customer coming any second. Gotta run.'

'Send him my way afterwards!' Mr Leghari shouted after her.

As she turned back into Jermyn Street, she saw a Bentley pull up to the kerb and park brazenly on the double-yellow line. The driver, decked in chauffeur's uniform, got out and opened the passenger door.

'Holy fuck,' whispered Esme as she saw who stepped out onto the pavement.

The man, dressed in a flat cap and tweed suit, was the very same figure she had stuck on her walls at boarding school. The person she worshipped more than anyone, after Robert Redford, had his hands on his hips and was staring through the closed door of the gallery.

All the other girls at St Mary's had gushed over David Cassidy or Donny Osmond. But she would fall asleep listening to 'Skyline Pigeon' on her Sanyo cassette player. This was the man whose songs had comforted her through homesickness and painted a world beyond the confines of the school gates. His melodies had given her hope. She had fantasized about meeting him in countless scenarios: bumping into him on the street, being pulled onto the stage from the audience, him singing at her death bed, even coming to her rescue at school. In her mind, they had been friends for years. And here he was like he'd just popped by to say hello. As friends do.

The incredible reality of her dream coming true made her want to flee. What if she made an idiot of herself? What if she was disappointed with the inevitability that he was, well, human? But her brain quickly calculated the regret she'd feel if she ran from this opportunity – and kudos she'd get from retelling the story. She felt herself shaking like a teenager faced with her crush.

'Oh gosh, I'm so sorry. The milk was – your tea—'

Elton John turned to her. 'I hate fucking tea. You must be Serena.' He smiled, showing the gap in his square teeth. How she loved that gap. His snub nose and clever eyes were more than she could cope with. Elton was a god. A musical genius who had come from nowhere and triumphed with raw heaven-sent talent.

'Are you Serena?'

'Yes, No. Sorry. No sorry, I'm Esme. Suki is at the dentist. She's going to be apoplectic she's missed you.'

Elton turned towards the door as if to say, 'Can we go in?'

Esme put the key in the lock but it wouldn't turn. She felt faint with nerves and fast rising humiliation.

'Fucking door. I'm sorry.'

'I think it's open. You didn't lock it, naughty girl. I won't tell Bill.'

She felt scalding embarrassment rush to her face. Was this really him? Why the fuck hadn't Bill told her the prospective buyer was Elton bloody John?

'Shit. Sorry.'

'Will you stop saying sorry and get us in?' he said with a hint of annoyance but continued to smile.

'Sorry. Urgh! Sorry!'

She laughed. Meeting her idol could not have got off to a shoddier start. She had already made an almighty fool of herself so things couldn't get worse.

Feeling she had nothing to lose she said, 'If Bill had told me it was you coming today, I would have called him a liar. You see, meeting you is a bit like you meeting...?' Who would an icon have as an idol?

'The Queen Mother?' Elton suggested. 'I shat myself when I met her but she was so warm and funny. Well, I'm not very warm but I am funny.'

'You've met the Queen Mother?' Was this a connection Esme could build on? She could tell him she knew Princess Margaret, but she was also aware dropping the Margaret bomb risked sounding like she was namedropping in a desperate bid to impress.

'Only formally. But given half a chance, I would love to get pissed with her. Bet she's got a filthy sense of humour.' He spoke with a clipped, clear pronunciation. Quite posh for a Pinner boy, she thought.

Esme imagined the two them in a grand drawing room at Royal Lodge, he at the piano and Her Majesty swaying with a gin and Dubonnet in hand.

'You see? Now you know how I feel meeting you. It's the best moment of my life,' she blundered, then almost to herself, 'I can't believe it.'

'Are we going to stand out here for the rest of the day or are you going to invite me in?'

'Sorr— Of course.'

She allowed the singer to enter first, taking note of his long hair and bushy sideburns. His glasses were round and understated but even off-stage and in civvies he was still indelibly Elton John. More recognizable than the Statue of Liberty and more loved than the tooth fairy and for the next few minutes, all hers.

'You don't want tea then? There is champagne if you prefer. It's not cold but I can find some ice.'

Bill wouldn't mind her cracking a bottle open for such a visitor, and she could do with a glass to calm her nerves.

'If it's pink, vintage and Laurent Perrier, I wouldn't say no.'

'We only have Bollinger, I'm afraid.'

'Poison.'

What else did she have to offer? Suki had eaten the ginger nuts and the bananas were brown.

'Do you want me to run out and get a coffee? Or Berry Brothers will have the Laurence stuff.'

But the moment for sharing a drink had passed. Elton was already wandering around the room looking at the displayed pictures. He seemed relaxed and ready now to get down to business. It was strange to see someone so famous this close. She wondered what it what like to be so well-known, so well-connected and to have enough money to indulge a passion for fine art. Never in a million years did she think a pop star – celebrated for his extravagance as a performing artist and transient lifestyle – would be the type of client to appreciate the kind of art Bill sold. Had she given it thought she would have assumed a more obvious admiration for Art Deco and Nouveau or the ubiquitous pop artists like Andy Warhol and Lichtenstein.

As if reading her mind, he said, 'I'm not a trophy collector. I've had my phases buying kitsch and I'm not known for my restraint, but with the Baroque and Rococo periods it's not about acquisition, It's about love.'

His steps were short and he waddled like a pigeon around the gallery, pausing at one of the landscapes and running a finger along the frame to check for dust.

'Too many fucking trees,' he said before moving on to the only portrait. 'Look at this Van Dyck.'

He surveyed the ugly man in red.

'Forget the face, they were all pigs in those days – but look at the fabric of his jacket. Its luminosity and verve. It's not cotton, it's not leather or silk. It's so clearly taffeta. Brilliant, absolutely fucking astoundingly well painted. And he's so clearly a poof, which I love!'

Funny how he had zeroed in on the most valuable picture on display. Of course, there were no prices on show, but she knew everyone invited to the gallery would have had the details of all the paintings.

'I'll arrange for someone to pick the old bugger up and pay for him after the viewing. Don't let Bill accept a higher offer.'

'I'll do my best but you know how much Bill loves the pound,' she said with a giggle, all restraint suddenly gone now she was giddy with the idea of making her first sale.

Elton didn't laugh. He looked at her as if for the first time, like he was surprised she had entered his orbit.

'Tell Bill to call me.'

And with that he was gone. In and out, just as Bill had said he'd be. Like the effect the cleaning alcohol had on Max's painting; for a second, bright and real then a figment of the imagination.

Had Elton been rude or was he just someone whose mind

was already on the next task? He had dismissed her and she was furious with herself for not having made a bigger impact on him. She looked at herself in the mirror. No surprise, she thought. But whatever the case, however swift his departure, she had met and conversed with Elton John.

Esme closed her eyes and did all she could to process a memory to hold on to. It was the details she must remember if anyone was to believe she had actually met him. He wore a fob watch. His shoes were brown and he smelt of a Mediterranean citrus grove. Irrefutable proof would have been an autograph but it would have been crass to have asked for one. She wasn't a simpering fan, she was meant to be a serious art professional. Anyway, Bill could confirm her story and swat away the doubters. And the first one she'd have to deal with would be Suki.

The left side of Suki's face was like a stuffed hamster's, swollen and already beginning to bruise. Blood had congealed in the corners of her mouth. She looked like a slab of raw meat that had been butterflied on a butcher's block.

'Oh my God, Suki. What did they do to you?' Esme said, trying not to laugh.

'The fucking dentist pulled two wisdom teeth out. I was awake the whole time. I didn't feel anything but the sound was horrendous. Like an eyeball being pulled from its socket,' She spoke as if she had a mouthful of pebbles.

'You poor thing. You should have gone home.'

'Nah. Been given fantastic painkillers. I look awful but I feel great! What have I missed?'

Hoping the pills had anaesthetized more than her tooth, Esme told her about Elton John.

'What? You've got to be fucking kidding me. Elton John? Why was I not told and what the fuck was Bill thinking, leaving you in charge of such an important client? I can't believe he put you in such an awkward situation. Poor you, Esme.'

Suki was gilding her jealousy with passive-aggressive concern that didn't fool Esme. She was just furious that she had missed out on meeting then dining out on the fact she had met Elton John.

'It was too much of Bill to expect you to make a sale,' Suki was simpering now. 'Don't worry, I'll back you up. It's his fault not yours.'

'But I did make a sale. He's bought the Van Dyck.'

'What was he…' She stopped, her head swivelling from her to the Van Dyck and back to Esme.

Esme might just have well slapped her. Suki's face reddened with surprise then rage. Swallowing the words on the tip of her tongue, she took a deep breath.

'Wow,' Suki managed, deadpan.

'I know. But to be honest, I had nothing to do with it. He just walked up to it and said someone would collect it after the show. We hardly spoke. It was business as usual.'

Inside Esme was bursting to share how excited she was. Bill's best painting had been sold and it was all due to her – well, kind of. Stupidly she had nothing to verify the sale, only a superstar's word and given his wealth and reputation for excess, his word she hoped, was his bond. She wondered now if she should have written up some sort of receipt or bill of sale.

'Well, aren't you a clever girl?'

Esme heard the sarcasm in her voice but continued to ignore it. Suki was only one of two friends she had made and given her short time at the gallery, she was bound to be pissed off. Time for damage control to make her feel she was still top bitch of the small working group.

'If you want, we can tell Bill that you arrived back in time to make the deal.'

'Don't be so patronizing. I have sold hundreds of paintings and anyway Bill told me Elton John is known to buy in bulk. Like the whole show, often.'

Esme's pride evaporated. She knew she shouldn't be so easily affected by other people's opinions but in this case, she hadn't even managed to give the star a cup of tea. She felt the sting of this deliberate, emotional sabotage and she was allowing her delight to be stifled by it. Piqued by Suki's childish conduct, she took hold of the building umbrage and used it to defend her success.

'Isn't it cheating if one person buys the whole exhibition? All our work gone to waste? Bill could have just sent the paintings to Elton John and given him an invoice if he was going to buy them all. But he'd be missing out on the publicity and the showcase for his area of expertise.'

'Don't be stupid, Esme. The paintings stay here until the exhibition is over, whoever buys them, and anyway Bill has enough paintings to put on ten exhibitions.'

It was like buying the dress off the mannequin in a shop window, thought Esme. She would never remain naked for long.

'Since it's clear you can manage better without me, I'm going to meet a friend.' Suki turned on her heel and left.

'Fine.'

Esme was relieved when she was alone again. She hated her new friend's mean-spiritedness even if she could understand why she was put out. But this was Bill's victory more than anyone's. He had found the Van Dyck and curated the exhibition. Suki could strop but Bill would be elated – and he was the only person who mattered.

The rest of the day passed uneventfully. Esme felt deflated and wished her boss would come back. The afternoon dragged. As irritating as Suki could be, she found that after a while she missed her company. For all petty jealousies, she was great fun and Esme admired how she never took things personally, especially when she was the target of Bill's baiting. She could be generous, and had been with Esme, so she hoped they would get over this spat. She couldn't afford both to lose a friend and make an enemy of her colleague.

She stared out of the window. The street was dead. Sometimes it felt like St James's was for dinosaurs, old people who had enough money to buy things they didn't need. A lone woman with too much make-up and an up-do pulled a fat Labrador behind her. The poor thing was panting with his tail at half-mast. He looked embarrassed and out of place. People shouldn't have big dogs in the city, Esme thought. It was cruel. They never got enough exercise and clearly this poor fella was mortified being walked by his owner's secretary. He cocked his leg on the wheel of a car. Old and unsteady, he was unable to hold his leg up long enough so he squatted like a bitch. The woman tugged at the lead but the dog wouldn't budge until he was done. Her own dog, beloved Digger, had been like that towards the end. Lost his dignity but Esme had done everything she could to keep him comfortable – she couldn't bear the thought of being without him. In the end, he had died whilst she was at boarding school, and her mother in full-swing mania, sent his body to her in a crate. It was both her best and worst moment at St Mary's. All parcels had to be opened and checked for contraband, like jail, and the nun who opened Digger was joyfully the vile Sister Ann. Word had it that she had screamed and cursed like a sailor. Good old Digger, looking out for her even as a cadaver.

There was nothing to do now except sit at her desk and answer calls. The only problem was that there were none. No customers to take her mind off things. She wondered what her sister Sophia was doing? It would be breakfast time in New York and she would be heading to the deli to collect a bagel. If she rang now she might just catch her.

Esme picked up the telephone. She considered reversing the charges but couldn't guarantee that Sophia would accept them. The call would be less expensive in the afternoon and she was sure Bill wouldn't mind if she was quick.

'Sophs?' she said when the familiar voice answered.

'Yes?'

'It's me. Esme.'

'Es! How are you? You just caught me.'

Esme could hear the jangle of keys and loose coins against something china.

'You'll never guess who just left the gallery.'

When she said Elton's name, Esme heard the china whatever it was crash to the floor and then a shriek from her sister.

'You actually met him? Christ, that's more exciting than Eric Clapton.'

Sophia had been introduced to him at a restaurant once. She had been thoroughly underwhelmed. But still liked to tell the story.

'What was he like?'

'Very rude in a funny way. I'm still in shock.'

Esme went on to tell her a blow-by-blow account of the meeting, with Sophia signing off with a demand that they become best friends.

'I'll probably never see him again,' Esme said wistfully, but secretly already hoping Bill's next exhibition would have more treasures to tempt the star with.

The sisters sent each other love and promised to speak in the next few days. As she put the phone down, Esme felt lifted. It had taken years for her and her sister to get to this kind of friendship – one where they were genuinely rooting for each other, not competing, comparing or begrudging. They might have both fled The Lodge but something clicked into place for Esme: being home wasn't always about who you shared your four walls with, but about who you shared your laughter with, your worries, your quiet moments. And she was lucky enough to have those people to call on. She made a mental note to call Mrs Bee tomorrow. It was amazing how a five-minute conversation could transform your mood.

She was just about to go to the loo when an exceptionally good-looking young man with an enormous portfolio came through the door. He was tall and slender with a whipcord leanness that dispelled any suggestion of weakness. Dressed head to toe in black leather, his black hair and pale skin would have made him look close to death were it not for his blue eyes. Irish, perhaps?

'Hi, I've come to see Bill Cartwright.' So, not Irish. American. 'I've got an appointment with him.'

Esme smoothed her hair and skirt self-consciously as she rose.

'I'm sorry, he's not here. Can I help?'

This was the second time today Bill's absence had left her to deal with the unexpected. So gorgeous was this man that she couldn't imagine any reason important enough for Bill not to be here if he'd known. Always one to fear the worst, a flash of concern crossed Esme's mind. Why was Bill missing the kind of appointments that he usually lived for? She worried that perhaps he was seeing a specialist for a dicky heart or something and had used the excuse of 'outside business' to cover up. Either that or he'd got arrested for something. She was being ridiculous, she told herself. Maybe he was actually just learning to trust her to do some deals and man the fort.

But this man was certainly no dealer, unless it was drugs he was selling.

'Yeah, well, maybe you could help.' He didn't look convinced.

'Are you here for a preview?' Esme ventured. He clearly wasn't.

He looked puzzled then smiled when he understood what she meant.

'Jesus, no. I can't afford to look at these paintings let alone buy one. Don't get me wrong, they are beautiful. But no. Painting isn't my thing. I'm a photographer.'

This made sense but Esme didn't recollect Bill wanting to have his portrait shot. Maybe it was for Javier? But most probably it was the man and not the photographs he was interested in. When it came to photography, she knew Bill only collected retrospectively.

'My agent said he wanted to see my work. I know he's an enthusiastic collector so I was like, wow, the great Bill Cartwright is interested in my photographs. He's a busy man, I'm sure, so I expect he's forgotten. That or maybe my agent was lying and this was all a ruse to get me through the door.'

'I'm sure Bill hasn't forgotten,' said Esme, but as it was blatantly obvious the 'great BC' was nowhere to be seen, she added hurriedly, 'But he was called out on urgent business.' And then, 'Hi. I'm Esme.'

She put out her hand which he took. His hand was rough, muscular and solid, like unpolished stone and the antithesis of his feminine beauty. Everything about his appearance was a contradiction. Effeminate but masculine. Hard yet open and warm. Battered old leather against scrubbed skin and casually gelled hair fashioned into a soft Elvis quiff. Esme considered Oliver's age. Early thirties? It was hard to tell.

'Oliver Maxey. Good to meet you, Esme. Are your parents Salinger fans?'

She didn't know what he was talking about and her ignorance must have shown in her face.

'"For Esme – With Love and Squalor". It's the story of a beautiful young British girl who captures the imagination of a US soldier during the Second World War. You should read it.'

Her father only read John le Carré and she'd never see her mother pick up a book. She, however, had always been a voracious reader, using fiction to escape. Stories of orphans with a happy ending and anything to do with running away were particular favourites. While Sophia lapped up the romance of

Danielle Steel, she flew on the wings of courageous young girls who prevailed against all odds. Sounded like Salinger's Esme might have been one of those girls.

'No, I haven't read it.' The phone rang, saving her from her embarrassment.

'I'd better get this. Might be Bill.'

'Hello?' She smiled at Oliver, mouthing, 'Sorry.'

It was Suki, calling to apologize. She said she was sorry she had been a bitch and blamed her temper on the dentist.

Esme smiled down the phone, a rush of forgiveness and relief making her sigh. She instantly felt renewed affection for Suki. True friends could screw up and then say sorry. True friends accepted apologies and moved on. When her parents had rowed neither ever apologized. Her mother retreated into another world and her father would extricate himself until the dust settled. Her childhood friend Lexi would go silent for days but Esme had always been quick to apologize whether she knew what she'd done or not. She could tell Suki's apology was sincere.

'Someone's come into the gallery. I'd better go. Hope you feel better soon.'

She put the receiver down before Suki had time to ask who. She had learnt a valuable lesson and this time Esme kept her mouth shut.

'Sorry about that, Oliver. Where were we?'

He shook his head and leant his portfolio against the desk.

'Hey, I don't want to take up any more of your time, so do you mind if I just leave my book here? Then Bill can look at it at his leisure. I can come collect it when he's done.'

'Or I could bring it back to you? It's no problem. We're used to handling fine art so I'll take good care of your portfolio.'

She liked Mr Maxey and she knew immediately she wanted to see him again. He probably thought she was just a bored society girl playing at working in the gallery, but if she could wangle another meeting, perhaps she'd convince him otherwise, maybe even add him to her admittedly rather small social arsenal. He was just the kind of individual who by association would make her more interesting. And she couldn't deny he was cute.

'That's super kind. Here. I'll write my address.'

He took an empty envelope from the wastepaper basket and scribbled his contact details. His writing was lyrical in its twist and flow.

'I'm afraid I don't have a personal phone so just drop it whenever. There is always someone hanging around. The studio I work in is a kind of co-operative for artists.'

This would not do. This would not do at all. She didn't want to run the risk of turning up at his studio to return his book when he wasn't there. She looked at the address. Lewisham High Street. She didn't know where it was and was damned if she was going to schlepp all the way over to an empty artist's collective.

'The thing is – what do we do if Bill wants to buy something? How will I reach you?' The 'we' sounded good, like they were already friends.

'I have this number, so I'll call you or Bill in a couple of days. He knows my show is next week, the gallery invited him. You should come too.'

'I'd love to,' she said without hesitation. She would definitely be there and perhaps she could take Cece with her.

'Can I bring a friend?'

'Sure. The more the merrier.' He shrugged and said, 'I'll see you around.'

As he turned, Esme caught sight of his profile. It reminded her of someone but she couldn't place the sharp, refined features. But as she waved him off she realized that it was Elizabeth Taylor he reminded her of. Something feline and mysterious.

Taking Oliver's portfolio, she laid it on the carpet and unzipped it. Carefully she pulled the top print out. It was black-and-white and printed with a clarity she had never seen before. She was visually assaulted by a full-frontal portrait of a woman. There was perfect symmetry to the face, architectural in its positioning and composition. Every hair, eyelash and both eyebrows were perfectly matched. There seemed to be a preoccupation with tonal variation which made it rich and physical. Yet despite immortalizing the subject in a photograph, the vulnerability in her eyes heightened her mortality. It was an incredibly powerful image.

Next – and again black-and-white – was a landscape. In the foreground, a branch jutted like a scar across a vista of undulating dunes. Esme couldn't place the topography. It wasn't quite a desert – clumps of vegetation clung together as if to try to survive the heat. The dunes rose and fell in natural ripples. It was still and peaceful apart from a small fish that disturbed the sand with its foraging. A fish? This wasn't land, Oliver had taken this photograph under the surface of the ocean and through the abstract composition, had deliberately confused the audience.

Until she'd seen that orchid picture in Bill's collection, Esme had never considered photography to be anything but capturing friends and family, fashion or product. Before her was an image that bridged the gap between photography and painting. It was a revelation and she knew she would be doing Bill a favour if she took Oliver's work straight round to his house at the end of the day. She fizzed with excitement – starting to understand how Bill or Max must feel when they stumbled across a hidden gem.

Chapter Thirteen

The hours dragged to closing time and in her impatience to see Bill, Esme shut the shop fifteen minutes early. She didn't have enough money for a taxi and, given she would be carrying Oliver's portfolio, it was too far to walk. Although it was rush hour, she'd take the bus which was only a couple of stops.

Office workers thronged the pavements outside pubs, still in their suits and court shoes. Esme wondered where all these people lived, how far they had to commute or whether they still lived with their parents close by. The mass of people in the city still felt strange to her – every nook and cranny of London filled with hidden lives. Passing a pub, drinkers spilt onto the road unwilling to spread themselves out along the pavement. Even en masse, there was a clear division of tribes. The bankers, the PAs, the proprietors and their workers huddled in groups pushed up against each other yet reluctant to mix. Esme fought her way through the hordes, head down and determined not to make eye contact with strangers. Someone tutted and shoved her out of the way. A man, half-cut and arrogant. She glared and he nodded at his friend and laughed.

'Asshole,' she muttered.

The bus was filled with what seemed to be the whole of the West End. She had had to wait for nearly half an hour before she was able to squeeze herself onto one. The only advantage of being one in hundreds was that she was wedged in and didn't topple when the bus braked. The man standing behind her rubbed against her back. She wasn't sure if he was getting off on it or an accidental pervert put into an awkward position by someone else ramming into him. She had to get off at the first stop to allow others to disembark but held on to the pole to secure her place. Everyone pushed and shoved with no regard for others. She'd learnt that in the world of rush-hour public transport, only the ill-mannered survived. If you were disabled, wrangling a pushchair or old, you didn't stand a chance, though. Esme saw an elderly woman who cried out when an elbow knocked her glasses off.

Quick to the rescue, Esme barged past the owner of the offending elbow, and grabbed the glasses before they were crushed underfoot.

'There you go.' She handed them back to their owner. 'Are you OK?'

'Thank you, dear, I'm fine now. I really can't see without my spectacles. I'm too old for this kind of thing – I hate getting in the way of the crowds. All you young busy people.'

Esme wanted to hug her but instead did her best with the help of the portfolio to protect the woman from the crush. It was upsetting that this woman was resigned to being ignored and invisible. People have no respect, she thought. God, she sounded like her father but she was grateful that he and, and to a certain extent, her mother, had drummed into her the value of a decent moral compass. Mrs Bee had always made sure she was aware of those worse off than her but Esme had never really seen how big that gulf could be until now. She was appalled by how desensitized some Londoners appeared to another person's vulnerability.

After what seemed like a lifetime, Esme prised herself off the bus and took a deep breath. Even the polluted air felt fresh after the fug of sweaty bodies. There was a faint breeze that dried her damp cotton top which clung to her back and the evening sun brought a golden glow to the streets as she set off for Bill's.

'Urgh… That feels *so* much better. I tell you, I'm never taking public transport in the rush hour ever again. I'd rather walk,' she shouted to Javier, who was, as night follows day, mixing something strong and delicious in the drawing room. He'd offered her a shower when she'd told him of her sauna-like bus trip.

'I'll be in the garden,' he shouted back.

Not wanting to put her filthy clothes back on just yet, she wrapped herself and her hair in towels and went to join him. He had a selection of Oliver's prints already laid out on the grass.

'Javier! You can't do that. Put them on the table. They'll get damaged.'

Javier laughed and said, 'Calm down! It hasn't rained for weeks and this grass is as dry as Margaret Thatcher's pussy.'

'And how would you know?' she laughed, sitting next to him. 'Aren't the photos stunning?'

Javier's uncustomary silence made her start to doubt herself.

179

Had she been more impressed by the photographs or the man who took them? She had questioned Bill's motives and now she was questioning her own. Talk about pot and kettle.

She watched a wasp hover above then land with intent upon Javier's shoulder. She flicked it off with the edge of her towel. Still, he said nothing, hunched over a photograph of a stingray flying silently through its watery underworld. It was a menacingly elegant representation of perfection only found in nature. Again, the symmetry of both subject and composition. She hoped Javier was quiet because he was mesmerized by what lay at his feet. It was hypnotic and swallowed the here and now into the shadows of the sea.

He finally cupped his hands around the back of his neck and stretched as if he had just woken up. 'My God, Esme, these are stunning,' he said quietly. 'Who's the photographer?'

'Oliver Maxey. He's American.'

'How could Bill have missed him? Or I? I know my photography too and this guy is a true artist.' He looked at her. 'Where did you find him?'

Esme felt she was witness to the discovery of something important.

'I didn't. Bill did – well, sort of. The guy came to see him this afternoon, except of course Bill wasn't there. I've got no idea how the appointment was made but he seemed to know all about Bill.'

Javier frowned and brought his face close to hers.

'Is he handsome?'

Reading Javier's mind that was already accusing his boyfriend of a secret affair, she said, 'Beautiful. In fact, sorry, Jav, but I pray he's not gay...'

Javier studied her then squealed 'OH MY GOD, ESME! You're in love!'

She grinned, pulled the towel over her head and kicked him in jest, blushing.

'I'm not! I've spent all of about fifteen minutes with him. Anyway, it's his photographs not him I wanted to talk about.'

'You lie!'

Jumping up as if the wasp had successfully stung him, he rotated his hips and stirred an invisible pot.

'Esme and Olly sitting in a tree, K.I.S.S.I.N.G.,' he sang.

The excitement of a galloping stomach made her shiver. She certainly fancied the leather trousers off him – Javier had worked that out immediately – but didn't want to invest her hopes in a man who, for all she knew, swung the other way. And anyway, he was an edgy American art-genius – what would he see in her but a Sloane babysitting someone else's gallery?

'I have only one true love and that is Elton.'

She told Javier about their meeting, embellishing and exaggerating the story until Javier was screeching with laughter.

'I can – not – believe you dropped milk in the street. So unsophisticated. What did he say?'

'"I hate fucking tea!"'

'This is too precious. I love it, Esme. I want you in my life forever! But forget everything else, *you* sold a painting. Bill will be ecstatico.'

Yes, it had been a pretty extraordinary day, thought Esme. She was doing things for herself, doing them her way, driven by her own ambition. But deep down, she knew she still longed for her parents to see her in action. She wondered if she'd ever grow out of the desire for them to be proud of her. Her mother would never be able to, but she hoped her father would be pleased to see his daughter making her way in the art world.

'You ought to get this Olivio to photograph you. Become a muse like your mama.'

'What do you mean "a muse like my mother"? Dad only painted one portrait of her.'

'No, *carina*. Your mother was once the toast of New York. Everyone was crazy for her.'

Javier went on to tell Esme how she might have become one of Andy Warhol's Superstars, had her father allowed it. 'Colin. Always so controlling.' They had met at a cocktail party given by a man called Fred Hughes who was Warhol's business partner and obsessed by all things British. He revelled in telling all of New York society that Diana was a more beautiful version of Jackie O. When her father was off 'getting down to business,' Javier said Fred would whisk Esme's mother off, put her in enormous sunglasses and a polo neck to see how many social-climbing wasps they could fool into thinking she was the former First Lady.

'Sometimes, I was invited,' Javier continued. 'Of course I was young and beautiful too back then. Bill and I were still just flirting and your mother would tease me about him when we went out. We got the best tables in all the restaurants and paparazzi would tail after her,' he laughed.

Esme hadn't realized Javier had known her mother so well. He was full of stories she'd never heard. He told her how there were two sides to 'darling Diana'. The ghost and the schoolgirl. The girl came out to play when she was apart from Esme's father. 'She had an aura, you know...' Javier put his forefinger on his chin, 'like… like a silent movie star. She didn't need to say a word to attract people. Fred was so happy to have discovered such a prize. He took her under his wing and introduced her to New York's movers and shakers.'

Because of Diana, he said, Warhol saw New York through fresh eyes. Apparently, when he and Diana were together, they would sit talking quietly and meticulously observe the superficial crowd that made up much of Manhattan's inner circle. 'Warhol's notoriety went straight over Diana's head. She simply found him a sweet, shy man. Like a white mole,' Javier said. 'The fact that she had no idea who he was made Warhol like her even more. He was sick of being brown-nosed. It was a pure friendship.'

Esme couldn't believe her mother had been friends – actual friends – with Andy Warhol. If Javier had told her the Contessa was to be ordained, she would have been less amazed. She'd assumed her mother had no inkling of American pop culture. The upper classes she'd been raised amongst were so narrow-minded. There was glamour in the higher echelons of society, yes, but the *beau monde* was considered brash and vulgar. But as Esme was beginning to learn these terms were used as weapons to keep at bay a world they misunderstood, excuses to remain pickled in aspic, righteously and stubbornly looking to the past for their standards and morals.

'This is so weird,' she said. 'So you think Mummy was cool?'

'Oh yes, my darling. She didn't try to be. She just *was* and we adored her. I think her time in New York was a happy one. She felt safe. She felt she belonged. New York celebrates the damaged. Andy loved that your mama was so beautiful but so sick. He said she was an incandescent star trapped by privilege. He wanted to set her free.'

Her mother might have been a star – but it was one that had since gone supernova. For a few fleeting moments, there had been light and heat, brighter than the rest of the heavens, but in her wake she had left nothing but darkness. Her mind had collapsed in on itself. Esme tried to push away a flicker of fear as she wondered if she would follow in her mother's footsteps. She was a similar age to Diana when she was in New York, trying to find the hidden life of a city, hanging out with artists, hoping to find friends beyond the stuffy society circuit. It was a warning, thought Esme – there was a fine line between burning bright and burning out.

Chapter Fourteen

It was the night of Bill's private view. Everything was going to plan. The waitresses had arrived, the canapés were plated, champagne glasses lined up on linen-dressed tables. Pulbrook and Gould had arranged and delivered exquisite displays of hydrangeas and peonies, blousy, extravagant and intrinsically English. But the stars of the show were European – the pictures themselves. Only six of them but each a perfect representation of the Baroque and Rococo periods. French and Italian scenes of exaggerated violence, rich and vibrant alongside light-hearted pastoral scenes. The thrill of being up close to such flawlessness never disappointed. She could almost feel the artists' brushstrokes caress her. She still felt amazed that she got to be their guardian, even if it was just for a few days. Side by side, they were glorious. Extravagant, grand and over the top. A bit like Bill, really, who had been delighted by the sale to Elton John. By his reaction, Esme suspected the sale had already been pretty much a done deal by the time the superstar had come to see the Van Dyck, but Bill still let Esme bask in the glow of her first sale. He was full of verve and generosity as his guests assembled.

Cece had said she was going to try and get there early, but also that it depended on Dan. He was on a deadline and wanted it done before he came.

'But don't be later than seven,' Esme had told her. 'It'll end around eight thirty and I want to see you for as long as possible and I'll be busy clearing up after.'

Having organized the event, tidying up was part of the job as well. Suki would normally be down to help but her boyfriend was on leave from duty in Northern Ireland and so Esme had told her she could manage by herself. After all, the guests would mostly be wealthy collectors more interested in swapping art world gossip than getting sloshed, so it was unlikely the gallery would be wrecked. Hopefully all she'd have to do would be empty ashtrays and lock up. The caterers took everything away dirty so she would only have to gather the empty glasses. It had cost extra but Esme had told Bill it would be cheaper than her breaking things washing them up in the bird-bath-sized sink in the kitchen.

On Javier's instruction, she had made extra effort with her appearance. She'd discovered a previous occupant of her bedsit had left behind a pale-blue shift dress which she had made more fashionable with a navy cummerbund of Javier's which she cinched in and tied with a double knot. She swept her hair back on either side with two tortoiseshell combs, like she had seen Princess Anne do, and put a dash of Rive Gauche behind her ears. Suki would doubtless be in something froufrou and frilly, especially around the collar and cuffs.

She clipped some gold knots on her lobes and checked her make-up. Not too much mascara but enough to thicken her lashes without clumping, a lip-gloss sheen and swipe of blush.

Looking back at her was the reflection of a sensible young lady. She looked like everything she was but didn't want to be. Bill was yelling for her from downstairs.

'Sorry, just getting ready,' she said as she hurried down into the gallery.

The upward trajectory of Bill's champagne glass stopped at his chin. He looked surprised.

'What's wrong? What have I done?'

'Darling Esme, you look…'

'Stunning!' finished Javier, tonight the very essence of English gentleman in his huge shirt collar and spotty cravat.

'What were you going to say, Bill?' Esme asked.

'I was going to say how sophisticated you look. It just surprised me, that's all. I'm used to the ruffian scurrying about and here you are all dolled up like…'

'Like what?'

'Well, like your mama.'

The awkward moment was broken by Suki, fresh from the poodle parlour. Every inch of her had been whisked into a frothy soufflé of pink.

'Esme, this is Johnny. Johnny Downes,' she said, presenting her boyfriend, who sauntered in behind her.

Johnny was everything and less than Esme expected. A jolly but chinless wonder, who swallowed his vowels and wore a signet ring on his left hand. Like so many 'gals' of her class, Suki punched below her weight when it came to boyfriends, but she was born to take on the role her mother had lived and father expected. Forget looks, it was all about the pedigree. Johnny didn't look like a soldier, thought Esme. In fact, he appeared more overgrown schoolboy than officer of the guard.

She then felt bad at being so quick to judge. If she was looking in from the outside, she would put herself in the same mould.

She'd never dream of letting on to Suki, but Esme did *not* want to end up with a Johnny. She wanted someone with fire, who inspired her and encouraged her to be the best version of herself. She supposed in a strange way, she had her mother to thank for opening her mind to other possibilities, because the life she had led – married to a man who ticked the right boxes rather than set her heart ablaze – had hollowed her out.

'Nice to meet you,' she said to Johnny, and they passed a perfectly pleasant five minutes engaged in dutiful small talk.

'Where did you go to school?' Eton, she predicted.

'Eton,' he replied.

'University?' She already knew the answer.

'Sandhurst.' Full of pride, as if he'd already been awarded the Military Cross.

'And when you've finished in the army...?' Daddy's firm, she bet. She was sure she'd guessed a hat trick.

'Downes and Ilford.'

'The estate agency?'

'Family business,' he said, rolling his eyes to feign he was being forced into it, as if nepotism had no part to play. Esme had had enough.

'Will you excuse me?' she said through a smile and a thumbs-up to Suki.

The gallery was filling up with older versions of Johnny and Suki, cut-outs of her parents and their friends. They spoke loudly, shouting to be heard over each other. It was a contest of show-offs, men and women who clung together like limpets, uninterested in anyone without a title or double-barrelled name.

Esme felt restricted in her get-up, hot and bothered. She needed some air.

It was a relief to get outside. She took off her belt which had left a tide mark of sweat. Javier came to join her.

'I feel sorry for Bill having to hobnob with these types. Braying ignoramuses with nothing better to do than boast to each other. What they don't realize is that they are all the same, just in different shades of bland.'

'I was brought up to become one of those idiots,' she said, peering into crowded showroom.

Javier laughed. 'You could never be them. Your parents were too glamorous. These silly people have spondulicks but no style.'

'Mum and Dad would be genuinely excited by these pictures, even if they couldn't afford to buy one. They were always on the lookout for similar things – although by lesser-known artists. Well, Dad still is.'

But Javier was distracted by something or someone behind her, Esme pinched his cigarette and took a drag. Javier was still staring ahead with a look of naked lust creeping into his face.

'Ohhhh,' he sighed. 'Who do we have here?'

Esme turned around. It was Cece and Dan, every inch the cosmopolitan couple.

'Cece! You came.'

'Wouldn't have missed it for the world, gorge,' she said, hugging Esme and then Javier.

'Hey, Esme.'

Dan remembered her name! Esme introduced him to Javier, chuffed that she could do so with someone the South American hadn't met before. Javier usually knew everyone. Dan shook

Javier's hand, complimenting him on his cravat and blazer. Javier took a step closer and gazed into Dan's eyes.

'Daniel. What a pleasure.'

'Great to meet you, Javier,' said Dan, pronouncing his name with a silent J unlike most Brits. 'Cece has told me so much about you.'

'All bad, I hope.'

Esme saw Javier give Dan's hand a squeeze and was now standing so close, the tips of their shoes were touching: Dan's cowboy boots to Javier's winkle-pickers. The latter gave his best Gloria Swanson come-hither look, hoping to bewitch its beneficiary. God, Javier was behaving like a bitch on heat. There was something delightful about his shameless flirting and Esme was amazed to see Dan was happily playing up to it.

'Not all. She told me all about your passage from Uruguay to New York. Sounds fascinating. I'd love to talk to you some more about it.'

Javier looked like Dan had cured him of leprosy.

'Pull yourself together,' hissed Esme, smiling, as Cece and Dan went inside.

'I can tell he swings both ways, darling.'

'You think everyone fancies you, Javier.'

Mind you, it was hard not to. When he turned his attention on you, Esme saw it must be pretty hard not to succumb.

Conscious of abandoning her friends and nervous they might tar her with the same brush as Bill's guests, she went back inside. Cece stood alone with an expression of awe, like she had entered a prehistoric tomb filled with cave paintings. Meanwhile Dan swanned around the room, schmoozing and smiling like a pro.

'Blimey, Es. So, this is your world,' said Cece.

'It's where I work. I don't know any of these people,' she replied. 'Do you want some champagne?'

'Is it free?'

'Of course it is.'

'Shit, yeah, I'll have two then.'

As she was waiting for the glasses, Suki sidled up to Esme.

'Who *are* those people, Esme?'

'They're my friends… And Javier's.'

'I thought so. He looks the sleazy type and as for her… I don't think Bill will be best pleased having a punk rocker at his opening.'

Esme wanted to tell her not to be such a snob, especially as she looked like an undercooked version of Barbara Cartland with her frosted make-up and bouffant hair. In her formalwear, Suki already showed the kind of polished Home Counties housewife she was set to become. Plus she wouldn't know a real punk if she had to pick on out of a line-up.

'I thought Johnny was lovely, by the way,' she said, changing the subject before saying something she'd regret. It wasn't Suki's fault that she had never been exposed to anything other than drawing rooms and shooting weekends but there was no need to be so judgemental.

'Isn't he just. He's not the most handsome but his wallet makes up for it. Got to marry money, Es, and his family is awash with it.'

Esme laughed. She was relieved to hear Suki's cynicism. Tough as old wellingtons and not afraid to admit it. It was good to be reminded that whilst Suki came from a privileged background, she could still laugh at herself.

'Hello, girls. How many paintings have you sold so far?' Bill draped his arms around the two of them, a wide smile on his face. Esme had all but forgotten she was here to help charm clients and help extract hundreds of thousands of pounds out of them.

'We've been plying everyone with alcohol to make the pain of parting with their cash easier,' said Suki. 'I think I might've sold one to Johnny's parents. He said they'd buy the Carracci.'

'Suki darling, there isn't a Carracci on show.'

'Well, you know, that one,' she said pointing to a Fragonard.

'God give me strength,' said Bill. 'And I met your friend Dan, Esme. Charming. He wants to write a profile piece on me in his newspaper. And he seems to know a lot about fine art. A lot about my area of expertise.'

Dan had clearly gained another fan. It didn't seem likely that an article on Bill in the Camden newspaper would have many readers but who was she to know.

Esme collected the champagne and squeezed through the throng, careful not to spill her drinks as people blocked her path, loath to break their conversational flow. She felt the heat of their bodies packed together like steaming lobsters. The air was cloying and damp, making it hard to breathe.

When she got to Cece, the girl already had a glass in hand from somewhere and was leaning against the wall surveying the scene. Esme wished that she had dressed up a bit. This wasn't a postgraduate show at St Martin's. One of the many things she liked about Cece was her defiant independence but given she had so many clothes, she could have worn something more appropriate. Then she mentally told herself off for sounding like Suki. She admitted Cece certainly stood out, with her bright pink top and silver mini that showed a bruise on her thigh.

'These people are like dinosaurs. I can't understand a word they say and they act as if I'm from another planet. One woman asked where the lavatory was. I mean who the fuck says that anymore? I said I didn't know and she told me to "buck up", if I wanted Mr Cartwright to hire me again. She then turned to her fat friend and said, "Only people like Bill would sanction the staff dressing like that." She thought I was the waitress. Must be in my DNA.'

'They're just ignorant, Cece. Here. I've got you another glass of champagne.'

'Thanks, honey. Their kind of talk doesn't bother me. Takes all sorts to make the world go around.'

She downed the remains of the first glass and put it on the windowsill and took a cigarette from her bag, a sort of kilim-type over-the-shoulder thing.

'Want one?'

'I'd better not. But you go ahead.'

Cece looked at her with raised eyebrows.

'Don't tell me you care what these people think. "Oh, look at that naughty girl smoking. How shocking."' She did a good imitation of a plummy English accent.

Esme laughed. But it was true. She did care what these people thought and she was furious with herself for it.

'Give me a cigarette,' she said, revelling in the tiny rebellion.

Cece pulled it from the packet and Esme lit it with one of the tea lights, there for effect rather than illumination as it was still light outside. She blew the smoke up towards the ceiling.

'Ah, that's good. You know I never smoked much before I came to London but in this atmosphere you're inhaling everyone else's anyway. My room is going to stink of it though.

I hate that. And waking up with my hair smelling like an ashtray.'

'I forgot you lived here as well. Nice part of town but it must be dead at night,' said Cece. 'I'm going to get more champagne. Want a top-up?'

'I'd love one. Rescue me if I get dragged off by one of these wankers.'

Esme's feet were hurting and she sat down. The evening seemed to be going well. Four paintings had red dots next to them, quite a coup considering each one was the price of a flat in Chelsea. Certainly, she hadn't brought anything more to the table since the Elton sale, making the fact that Bill had taken her on as a favour feel even more apparent. But Suki was in the same predicament and Bill was a one-man band at heart. More of a one-man orchestra, she thought as she watched him buzz around the room, flattering and fawning over potential buyers. They loved his flamboyance and paid to step into his exotic world, even if she knew some of them still viewed homosexuality as a disease. But what they didn't realize was that he saw through their bullshit and used it to his advantage. He was sharper than any of them.

Esme looked at her watch: 7.45. She hoped there would be no late-comers as the gallery was bursting at the seams. Despite the sweltering heat, no one went outside. All the men – apart from Javier – were buttoned-up in suit and tie, and the women wore flesh-coloured tights, sweating like pigs in a sandwich bag. God forbid they let respectability slip even in this temperature. The acidity of champagne mingled with smoke, cologne and syrupy perfume. It was the smell of money and it stuck at the back of her throat.

'Penny for your thoughts.'

Dan sat down next to her. She automatically clocked Cece's whereabouts and saw she was chatting to Javier.

'I was just thinking how these people see Bill as some kind of novelty, some kind of entertainment.'

'Dog eats dog. Bill seems the kind of man to use this to his advantage. No flies on him.'

'He's one of my father's best friends.'

'Is that how you are working here? I had you down as more of a fashion magazine girl. Organizing photo shoots and running around town with rails of the latest collections. *Vogue* or *Harper's*.'

Esme laughed, 'I don't think so. Growing up I was more likely to be seen pushing sheep into their pen than dreaming of styling a fashion shoot. I'd be hopeless. Paintings are the only thing I've ever really understood. I love art.'

'I'm sure you do. I bet you are knowledgeable, too. Bill mentioned you grew up in one of the great houses of Scotland, surrounded by Old Masters. He said you have an instinct.'

'You asked about me?'

'Of course I did. You are the most interesting person here.'

Esme took a gulp of her drink, embarrassed and ill-equipped to deal with this kind of flattery.

'There you are, Esme.'

Bill was clearly pissed. His face glistened like a doused newborn, his hair sticking to his scalp. Sweat had soaked into his shirt collar turning it a shade or three darker than the rest.

'I know, I know, I'm tipsy but I need to be to be pissed to spend time with these fools. I was rather hoping you'd invited your friend Princess Margaret. At least she's intelligent.'

Dan's eyes darted between her and Bill. It annoyed her that everyone got so wound up by the royal family. They were just people born into extraordinary circumstances. She was embarrassed that Bill had mentioned the Princess and Dan would get the wrong idea about her; think of her as one of the entitled 'fools' Bill had to put up with or worse, that she was only worth befriending because of her contacts.

'I only know her through my parents, Bill. It's not like I hang out with her. And anyway, I haven't seen her for years. She doesn't even know I'm in London.'

'I was joking, blossom. We don't want young Dan here thinking you're an airhead heiress, do we?' He winked at her. 'You are now an independent young woman who likes to frequent the seedier side of London. Camden, wasn't it?'

How the hell did he know? But she was grateful that he'd given her a get–out–of–jail–free card after his indiscretion. She could try to show Dan she had at least some street–smarts.

'It's great up there. You can find some cool stuff in the market, but you have to haggle. And they can spot money a mile off. They'd see you coming, Bill,' she said.

'I, my dear, wouldn't go there if my life depended on it. All that dirt.' He shuddered. 'It's a third–world country outside of SW1 as far as I'm concerned. Horrendous!' And then to Suki who had teetered over to join the party, 'What do you think of Camden, Suki Su?'

'How would I know?'

'My point exactly,' said Bill.

It occurred to Esme that Dan was keeping very quiet on the subject. She'd expect him to stick up for the place, given it was where he worked.

'We haven't met,' said Dan standing up to shake Suki's hand.

'No. I'm Suki.'

'I gather. Nice to meet you,' he said with a smile. 'I'm Dan.'

'So, you're a journalist, are you?' said Suki. 'Who do you write for, *Apollo* or *Burlington*?'

'There are other periodicals beyond art magazines, Suki,' said Bill. 'I'm sorry, Dan, the girl has been brought up in a padded cell.'

Dan came to her defence. 'Not at all. You put two and two together and assumed that as a writer I would be doing a piece on this exhibition.'

'Well, sort of,' she giggled, then swayed. Dan caught her elbow.

'Oops, I'm a bit squiffy,' she mumbled.

'Let's get you something to eat, honey,' said Dan.

Honey? Since when did Suki become a honey? He'd only just met the girl and was coming over all charm and concern.

'I'll get your boyfriend,' said Esme. 'I can see him over there.'

She shouted Johnny's name and for a beat the room went quiet – all the better to hear the sound of breaking glass. Cece – alone and holding onto the frame of one of the paintings – had dropped her glass splattering champagne everywhere. With exaggerated shock and disgust the people close to her backed away as if the tide was coming in. The whole room turned to look, the spotlight of their gaze highlighting her difference. Against the sea of matching navy and regulation chiffon, her cheap clothes and bottle-dyed hair stood out. All strength and defiance left her eyes as she raised her hands in surrender, mouthing 'Sorry' and staggered towards the door.

How could Cece of all people have got so plastered? Esme wondered. She thought she could take her drink better than most.

Alarmed, Bill rushed over to the painting with the speed of a cow elephant protecting her young.

'Jesus-fucking-Christ-be-CAREFUL!' he shrieked and then turned to Esme and hissed, 'Get this girl out of here. Now.'

But Esme looked to the door and Cece was already gone. She followed her out found her throwing up in the gutter.

'Hell, Cece. What got into you? How could you have got so bloody drunk? Especially tonight.'

'A case of that grog, I think,' she groaned and threw up again, making Esme jump back.

'I'm going to get you into a cab. Stay here while I grab some money from petty cash. Shall I tell Dan?'

'Fuck no. I'm so embarrassed. He'll never want to see me again.'

She was crying now. Drunken tears and self-pity washed away her last vestiges of dignity. She leant against the lamppost, head back taking in gulps of air.

'Fuck, fuck, fuck. I'm sorry, Esme.'

Esme suddenly saw Cece as she really was. This girl was not just her guardian angel, invincible and full of courage. She was as fallible and vulnerable as anyone. She'd been so focused on feeling out of place in Cece's cool Camden world of nightlife and alternative fashion, that Esme had never stopped to think that Cece might get the same anxiety when dropped into the middle of her world of free champagne and paintings worth more than Cece would earn in a lifetime of waitressing. Was a friendship possible if they felt so alien in each other's respective habitats? Or would they always feel like tourists, doomed to be stuck in the worlds they came from?

'Stay here. I'll be back in two minutes.'

Inside the gallery, Bill was clearing up the glass with a dustpan and brush. Suki had Dan trapped in a corner and was screaming with over-enthusiastic laughter at something he was saying. He looked smug and relaxed as he surreptitiously tried to take her hand. Esme took a tenner from the red box. The gallery felt like a greenhouse and she was suffocating with an overbearing sense of anticlimax. The evening was meant to be her arrival on the arts scene, she'd wanted to talk to prospective buyers, show Bill that she was indispensable. But instead she hadn't even been able to clean up properly. Bill wouldn't be happy at having to wield the dustpan himself. She began to ask herself why the hell she was still there. But escape wasn't easy when she lived above the gallery. She wished she knew more people here. If Max had come she could have used his straight-talking right now, or if Oliver had been present her defeat might have given her the confidence of having nothing left to lose and she could have summoned the nerve to ask him out for drinks and dragged him off into the night.

At least if she gave Cece the money for a cab and saw her set off home safely it would give her a chance to cool down before returning to tidy up. But outside, Cece was nowhere to be seen. Esme supposed she must have found her own taxi or decided to walk the alcohol off. She hoped she was OK – though she would surely have a sore head in the morning. Thank God it was the weekend and the gallery was shut tomorrow, Esme thought. But she'd have to get out – she needed a change from Jermyn Street. She remembered the poster for the Wallace Collection. The prospect of seeking solace and anonymity in a museum felt good. At least it would take her mind off the calamity this night had turned into.

Chapter Fifteen

It was a relief to leave the heaving swell of Oxford Street the next morning, with its Saturday shoppers and stationary buses. Esme turned the corner into a small, quiet, leafy square. Silent calm, yards away from the crowds. There was both beauty and excitement in London, she knew that now, but so often the best bits lay hidden. She considered the actual land lying concealed but not entirely changed or destroyed, beneath the surface of concrete. London was simply disguised countryside, after all. The street she walked down veered off at an angle, perhaps to avoid where the wall of a manor house once stood or even a stream once ran. She thought of paintings she studied, created when London was still a succession of villages. Street patterns had been determined by the holdings of individual farmers and landlords, parcels of land that could be traced back centuries. Only now they'd joined up and merged in towers of brick and glass, you had to look a little closer to feel that living history.

Tourists flocked to the city like a theme park, a Disneyworld of cobbled streets and grand architecture with its kings and queens in lieu of Mickey Mouse and Goofy. So often they came not to see what London was, or even what it had been, but to confirm a kind of picture-postcard view, all red telephone and letter boxes and The Beatles. She supposed she'd done the same – except she hadn't come looking for palaces and parliament, but clubs and counterculture.

Lost in thought, she became aware that she had missed the Duke Street turning. She pulled out her *A-Z* and ran a finger over the page seeing that she could get off the human highway at Regent Street and double back through Cavendish Square. There would be no window-shopping that route but at least she'd be able to move without being battered by the crowds. Feeling like she'd been squeezed free from a tube of toothpaste, the air was less choked once she'd turned off and looking up she could see the sky through the latticed branches of plane trees with their balls of clustered seeds. Funny how no birds seemed to like these trees, yet pigeons patrolled the ground. She took off her cardigan, tied it around her waist and headed uninterrupted towards Manchester Square.

Before setting off that morning she'd skimmed through one of Bill's many books on London's museums and collections, but she was still amazed when she arrived at the Wallace Collection and looked at the grand building. It was hard to believe that Hertford House had once been a private residence and that one family could have made their home in such a vast and opulent space in the centre of London. She remembered Max telling her the contents were predominantly made up of an extraordinary array of eighteenth-century French art, bought at knock-down prices post-revolution and some fine works by Dutch masters. 'Elegant and sensuous' was how Max described them. She wondered how many of them had passed through his studio for restoration.

Upon entering the museum, she felt a calm fall over her. Despite its size and the grandeur, it was an ornate but unintimidating entrance. The stillness made her step back into a leisured, more graceful age when time moved at a gentler pace and there was no shame in privilege. The sense of power and quality bathed her soul, wrapping her in a protective shield. She could just take in the peace of a bygone era for a few hours. Esme let out a sigh and felt her body relax. This was an environment that was more familiar to her than the hectic London streets. There was no pressure to pretend to be worldly and sophisticated, no need to have something new or clever to say about the paintings, she could just appreciate the beauty that surrounded her. She felt she knew at once why this was her father's favourite gallery. Apart from Frans Hals's *Laughing Cavalier*, there were no 'superstar' paintings to entice the hordes, instead the gallery attracted either those with a pure love of art or else lost souls looking simply for a some quiet and contemplation.

Every single piece was flawless. By contrast, the few visitors looked incongruous and out of place in their modern dress and casual clothing; paupers allowed to enter for the briefest of visits. Esme was almost ashamed she hadn't dressed in accordance with her surroundings. It felt rude to be in cotton and not silk and lace.

She climbed the stairs, imagining what it must have been like when it was a home. Whilst Culcairn was several times the size and valuable masterpieces were scattered in state rooms like cushions, there was nowhere near the concentration of affluence. Had it not been so thoughtfully laid out, Herftord House might have appeared cluttered and individual pieces would have got lost, but each item had the space to shine even though its neighbours were of the same quality or superior. Alongside the paintings, exquisite furniture, porcelain figures and assorted snuff boxes of gold and precious stones sparkled. Chandeliers of all kinds and hanging lights in the shape of jelly moulds threw a subtle glow that exaggerated the romantic atmosphere. Each room boasted a fireplace of such magnificence they felt like exhibits in their own right. Every one was decked with clocks adorned with flying putti, candelabra and delicate sculptures. The depth and breadth of the collection was extraordinary; a treasure trove beyond anyone's imagining.

Esme joined a small group of visitors clustered around *The Rainbow Landscape*, a Rubens she'd seen so many times in her textbooks. In the flesh it had a depth and subtlety of colour that transfixed her. A guide was pinpointing details with the precision of a surgeon. It was extraordinary that none of the paintings were covered by glass to protect them from people who stood too close – to Esme the best way of viewing a great landscape such as this was to stand back and take in the image as a whole. And they'd never get around the collection in one day if each work was going to be scrutinized in such detail.

Entering the Oval Drawing Room, it was clear to see where her father got his inspiration from. Stuffed to the gills with bronzes, wall sconces, gilt, gold and intricately carved wood it was extravagant, designed with tasteful greed. Pale-blue damask lined the walls and swagged either side of the windows in garlands. Pelham Place had emulated this style in miniature. Decorating had begun on a budget, but as Munroe Fine Art Removals grew, so did the house's contents – and insurance policy. But the house had never seemed jumbled. Everything was placed in perfect symmetry having its own spot that her father had spent hours if not days analysing and measuring. If something wasn't quite right then he would buy a replacement that cost more money and usually involved a trip to France.

Looking around her now, it was a wonder the Hertford and Wallace families had left anything behind in France for future collectors. The majority of the art here had been plundered after the fall of the French aristocracy – from people who had either been slaughtered or needed quick cash in order to flee the country. Beautiful they might have been, but they were ill-gotten gains that took advantage of dire circumstance. She was surrounded by unapologetic beauty that had endured unspeakable bloodshed and violence. She thought of her own family: her father's relentless buying sprees with a Coutts' chequebook that belied the size of their overdraft; her mother's designer clothes that shrouded her inner turmoil. There were two sides to every story including her own and she was yet to discover which was closest to the truth.

Esme came now to *The Swing*, Fragonard's iconic painting. She sat down opposite in and studied its energy and frivolity. A carefree young woman was tantalizingly positioned mid-air on a swing between two men. It occurred to Esme, one was the husband and the other her lover, the latter being in the privileged position to see right up her skirt. She was conflicted by what it stood for. The rich pink silk of the woman's dress and her carefree demeanour seemed like enough to drive any disaffected pauper towards revolution. Had she been alive in the eighteenth century, would she have joined them or run for the hills along with her family and friends?

A couple of grey-haired ladies entered the room clutching

guidebooks and reading glasses. In their loose-fitting clothes and comfortable shoes, they looked the type to object to talking in a library, and indeed they spoke in reverent whispers, pointing at things then referring back to their books. Esme felt their disapproval and realized they were tutting at her sitting in a roped-off chair. She hopped back over and gave the old dears an apologetic smile, feeling embarrassed. At Culcairn, she was allowed behind the velvet ropes. Here she was the same as every other visitor.

Still hot with shame, she sidled away to take a closer look at the frame of one of the Watteaus hung nearby. Max had told her that a mediocre painting could be greatly enhanced in value with a decent frame. Genuine gold leaf never lost its shimmer, he had said, whereas imitation gold always darkened in time.

In the opulent Great Gallery she felt like its magnificence knocked her sideways. Nothing had prepared her for the stupendous scale, its size and grandeur. It was hard to believe she was only a matter of metres from the grubby neon reality of Oxford Street. Even compared with the previous rooms she felt like she had moved from a very grand house and into a palace. She thought of the shops nearby, their gaudy clothing in artificial colours replaced by Titian's burnished red-pinks and the blue robes of the Madonna sang softly against the damask walls. The vast canvases complemented one another, swathes of nude flesh flashing from silk and satin and blue sky. She felt she was seeing paintings she had known all her life for the very first time. Her eyes flew from one picture to another making her feel dizzy. It was breathtaking.

One thing was certain: she had saved the best for last. A group of school children sat beneath *The Laughing Cavalier.*

The small troupe of boys – dressed in uniform burgundy and mustard – looked bored, finding their friends more interesting than the iconic painting their teacher was describing in dull tones. She wanted to take her place and tell the kids instead to move around the gallery to test the theory that the eyes follow you and to focus on the rich gold-and-black pattern on his sleeve. Esme thought she could see a face in there; a lion; a monster. She wanted the boys to feel the same fun and intrigue she did when she looked into the eyes of the mysterious cavalier. She was enthralled to see up close the spun threads of spittle-like white paint and broad smears of silky black that made the painting such a tour de force. Who was this man, she wondered, and what would he make of having gone down in history for his portrait? It was 350 years old yet this portrait made her believe, against all reason, that a conscious mind was looking back at her from the picture. Then she smiled. There was something about him that reminded her of Dan; a slight smugness in the smile that hinted at a Machiavellian soul.

Chapter Sixteen

A full day in the Wallace Collection had cleared her mind but she was exhausted, completely and utterly drained when she got back to the flat. Her lower back ached, her sockless feet were sweaty and raw and she had a thumping headache. What was it about museums that made one so tired? The last thing she wanted to do now was go out but she didn't want to let Max down. Max hadn't come to the exhibition but had called to decline and invite her to his own party and she didn't want to quash their new friendship. A party with all his neighbours wasn't what she was in the mood for – it took energy for her to play the extrovert. What she really wanted was a relaxing bath with a glass of chilled wine and an early night. But kick-off was at 7.00 so at least she had time to take it easy before heading back out. She stopped off at Europa and bought a bottle of cheap plonk and a bag of ice, a tube of Primula cheese and some TUC biscuits. Enough to keep her going until dinner and the alcohol would medicate her weariness with a much-needed shot of energy.

As the bath filled, she ran downstairs to get a bottle opener and glass. The caterers had left the kitchen clean and in order, with everything replaced as it had been found. She had forgotten to take the last bag of rubbish out and the place smelt of the night before; a whiff of stale canapés, champagne-soaked cigarette butts and the sweet-scented flowers. A pool of the nicotine-infused booze had leaked from a binbag onto the floor making it sticky underfoot. The smell brought on a wave of guilt and a vision of poor Cece, stumbling home. Esme hoped she hadn't felt too rough this morning. Not wanting to make a big deal of it, she hadn't called her but now she felt awkward. Hopefully, like her, Cece just wanted to forget it. There was no point in phoning her now. She'd probably be getting ready for her shift at the club. Instead Esme vowed she'd call Cece tomorrow. Her bath was beckoning.

Dumping her clothes on the floor she sank into the bathtub, her glass of wine propped against the empty soap dish. The blonde hairs on her arms swayed like grass in a summer breeze. Slowly she gave in to the cooling water, fully submerging herself from the mouth down. She lay quietly waiting for the water to still until it was only her breathing that rippled the surface. Gradually she felt the wine begin to take effect and her muscles relax. She lay in there, along with the sliver of Imperial Leather she had no energy to fish out. Bliss.

By the time Esme got to the party she was an hour late. Conditioned by her father *never* to be 'tardy' but persuaded by her mother, on good days, that 'It's always best to be fashionably late', she was comfortable with neither one. She had panic-dressed but at least she was clean, and a cat's whisker away from being fuelled by Dutch courage. Max seemed pretty relaxed about most things so she assumed timekeeping wasn't high on his list of priorities but knowing no one, she would be at a disadvantage arriving too late.

It turned out Max lived close to his studio in a converted distillery. Expecting a front door with a number, it took her a moment to realize the entrance was a wooden door cut into a wall. The sound of laughter and music gave it away. There was no bell to ring, so she knocked knowing the sound would get lost in the revelry beyond, then pushed the door open, tripping over the frame into a courtyard. A small gathering sat and mingled under fairy lights and hanging lanterns. But as she saw the other guests, she already felt like an idiot in her nightclubbing garb. Compared to the assorted flowing fabrics and rainbow colours preferred by this gathering of artists and freethinkers, her outfit was too tight, too black and too short. All the French windows on the ground floor were open where residents had dragged out sofas and armchairs. Flagstones had been covered with rugs, carpets and bean bags. An upright piano topped with candles sat up against a wall of honeysuckle and clematis. Outside had been converted into a room of its own under the twilit sky.

'Esme!' shouted Max, peeling himself from an attractive brunette with huge unrestrained boobs barely covered in a vintage slip.

'Come. Come. Let's get you a drink. Red or white? I'm so pleased you came.'

Max had transformed. No longer the dusty picture restorer, he wore an open floral shirt, an arrow of chest hair pointing towards his belt buckle, no shoes and flared jeans. His hair was wet and he smelt of soap and rosemary.

'This looks amazing,' said Esme.

'Just another night at Burlington Lodge. We do this once a month in the summer. Everyone pitches in. The joy of nice neighbours.'

'How many people live here?'

'There are six apartments. We don't call them flats because the rooms are too big. More like lofts, I suppose.'

Max filled an extremely beautiful glass with white wine.

'Here you go. Italian, of course.'

Esme held the glass up to the fading sky and turned it around. The crystal threw fragments of brilliant light across Max's face.

'I found six of those at Bermondsey Market. In perfect condition and worth a small fortune.' He laughed as if their value was a happy accident. Esme was sure he didn't buy them by mistake.

'So pretty.'

'Yes, they are,' he said, looping his arm through hers. 'Come and meet everyone.'

The names of twenty or so people went in one ear and out the other. Everyone was much older than her but Esme felt comfortable in their company. She found that people made an effort with the baby of the crowd, interested in what she did and it provided them with an excuse to talk about their own children. They all seemed happy to include her in their conversation as an equal.

'Leo, this is Esme. The girl with the painting,' said Max, introducing her to a giant character with tiny pig eyes above a gnarled snout. His voice was very grand but he had an air of destitution about him.

'Ah,' Leo said, 'the owner of the Romney. Max is frightfully excited by it. I understand it was left to you by the Earl of Culcairn. He must have been very fond of you, my dear.'

'Well, I don't know about that but, yes it was extremely kind of him,' she said, embarrassed that Max had defined her as 'the girl with the painting'. The bloody thing was an unavoidable sign of her privilege and meant people would judge her instantly. She knew that her past – and her privilege – would always be a part of what had shaped her, but that didn't stop her from wishing she had the choice of when and how much of her story to share with strangers. It was as if the Romney's frame had replaced Emma for Esme, trapping her inside its gilded boundary.

'Are you in the art world?' she asked.

He laughed, projecting his voice into the night, 'Christ, no. I'm an actor and I also write books. It helps to keep my cellar full.'

Too much Shakespeare and bit-parts playing the local laird, she thought. Esme didn't recognize him.

'I can see you are thinking who the hell is this ugly, old wanker, and quite rightly so. I do theatre mainly, and there's fuck all money or fame in that,' he said.

Despite his height, he held his head high and looked down at her over his fleshy cheeks. He was a mountain of a man, built like a cement mixer churning his way through life.

She knew nothing about the theatre and couldn't think of a thing to say. Her silence spread like a stain and she felt as awkward as he looked.

'How do you know Max?'

'I'm one of the neighbours. Lived here with my cats for aeons,' he said.

'It's lovely.'

'Isn't it just? We all rent, which is marvellous as we aren't imprisoned by owning a property. Nothing more suffocating.'

Esme wondered what it was like living on top of your neighbours, surely that was claustrophobic. She couldn't imagine being sandwiched in with people above and below. But then she thought of Cece and Mabel, and all the other countless flats she'd passed. Collective living was necessary in the cemented confines of a city. It was she who was the odd one out, used to whole houses or even the expanses of the Highlands.

'Well, I might get something to eat. Smells delicious. Nice to meet you,' she said.

Small talk wasn't her thing. She'd rather keep quiet than talk nonsense for the sake of it.

'You too, ducky.' Leo gave a watery smile, trying not to look relieved to be released. Not such a great actor, after all, thought Esme.

As darkness fell, the candles and Christmas lights came into their own, casting elongated shadows, leaving corners veiled in secrecy. Not knowing where Max was she went through the nearest open door and straight into a huge open-plan kitchen. At its centre was a large kitchen table where Max was beating the crap out of something in a pestle and mortar. Wine bottles, spices, herbs and a huge pepper grinder crowded around him. The aroma of nuts toasting came from an ancient-looking oven and a pan of boiling water spat and hissed on the hob. Whatever he was preparing and however typically unhygienic his work surface was, it smelt utter heaven. Basil, garlic, strong cheese. Next to his utensils were two enormous bowls, one fired and glazed in blue-and-green flecks and the other wood.

A mound of grated parmesan rose and tumbled directly on the table surface like a pile of gravel in waiting to be laid. His slapdash cooking was a far cry from the precision of restoration.

'Oti, can you put the linguini on?' said Max, not looking up from whatever it was he was persecuting.

A tall, languid woman uncurled herself from the nearby sofa, leaving Flea to stretch out in what was clearly his spot, judging by a still-bloodied marrow bone tucked down the side of a cushion.

'It's OK, Fleabag, Oti will be back soon.'

Oti was one of those women that you couldn't help but admire. No wonder Flea was besotted. Esme wondered if Max was too. She was tall with an athletic grace that demanded attention, though she sought none. Charisma, thought Esme. Powerful femininity that was impossible to manufacture or emulate; something you were born with.

'Isn't she gorgeous?' said Max, catching Esme's gaze.

Esme nodded.

'Oti!' he shouted. 'Leave the pasta and come and meet Esme.'

Oti turned and grinned. 'Hi, Esme. Give me a second,' she said, wiping her hands on a beach towel. Her rich voice was full of music.

'Oti is from Somalia. She was discovered by Peter Beard. The artist.'

Oti gave Esme a light hug and two air kisses.

'Max is so old-fashioned – he talks about me like I was found in the jungle but I met Peter in Nairobi where I went to university.'

Esme knew his work and reputation, a photographer famed

for his pictures of African elephants and his journals that he integrated into his work. She also knew Peter Beard happened to look a lot like Max.

'How did you end up in London?' asked Esme, assuming Beard had scouted her to model for him.

'It's a long story. I'm a psychiatric doctor based at the Maudsley.'

'When Max said he had met you I asked if your mother was Diana. He didn't know. Is she?'

This was too much. How did this woman know her mother? Everywhere she went, Diana reared her damaged head.

'Yes, she is, in a manner of speaking.'

'She either is or she isn't, Esme. You can't have a "sort of" mother,' said Max.

If only she did have a simple relationship with her mother, she wished. She felt like she had already half mourned her, since she would never get back the maternal figure she once had. But even so, the ghost of her mother seemed to constantly appear in the least expected places.

'Max, you are an emotional philistine. I know exactly what you mean, Esme. My father suffered in the same way, which is why I became a doctor.'

Anxiety ransacked Esme's tipsy haze like a ferret in a haynet. How much did Oti know about her mother? Had she been a patient of hers? She wanted to ask but not at the expense of the chance of being anonymous tonight. In amongst a crowd of people who knew nothing about her, she could be accepted on her own merit, rather than defined by her mother and her illness.

'I haven't seen my mother for some time and I was sent

away to boarding school, so we never had a close relationship. I'm more of a daddy's girl,' she said with an awkward laugh.

Oti gave her a look filled with compassion and stroked her arm as if to say, 'Your secret is safe with me.'

'Enough talk about the past,' said Max, 'let's eat, drink and focus on the future.' He raised a small glass filled with something stickier than wine. 'To new friendships and a night we won't remember tomorrow. *Saluti!*'

Flinging his head back, he tipped the contents down his throat in one and smacked his lips. 'Christ, that's good. Try some of this, Esme. Grappa from my friend's vineyard outside Florence. It's made from pressed fermented skins left over from winemaking and its absolutely lethal.'

The fumes alone made her eyes water. She took a cautious sip of the fiery liquid that scorched then numbed her lips.

'Wow, that's strong,' she laughed, following suit with a clean slug.

'Another!' Max refilled her glass to the brim and beyond, slopping it over the table and wiping it with his shirttail.

'Max, go easy,' said Oti. 'Remember you tried to hump Coralie the last time you drank that stuff,' she laughed.

'I have absolutely no recollection at all, thank God.' He went on to inform Esme that Coralie lived next door and was what he termed 'a raging, man-hating feminist'. Before Esme could butt in to defend feminism (or at least channel what she thought Cece would say), he continued unabashed. 'She thought I was going to have my evil way with her. She would be so lucky. I'd rather fuck a holly bush.'

'Did I hear you a-calling, my love?'

A round woman with wild grey hair and mad eyes put her arms around Max and squeezed him from behind.

'I know you want me, Maximillian, even if my cunt is haunted cos I'm so old.'

Max spun around and embraced her. 'Talk dirty to me, baby,' he said, laughing. The woman's body wobbled with mirth under her striped man's shirt.

'Where's that grappa?' the woman asked and then added, 'Oh hello and who are you, Cinder-fucking-rella?'

Esme introduced herself.

'Max, she's far too young for you. I'm Coralie Laing, by the way.'

Esme laughed but didn't quite know what to do or say next. She wasn't used to this kind of chat coming from the mouths of respectable adults but as she was learning fast, this lot had no filter when it came to friends.

Not wanting to appear prudish, Esme chucked her grappa down then slapped the glass on the table as an invitation for a refill.

'One more, please,' she said, grinning broadly at Coralie.

Without taking her eyes off Esme, Coralie held her own glass out to be filled.

'Oh, I like you, Esme. A girl with balls. Cheers!'

'I think it's time we put the pasta out,' Oti said quickly. 'The pesto is our contribution to soak up that poison,' she said, pointing to the moonshine.

The four of them each collected something from the table. Coralie swept the cheese onto a plate and took some serving spoons from a drawer in the table. Max got more bottles and some napkins and Oti and Esme carried the two oversized bowls of pasta.

'Watch out for Flea,' shouted Coralie over her shoulder, but it was too late.

The bowl flew out of Esme's hands and landed with an almighty crash on the floor and rolled towards a bean bag. Bred to race, Flea was on and into the pasta in a flash.

'Get off, you pig,' said Max, kicking Flea away.

'Oh God, I'm so sorry,' said Esme, mortified to have made such a spectacle of herself.

'Don't worry. We'll scoop it back into the salad bowl. Bit of dirt won't hurt anyone,' said Coralie.

Max fetched the bowl and shovelled the pasta back into it, licking his fingers.

'God, I'm a good cook,' he said, then he shouted, 'Grub's up. Let's eat!'

No drama about the dropped food, then. No frosty stares or catty remarks. Just a few jokes and a round of applause. Esme could get used to this live-and-let-live atmosphere. Although she didn't know if she could bring herself to eat the pasta she'd dropped. She decided to stick to the other offerings.

The Burlington Lodge community and assorted friends gravitated to a long table weighed down by food. Grapes, cheese, ciabatta, radicchio, olives, oil and balsamic vinegar; a quintessential Italian spread down to stemless wineglasses and an absence of butter. A mismatched assortment of kitchen chairs circled the table but there weren't enough for everyone. It was a case of first come first served, but no one was in a rush to sit down apart from Coralie and a bearded fellow smoking a roll-up.

'Esme, come sit next to me,' said Coralie.

This public approval from the woman who was clearly

the queen bee of the group drew a line under Esme's mishap. She gratefully took a position at the head of the table, a place normally reserved for the host but there was no hierarchy here. This was no place for airs or social protocol. In fact, Esme would go so far as to say the rejection of bourgeois values was a badge of honour here. There was clearly no cloying unspoken etiquette, no judging people by their name or old school tie, no flashing of money. If tonight was anything to go by, they were a passionate bunch living a carefree lifestyle, not just accepting but celebrating their marginality. She would love to see them parade their bohemian ways under the Contessa's nose. The woman wouldn't be able to cope because none of this lot would give a shit about her and her snobbish rules.

Coralie piled her plate with linguini, picking out a couple of stones collected on its fall from grace and dropping them back on the ground.

'So, sweet Esme, which star have you fallen from?' she asked, holding a cigarillo in one hand and a fork in the other. Her teeth were stained with nicotine and her skin rough and lined but she had the most startlingly blue eyes that bore into Esme's with an intensity that made her feel naked.

Esme poured wine into her tumbler and drank deeply.

'Oh, you know, that distant planet called Scotland.'

'So you must be the daughter of clan chief or laird presiding over his grouse moor?'

Esme laughed. She felt welcomed enough by this diverse crowd. 'I might have been born with a silver spoon in my mouth, but it turned out pretty tarnished so now I'm trying to find my own way.'

'And how do you plan on doing that?'

'To be honest, I have no idea. I love art although I don't really paint myself. I'm more interested in other people's work, especially Old Masters. It's how I met Max. Introduced with a painting as my calling card. A friend of my parents left it to me in his will, but it's damaged so I fear it's not worth a bean.'

'Well, it must be if Max has found the time of day to look at it. That man comes across as fey and whimsical but he has a nose for a good painting and he's never wrong. I assume you took it to him for restoration?'

'Yes.'

'And he has agreed to do the job?'

Esme nodded.

'Then he must have an inkling it's worth more than you think. He gets terribly bored restoring the same old shit museums send him and rarely takes private clients now. Don't get me wrong, he loves what he does, but he has two very greedy ex-wives and needs the money for God knows how many illegitimate children he has running around. Can't keep it in his trousers.'

Esme wondered for a moment why he hadn't made a pass at her but looking at Oti, his standards were high and women seemed to materialize around him like mushrooms after rain. He had the pick of the bunch, she bet.

'Oh no, Max and Oti aren't an item,' Coralie said, following her gaze. 'He's shagged her, sure, but she's too immersed in her work for anything long-term. Shame, really because they are perfect together and Max is desperate to settle down again. He was broken after his last divorce and, like all men, once they've been married they can't survive alone.'

'How long ago did he get divorced?' asked Esme.

'Only recently, but things started going wrong from the start and then the bitch ran off with his best friend. Good riddance to them both, but it crushed Max. He's been consoling himself with work, booze and women ever since but I think he's coming out the other side now.'

'Poor Max.'

'Don't feel too sorry for him. He's his own worst enemy. If I was straight I wouldn't touch him with a barge pole. And nor should you. Too capricious, but that's his beauty and his downfall. Women want to rescue or tame him.'

'Oh no, I...'

'Don't worry, you are too young for him. If he was interested he would have slept with you by now. Completely irresistible once he's set his sights on someone.'

She really liked Max but genuinely hadn't considered sleeping with him. It dawned on her that she saw him as a friend and nothing more. A genuine friend, who she was learning to trust. How refreshing to have a relationship with a straight member of the opposite sex without sexual tension or regarding him as a candidate for possible marriage.

'What do you do, Coralie?'

'I'm an artist. Ceramics and sculpture. And I teach at Camberwell. Made my name with a series I did of life-size female torsos, naked, of course,' she laughed. 'You can imagine the enjoyment derived from smearing tits with plaster.'

'I bet the women loved it too,' said Esme.

'Some, but most did it for their husbands and withstood the process as if they were Joan of Arc; martyrs to their marriages,' she said with a wry smile.

'Do you know where there's a loo I can use?'

'Use mine. But bring back a couple of bottles of wine. There are loads in the bath.'

When Esme returned, everyone had gathered around the piano where someone was playing the theme tune from *The Sting*. Pushing her way in, she saw Max performing with the energy of Jerry Lee Lewis. On cue, he seamlessly banged out 'Great Balls of Fire' and people started to dance. Esme felt a hand grasp hers.

'Come on, Esme,' said Coralie with an immense grin.

She pulled her away from the small audience and began to swivel her hips and spin Esme around, their bodies bumping and twisting to Max's frenetic playing. Others joined them, holding hands in a big circle and jumping up and down like five-year-olds. She could hear Max singing and whooping, stamping his feet on the pedals, pushing his friends into a fever of joy and laughter. Surrounded by his companions, he radiated vitality and heat, sweat pouring down his face; his cheeks aflame with the force of his playing. His vigour was catching as it released itself into the hearts of this ragtag gaggle. The ambience was euphoric and Esme felt uninhibited and absolutely at home here. She could have been dancing with a man, woman or milkmaid for all she cared.

'Come on, Esme, do the flick,' said Coralie, flinging her scarecrow hair back and forth.

'Oh Coralie, you are wonderful,' she said, laughing and giving the woman a massive hug. 'Thank you. I feel like I could dance all night.'

Chapter Seventeen

'Christ, you look rough, Esme. Did you get mugged over the weekend?' said Bill on Monday morning.

'You're a fine one to talk. Have you been training at Stamford Bridge?'

Bill was not his usual impeccable self. He was dressed in a tracksuit although he'd never willingly exercised a day in his life. The jogging trousers sagged at his bum and he wore a Chelsea football strip underneath.

He roared with laughter.

'No, I had a "naughty" last night. In a rather lovely hotel, actually. One of the gentlemen in question *swapped* his clothes for mine. My house keys were in the pocket and Javier is out so I've come to get my spare pair.'

Esme's eye's shot open.

'I only watched, blossom.'

'But, Javier? Won't he be furious?' she asked, thinking back to his reaction to Oliver.

Bill laughed again, 'Just as long as I stay in the viewing gallery and I don't mix pleasure with business, we're fine and dandy. Anyway, he was with me until things got, shall we say, frisky.'

Esme relaxed. She had grown very fond of this couple and hated the idea of either of them being deceitful.

'The party went well, don't you think?' he asked.

They hadn't had a chance to catch up since the night of the private view. By the time she had got back after looking for Cece, Bill had gone, which was just as well as she had been in such a foul mood. She still felt bad that she hadn't contacted Cece since then, she'd been too tired to do anything much but sleep since Max's party.

'Yes, I do. You are amazing, Bill, and everyone loves you. The night was a triumph and there are red stickers on every painting.' She hadn't noticed until she came down this morning and felt guilty for not checking before.

'I know. I am adored and my reign of Jermyn Street is secure once more. And you, my sweet, sold the first. Always encourages others to see a painting has been pre-sold. They get scared they might miss out,' he said. 'So, what did you get up to at the weekend to be rewarded by an attack of the uglies?'

Esme laughed because Bill was right. The volume of grappa consumed had left her face puffed-up and blotchy. The blotchy she had hidden behind a layer of concealer but there was nothing she could do to about her swollen eyes.

'Max had a party.'

'No wonder! All those sex-crazed Bolsheviks. Bet you had fun, though. If nothing else, they throw a fabulous party. I went once and vowed never to go again. Did you meet Coralie Laing?'

'Yes. I love her. She was so sweet to me.'

'A fine artist too. You know her work is at MoMA?'

'Wow. She didn't give that away.'

'It's why I don't work with living artists. They are so insecure about their work.'

'Shit!' She remembered Oliver's portfolio. Had Javier
showed it to him?

'What?'

'A photographer came in the same day as Elton John. Oliver
Maxey. He left his portfolio for you to look at.'

'Who?'

'Oliver Maxey. He said you had contacted his agent?'

'Must be getting old. I don't remember any Oliver whats-
his-name. No, wait a minute – Javier said you had a crush on
some hot young photographer and you'd brought me his book
to look through. I'd clean forgotten.'

But a wave of panic hit Esme. She had no idea where she'd
put the envelope with his number on. Hopefully the caterers
or Suki must have put it aside for safekeeping. She'd ask her
when she got in.

'You'll want to meet him because his photographs are
extraordinary. Truly.'

'Barely a week in my company and you're now an expert,
hmm?' said Bill.

'I didn't say that…' Esme began, embarrassed by her enthusiasm.

'I was joking, darling. You know I respect the Munroe
eye. I'm sure they are wonderful and I'll take a look when
I go home for a shower. I feel like I've spent a week down
a mineshaft,' he said.

★

She was on the telephone, trying to reach Cece to see how she was, when she heard Suki arrive. Oliver's number was still nowhere to be found and she prayed it hadn't been stolen or thrown out, as it could easily have been mistaken as rubbish.

'Esme?'

'I'm here. Have you seen an old envelope with a phone number on it?'

Suki appeared in the doorway with a jubilant look on her face. She was waving her hand around.

'Guess what?' she trilled.

'I really need to find this thing, Suki. Bill will need it and I can't remember where the fuck I left it.'

Suki's smile turned to a pout.

'What?' said Esme, irritated that she wasn't helping.

Suki continued flapping her hand like a demented puppet.

'I *can* see you,' said Esme.

'Do you see anything different about me?' Suki persisted.

Not in the slightest. She still looked the archetypal Sloane Ranger; prim, proper and oh-so-respectable.

'My ring. I'm engaged!'

'What?'

Remorse filled Esme. She felt a bitch for being so wrapped up in herself and jumped up to hug her friend.

'Oh, Suki, what fantastic news! When? How? You have to tell me everything.'

Johnny had apparently proposed after the exhibition.

'I knew something was up when we arrived at Harry's Bar. He's not a member but his father is and… oh, it is so romantic, I can hardly tell you.' Tears dripped into her beaming smile.

Suki told her how she had ordered her usual G&T and after

she had finished it, Johnny had refused to let the waiter take away the empty glass.

'He got quite cross and I told him to stop behaving like an arrogant twat.'

It wasn't until the ice had melted that she had seen the ring that was now on her finger. A huge sapphire flanked by two diamonds.

'He had got the head barman to freeze it in an ice cube the day before and voila! I'm going to become Mrs Downes. Not the Marchioness I once hoped for but at least his family have more money than God.'

High five to Johnny, thought Esme. The boy had more oomph to him than she'd thought and she was genuinely happy for her friend.

'This is cause for celebration. Does Bill know? There's some champagne left over in the fridge. I think we need to open it,' said Esme.

'Let's wait for Bill,' said Suki.

The two girls talked through wedding dates and plans, the kind of dress she wanted, who would do her hair. How many bridesmaids, a dance, dinner, or both. What about an engagement party? Suki said that Johnny's parents were going to pay for the wedding because 'they know I come from a poor, deprived background. Isn't that the sweetest thing ever? No expense spared,' she said. 'It's going to be the wedding of the year.'

Esme had no doubt that she would make sure the ceremony was in every society column and the main event in *Tatler* magazine.

'You ought to get this photographer I met to take your

portrait,' Esme suggested. 'He'll make you even more beautiful than you already are. He's left his portfolio with Bill but I can't find his phone number to get back in touch.'

'Oh, that thing. I wasn't sure if it was important or not, so I put it in the desk drawer just in case.'

Esme kissed her. 'You goddess, Mrs Downes-to-be. Bill would kill me if I'd lost it.'

The doorbell tinkled and Bill walked in, back to his impeccable self, complete with kerchief in his suit pocket and an umbrella. Under his arm he carried Oliver's battered portfolio.

'Hi, girls. Forecast is rain.'

'Not in my world. Guess what, Bill? I'm getting *married*!' Suki's voice had gone up at least an octave.

She flung herself at him and he picked her up and did his best to spin her around, her legs beginning to revolve like the spokes of a slow-turning wheel. Esme was impressed as she watched Bill's face turn scarlet with the strain. Suki was a good couple of inches taller than her boss and it must have taken all his strength. His eyes started to bulge and Suki squealed.

'Suki Su! How marvellous! And you've snagged a rich one too. You clever old thing,' he said. 'We must crack open the champers!'

Esme left them to gossip and went to retrieve a bottle and Oliver's book from where Bill had propped it up in the doorway. She imagined that wedding photos were not part of Oliver Maxey's remit – unless he needed the money – but it was a good excuse to look through his work again without stealing Suki's thunder.

Bill was mopping his brow when she returned to the showroom.

'I've sent Suki off to buy every wedding magazine she can find. I said she's too tasteless to pick a wedding dress. She'll end up looking like Madame de Pompadour's pavlova left to her own devices.'

Esme laughed and put Oliver's portfolio on the desk.

'So, this is your photographer? I thought I'd bring the book back here so we can look it together since you're so excited about your new discovery,' Bill said.

'He's not *mine*, Bill, but I think you'll be blown away.'

The zip snagged and stuck as she tugged it open. It wasn't the most salubrious introduction to Oliver's work, but served to give added surprise when Bill lifted out the first photograph. Like Javier, he said nothing even when Suki came back weighed down by two shopping bags full of glossy monthlies.

'He's good, don't you think?' she said, hoping to encourage a response.

As if hypnotized, Bill took out another image and after what seemed a lifetime he finally said, 'Just look at his handling of light. It's masterful.' His voice was filled with emotion. 'The way he has immortalized fleeting images.'

He looked up, his expression serious and bemused, as if he had witnessed a tragedy or a miracle – Esme wasn't quite sure. Either way, he was moved, almost to tears.

'You like them?'

'My God, Esme, I don't know what to say? I haven't seen such hauntingly luminous images for a very long time. And certainly not ones taken by a living photographer.' He breathed, then laughed. 'I'm having an epiphany.'

'What's an epiphany?' said Suki, lifting her bags like an announcement.

'A religious moment,' said Esme. 'This is the photographer I told you about.' She picked up the portrait of the woman. 'This could be you,' she said to her colleague.

No lightbulb moment registered on Suki's face. In fact, she looked completely confused and then pissed off. She dropped her magazines on the floor with all the theatrical flourish of a four-year-old.

'But she's got no make-up on? And her face is dirty. Imagine how a photo like that would appear in *Country Life*. I mean, honestly.'

'Step out of your pigeonhole for one second, Suki,' said Bill.

'OK, well maybe not for your engagement, but you could give one to Johnny as a wedding present,' Esme suggested.

'You could do a lot worse, Suki Su, than getting this Oliver fellow taking your portrait. Much classier than that poufy-haired Litchfield, who I'm sure will be your first choice. His photographs are already dated,' said Bill.

'These portraits are beautiful, Suki. You've just got to have the balls to be photographed without make-up. You've got the bone structure to carry it off.' Esme knew Suki would look beautiful if she ever let Oliver turn his lens on her.

Suki ran a finger down her cheek, looking ever so slightly smug with this compliment and happy to have the focus back on her.

'Maybe,' she said.

'Personally, I think his abstracts are more interesting,' said Bill. 'Look at the moody atmosphere here.' He was examining one of the underwater photographs. 'The daylight through water and the silhouetted coral is so delicate. Like a mere trace rather than a documentation of the real thing.'

He put his glasses on top of his head and rubbed his eyes, replacing them to re-appraise the image.

'This man is seriously talented,' he said. 'You said he is having a show?'

'I didn't, but yes he is actually. I don't know where but it's on Wednesday. You are invited. He's given me his studio address and a number.'

'Well, you've picked a winner, Esme. I think you should go and follow this through as he's your discovery,' Bill said. 'And Suki, I will commission him to take your portrait as a wedding present.'

Chapter Eighteen

Bill's excitement quickly turned to frustration.

'I can't call the fucking artist direct,' he said when Esme gave him the envelope with Oliver's number on it. 'It's totally unprofessional. I need the agent.'

Bill vanished into the back office and emerged a few minutes later, smiling. Bill knew everyone and it had only taken a couple of calls to find Oliver's agent. It turned out that there was a private view tomorrow night before the public opening on Wednesday. He'd arranged for Esme to go.

'It'll be much better this way. They see me coming.'

Hard not to, thought Esme. She could only assume that such a swift turn-around from football hooligan-ette to Savile Row gentleman – albeit one dip-dyed like a bag of sherbet – indicated he'd laid out his clothes the night before.

'You can go straight after work tomorrow. Be my eyes and ears – pick out a masterpiece or two.'

Good, thought Esme. This could be a big break. And if Oliver was there, all the better. She was glad the opening wasn't that night. Time for her to lay out her own outfit.

Work raced by the next day. Before he vanished off to

another meeting, Bill had handed her the money to go and buy as many of Oliver Maxey's photographs as she could with the sum, especially his underwater visuals. She had been given the go-ahead to choose the ones she felt were his best and was now on a high, basking in Bill's trust. With her 'instincts and inherent taste that money can't buy', as Bill called it, she had a future. The art world was starting to feel like her natural milieu and for the first time in her life she felt valued and able to contribute more than just being a conduit to her society connections.

Esme was pleased with the way she looked. Not too try-hard and her hair had behaved and dried into a gleaming shank of gold. She was just locking up when the phone rang.

'Hello?'

'Es, it's Cece.'

She'd been trying to call her for days, but there had been no answer. She was relieved to hear her voice.

'Es?'

Esme paused, she still felt guilty that she'd let Cece vanish off into the night, half-cut.

'Yes. It's me.'

'How are you?' The question sounded a perfunctory one. She couldn't tell if Cece was pissed off or embarrassed by the events at the gallery.

'I'm well. I was just leaving. Got to get to an exhibition.' Her mind fast-forwarded to Oliver in his leathers, but her voice didn't follow.

'Oh? That's exciting.'

'Yeah. It is. Not paintings but these stunning photographs.'

Esme realized as the words came out of her mouth, she still wanted to impress her.

'I was wondering what you were up to later? There's this party... and well, I thought you might like to come. It's a friend of Dan's. But it sounds like you're busy.'

'No, I... well, yes, I am...'

'There's a cool bunch of people coming and well, you know...'

Esme decided she should accept the invitation by way of an olive branch. Make peace and move on. She realized she'd judged her friend harshly because she had built her up to be this all-powerful tower of strength and invincibility and it had been a shock to see that Cece had weaknesses too.

'That'd be nice. I'll come on the way. I won't be able to stay too long as I have to get to North London for the launch.'

'Everyone's contributing to grog and grub so maybe pick up some supplies on the way. It's not far from your gallery.'

'OK. I could swing by Harrods and stay for an hour or so.'

Esme felt like she had robbed a bank as she left the gallery. She clutched her bag close, fearful it was obvious she was carrying £500 in cash. The money was disrespectfully bound in a rubber band and was an unsightly lump. Every passerby was a potential mugger. There had been a spate of attacks in Knightsbridge, with one woman even having a finger chopped for the diamond she was wearing. It wasn't until Esme had passed under the green-and-gold awnings of Harrods that she felt safe.

The Harrods Food Hall was comfortingly familiar – her

mother had used it as her local grocery store when they lived in London. She fondly remembered the excitement of a trip she had accompanied Diana on once to buy ingredients for dinner. When she was well, her mother had been a good cook; a natural with no need for recipe books. Esme must have been about ten years old at the time and when she thought back she could still taste the frothy smoothness of her chocolate milkshake at the Soda Bar. Her mother had Earl Grey, which she 'cooled down' with the contents of a small ornate bottle. 'I always bring a little water in case I get thirsty,' she explained. Looking back, Esme now understood why the water smelt of gin.

The Art Deco opulence remained, with veined marble sprawling across surfaces, wall partitions and internal columns. Piles of fruit and vegetables were positioned with artistic precision. Some of the produce Esme had never seen before, imported from hotter climes, and now looking exotic and unseasonal in the heart of a Northern European metropolis. Lychees and grapes were coated in a powdery bloom. Families of cherries, figs, citrus fruit, apples and pears were piled high in gleaming heaps. Squash, peapods, lettuces, asparagus, tomatoes, bunches of chives, rosemary and basil filled displays. Overflowing wicker baskets were the main focus, positioned with the painterly flair of Caravaggio. She looked at a bowl of bicoloured peaches with a bright red blush that, Esme observed, had an uncanny resemblance to a dimpled derrière. Next to them, split-open pomegranates lay, disgorging their jewelled seeds. Bunches of grapes were heaped next to curved cucumbers and courgettes that looked like some kind of sea monster. Huge speckled vine leaves displayed warty melons that looked nothing like the smooth fruits Esme was used to. It seemed the whole world's offerings were stacked up and offered for sale here. But this harvest was so profuse it seemed almost symbolic. The ripeness, the burst fruit, the tempting red apples speaking of original sin and their blemishes hinting at the transience of human life. All very Baroque, she thought – or perhaps she'd been spending too much time with Max.

Cece had given her a small but expensive shopping list after Esme said she could try to use her mother's account card. She'd held onto it when she had gone into care. It was the only thing she had of her mother's with her in London, apart from the old shirt, and she had no idea if the last bill had been paid. It seemed worth a try. The gold and green piece of plastic had her mother's signature on the back, the uncertain scrawl and flamboyant capitals. Even her writing was a contradiction.

Esme was to meet Cece at a house in Eaton Square belonging to some 'loaded' friend of Dan's. She had agreed to pick up Stolichnaya vodka, cigarettes and shell-on prawns. As she stared at the fish counter, she found it hard to believe a world of variety had been caught and delivered to the heart of London. A huge taxidermy marlin of record-breaking weight hung above a fishmonger in his straw boater.

'What can I get you, miss?'

Not knowing how many a pound of prawns would be, she said, 'Three double handfuls, please.'

He weighed up the prawns and tipped them into paper and then a bag. There were enough to feed an army, but she was too embarrassed to say there were too many, even when he stuck the price on.

'Thanks,' she said awkwardly, feeling like she was playing at being grown-up.

She added two bottles of vodka to her basket and strode over to the check out, ready to forge her mother's signature.

'That'll be £25.46, please.'

She found her purse in the bottom of her bag and without a beat, handed over the card, praying the payment would go through. Poor Mum, thought Esme, she should be the one to be buying delicacies for dinner, not dining on hospital dinners in her care home. But she also knew her that if they had been together, her mother would have encouraged her to take nothing but the best to the party.

Esme was amazed when the card went through. She felt a buzz of adrenaline at having got away with it. An idea fizzed into life. It was late-night shopping in Knightsbridge, so she'd still have time to go and browse the fashion rails in Way In, upstairs. Surely her dad would forgive her the odd indulgence when he came to pay the bill on the card.

By the time she left Way In with a new dress and pair of wedge espadrilles, it was later than she'd thought. Cece had said she would meet her at the party and as she hurried in the direction of Eaton Square, Esme was looking forward to seeing her again and laughing off her drunken behaviour and Esme's overreaction to it.

She felt good in her new mini wrap-dress and her shoes, though high, were easy to walk in. It was a lovely evening and London had never looked better, bathed in gold and harbouring smiling faces enjoying the balmy temperature. Esme paused to take in the magnificence of Pall Mall and its majestic Regency architecture, the clean lines and uncomplicated façades. Then she dashed on, the vodka bottles clinking.

Number 81 was on the corner of Eaton Square and Elizabeth Street. The house was a larger version of Pelham Place, three times the size and with cleaner windows that reflected the communal gardens behind her. The entrance was flanked by two leafy orbs in cubic urns and there was an oversized knocker cast in the shape of a lion's head. Buoyed by the reassuring familiarity of this kind of place, she was slightly surprised that Dan swam in such circles. He'd given the impression that he was a class warrior, the kind of person to despise such wealth and opulence. She hoped Cece hadn't been as intimidated as she'd been at the gallery and legged it back to Camden. Checking her reflection in the window, Esme smoothed her hair, retouched her lip-gloss and rang the bell. After a beat, a butler in full livery answered the door.

'I'm here to meet Dan.' Esme realized she didn't know his surname and was going to ask for Cece but she didn't know hers either.

'Would you like me to put your bags in the cloakroom, or will you be taking them with you?' the butler asked.

Thank God they were Harrods bags.

'I'm not sure. I've bought prawns and vodka with me,' she said, feeling foolish. Who brought prawns to a party? 'And cigarettes.'

'We have plenty of those. I'll take the food and drink to the kitchen.' His voice was monotone and weary. 'May I offer you something before you go in?'

'Vodka and tonic would be lovely, thank you.' Assuming a drink was what he meant.

He nodded his head, and she waited in the hallway. She could hear voices upstairs. The doorbell rang again, just as the butler returned with her drink. She hoped it was Cece but a tall, sleek man wearing an expertly cut three-piece suit in material more fitting for soft furnishings made his way in. He seemed to crackle with an odd mix of watchfulness and obstreperous confidence. Esme put his age at somewhere in his late twenties despite his precocious get-up. She took in his cartoonish oversized coronet tie-pin, like something you'd find in a Christmas cracker, and shiny patent leather shoes. He was flashy and overbearing with whiff of used-car salesman, she decided.

'Sorry, Maynard, I left my keys at the club.'

'You didn't take them, sir,' said Maynard scooping a set from a silver tray on the hall table. 'Some of your guests have arrived and I have shown them to the drawing room.'

'Guests? Are we having a party, Maynard?'

'It appears so, sir.'

'Are you one of them?' he asked Esme. He put out a pale hand that Esme shook. It was cold and clammy.

'Yes. Well, I think so. I was invited by—' She stopped abruptly as the man reached over and took a sip from her glass.

'I'm Esme,' she said, nonplussed.

He introduced himself as 'David,' returning her glass. 'Come, I'll take you upstairs.'

The light in the drawing room was low, the curtains drawn for a premature nightfall. It was difficult to make out who or how many people populated the sofas and seating areas. Stained-glass lampshades threw shards of colour across the walls, papered in bordello red which created a sense of womb-like security, detached from the real world. The air was thick with smoke and the sweet aroma of marijuana. It was far too intimate for comfort.

239

David left her and went to join a group of bright young things who Esme instantly clocked as restless trust fund children. Their earnest conversation was punctuated by bursts of laughter and wild gesturing. Smooth music issued from two speakers hidden amongst the bookshelves. The rest of the room was a murky snapshot of London in all its diversity. Both the worlds she'd been trying to inhabit were colliding – moneyed society and a fashionable edgy crowd in one room. There was a heightened gaiety, an artificial insouciance which made Esme feel uneasy. High and low life mixed with handsome clingers-on, somehow familiar faces, outcasts, wasted self-destructive exhibitionists and ambitious voyeurs watching from the shadows. It was an exclusive group, based less on family name and wealth, and more on glamour, style and street cred.

Esme scanned the room and to her relief saw Cece sitting talking to a girl with crimson lips and a cloud of red hair teased and sprayed into a grand explosion. Stepping over legs and lounging bodies, she made her way towards her.

'God, am I glad to see you,' she said, bending to give her a hug.

'Oh. Esme. Hi,' she said, like she was surprised to see her. It wasn't the welcome she'd expected and certainly didn't match her own relief in finding a familiar face in this sea of strangers.

'When did you get here?' she asked.

'A while ago. This is Vicky. She's a trapeze artist. How fucking cool is that?'

There was no reciprocal introduction and Cece went back to talking to Vicky.

Esme tapped Cece on the shoulder.

'I've got to get to Oliver's private view soon. I hope you're going to come. It'll be really cool.'

Cece didn't even glance at her.

'I got the vodka and fags. Gave them to that butler. I mean, who has one of those at our age? Is this David's parents' house?' asked Esme as she watched him holding court across the room.

'Who's David?' said the redhead, looking at her with blank eyes. 'I thought this was Dan's place?'

'No, David is Dan's friend. He told Dan to invite a bunch of mates,' Cece explained impatiently.

'Don't tell me you're still cross about the other night?' said Esme.

Cece looked at her and laughed.

'Why would I be? It's not the first time I've got shit-faced and it won't be the last.'

'Well, that's good then, isn't it?' said Esme, at a loss to know why Cece was giving her the cold shoulder.

It seemed that her friend's head had been turned by the allure of the cool crowd and that she was in no mood to be extracted from this party to go with Esme, despite the hip crowd she anticipated to be at Oliver's show. Esme wondered whether she had only been invited for the booze she could bring. Or did Cece want an opportunity to show she felt that Esme had let her down at the viewing?

With a rush of relief, she spotted Dan sitting on the floor amongst a circle of friends. She left Cece, navigating the room and its rapid descent into debauchery, people openly snorting cocaine, smoking expertly rolled joints and foregoing glasses to drink straight from the bottle.

Dan appeared slightly the worse for wear but looked all the better for it. The light sheen of sweat on his skin made it seem like he was dripping with unbridled masculinity and sexual desire.

'Esme!' he hollered, kissing her full on the mouth then dancing to the barely audible music. His cheeks were flushed and his eyes glimmered with heightened excitement.

'Do you want a line?'

Esme had never done coke. Never even been in a situation where it was on offer. She didn't feel like starting now.

'I'm fine, thanks,' she said, pouring what she hoped was vodka into her empty glass from a decanter nearby.

Dan smiled and said, 'All the more for me.'

Was Cece on coke too? Did this explain her distance or was she still angry that Esme had tried to dispatch her from the gallery? She'd tried to help so it was unfair that Cece might blame her for wandering off before Esme could find her.

'Come and join us, Esme! We're about to start a game of strip poker.'

She knew she'd need to get going to Oliver's soon, but before she went, she was determined to show Cece she didn't need her to have a good time. She was quite a dab hand at card games, having played endlessly with the Culcairn children at the castle. The others looked off their trollies so it was likely she'd be the stronger player and the game would eat up the time before she had to leave and avoid being left alone with no one to talk.

'The rules,' announced Dan. 'Socks, tights and underwear count as clothes but I'm afraid jewellery doesn't. The player with the best hand doesn't have to take anything off but the rest of us do.'

Esme would only have to lose her shoes and dress before she was down to her bra and pants. Maybe this wasn't such a good idea.

As if reading her mind, Dan clapped his hand on her shoulder.

'Don't you dare,' he said, putting an arm around her and resting his chin in her hair. Esme didn't pull away, liking this move of intimacy. 'Now. Let's play poker!'

He took a long toke from a joint then passed it to her. She watched the smoke, more dense than plain tobacco, curl lazily upwards. Not wanting to appear square in front of Dan she took a puff and held both the smoke and her cough down.

Dan dealt the cards with dexterous speed.

Esme lowered her cards, hiding them against her chest.

The first round was quickfire and she came out of it having surrendered one shoe.

As the cards were dealt again, she looked at her hand and was sure she could win, saving her dignity for another round. 'I'll raise you.'

The guy opposite regarded his cards with a quiet, steady look. His eyes were glazed, his pupils contracted but they were as cold as steel and gave away nothing. Blank and unblinking; a spaced-out waste of space. She would crucify him. He extended his hand, nails ringed in dirt and put the chips to match hers.

'I'll see you,' he slurred.

A tiny smirk appeared in a flash and Esme knew she had been too quick to dismiss him. He'd got her.

Clutching her cards, she kept her breath even as she unwillingly put her hand on the table: a five alongside a pair of aces and two queens.

Mr Grimy Slimeball raised his eyebrows and she squealed in triumph.

'Well done, Esme,' cheered Dan.

'A fair hand,' conceded Slimeball.

Esme grinned, elated that she was still in possession of her dress, when he put his cards down and she looked at them, furious.

A straight. One more shoe and it would be her dress. The greasy little fucker had beaten her. He sat back to watch the rest of the players take off the requisite item.

A pretty, dyed-blonde undid the buttons of her shirt with the slow suggestiveness of a burlesque performer, even though she had a kerchief around her neck and was still in possession of her trousers and shoes. Dan started humming 'The Stripper' and, rising to the moment, blondie swung her blouse around her head then released it into the room. Everyone cheered and she stood up to take a bow, shaking her shoulders and rotating her fingers like nipple tassels. Show-off. Esme downed her drink and held it out for anyone to refill whilst simultaneously taking a long drag on another joint.

In that moment, she decided she would not be outdone. The melodious song playing softly mesmerized her and cloaked her discomfort. The drink and the joint had enveloped her and smothered her shyness. Standing up, she slowly untied her dress. First, she popped a shoulder and then revealed a flash of thigh. She leant forward and pushed her breasts together then flicked her long hair back. She felt the eyes of the room on her and the guests' slow clap as she moved and swayed, but it was Dan she was doing the striptease for, holding his gaze with seductive intent. As the dealer, Dan was the only member still fully dressed and he was goading the near-naked Esme by yelling, 'OFF. OFF. OFF.' Out came the second shoulder then an arm, which she ran her fingers along. She wiggled her bum and allowed the dress to slide over her body to the floor, landing around her feet. Licking her teeth, she stepped out of the pooled cloth. Someone wolf-whistled and another whooped, 'Encore!' She finished with a bow and sat back down as gracefully as the whirling room would allow.

He dealt again and Esme looked at her cards. Diddly squat. Nothing and everything that would force her to take her bra off but she was now so stoned, she didn't care. Oliver and his photographs could wait a while longer. The great Bill Cartwright's money would keep the doors open. One more drink, one more round of poker.

Chapter Nineteen

Esme awoke to soft snoring in her ear and the weight of an arm and a leg across her stomach and thighs. Whoever it was spooned her back and stank of booze, their body warm against hers. She lay rigid, hardly daring to breathe let alone roll over for fear of seeing who it was and waking them. Opening her eyes, she was in a room she didn't recognize. Not the bedside table, weighed down by books. Not the satin sheets or the velvet curtains. The pillows were huge and expensively soft.

Nothing was familiar. Desperately trying to piece together the night before, fragments came and retreated; wide eyes, contorted faces, jaws clenched, skins oily with sweat. People clapping. Red lipstick. Red hair. Red wallpaper. Hearts and diamonds. Nakedness. Had it been hers? She felt her breasts. Still in their bra and her dress was on but open. She remembered cards. A creepy man leering at her. Slow dancing, her arms waving and hips undulating. She felt the sickness of self-loathing in her gut. Strip poker. Someone stopping her from taking her underwear off and Esme shouting at them. Shame shot through her. Christ, what had she done, or not done, for that matter? All she knew was that she needed to get up and get out. Fast.

Sliding from the nameless person's embrace she tried to stand but her brain felt burnt-out and her legs stiff and cramped. She turned to look down at the person who had slept behind her. It was Cece. She was naked from the waist up, her face smeared with make-up. Dan lay the other side, his chest exposed under the slippery sheets. Esme made a half-hearted attempt to wake Cece with a gentle prod but she was completely out. She thought about leaving a note but the urge for flight was stronger. What time was it? A glance at the light seeping through the curtains. Panic ripped through her. Oliver's show. Missed. Lost to the night.

Her shoes lay on the floor by the bed and she picked them up and tiptoed out of the room. She needed to pee and went to find the loo. Lifting her dress to pull down her pants she was horrified to realize she had none on. It was then she remembered allowing the poker-playing creep to kiss her. She could taste the furry plaque coating his teeth, feel his hands venturing under her knicker elastic. She remembered slapping away his hand. They had been in this bathroom but her underwear was nowhere to be seen. Although she was reassured they hadn't gone the whole way, the agony of humiliation spread through her. She just had to find her bag and then she'd be gone.

The scene in the next room was carnage. Bodies were strewn across the drawing room. Broken lines of white powder and rolled-up notes, pieces of tinfoil and dirty spoons scattered the surfaces. Empty and broken bottles were everywhere, as though washed up on the tide of immorality. It looked like something from a nightmare.

Who were these people and how could they live like this?

More to the point, how could David allow them into his house? Esme was disgusted by the whole night but she was even more disgusted with herself. It was seedy and revolting. Depraved but not deprived, which made it even worse. And she had been a willing participant. She wanted to throw up.

She picked her way over slumbering corpses, her eyes flicking into every corner, searching for her bag. The creep was on his back, unconscious in the middle of the carpet. Someone had emptied the contents of an ashtray onto his chest, which was rising and falling gently, covered with butts and ash. She pushed him softly to see if he was on lying on her bag. It had to be somewhere. She rewound her movements, retracing her steps and then remembered that she'd left it in the hallway. Relief swept over her. She ran down the stairs and searched through the coats on the stand.

'Looking for these?'

The butler had appeared, silently, holding her handbag by its strap with one finger and the Harrods bag dangling from his other hand.

'Are you and your prawns leaving? They'll smell if they hang around for too long.'

Shame washed over her again reddening her cheeks. How much had the butler seen?

'Yes. Thank you,' she said. He looked at her with disdain.

Oh, Christ the money. Dread sucked the blood down to her feet. She put a hand out for a solid surface to keep her upright. She was a child again, waiting in fear of being caught out by her parents for something she may or may not have done. She didn't dare open the bag to check its contents under the gaze of the butler. Her brain scrambled for excuses to tell Oliver.

The truth was too embarrassing. She had missed the show for what? A horrid, sordid night that she could barely remember.

A stream of black cabs passed by, like buses arriving in clusters, but none had their light on. She prayed to the patron saint of lost things for a taxi to appear and fast. Although the invite-only launch party had been and gone last night, she'd still be able to see the exhibition today before it was open to the public this evening and in hopefully have her pick of Oliver's work.

'Dear Saint Anthony, please find me a cab.'

No sooner had she uttered 'Amen', when a cabbie stopped at the zebra crossing and she hopped in.

'Oh, thank goodness you turned up.'

'Where you going, miss?'

'Farringdon Road, please.'

The driver was ancient with a creviced face that mapped out years of smoking. He wore a flat cap dusted with a dusting of fallen cigarette ash on its brim. Her father always said that women and people wearing hats in cars were terrible drivers. She was glad she was learning to ignore many of his similar pearls of wisdom. She sat back and breathed a sigh of relief to be on her way. Perhaps it wasn't so bad. Maybe it was even a good thing she had missed the party? It would have been full of people and now she'd be able to view his photographs in peace and select the best with Oliver's focused guidance.

She looked at the meter and then checked her purse to make sure she'd have enough for the fare. Unzipping her wallet there was barely enough for a coffee, which she desperately needed.

'Fuck.'

She'd have to break into Bill's money and pay him back. Digging to the bottom of her bag, she fished out some loose notes and counted. Fifteen pounds. Shit. She dived back into the mess and tipped everything out and peered inside. Empty. Nothing. The rest of the cash had gone.

Her heart began to beat like a gloved fist against her ribs. She felt a horror so intense it yanked all hope from her. Swept clean of delusion now, desperation boiled through her hangover, reducing it to a glaze of concentrated panic. Her hand returned to the innards of her bag, feverishly searching for the money that she knew wasn't there. Trying once more to piece together the events of last night she was sure she hadn't told anyone about the cash. The only person who knew about Oliver's show was Cece, or maybe she had mentioned it to Dan? Could one of them have taken the money to look after it? Or the butler… God, this was beginning to sound like a farce. The trouble was, this was reality. She had left her bag unattended for any one of the partygoers to help themselves.

'Stupid, stupid idiot,' she said out loud.

''Scuse me?'

'Sorry. No. Nothing.'

She glanced at the bleak part of London she was travelling through. Her despair deepened at the sight of nondescript office buildings and she suddenly felt wretched, empty of everything other than the desperate need to get to Oliver's. She fiddled with the belt of her dress, coiling and uncurling it repeatedly.

The traffic was appalling. She slipped the partition window to one side, releasing the driver's fag smoke through the gap.

'Sir? Could we take another route? Perhaps through the back streets,' she asked, knowing that he would be selectively deaf or come back with the sarcastic retort of someone who wanted to retire but a nagging wife at home kept him behind the wheel.

'Ah… another passenger who has done the Knowledge. Which way do you want to go?'

Esme had no clue and sat back in her place.

'It's OK.'

But it wasn't OK. Her fears were gaining momentum with each passing mile.

They travelled along the Thames before turning northwards into an industrialized part of town that reminded her of Camden without the people. Most of the buildings looked disused with tall windows running along the first floor and seemingly no way to get in. She had given the driver the street number but there appeared to be none.

'Is it a studio?' he asked.

'I'm not sure but yes, it probably is. My friend is a photographer.'

'Well, the only studio on this street is Lemonade. The entrance is down the side there – look,' he said, pointing to a narrow alleyway with fire escape steps climbing up the side of the building.

This must be it, hoped Esme and paid the taxi man, leaving her nothing to get home.

'Thank you,' she said.

As the cab pulled away, she stood and looked up and could see there were spotlights set into a brilliant white ceiling stretching along of five of the windows.

She began to climb the stairs but after a few seconds felt light-headed and sat down, head between her knees. The heat was insufferable and sweat sprang from her scalp. She rucked her dress up to sit on the cold iron step. After a moment, she stood again and taking a few deep breaths, continued at a slow, grinding pace. On the first landing, she peered through the bevelled glass of a door and could see a silhouette moving across the room. She knocked and waited. There was the sound of a bolt sliding back and a peroxide blonde with a studded dog collar around her neck and heavily kohled eyes stood there. She was beautiful in a dominant, unapologetic way.

'Hi. May I help you?'

'I'm here to see Oliver Maxey's exhibition,' Esme said, trying to keep her voice steady.

The woman turned and shouted, holding the door, barring her way in and obstructing her view.

'Ollie, there's someone to see you.'

'Is that Esme?' he yelled back.

'Are you Esme?' said the woman, looking her up and down.

'Yes,' she said, suddenly feeling out of her depth. Esme wanted to say no and make a run for it. She was late, had no money and all her hangover-induced insecurities were hyper-sensitized as she compared herself to this alpha-female with a look of possessiveness written all over her face.

The woman stood to one side as an invitation to enter and Esme stepped over the threshold. Nothing prepared her for the interior – the highest, longest room she had ever seen, so bright and white she had to shield her eyes until they acclimatised. Vast black-and-white photographs had been placed between two sheets of Perspex with nothing to distract the eye from the pure majesty of each photograph. No frame, no sign of nails, hooks or hanging wire broke the illusion that they were hovering in mid-air. The impact and power of Oliver's work was a throbbing visual baseline. A shot of rocket-fuelled adrenaline recharged her waning energy. Esme was stunned.

'Hey.'

Way down at the end of the gallery stood Oliver as if he had miraculously appeared from out of the whiteness: a black, leather-clad shadow against a blank canvas.

'I'm so please you made it. I thought maybe Bill didn't like my portfolio,' he said.

'These are…' she mumbled, genuinely lost for words.

'It looks great, doesn't it?' he said. 'This is Nancy, by the way.'

Esme was unable to take her eyes off one picture of – what was it? A lily shot through wet glass?

'Is this who you were telling me about?' said Nancy.

'Yeah. Esme. She works with Bill Cartwright. The collector everyone wants as a patron.'

'These are incredible,' Esme said finally, looking at Nancy. 'I mean, really, really incredible. Bill is going to go nuts.'

Fading flowers, rotting fruit and skulls recurred in the photographs. They were gloomy symbols of the brevity of life and the inevitability of death. Beautiful but damned. At the centre of one wall hung a huge still life of a lotus flower. It was the only colour in this snowy oasis and sprang – in all its purple glory – with a restrained eroticism.

The studio itself offered cool relief from the burning day and was as icily clean as a surgical theatre. There were no skirting boards or cornicing to mar the sanitary lines and the floor was a piste of glacial resin that sucked at her shoes as she moved towards Oliver.

Nancy was planted with her legs apart, arms folded. There was a hint of suspicion in her eyes. 'Bit late for that,' she said and walked away.

'I'm so glad you came,' said Oliver. 'Let me show you around.'

He wore a blue-and-white-striped T-shirt under his jacket which made him look younger, somehow more familiar, less New Yorky and more like an image from her childhood holidays in the South of France. For a second she forgot why she was there – there was something about him that made her feel at home, even in this alien environment.

'I'm so sorry I'm so late, Oliver.'

'Jesus, I'm never on time for anything. Try getting around the grid system of Manhattan. It's a fucking nightmare. I used rollerskate everywhere until my work got too heavy to carry twenty blocks,' he said.

He came over and reached out to put an arm around her shoulder to show her the exhibition but something stopped him. His eyes travelled down her body and back up to her face.

'Late one?'

Esme nodded, freshly conscious of how she must look. Smudged mascara, crumpled dress, matted hair and bloodshot eyes; a wreck of lost control. She hung her head, wanting to hide but wanting to explain. Instead she started on what she hoped was a happier topic.

'Bill has authorized me to buy all of your best work. But I don't know where to begin because it is all... well... it is all so incredible,' she said hopefully. Surely he would let her reserve some pictures for Bill, giving her enough time to see if Dan or Cece had the missing cash. 'He is in awe of your ability and got completely over-excited when I showed him your photographs. In fact, he was struck dumb. Literally didn't speak for two minutes. Bill never stops talking but he couldn't say a word when he saw your work…'

Now she was with Oliver – soothed by the serenity of his work and the fact he seemed genuinely pleased to see her – she felt a moment of hope.

'That's a pity. They've all sold,' said Oliver, matter-of-factly.

'What…?' A chill ran through her. She looked more closely. Sure enough, little red dots of stickers were there, blinking against the whiteness surrounding the big prints that flanked here. 'All of the best pictures have been reserved already?'

'No, not just the large ones. I mean they *all* got sold last night. I couldn't believe it. Esme, when you are trying to make it as an artist, you don't bite the hand that feeds you. Two collectors came by and between them they bought up the entire show. Obviously I wasn't going to refuse them.'

The room and – in particular – Oliver's face, came into sharp relief. She wanted to get back into the sun to take away the sense of foreboding blossoming in her – the certainty she had that Bill would fire her for such catastrophic failure. She could smell the stale odour of disgrace from her clothes, her hair, her future. Bill had given her a chance and she had screwed it up.

'No. Of course not! Of course, you wouldn't,' she said faintly. 'I'm really pleased for you.' Esme wanted to be happy for him, but as the magnitude of her mistake hit home, it was all she could do not to collapse to the floor. First she'd lost Bill's money, and now she'd missed out on more than the photographs – she'd lost the chance to prove herself to Bill.

Please say something, she thought, but Oliver just looked at her, those blue eyes filled with – what was it – disappointment? Regret? Scorn?

'I've been an idiot,' she said.

'Yeah, well…' He pushed his fringe back but it wilfully flopped back and seemed to cast a shadow over his features, or was it a shadow rising within them? 'I'm still flattered that the great Bill Cartwright wanted to own my work. I'm just sorry it wasn't to be.'

A phone rang from deep within the bowels of the gallery.

'Ollie! It's the journo from the *Observer*,' shouted Nancy.

'I have to take this,' said Oliver, with the bewildered slight smile of someone getting used to the smell of success.

'Of course.' Esme walked to the door turning to say, 'Good luck.' But the photographer had already vanished through a white door in the white wall.

Esme ran down the steps, clinging to the railing for support. Blinded by tears, she missed the final step and fell onto her knees. And there in a messy heap the sobs began; long, scalding ones that came again and again. Crawling to the wall, she sat and drew her legs in to her, wrapping her arms around them to become as small as possible. Blood trickled down her shin and she dabbed the graze with her dress. One of her heels had snapped and fallen under an overflowing wheelie bin and she took off its pair and threw it in the same direction. Resting her head against the sun-soaked bricks, she wept silently and unabated. From inside the gallery she heard a shutter clicking but the sound only reminded her of what she had lost.

Chapter Twenty

It took her nearly two hours to walk back home. Two hours of smothering car fumes and unbearable humidity. It had been very hot for too long now; the Embankment, for all its dazzlements, stank of the stagnant Thames, emptied by the tide. Everything glistened with a hard, brittle light, the intensity of the sun bouncing off car bonnets and firing the temperature to boiling point. Esme felt that every passerby saw through her demolished appearance, sensed her shame. At each pedestrian crossing she held her breath, aware that she stank of booze. Busy streets in the heat of the day were no place to be with a hangover. Everything felt far away and then suddenly she was ambushed by an unseen lamp post or car, briefly shaking her out of her trance.

Any hope that Bill might not be at the gallery was quickly dispelled by his Bristol parked outside. She pushed the door but it didn't open. She normally loved letting herself in and locking the door behind her until Suki or Bill arrived, feeling the still security of the gallery. She rummaged for her keys which, thank God, had not been of any use to whoever had ransacked her bag.

The second post was still scattered across the door mat and there was no sound from within; but she felt a charge in the air, that she wasn't alone. Gathering up the letters, she saw that her father had sent a postcard. It was a photograph of the amphitheatre in Arles. Provence had always been a favourite place for him to paint. It was the light, he said. Seeing his large, lazy handwriting made Esme realize that she hadn't given her father much thought. Even when he was in the same country, or same city as Esme, he had felt absent. He had never written to her at school and as she read the card now – *Having a marvellous time and painting like a fiend. Sending you much love, my darling girl* – Esme felt an unfamiliar spark of affection for him. As her life was about to implode, she was grateful for the momentary distraction.

'Bill?' she said too softly for human ears.

Silence.

She went into the kitchen where Suki, most likely, had already made a mess since the cleaner's early-morning visit. The cutlery drawer tilted heavily open and milk curdled idly on the counter. She checked in the office and the vault was locked. Part of her guiltily wished there had been a burglary to deflect from her mistakes. She ran the tap until it was cold enough to drink and downed two mugs of water after rifling through the cupboard for aspirin.

'So how did you get on?'

'Christ, you made me jump.' But she didn't turn to face Bill, wanting to postpone her fate for a few seconds longer. She felt dread and self-disgust as palpable as seasickness.

'Have you seen it? A double page in the *Evening Standard*. First time I've ever known a photographer to get a write-up like this. You picked a winner, blossom – your friend Oliver is being hailed as the next Man Ray.'

Esme's heart sank as she turned to face him. Death itself began to look welcome. Bill would kill her anyway once the truth was out.

'Jesus, Esme.' Bill's eyes widened as he took in her dishevelled state. 'What on earth happened to you?'

'Oh, Bill. I'm so sorry.'

He knew she hadn't come back last night; it only took a few stuttered words to fill in the rest and tell him she'd missed the preview. Her body went limp with defeat and the weight of letting him down.

'Bill, I'm really, really sorry. I've fucked up big-time, I know. I'd didn't think they would be sold so fast.' She began to cry, more genuine than the fake tears she squeezed out as a child to avoid punishment.

'They've sold already? How many of them?'

'Yes,' she said quietly. 'All of them.'

He stared at her, puce-faced with eyes bulging, his veins like fat blue worms etched on his neck. His fists were clenched with the strain of keeping his emotions in check.

'Do you realize what you've done? This guy is no longer a rising star, he's the full-blown fucking midday sun after this article and I gave you the *opportunity* to choose those photographs on your own – to get in there before the vultures – and you've fucking spunked it up the wall,' he hissed, spittle flying from his mouth like sparks.

'I know. I know. I'm sorry,' she said.

'If you *knew*, you wouldn't have missed the fucking appointment. Jesus, if there is one thing I *hate*, it's being taken for granted.'

He paused and rubbed his face, taking deep breaths like a swimmer before a dive.

'I've done so much for you, Esme, and the one time I ask you to do something for me, you screw up. Not because you got run over or had a family drama but because you stayed out all night getting fucking pissed. You look like you've been dragged through nettles and you stink like a fucking beer mat.'

He looked at her like she was diseased.

'You need to pray one of those sales fall through and that he realizes the value of being part of my collection…'

Esme remembered Oliver's excitement in Bill's interest and she wanted to kick herself for not actively pitching her boss when she had been at the studio. But then she remembered she had had no money. Shit. She was going to have to tell Bill about the money and it was better she did so before he asked for it back.

'The other thing is…' she stalled, preparing herself for the human hand grenade to explode.

'Now what?'

'Your money. Someone stole it out of my bag,'

Bill looked at her and put a hand up like a policeman flagging down a speeding vehicle and went very still. The edge of his pursed mouth went white and he shook his head, advancing to the door. When he turned around his face held a look of utter blankness.

'I've got an important client coming in tomorrow, so I suggest you make yourself scarce for a while.' He stalked off.

'Bill, wait! Please wait,' she banged on his car window but he ignored her and drove away down the street.

She slammed the door and screamed into the empty gallery.

Rage at her uselessness boiled inside. She wanted to punch the wall. Bill had given her the responsibility for her discovery and she had let him down. Oliver had been her golden ticket. If she'd bought those photographs when she was meant to, it would have been another rung up the ladder in the art world. If Bill sacked her now, it was all snakes and no ladders. And she didn't blame him. It would be a fair consequence for her foolish behaviour. She would sack herself in Bill's position. Then another thought struck her. With her job would go the roof over her head. What a mess. What a fucking mess.

If she didn't feel so ashamed she would have called Sophia. She couldn't decide if she needed to be alone to ponder her shame and despair in seclusion or whether her problem shared would be a problem halved. Where was Suki when she needed her? Although Suki would probably just tell her to follow her footsteps and focus on finding a man and settling down rather than trying to slog it out in the art world. Cece might be a better option. Yes. She would go and find Cece and be united in the rueful bond of a shared hangover. Esme still clung on to the hope that she might know something about Bill's money. Cece's no-nonsense, worldly-wise attitude was what she needed right now. Plus her sofa might be available until she found somewhere else to live. But first, she had to clean herself up.

The breeze had blown her bedroom door shut and the room was like a furnace; books and papers on the table by the window curled like old sandwiches. She threw her dress on the bed and went to wash, wondering if there was anything clean to wear. She still had a couple of tops lent to her by Cece and a borrowed striped shirt of Suki's hung on the back of the door. After towel-drying her hair, cleaning her teeth and spraying deodorant on her stubbled armpits, she re-applied a light face and opted for the reassurance of her mother's shirt and a pair of white shorts. Thankfully Bill had paid last week's wage in cash which she pulled out and stuffed into her back pocket. The notes were covered in pencil shavings glued in place by ink from a leaking biro which got all over her hands. It felt like everything she touched was stained right now.

The closer she got to North London, the more she craved the comfort of Cece's pragmatic outlook. She'd been there, seen it and done it, she was sure. At some point, she bet Cece must have been sacked and faced the prospect of destitution. Her empathy and sound advice was exactly what Esme needed.

Mornington Crescent was like a hairdryer, the hot air scooping up dead leaves and litter. Mini dust tornadoes swirled at her ankles, the grime settling on her hair, still damp. Esme used one foot to brush aside crisp and sweet wrappers from the entrance to Cece's house. She rang the bell.

'She's not in, love.'

Esme turned around. It was Mabel, pushing a shopping trolley, a saggy sleeveless dress exposing her lack of bra.

'Effing windy. Storm's coming, they say.'

'Did Cece say when she'd be back?'

'I'm not her bleeding secretary.'

Esme thought she would wait for a bit and she sat down on the step, her face feeling irritated and clammy as dust gusted into her eyes and up her nose.

'You might be there all night, love. She's always out, that one. Right slapper.'

Esme didn't fancy getting stuck in an argument with Mabel and got up to leave.

'Will you tell Cece I came by?' she asked.

'Who are you?'

'Esme. Tell her Esme came to see her.'

Mabel raised her giant arm in acknowledgement and Esme returned to the Tube station, faced with a miserable night alone.

Given her possible eviction, Esme began to pack, readying herself for a swift and clean exit. As she folded her new, newly soiled dress that reeked of smoke and was sticky with God knows what, she began to weep. Her misery came from an emptiness inside that she felt had been carved out with a knife; the emptiness you get when you've broken something very important to you. She'd lost her chance at breaking free from her past. She pressed her face to the cool glass of her mirror and had an overwhelming sense of the loneliness of London. Thousands of souls in their bedrooms, high in the cliffs of windows.

Exhaustion began to creep in, wrapping itself around her bones, squeezing her so tight she could barely breathe. She'd have to finish packing tomorrow. As she went to turn out the landing light she clocked an envelope propped against the opposite wall. Parchment-thick, it had a red crest on the back and her name handwritten on the front. Opening it, the note inside was from Kensington Palace requesting her to join HRH Princess Margaret for lunch at her home.

Well, this was a first. To get an invite from the Princess in her own name, especially when her parents were out of mind and out of town, was something she never expected. How on earth did the Princess know she was in London? Esme thought back over her movements. The only thing she could think of was that one of the guests at Bill's exhibition must have told her. The summons, whilst a surprise, did little to lift her spirits. She would have to lie about her circumstances and pretend to the Princess that all was rosy.

Chapter Twenty-One

The next morning, despite longing to stay in the oblivion of sleep, she woke early. Her hangover gone, she could feel the misery of the past twenty-four hours in even sharper detail. She kept replaying the last few days obsessively but try as she might, she could not conjure any vision of the future that didn't involve feeling lost and in limbo. All she knew was that she had to get out of the flat. Bill had told her to make herself scarce and she couldn't think of anything more miserable than cowering in her room above the gallery, hearing him downstairs, waiting for the axe to fall. But where was she to go? Cece hadn't called her – if Mabel had even delivered her message. She should have pushed a note through the door. And then she remembered Dan had said he was covering a story at Battersea Dogs' Home today, the last Friday of the month, and decided that was how she would spend her day. The way she felt right now, she'd definitely prefer to be around dogs rather than people. Plus she could ask Dan if he'd seen anyone pickpocketing and going through bags at Eaton Square.

Aware she was going to have to make her pay packet last, she decided against coughing up for a bus or Tube fare, and so Esme walked to Buckingham Palace Road and started for Battersea.

The pavements were hot enough to have shimmering heat hazes in patches. The unrelenting heat had been absorbed by the roads and buildings and now it felt like they were pumping it back out. The tar was like poured liquorice in the streets. In the distance, she heard the growl of thunder rise up over a bank of building cloud. The parched stony soil in the park showed through the thin grass which was balding in great swathes that had been exploited by too many picnic rugs and sunbathers. Gold-crested bins were overflowing with waste. City dwellers had no respect, she thought, chucking their rubbish wherever they felt inclined, be it out of a car window or here in Her Majesty's garden.

As she eventually approached Battersea, Esme thought it must be close to feeding time as she could hear the dogs barking and howling across the rooftops. The closer she got to the refuge the more intense the noise became so she had to shout at the lady in reception.

'I'm here to meet the journalist from the *Camden Journal*; Dan is his name.'

The young woman played with a piercing in her nose. Her face was set in a mean expression of confrontation. A woman not to be charmed by anything unless they had four legs and a tail. The woman – 'Tricia' it said on her name badge – looked at Esme with unsympathetic eyes.

'He's in the canine block. Sign in,' she said pointing at a form.

'May I borrow a pen?'

Tricia sighed heavily and took a biro from the bun at the back of her head.

Esme squiggled a signature and asked directions.

'Out the door, through the green gates and left. Ring the buzzer and someone will let you in. We close at five thirty sharp.'

The flagstones in the dog run were slippery and wet with undertones of ammonia that had been mixed to disinfect the compound. As a child Esme had harboured a dream to work here, inspired by her own dog Digger, himself a Battersea boy. The chemical residue made her eyes sting, adding to the combined misery of messing up her career and losing the roof over her head.

Suddenly, all was peace and stillness, as though the elements were obeying that sacred law of calm before the storm. For a moment, the birds had stopped singing, the dogs barking; just the clanking of metal grilles and the distant hum of traffic.

She pressed the buzzer which sounded off someway in the internal workings of the pound and she soon heard the soft pad of rubber-soled shoes. Then the click of a switch and the door unlocked.

The corridor was pleasantly cool and bright with a bank of cages along each side. As soon as she passed the first kennel it set off an alarm of barking, whining and yapping. Every dog had its own stark kennel with a bowl of water and a solitary toy. Some leapt snarling in terror wrapped up in aggression, others sat quivering in a corner with uncomplaining acceptance of past suffering. Snarling dogs had been owned by snarling people and dangerous people had dangerous dogs. A dog was never sad in a happy family and so many of these dogs carried the trauma of beatings or abandonment. It was terribly sad to think there was such cruelty and for a moment Esme understood Tricia's distrust of people. After all, Esme had never had a human relationship that was as free from strife, disagreement or frustration as the one she had had with Digger. Bending down to make eye contact with a scruffy cross-breed possibly of spaniel/beagle heritage, the skewbald mongrel crept towards her, his tail wagging timidly and head down in submission. He sniffed her hand and gave it a small lick.

Just then, Dan appeared and sat down on his haunches next to her, putting his own hand through the grille to stroke the dog.

'He's adorable, isn't he? Frisky is his name.'

'Yes, he is. He's the only one not barking or whining,' said Esme.

'I'm glad you came. I didn't see you leave the party the other night. Did you have fun?' he asked with a knowing smile.

'Well…' Esme didn't know where to begin.

'I did. A lot,' he said with a look that was coy but persistent, as if to show that they could be candid with each other.

'To be honest, I don't remember much about it,' she said in an attempt at diplomacy. She didn't know how good a friend David was to Dan so she felt she could hardly say how ghastly she'd found the whole night. And that would only draw attention back to her antics.

'I can reassure you that you were magnificent.' He laughed salaciously. 'I tried to find you after the poker game but you had disappeared.'

'What about Cece?'

'She was a mess. I don't know what she'd drunk or snorted but I saw a different side to her. All her jealousy came out as a kind of disdain for what she longs for: class, breeding.

She's so envious of everything we have and coming from her background she can't bear to see inherited wealth or people enjoying it.'

She was glad the memory of her own conduct was still fuzzy. She'd been so busy thinking about her mistakes that she'd forgotten how off Cece had been with her.

'All I ask of a friend is loyalty and she kicked off on one, accusing me of things she has no right to concern herself with. It was embarrassing,' continued Dan. 'There's no place in my life for chippiness and envy. I told her if she felt like that we should probably cool things off. I want a girl who loves me and loves a good time.'

Esme nodded, glad the focus was on Cece rather than her own drunken striptease.

'She told me to bring all this vodka and stuff and then proceeded to ignore me all night,' Esme said, and then felt the guilt of disloyalty as a snapshot memory of Cece covering her up with her dress and taking her to the bathroom flashed before her. She struggled to remember at which point of the night it was.

'When did you leave?'

'Too late.' She wondered if he didn't realize they had slept in the same bed, with Cece between them. Did she pass out after him and Cece? She tried to recall going to bed but had no memory of anything after being kissed by Scumbag. She shuddered.

'What's wrong?' he said, running a finger down her cheek.

'I only meant to drop in at the party. I was meant to be going to a work thing. Bill went fucking berserk when he found out I'd missed it.'

'What was it?'

'It was with this photographer. Bill asked me to buy some of his work but it had all sold when I finally got there. Bill shouldn't have trusted me. I've let him down. No wonder he went mad. It's entirely my fault and I missed a golden opportunity for him. He's done so much for me.'

'Sounds like he seriously overreacted. And what was he thinking in giving you so much responsibility? I'd say he's the one at fault for asking so much of you. Bit like putting an anemone in a tank with circling sharks. I'm sure he'll calm down and see it was a big ask. It's not your fault.'

Esme steadied. She felt the relief of being supported by someone who had walked into her life when the rest of the world had walked out; a sense that someone strong was on her side. Under the warmth of Dan's opinion, a seed of resentment towards Bill sprouted.

'And he gave me all this cash which I had to carry around like a human piggy bank. I was a walking target for muggers but in the end it was someone at the party who took it. You didn't see anything, did you?'

Dan shook his head. 'Afraid not.' He gave her a concerned glance and Esme felt encouraged to go on.

'When I told him the money had been stolen he drove off in a huff. For all he knew, I might have been attacked or beaten up but he was only concerned about his sodding pictures.' Esme stopped, aware how self-pitying she sounded and tried to backpedal. 'But I still can't believe I let all this happen. Honestly, I'm more furious with myself than poor Bill.'

Dan assessed her as though her welfare, her fearful heart, had long been his concern. His idling gaze was hypnotic, the huge dark pupils seemed to fill his eyes like he was working on a scheme of imminent gratification. There was something confidently patient about him, neither lecherous nor rushed but predatory all the same.

'Why don't we go and meet some more canine friends?'

He put his arm through hers and they continued along the corridor.

'Want one?' he said, offering a packet of cigarettes.

'We can't smoke in here.'

'The dogs won't tell,' said Dan with a conspiratorial grin.

'But it's not good for them.'

'Do you remember that scandal about the smoking beagles a few years ago?'

'Smoking dogs?'

'Yes. An undercover journalist took pictures of beagles being forced to smoke in an experiment to test a new cigarette. The scientists trussed the dogs up, attached the cigarettes to their muzzles so they couldn't move.'

'Oh my God, that's horrendous,' said Esme, not wanting to imagine such brutality.

'Truly shocking, no? But it shows you what good journalism can reveal.'

'It's an appalling story. Have you ever had a dog?'

'No. I'm too selfish but I do love them. You?'

Esme told him about Digger; how he had shared in her sorrows and stuck by her through thick and thin.

'I think a dog is the only thing on Earth that loves you more than he loves himself.'

'That's so true,' said Esme. Digger had been the only creature who understood. Tears welled in her eyes.

'I've upset you. Come on, let's go and have a smoke outside.'

The storm was rolling in now, heralded by claps of thunder and lightning and dark clouds that held a well of tears far greater than Esme's own. There was an ominous majesty in the sky that managed to overshadow her brooding self-pity. The temperature had dropped at long last and the wind increased. The dogs began to howl from within. A boom of thunder crumpled the sky, nearer than before.

''Scuse me, can't you read?' It was Tricia, pointing a ring-laden finger at the 'No Smoking' sign. 'If you're going to do that, I suggest you scram before I throw you out.'

She wore a high visibility jacket with the hood pulled over her head. Every time a flash of lightning streaked across the sky she lit up like a beacon.

'We were going anyway but thank you for your time and co-operation. I'd like you to know that you will be the headline of my feature,' said Dan. 'There is only one Bitch at Battersea.' And with that he grabbed Esme's hand and they ran out the gates, not stopping until they reached the park.

'I can't believe you said that!' said Esme, laughing and out of breath.

A plop of water hit her on the face, one of those early raindrops that turns up a few seconds before a deluge. And then it came. The rain thundered down so heavily that she could imagine that the park itself was made of water and an ocean had come to wash away the angry summer heat. Within moments she was wet through. Her shirt clung to her and hair streaked around her face. She felt unsteady and held on to Dan as they took cover under a tree. Water collected in the ossified leaves like sinking boats and spilled out as the wind tugged at its branches.

Hauling in a breath to steady her thumping heart, Esme held it, then turning to Dan, she found him standing so close they were touching. Shutting her eyes, she let her head tip back and fleetingly she felt Dan's lips brush hers. Sensation flared at the brief contact and Dan's mouth curved upward, as she heard a low teasing laugh. A small part of her mind tried to warn her that this was not a good idea but she was past listening. His mouth met hers again, slowly this time, with an assured arrogance that it would not be rejected.

Chapter Twenty-Two

Dan looked down at her, his eyes as dark as the thunderclouds.

'We need to get out of here before lightning strikes. We don't want to burn to a crisp and ruin this magical moment,' he laughed.

By the time they found a cab, the rain had drenched Dan's jacket, which he had given her in a futile attempt to protect her from the storm. As he cast aside the now heavy denim, Esme didn't question where they were going. The heat of her desire and strength of the rain washed all caution from her.

They tumbled into the back of the taxi and Dan chucked his jacket on the rubber matting, still branded with a previous passenger's footprints. The windows steamed up so Esme only had a vague notion that they were headed north. She could see from the glow of the driver's dashboard that he had had to put his headlights on. The rain hammered on the roof, skittering across metal, then tipped onto the windscreen as the wipers tick-tocked frantically in a frenzied bid to swipe away the water. Visibility was murky at best and every now and the wheels tugged through surface water already overflowing from drains.

Esme shivered.

'I need to get you into a hot shower,' said Dan, pulling her into him. ''Scuse me – it's just here on the left.'

The driver pulled over and Esme and Dan made a mad sprint down a dicey stairwell. Dan rummaged in his pocket and fumbled with the lock.

Inside, the flat was dark and smelt musty and dank with a pinch of dust – a little acrid, as if it were haunted by the ghosts of long-dead hops.

Assorted coats and shoes lay in a pile at the end of the narrow entrance hall to which Dan added his wet jacket and cowboy boots with white stitching. Esme followed suit and took off her own shoes, placing them neatly against the skirting.

He turned on a naked lightbulb that hung from the ceiling and shone its prying beam over the dilapidated state of his home. There was nothing to be proud of here, thought Esme. Nothing that represented the ego-driven polish of the man who presented himself as a quasi-intellectual. It was filthy and unappealing in every possible way.

'There are towels in the bathroom,' he said, picking up a shirt that had been flung over the back of a worn sofa. 'Here. Take this to change into.'

'Thanks. I won't be long.'

The shower room was like the rest of the flat – small, dingy and cluttered. Clothes filled bin liners, empty bottles lay discarded and the place reeked of damp. She turned on the shower, took off her clothes and stepped into the cubicle, careful not to brush the plastic curtain speckled with mildew. So much for hot water. The tepid dribble did little to warm her up but she was able to wash her hands and face.

Still shivering, she gingerly dabbed herself with a towel that hadn't had a chance to dry since it was last used. The shirt Dan had given her to wear was scarcely large enough to do up over her chest. Was it Cece's? She told her conscience to be quiet and dried her feet with whatever was hanging over the towel rail. Too late she realized it was a pair of boxer shorts – but her phobia of walking on a dirty floor with wet feet required desperate measures. At least he didn't wear Y-fronts.

Once dry and semi-dressed, she inspected herself in the smeared mirror. It still showed bloodshot eyes and her mouth was dry and claggy. She found some toothpaste poking out amongst aftershave (Vetiver), deodorant, hair gel, an incongruous lip-gloss and a stash of condoms carelessly chucked into a shoe box at the foot of the sink. The toothpaste was Signal (not Colgate, which was more expensive), and had a bead of dry stripy paste at its opening which she wiped off, then squeezed onto a finger. She put her mouth to the tap but changed her mind when she saw the limescale. Taking one last look in the mirror, she smoothed back her hair and took a deep breath.

When she came out, she found Dan had done a speedy clean-up. The flat no longer looked as though it had been inhabited by a pack of wild cats – with books hastily stacked and rubbish dispatched away from view, it was still squalid.

'Dan?'

She saw a note on the kitchen counter.

'*Gone to get a cure. Back in 10. D x*'

A cure for what? Looking at the table, it could be for any number of things, with food poisoning getting top billing. A half-eaten tin of baked beans, topped with a crusty coating had obviously been opened for a very long time. The fork used to eat the beans had oxidized to a lethal shade of green. Was it the fork that had done that to the beans or the beans that had done it to the fork? She opened the tiny fridge to find nothing but Heinz Salad Cream and a wedge of mouldy pork pie. Esme was starving but even the butter was she found on the worktop was rancid and the sliced bread next to it was flecked with mould. There was a smell of decay that must have intensified during the heat wave and Esme lifted the venetian blind to open the window. The slats were covered in grease and most were bent at sharp right angles so that it couldn't be raised. Outside the downpour had strengthened and Mother Nature was doing her best to douse the heat. It was dark and raging. A storm where diabolical deeds are done. She saw a figure moving down the street holding their coat over their head with one hand and carrying something in the other. Despite the rain, he walked in long unhurried strides.

Esme sprang back from the window as Dan approached his front door.

He shook himself, tossed his jacket on the ground and used his shirttails to dry his face. His curls hung straight with the weight of the rain. All that was missing was an ark and his pairs of animals.

'I mean, we needed the rain but this is insane. The canal looks close to bursting its banks,' he said, grinning. 'But it meant there was no queue in the wine shop.'

He hand-opened a bottle and handed her a shot of something black that smelt of fermented mouthwash. She gagged.

'Trust me, it will warm you up.'

She took a sip and felt her face flush with the burn of alcohol. 'What *is* that?'

It was so foul she worried it would produce an instant hangover whose chemical legacy would leave its taste on her brain forever.

'Fernet Branca. It has its roots in the unlikely crossroads where centuries of herbal remedies collided with robust capitalism. Mr Branca sent it to a Milanese hospital during a virulent outbreak of Asiatic cholera. It wasn't a cure but the stuff seemed to help.'

'Probably because it got the patients drunk.'

'It's also good for the digestion,' he said, 'and curse pains. Allegedly.'

'Bottoms up!' saluted Esme and drained the glass. She immediately felt a warmth coat her throat and a sting of medicinal wellbeing. 'Wow. I already feel better.'

Dan refilled her glass and she began sifting through a pile of books; Kafka, Hemmingway, Orwell and lots of names she didn't recognize ending in '-sky'.

'No Harold Robbins, then.'

Dan laughed, 'Trust me, I love a good blockbuster as much as the next person. Who's to say what great literature is? It's so subjective and as long it gives pleasure it doesn't matter if it is Jackie Collins or Joseph Conrad. I learn from both and as long as I am writing often, and writing well, I don't need to be hanging out in the British Library all the time. Nightclubs and dog homes are just as great as literary research centres.'

It was Esme's turn to laugh. 'Cece says you are going to be the next big thing. Have you begun your novel?' She immediately felt awkward having mentioned her name.

Dan looked slightly irritated. 'I wish she'd shut up about that. There is nothing worse than being under someone else's pressure and there is still a long way to go.'

An answer but not an answer, thought Esme, 'Well, I'd love to read it when you're done.'

'Nah—' Dan looked away with a reluctant smile and Esme saw that he was embarrassed. 'You wouldn't be able to read it. I hardly can myself.' This first hint of shyness and uncertainty made Esme want to kiss him again. 'My handwriting's terrible,' Dan said, with a short, defeated chuckle.

Instead Esme said, 'Is that an excuse?'

'Yes,' he admitted.

'Stop being self-conscious about your writing. You are the expert when it comes to the world you are creating, no one else. So be bold and write on,' she said in a raised voice, like a war cry.

She blushed, and in the silence that followed, she felt the crackle of lustful static pass between them. She couldn't bring herself to meet his gaze – doubtful, encouraging, embarrassed, she couldn't tell.

Before she had time to look up, his mouth came down on hers. And that was it. All the self-control went, like water crashing through a broken dam. Esme put her arms around his neck and he pulled her against him... His hands flattened against her back... and she was up on the tips of her toes, kissing him as fiercely as he was kissing her... He clung to her more tightly, knotting his hands in her hair, telling her, with the press of his mouth on hers, all the things she had thought but could never say out loud.

There was always one glass that tipped her over – unfairly and jokingly – into being drunk and afterwards, she decided that was the glass that was responsible for her going to bed with Dan. The sex had been good, great even, but it was a consolation prize compared to the desire she had felt for him. He had fallen into a deep post-coital sleep and she lay rigid, staring up at the ceiling listening to the white noise of wheels and water spray; the rhythmic splatter of rain. Esme tried to do up the borrowed shirt but it no longer had any buttons after Dan had ripped it off. The fabric was in tatters.

What had she done?

Loyalty was one of the things Esme valued most and yet, here she lay, next to the evidence that she had betrayed her friend. And even more than the betrayal of sleeping with Cece's boyfriend, Esme was a thief. She had stolen her friend's trust in Dan and herself. This could never be repeated, she swore. She would have to lock this secret away and would always have to dodge and skirt around the deceit.

Dan stirred and turned, throwing his arm over her, a heavy weight that pinned her to the bed. As she began to ease herself out, she heard a key scrabble with the lock. She stopped, alarmed, feeling that it was she who had broken and entered rather than whoever was trying to get in. Slowly she slipped back under the covers, peering over the sheets hoping to see who it was without them being able to identify her.

'Dan?'

It was Cece. Esme recognized that Australian twang at once. She had a key to Dan's flat and Esme was in bed with her boyfriend? Ex-boyfriend? Whichever it was, hot shame shot through her. There was nowhere to hide as the only way out was the way in. If she moved too suddenly Dan would wake up and if she stayed put Cece would find her. She opted for the latter, stiff with panic. The light went on in the living room.

'Dan,' she said in a yoo-hoo voice. 'Sorry it's so late but I've only just finished work. The club was heaving.'

The bedroom door was flung open and there was Cece with her shining smile of devoted excitement, her wet clinging clothes and bedraggled hair like some resplendent goddess of the deep. She had never looked more beautiful. Esme hoped she was invisible under the tangle of sheets.

'Cece! What the fuck are you doing here?' said Dan, waking and automatically turning on the bedside lamp, going from lifeless form to warrior on the attack in a split second.

'Oh God,' Cece muttered as she realized there was a third person in the room.

Dan scrambled off the bed and grabbed his shirt off the floor, his face glowing scarlet. Esme retreated further into the bedclothes. 'Cece, how did you get in here?' Dan demanded, playing for time.

'With a key?' she said, like he was stupid. 'I knocked first and you didn't answer… and you'd given me your spare set the other morning. Don't you remember?'

Then she came towards the bed and hovered over it for a second. Her face questioned what she saw. She stepped back quickly, trying to step out of the moment. And then she glanced back and locked gazes with Esme, no longer able to hide at such close quarters.

Her dark grey eyes were huge with what Esme could only guess was shock, dissolving quickly into disgust, and they stared directly at Dan. She stood there for a second, disbelief holding her rooted to the ground.

'I can't believe this is happening' she said, her voice filled with hurt. 'You are both pathetic.'

She threw something at Dan. A gift. Wrapped in blue paper with green ribbon.

'Happy fucking birthday. I hope it strangles you,' she shouted as she turned about and left, slamming the front door so hard that something crashed to the floor.

'It's your birthday?' said Esme, stunned, unable to ask the bigger questions. How had she been so gullible? Such an idiot? How had she believed Dan's line about him and Cece having called it off? In her desperation to find an ally – to not be alone and have someone want her – she'd taken everything at face value. Enraged by herself as much as Dan, she drew back her hand and slapped him across the face. The sound of flesh striking flesh bounced off the walls. Raising her voice to a level just below a shout, she snarled, 'You asshole.'

'Oh, grow up, Esme.'

She was about to reply when they both heard the screech of tyres and a sickening thud.

She didn't have to look. A part of her somehow knew. 'Cece,' Esme whispered, then her voice rising to a strangled scream, 'Oh my God. For fuck sake, *Cece*!'

She leapt up and ran out the flat, oblivious to the fact she was half naked. The dawn light had begun to arrive and she immediately saw Cece's motionless body lying in the road, a man standing over her. Esme started to tremble. She staggered and fell off the kerb, her panicked breath coming in shallow bursts. Her eyes welled up, and for a second she couldn't see anything, just her own tears. She couldn't breathe and she began shaking all over, jerky and painful. It was cold. So terribly cold. She was swimming and wanted to put her feet down on something solid but the water was deeper than she thought and there was nothing there.

The scene before her was both sharp and fuzzy. Time stretched and distorted. The car came rushing into focus and seemed huge and terrifying, yet Cece looked like a speck in the bloodbath of this scene. For a second the scene appeared frozen in time. Esme was rooted to the spot. None of this was happening. It couldn't be. She held herself as if only her arms could keep her pieced together and watched the driver go up to a woman in a pink dressing gown putting milk bottles out. He gesticulated wildly and turned to point at the limp form by his car. The dressing-gown woman dropped her bottles, a painful, injurious sound that rang down the empty street and she rushed into her house and after an age came back out with a blanket which she placed over Cece.

That won't keep her dry, thought Esme, her face, her eyes, soaked with tears and rainwater, her hands and legs vibrating like plucked strings. She wanted to disappear into the thin air but was immobilized by guilt so heavy she couldn't move. There was no noise. It was as if the rising dawn ate the sound. It swallowed the quietly spoken words of the driver's inadequate apology. And whatever blame he took, Esme felt her responsibility at the root of it all.

I put her in front of the car. It's my fault she got mown down.

In the distance, she heard a siren. Ambulance. Dressing-gown lady must have called 999, Esme thought, realizing she hadn't even been able to do that for Cece. The blue flashing lights flung shadows along the street that grew longer and hungrier the closer the vehicle got. A female paramedic knelt down beside Cece. She was talking to her, running her hands down her body, shining a torch in her eyes held open with latex-covered fingers. A male paramedic helped lift Cece onto a stretcher and into the back of the ambulance. Somewhere deep inside, Esme registered that their frantic efforts suggested hope that Cece was still there, inside that motionless body, fighting to come back.

Esme felt fairground activity swirled about in a blur. It seemed like no one else could see her. She felt split in two. Her real self standing here, horror-struck, but it felt like she'd left the ghost of her body in Dan's flat. She could almost feel it, looking at her and not liking what she saw. She knew she could never escape her own judging gaze.

A guilty person can still love someone else, can't they? Even when they've hurt them and let them down?

Chapter Twenty-Three

Police had joined the small cluster. One officer was talking to the driver, writing down his words while another two were taping the area off. They spoke to dressing-gown lady, who shook her head, clasping her hands in prayer, dabbing her eyes, her robe darkening in the rain, a wet red shroud around her shoulders. She made a sign of the cross and bowed her head at the ambulance as it drove away.

The departure of the ambulance broke the spell and Esme realized she had to move, had to do something, had to find out where they were taking her friend, if she was all right. She thought about going back inside Dan's flat but knew she would rather die of hypothermia than come face to face with her co-perpetrator. He was no friend. Friends ask you questions; enemies question you.

Shoeless and naked from her pants down, she tugged at a cuff of her shirt, trying in vain to cover herself. The police had cordoned off the area with blue-and-white tape that said POLICE LINE DO NOT CROSS and all of a sudden this was a crime scene. Esme didn't know whether she should identify herself but she didn't know what to say. Although she hadn't been a witness to the accident, she still felt she had caused it. Maybe she could just ask the officers what had happened – see what they said about Cece, but she wasn't ready to hear what they had to say in case it was the news she dreaded. The police tape whipped and snapped in the wind and she started to stumble away. But her guilt tracked her as she walked, an ugly shadow made by herself. She could feel tears stream down her face – in some kind of frenzied competition with the rain.

She had no coat, no bag, no money to get her anywhere. Even if she had, there were no taxis at this hour and anyway, where would she go? Not back to the gallery. Not to Bill and Javier's. For a crazy moment she thought she should head to Cece's. Cece would scoop her up, she thought – then remembered with a sick jolt that Cece was in an ambulance, fate unknown.

In the end, she didn't flag a cab down. One stopped without her hailing it and she got in, almost faint with relief. The driver could recognize a woman in distress, but she was even more thankful that he asked her no questions. He didn't ask about her tears, her state of undress or obvious lack of money. She gave the driver Suki's address.

The London streets were beginning to stir with early risers and night-workers at the end of their shift, going about their business as if nothing had happened. Each time the taxi turned a corner Esme slid across the seat, her legs slippery and wet.

She should have done something. The thought of her friend lying in the middle of the road, unconscious, burrowed into her heart. It coiled in her guts as she wedged herself further into the corner of the cab and clung on to the armrest. Guilt wound her shoulders as she climbed out of the cab, hungry and exhausted from the nightmare. She felt unbalanced, like she'd crossed a line she hadn't known existed.

'Fucking hell, Esme.' Suki pulled her inside when she answered the door, confused to have been woken at such an hour. She put a coat around her. 'What the fuck happened? Have you been raped?'

'Will you pay the taxi?' Esme asked automatically, but the driver had already gone.

Staggering into the living room Esme fell onto the sofa, her teeth chattering.

'It's Cece.'

'Cece?'

'She's been run over.'

'What?'

Esme pulled Suki down next to her, and held on to her arm for fear she might run off when she was told what happened.

'Is she OK?'

Loud sobs: 'I feel so terrible… It was my fault…'

'Where have they taken her?'

'Hospital.'

'Which one? How badly was she hurt?'

'I don't know.'

'How do you know it happened?'

'I was there.'

'Well, you must know how she is then.'

Esme shook her head and saw a flash of surprise in Suki's eyes. 'What do you mean you don't know?'

'I didn't see it happen. Just heard it.'

Questions registered in Suki's face.

'I was staying with a friend of hers and she just turned up

and then ran out of the flat. Then came the noise. I knew it was her,' said Esme, her brain scrambling the details.

'Why did she run out of the flat?'

Esme put her head back and took a deep breath.

'I was in bed with her boyfriend. Dan.'

'You what?'

'It just sort of happened.'

Suki nodded quickly, her eyes wide, mouth open, ready to catch the next revelation.

'I ran after her.'

'But you didn't go to her? I mean, she might be dead. Shit, Esme.' Suki's voice had risen an octave.

'I froze. I didn't know what to do. The door locked behind me, I think... That's where my clothes are. My bag, money, everything...' Then Esme ground to a halt. 'What if she's dead? She didn't move and then the ambulance came. Oh Suki, she can't be. She can't be.'

Suki stiffened and pulled away.

'Suki, you are the only person I can trust.' She broke down again, terrified that Suki would abandon her. 'You are the only friend I can turn to. Please. I mean, look at me. How could I have gone to the hospital like this?'

Something seemed to click in Suki and she suddenly sprung to life. She put her arm around Esme and gave a squeeze. 'It's ghastly but sitting here won't help. You'll be in shock. And you're frozen to the bone,' she said, holding her hands and blowing on them. 'We need to get you into a bath and then we'll sort everything out.'

This kindness made Esme cry even harder, swallowing back spasms in her throat, struggling to breathe. Her tears were an ocean trying to drown her from the inside out. Suki handed her a box of tissues.

'I'll be right back.'

Esme feebly dug into the sofa, pulling the cushions around her. She jumped when Suki returned and gave her a mug. She took a sip; a nice warm mouthful of regret and self-loathing.

'Hot sweet tea. I'm running the bath. Let's get you out of these wet clothes.'

Suki guided her into the bathroom and undressed her. There wasn't much to take off. Just a shirt and underwear. Esme stepped into the bath. It could have been scalding, lukewarm or cold. She felt nothing.

'Here's what we are going to do,' announced Suki. 'I'll cover for you at work, say you are ill. Bill doesn't need to know what happened. You can stay here and rest.'

'What about Cece?'

'I'll ring around the hospitals. What's her surname?'

'I don't know.'

'Well, there can't be many girls of our age who got run over this morning. Where did it happen?'

Esme realized she didn't know the name of the street; had no idea of Dan's address.

'Camden,' she said looking up at Suki.

'I'll find out what the local hospitals are. There's probably only one or two up there.' She put a clean towel on the radiator. 'I had better get going. I've left some clothes for you on my bed.' Suki bent down and kissed Esme on the top of her head. 'Don't you worry. It's going to be fine.'

'Thank you, Suki.' And Esme meant it.

'Don't be silly. You would do the same for me.'

Esme hoped she would have done. She had always thought of herself as a good friend. Until yesterday. Until Cece.

The towel was stiff and Esme rubbed her body with a ferocity that burnt her skin, wanting the pain to override her wretchedness. Her fevered skin made her feel less alone, a welcome sting that helped briefly blank out the horrifying image of Cece's lifeless form. She rubbed harder, replacing the agony of her actions with a pain she could control. Thunder clapped overhead, a mocking reminder of the previous day. The clouds burst open and rain cascaded down. It made her feel better that things in nature could break, too.

Suki had left a nightdress and dressing gown for her to use. She put them on and crawled under the bedcovers, burying her face in the pillow. Her body ached with tiredness but her brain raced. She felt the splintering mortification of having done nothing to help Cece growing worse every minute. If she hadn't screwed up with Bill she wouldn't have gone to Battersea and if Dan hadn't taken her home, none of this would have happened.

She knew she was to blame but she saw Dan in a new light too. Sensing her weakness he had taken advantage, and dazzled by his attention she had surrendered to her loneliness and fallen into his bed. When Cece had run out of the flat, he had done nothing. She wondered if he was somewhere racked with the same guilt and agony as she was, or if he was going about his selfish ways without giving her or Cece a second thought. Everything had been going so well until he came along.

That she had been a bystander seemed unforgivable; even

though others had been taking care of her friend, it should have been her. She wanted to hide her shame but she knew being honest with Suki was only decent thing she'd done that day. She still had no idea what to do, but she knew only by facing up to the truth would she even begin to find a way forward. But right now she had to live with her failure to act and she hated herself for it.

All her life, Esme had been in the presence and at the mercy of two damaged women: her mother and the Contessa. Both would have dealt with this drama in the same way but for very different reasons. The Contessa would have felt nothing and her mother would have made it all about her. At least Esme felt guilty and this let her know that her moral compass was pointing in the right direction. But what she had done was unalterable. She was blaming Dan in the same way Diana would have blamed Cece. Part of Esme's motivation in leaving the Highlands had been to break free from these two dysfunctional women.

In befriending Cece, she had hoped that some of her natural charisma would rub off onto her and that moving in artistic circles would open doors. But despite trying to ride on the personalities of others, she had messed up with the people she cared about most. She had tried to outrun her demons by upping sticks but unless she learnt from what she had done, she would never be free of her past.

It was easy to see how she had been seduced by Dan – he was sexy as hell, but it had been more than that. Her desperation for a man to replace the ones she had lost – her father, the Earl – had clouded her judgement. And she had fallen for the first guy who had shown interest in her. She didn't care about Dan but she was heartbroken at having derailed her best chance of a real friendship. And for what? A shoulder to cry on because she had jeopardized her job through being selfish and unreliable.

Her shiny new life had turned to shit but she felt more grateful to Suki than ever. Esme had been too judgemental of the girl who had taken her under her wing. In her eagerness to escape the society world and husband-hunting, she'd refused to see Suki as more than a stereotype. Yet when Esme was alone, disgraced and lost, she had been warm and practical in her hour of need.

'Esme? I'm home. Got good news.'

Esme was almost afraid to open her eyes, because once she did, she would know one way or the other. Perhaps she could just lie there forever. Perhaps that was her punishment; to simply reside in hell with her eyes closed afraid of opening them lest things had deteriorated even further.

'Es. Wake up!'

Her voice didn't have the tone of someone about to deliver bad news. There was pride in it and the excitement of a soon-to-be-shared secret.

'What time is it?' Esme struggled from the bedclothes. How long had she been sleeping?

'Five thirty,' said Suki. She took a deep breath. 'I found Cece. She's going to be fine. Small head injury and a broken wrist but other than that... she'll be out in a few days.'

Relief swept over her. 'Thank God, Suki. Oh my God. You are amazing, Suki.' Esme leapt up to hug her friend. 'Which hospital is she in?'

'The Royal Free.'

Esme wondered whether she should send Cece a note and some flowers or would they be chucked in the bin? Should she just show up in person or was she the last person Cece would want to see right now? How would she even begin to show how sorry she was?

'She was bloody lucky. Could have been fatal.'

Cece could have become a statistic – in the wrong place at the wrong time. In a flash, her life might have been snuffed out. She could feel energy flowing back into her. It didn't matter what happened tomorrow, because it might never come. What mattered was the here and now and Esme had to find a way to apologize; she had to start making amends and she had to start now.

'Was Bill OK?'

'In the end,' said Suki. 'He told me about you missing the show, and losing the money. I was going to just tell him you were sick, but I figured the truth would go a long way. So I told him about Cece getting run over. And before you ask, of course, I didn't tell him about Dan. At first, he was a bit off – like he didn't believe me – but I reminded him how hard you work and of all the times you've covered my ass. And then he calmed down. A bit.'

There wasn't much conviction behind her delivery, but Esme chose to believe it anyway.

Yesterday her fuck-up at work and Bill's fury had seemed like the end of the world. Although she still had no clue how she was going to deal with that ghastly mess, Cece nearly dying put her own woes into perspective.

She felt like she had been released from a nightmare, given a second chance and was determined to find a way of convincing Cece how sorry she was. If she could do that, then apologizing to Bill wouldn't seem quite as hard.

She had been so busy trying to forget or rearrange her past that she had forgotten to work out who she really wanted to be. She knew now that the essence of herself could not be changed and that that was all right. She'd been so impatient, so told herself that in time she would become less naïve and gauche. The problem had come from wanting to change overnight by flying on the coattails of those she deemed sophisticated and worldly. She needed to grow up at her own pace. If she didn't, there would always be disaster waiting in the wings.

Right now she wanted to repay Suki for her loyalty and to make amends for labelling her a brainless Sloane. Then an idea struck her.

'What are you up to tomorrow?'

'I was meant to be having lunch with the future in-laws but Johnny's had to go away,' she said, rolling her eyes. 'You?'

'I'm having lunch with Princess Margaret tomorrow at Kensington Palace.'

'Seriously?'

'I'd love it if you came with me, Suks. PM will adore you and I'm sure she won't mind if I bring you along.'

Suki looked like she had just been knighted. 'Are you sure?'

Esme nodded and felt for the first time in a long while that she'd done a kind thing.

Chapter Twenty-Four

The first thing Esme did when she got back to the gallery was order the biggest bouquet she could afford with the last few pennies she had until her next pay cheque. (If Bill was still going to pay her final wages – he'd be within his rights to take it as debt repayment, Esme knew.) She chose pink and blue blooms with a note saying 'Forgive me'. She prayed that this would ease things before she went to visit Cece in hospital.

Johnny's father had offered his driver and Mercedes to take them to the Palace and Suki was coming to collect her at noon. She must have phoned at least five times fussing about what to wear and when she arrived – on the dot of twelve o'clock – Esme thought Margaret Thatcher had done a detour via Jermyn Street.

Suki – in all her sartorial lack of wisdom – looked a decade older than her twenty-five years. Pussy cat shirt, bouclé skirt suit in dusky rose, nude tights and a pair of black capped sling-backs from Chanel. She even had the Mrs T handbag, a smooth leather tote with gold buckles capable of biting your fingers. Hours of thought had gone into this outfit and Esme didn't have the heart to tell her that it was lunch not the opening of parliament. How she had managed to pull together such staid formality at short notice was nothing short of a miracle. Where the hell had she got these clothes?

'Wow, Suki, you look so smart.'

'Thank you,' she said with the confidence of someone who knew she was wearing all the best labels.

Esme had asked to borrow something, as her only dress was soiled and her mum's shorts were lying on the floor in Dan's bathroom – and would stay there. Suki proffered a holdall and she feared what was inside.

'Hurry up and put these on. We don't want to be late.'

'These' were a white lace off-the-shoulder peasant dress and espadrilles. She would look like Suki's daughter. But whilst dated, it suited her more than if Suki had brought her an outfit that matched hers. When she put it on she looked less maid of honour and more the romantic subject of a David Hamilton photograph. There was something slightly erotic in its innocence and once she'd added gold hoops, Esme was pretty pleased with her appearance. It had a fresh cleanliness that she certainly wasn't feeling after the last twenty-four hours.

'You look lovely, Esme. Really pretty,' said Suki.

'Mother of the bride and her virgin daughter,' Esme said, smiling.

Suki laughed and pulled a small can of hairspray from her bag. Lifting her hair in sections, she hosed it down with lacquer until the tin ran out of breath.

'Right. The Palace, here we come!'

The Downes's chauffeur was a woman. She wore a green uniform and cap with some kind of black resin plume stuck on the front and she didn't say a word. Esme put her well past retirement age and wondered what circumstances had led her to driving two giddy girls across London on the weekend.

'So, what do I call her?' Suki was aflutter with nerves.

'Ma'am, pronounced "damn" not "darm". When you talk about her to someone else you call her Princess Margaret and if you introduce her to someone you say "Her Royal Highness, Princess Margaret", which I'll do when you meet her.'

Suki looked petrified. 'I'm never going to remember all this. What about curtseying. Do I have to do that?'

'Of course. She'll offer her hand. You take it then curtsey nice and low. Men only have to bob their heads.'

'What happens if I head-butt her when I rise?'

This had been a recurring concern of Esme's, but it hadn't eventuated.

'Unless she bends over you, that will never happen.'

The car turned right off High Street Kensington and into the Palace drive.

'We're here. Now don't worry, Suki. I wouldn't have invited you if I thought you'd fuck things up. She's lovely and very funny, so just relax and enjoy it.'

Suki took Esme's hand and placed it on her lap, peering through the windscreen with all the wonder of a six-year-old.

'Oh God, it's closed. Look. The barrier. Are you sure we've got the right day?'

Esme giggled and whispered, 'What's the chauffeur called?' nodding towards their driver.

'I don't know,' said Suki grimacing.

''Scuse me, Mrs—'

'Slack,' said the chauffeur. 'Don't worry, I've done this

before.' And she wound down her window to speak to the policeman in his little shed.

'I have Miss Esme Munroe and her friend for luncheon with Her Royal Highness.'

The policeman looked down a list and said, 'Her Royal Highness will be in the garden. First right. Her Royal Highness's equerry will take care of the young ladies.'

'Thank you, Sergeant.'

'She didn't say my name. How will they know who I am?' hissed Suki.

Esme ignored her and squeezed her hand as they drove under an arch, where a man in chef's whites stood in the doorway wiping his hands on his apron. He waved and Esme waved back.

'Who's that?' Suki asked.

'The chef, I presume. It's not like I know the whole staff! This is my first time here since I was little.' Esme had seen the Princess socially more often than at home here at the Palace.

Mrs Slack did a grand sweep around the cobbled quadrangle, stopped in front of the entrance and got out to open the car door.

'Oh my God, it's *her*... look, Esme, it's Her Princess Highness.'

Princess Margaret was in position in the doorway, small and perfectly formed with an enormous smile. She posed, Cecil Beaton ready, with her cigarette holder aloft in one hand and whisky tumbler in the other. Her 1950s cotton dress, with its tiny waist, flawless cleavage decked with pearls and large turquoise pattern, billowed in the light wind. She had aged since her divorce but still owned an old-school glamour that set her apart from her sister.

'Esme,' she cried, 'how wonderful to see you, darling.'

Esme bounded up the steps. She had never been so happy to see this woman who'd been part of her family's circle since before she was born. Out of all her parents' friends, the Princess was her favourite because she never talked down to her and had stood by her mother through her illness. On more than one occasion PM had stepped in as her Princess in Shining Armour and although Esme played down their relationship in public, she felt they were genuinely fond of each other. Overcome by the nostalgia and security the Princess represented, Esme could have cried. Grateful to find that some things didn't change – however messed up her life had become – Esme wanted to hug the life out of her but gave two efficient pecks on each cheek then curtseyed.

'Oh, ma'am, I've missed you.' Then unable to resist, Esme flung her arms around her, to which Princess Margaret laughed.

'Only you, Esme. So full of love. Just like your darling mama.'

For a beat Esme forgot Suki, who stood starstruck as if waiting to get an autograph.

'I'm not Elvis, dearie,' said the Princess, smiling at Esme's friend.

Esme knew that one thing she couldn't abide were those in awe of her. Esme should have told her to act normally, worrying that the Princess, sensing her weakness, would choose her as the scapegoat of the day.

'Ma'am, this is Suki. We work together at the gallery.'

The Princess took a long pull on her cigarette holder, giving her time to come up with a cutting or witty comment. Esme hoped it was the latter.

'Suki? Isn't that Sooty and Sweep's friend?'

At the address, Suki bent double in her deepest curtsey.

'Her real name is Serena,' said Esme quickly.

Suki hadn't moved, frozen in her curtsey.

'I will call you Serena. Suki is the most ridiculous name.'

Esme gave Suki a sharp kick to get up which she did with a fixed plastic smile that didn't mask the terror in her eyes.

'How do you do, your majesty?' said Suki, curtseying again.

Oh Christ, she's forgotten everything I told her, thought Esme. She's in for a bruising.

'I'm *not* my sister but thank you for the promotion,' said Margaret.

The girls followed her into the drawing room, an overly stuffed chamber with a grand piano and a wall of French windows open onto the garden where a dozen or so people mingled. It was like entering into the depths of the Princess's eyes. If she were a room, this would be it. Painted in cornflower blue and edged with white voile curtains with aqua trim, it was warm and homely but maintained a certain look-but-don't-touch extravagance. To the left Esme saw the dining room laid for lunch. The rain had finally stopped but the air was damp and would frizz the Princess's carefully trained curls.

Suki pulled Esme back and whispered, 'She hates me.'

'Just be yourself. Don't suck up to her because she'll see through it in a heartbeat. And for fuck's sake don't ask if Snowdon will take your engagement photographs.'

'I'm not that stupid,' said Suki, through her painted-on smile.

Drinks were being served on the long terrace above the garden, and when Esme and Suki went out through the French windows there were two or three small groups already mingling and laughing. You could tell that everyone had been drinking for a while and like the roses and lilac, they seemed to sway in the breeze. It was still hot but after the recent storms the stifling humidity had been replaced by a vague sense of steam rising from the baked ground. The garden was busy with life – not just bees, but butterflies and ladybirds that flitted in the rain-soothed air; a haze of activity that no one else seemed to notice but to Esme it signified a world resurrected by the downpours. The Scottish lass in her missed the natural world and fresh moorland air.

A cocktail cabinet had been wheeled out onto the terrace for those wanting something stronger than Pimm's. Large fruit-laden jugs sweated on a trestle table dressed with a white tablecloth and vase stuffed with sweet peas. A liveried butler filled a couple of highballs and Esme handed a glass to Suki and took one for herself. She dipped her fingers into the drink, popping a slice of alcohol-infused cucumber into her mouth followed by a handful of the stale crisps that were laid out in little bowls. At first glance, there was no one else of her and Suki's age but she did at least recognize one of the Princess's ladies-in-waiting. Lady Ann was talking to a somehow familiar man and his blonde-helmeted wife. Esme could see from his smiles and guffaws that he was being greasily agreeable and was surprised that an asslick of his calibre was there at all.

'Come on, let's go for a wander,' she said, and strolled off into the knee-high maze of the parterre with Suki crunching over the pea gravel behind her.

'I thought there would be some famous people here,' said Suki, whose suit had warmed up and gave off a sharp stale smell, the re-awoken ghosts of numberless long-ago weddings in the Home Counties. It must belong to her mother, thought Esme.

'There are. You just don't recognize them.'

They walked on a pace or two, round the plinth of a large urn, and looked across the roses at the assembling guests.

'There,' said Esme, pointing discreetly to a tall man in navy blazer and fawn slacks. 'David Frost.'

The famous TV interviewer was exerting his charm over a group of flattered middle-aged women. 'It's a distinguished crowd rather than a café society one,' Esme said.

Although she didn't admit it, she too had expected a more glamorous guest list but surmised that the Princess was content being the star of her own show. She sat on a chintz-upholstered swing seat, holding court within a circle of admiring syco-phants who were basking in her status like the rays of the sun. It was true that the light that seemed to radiate from her shone more brightly into male eyes – with one in particular trying unsuccessfully to capture the shade of the seat's fluttering canopy so that he might gaze more intently into the Princess's face. Esme recognized him as head of the furniture department at Christie's. He was large and round in the middle and in his tight suit seemed to taper from a long, jowly head towards narrow feet. He looked pop-eyed and sweaty, no doubt from the effort of fighting between an impulse towards pompous discretion and a natural love of intrigue. No one could beat the Princess for the most scandalous stories.

Margaret caught Esme's eye – rolling her own – and waved her over.

'Do you know Esme Munroe?'

The male collective dutifully introduced themselves and Esme in turn introduced Suki. They were spare parts in a group of people bound not by their affection for each other but purely by the love of their hostess. Anyone seen as new, including Esme, was regarded as a cuckoo in their nest. They'd all no doubt scrambled to get to the top of the social ladder and they guarded their place in the court of Princess Margaret with badly disguised jealousy. Esme understood the glamour and appeal of the Princess but these were the kind of social climbers she didn't like; bitchy and petty-minded, caring more for the Princess's title than the woman herself. And they clearly felt that since ma'am hadn't mentioned Suki's name, she was not worthy of so much as a look. It reminded Esme of how the Contessa had treated her when she was a child. Like she was invisible. Esme took Suki's hand to include her in the throng.

'We are trying to get Charles to reveal who the headless man was in Margaret Argyll's Polaroids but he won't tell,' said the Princess. She inhaled tolerantly and blew the smoke out in a long hissing jet. 'You probably don't know, do you, Charles? Just teasing us, which I find frightfully dull.'

Encouraged, Charles said, 'Ma'am, you know how important it is to string out the punchline, how *dull* would it be if I told you from the off?'

Princess Margaret swashed a non-existent fly from her face, 'For God's sake, Charles, just tell us,' she said with a concentrated look of mischief.

'My father told me it was Douglas Fairbanks Jnr,' said Esme, deciding to show the group she was not the kind of know-nothing girl they'd probably pegged her as. She turned to

Suki to explain, 'We're talking about this scandal of a duchess who got photographs stolen of her giving—'

'Giving a man a blowjob, but his head is cut out of the picture,' finished Margaret.

One member of the crowd – with a serious comb-over and navy shirt with white collar and cuffs – pretended to faint and gasped, 'An ugly word like that should never spew from such a beautiful mouth, ma'am.'

'Oh, shut up, Lionel. I have conceived two children, you know.' To which Lionel bowed in apology, befitting his already oleaginous manner.

'Come on, out with it, we're getting bored,' she said, rapping Charles on his knuckles with her cigarette holder.

'Bill Lyons.'

Delighted, Princess Margaret clapped her hands, 'The Pan-Am director?'

'The very one. I'm not surprised. I would have done the same had I managed to corner him,' said Charles.

Much laughter erupted. Esme was surprised that the Princess was engaging in such a conversation, but she seemed to thrive on gossip and soon the men began competing to tell the most salacious stories about people Esme had never heard of.

'Esme, darling,' the Princess turned to her, 'have you got any delicious secrets about the ghastly Lucia? Is she as poisonous as ever?'

'Well, actually I did find something out…' She went on to tell her hostess what Javier knew of her humble beginnings.

'Oh, my. What is it about aeroplanes that the aristocracy find so attractive?' asked Margaret.

Although Esme hated the Contessa she felt bad about her

indiscretion as she knew the information would pollinate far and wide on the wings of this lot and she didn't want to be known as the source. It would only add to her nemesis's arsenal of vitriol against her and her mother. Too late now, she admitted.

'Why is everyone so frightfully dreary these days? We may all love to talk about Margaret Argyll or your wicked Contessa, Esme, but I never hear what misdeeds you young people are getting up to. Won't someone tell me something new?'

'I've got a story.'

Everyone went quiet and turned to Suki as if she had risen from the dead.

'Do tell,' said the Princess, addressing her for the first time.

'Well, Esme's been on a mission to find out how the other half live, haven't you? But that's all ended up in disaster. Her Aussie friend got run over because of that little love triangle...' Suki laughed an uncomfortable laugh.

Nobody said a word and it became so silent that all Esme could hear was the low buzz of a bumblebee. Her heart raced and she felt her blood turning to ice.

'She got caught in bed with her boyfriend. But...' she added quickly, 'the guy's a real cad. He's the one to blame.'

Suki looked surprised by the words flowing from her mouth but seemed unable to stop them.

'Esme turned up at my house almost naked. It was lucky she got to me before anyone that mattered was awake.'

Princess Margaret's expression faded to one of shock as she whipped from Suki to Esme and back again.

Esme felt her vision turn to darkness and her head swam. Determined not to faint, instead she headed inside as fast as she dared.

How could she? How could Suki be so disloyal? She shuddered as she realized how it felt to be on the receiving end of betrayal. The pain of the fact of her crime rose in her throat and she let out a sob. Unaware of where she was going, she went into the room nearest the drawing room – a kind of annex with a desk – and collapsed on the sofa.

'Oh, Cece, Cece.'

Esme felt the sofa dip as a soft puff of air released from its feathers.

'Is Cece the friend you…?' a kind voice asked.

'Yes and I can't believe Suki told everyone,' sobbed Esme.

Princess Margaret sat next to her and stroked her back.

'Darling, tell me exactly what happened.'

Esme spoke, her words rushed. She left nothing out. Cece, Suki, Bill, the photographs, sleeping with Dan, her terror. She told her how kind Cece had been, how down to earth and unspoilt she was. What fun. How hard-working.

'Esme, Esme, darling girl. Serena is right. We've all fallen for men who turned out not to be quite what we thought. But you must learn to see through people.'

Esme looked at the Princess, confused.

'Friendship, in my opinion, is built on two things. Respect and trust. Both elements have to be there. And it has to be mutual. You can have respect for someone, but if you don't have trust, the friendship will crumble. Serena's not cruel, I can see that, but I fear her mouth works faster than her brain. She's too eager to please – at any price.'

Esme nodded her head, her eyes welling with shame.

Princess Margaret wiped a tear from Esme's cheek and went on, 'Don't let that silly girl upset you. You can't be chained to the mistakes of your past. It sounds like this girl, Cece, is lucky to be alive – and that means you have a chance to make amends.'

Keen to allow the Princess to advise her further, Esme told her how Cece had behaved at the gallery opening and fateful night in Eaton Square.

'People aren't always what you want them to be. Sometimes they disappoint you or let you down, but you have to give them a chance. You can't just meet someone and expect them to be everything you're looking for and then be angry when they don't fulfil every hope and aspiration you projected onto them. It's foolish to believe that someone will be exactly what you imagine them to be. And sometimes, when you give them a chance, they turn out to be better than you imagined. Different, but better.'

The Princess walked over to a side table with two decanters and a jug of water.

'Would you like a whisky? It's all I have in here, I'm afraid.'

'No, thank you,' said Esme.

As the Princess fixed herself a drink, she carried on.

'I despise the rituals of fake friendship. There are many people who can't stand me but because I'm the Queen's sister they'll put on radiant smiles and spout compliments until their teeth hurt from their obsequious effort. All that insincere familiarity. If you and your friend – what is she called again?'

'Cece.'

'If you and Cece were identical, what would you have to

307

give each other? And if you can't give a person something they don't have, how can you ever be friends? Enjoy the different worlds you come from, don't fear them. But enough lecturing. You need to get to your friend. Don't leave it until it's too late. My driver, Griffin, will take you. You know which hospital?'

'Yes. Thank you, ma'am. If you don't mind my saying, I needed a kick up the arse and there is no one better at delivering it than you. Suki really dumped me in it, but you're right, she's not a bad person.'

'I'm sure she's not. I've become cynical in my old age. She's just a little too keen to be in with the in crowd, and I suspect she's not had enough adventures of her own so she has to tell stories about other people's,' laughed the Princess.

Hospitals held upsetting memories for Esme: the fear of not knowing if her mother would die or remain damaged by whatever her chosen method of attempted suicide had been that time. The waiting was the worst, the uncertainty of what lay ahead. The fact that losing a parent happened to pretty much everyone, sooner or later, didn't make those hospital visits any less hideous. But she was determined not to dwell on the past. Today was about Cece.

Visiting hours weren't for another thirty minutes so she took a seat on some plastic chairs she'd been directed to. It was just a little too cold and smelt just a little bit too sharp and clean. Esme could hear the constant humming of fluorescent lights in the silence. As everyone else there seemed to be in the same predicament – anxiously waiting to visit loved ones – there was no cheerful conversation. She looked at the clock, which had superpowers such that it moved only two minutes in what seemed to be at least twenty. It made her acutely aware of how little time she might have had with Cece.

She clutched a bag to her. Princess Margaret had given Esme what looked like a baby pillow with a pink-and-white embroidered case. 'Hospital pillows are like cement. This will make Cece more comfortable.'

As she sat and waited, the Princess's words had deeply reso-nated with her. Esme understood now why she had been so drawn to Cece when they met. She was truth. No affectation, no entitlement, just herself. Of course she wasn't perfect. She had vulnerabilities and quirks like anyone. But Esme now felt foolish to have allowed her instincts about Cece to have been clouded by other people's judgements and superficial standards. It didn't matter that Cece had got drunk; she was ashamed to think how all this had stemmed from her panicking about what others would think. Bill hadn't given a rat's arse about Cece's behaviour – he'd no doubt seen worse from his super-rich clientele – his only thought had been to protect the paintings. And now Cece was lying in the depths of this vast hospital, with no family at hand and probably scared out her wits. If the shoe had been on the other foot, Cece would have come to her aid, Esme knew. Boyfriends were expendable but friends were not.

After an eternity, her fellow visitors began to gather their bags, gifts and flowers, shooing young ones towards a bank of lifts. Cece was in a ward on the third floor, apparently.

Peering through the reinforced glass window in the door, she saw Cece propped up in her bed chatting to an ancient woman with chaotic hair and her teeth in a glass on the bedside table. Her head was dressed and she had her arm in a sling across her chest. A black bruise circled her left eye. Esme smiled. Only Cece could look so recklessly cool bound and bandaged in hospital. Just seeing her awake and talking made Esme's heart swell with love and relief.

Esme didn't want to approach while this other visitor was there. She waited outside the double doors for a few minutes and felt her courage failing. Maybe she could just leave a message with the ward sister, to say she'd been but didn't want to interrupt. But just then Cece's visitor left the ward. One more glance through the glass at her friend – now looking quiet and pensive – was enough to remind Esme that courage was the only way to start making amends. Still with no idea what to say, she went over to the bed and put the pillow on the tray table next to the flowers she'd sent. She took Cece's free hand and squeezed it gently, then harder as she tried to hold herself and her emotions together.

'I'm so sorry,' she whispered.

Cece didn't pull her hand away so she carried on.

'I behaved appallingly and quite understand if you never want to see me again.'

'Shit happens, Es.' She didn't smile but there was no anger in her voice.

For the first time, Esme wondered if Cece's disappointment might hurt more than her anger.

'Can you forgive me?'

They stayed silent, holding hands for a few minutes. Esme didn't dare speak for fear she'd say the wrong thing.

'Sometimes people let you down,' Cece finally said.

Did she mean Dan or herself? Esme wondered.

'The thing about nearly dying is suddenly you don't care about the small stuff. And anyway, everything hurts too much for me to get mad.'

Was this forgiveness? Esme knew she was walking on thin ice – a thin crust of what possible friendship remained.

'Yeah, I was pissed off you screwed my boyfriend and yeah, it sucks that I got run over but you weren't driving the car and Dan is hard to resist with his headlights on and trust me you weren't the first,' she said. 'The guy's a fuckwit and it seems it took a broken arm and concussion to make me realize this. I bet he told you he discovered The Clash. What a tool. Hit and not run aside, you did me a favour. You aren't perfect. I'm not perfect. It happened. It was awful. It's over.'

Esme couldn't believe Cece's generosity. She didn't deserve it. 'I still shouldn't have done it, Cece. It was fucking thoughtless. I feel such a trollop. You must have been terrified. I should have been there for you. I watched you get put into the ambulance and I was so ashamed I just fled. I should have followed and been here when you came round.'

'Trust me, it was no worse than waking up with a shit-house hangover and in here they give you morphine.'

'Shall I call your boss…' – Esme tried to remember his name – 'Clement, and tell him what's happened?'

'That would be great. Hopefully he hasn't filled my place already but he knows I'm good for business.'

'Maybe I could stand in for you… until you're better, that is.'

Cece burst out laughing, 'You wouldn't last a night. Fuck him. There are plenty of bars that need a great Aussie waitress. And if I can't find one, there's always a doorway and soup kitchen.'

'Don't say that!'

'I'm joking. It's not the first time I've lost a job and won't be the last. I'll be fine.'

Reality hit home for Esme. Cece had no other place to go to and no family to pick up the rent. Did Javier even know she was here? Her job at the club was her sole source of income and there was no safety net for her. Losing everything for Cece was a world apart from her own fear of being sacked by Bill. Back up North, there was The Lodge and Mrs Bee to go home to – and worst-case scenario she could raid her father's art stash at the warehouse. Her bank account might be in the red but she would always have access to wealth.

'This is all my fault.'

'Come on, I was a cow to you that night at Eaton Square. I wanted to get high and party and show that you weren't the only one who had friends who threw crazy parties. I was still embarrassed after puking outside your gallery, and I thought Dan's mates would show us a good time. But they were just stoners and lechers. Anyway' – Cece smiled, the old irreverence creeping back into her eyes – 'to be honest, I'm more worried about having to spend another night in this fucking room. I've got to sleep mere metres from a woman whose ailment is unknown to me but she stares at me her every waking hour. For all I know she might be a cannibal. Except her teeth are in that glass.'

Both girls burst out laughing.

Chapter Twenty-Five

Predictably, the hospital food was disgusting and lacking a kitchen to rustle up the chicken soup which Mrs Bee always swore was a cure-all, Esme went in search of sustenance. The only shop open nearby was a mini-market. She returned with a small offering, knowing she still had a very long way to go to make amends; magazines, fruit and some Lucozade. When she got back Cece was asleep, so she scribbled her a note and tiptoed out.

As she walked away from the hospital, there was the sense of relief to have made up with Cece but her forgiveness left Esme feeling worse than ever about her own betrayal. How typical of Cece not to feel exploited or that sleeping with Dan had strained their friendship beyond repair. What Esme had done was reprehensible but Cece – in all her grace – had chosen to show that it wasn't the burning of bridges that mattered but the rebuilding that counted. A broken friendship that is mended through forgiveness can be even stronger than it was before, she thought.

But Esme still felt broken. Like she didn't fit together; that there was no room for her in London anymore. After her catalogue of errors she wondered if it was time to leave. She had outstayed her welcome at the gallery, she was sure – but was relieved that no one was there when she arrived back and let herself in to the bedsit. The sad little pile of her belongings packed and ready to go felt like a sign that she should just go straight back to Scotland.

This might be her last night in St James's. She was exhausted, wrung dry and prayed that a good night's sleep would dissolve her self-pity and that the darkness would wipe the slate clean enough to let her to make things right with Bill before she left.

It was a fitful night filled with uncertainty. At one point, Esme woke with a start, soaked in tears. But she found no relief in the peaceful silence of her room, because there everything was real; solidly, unrelentingly real. Each time she opened her eyes, she quickly shut them.

She woke up early, and took a long time persuading herself to get up, staring at her ceiling for a good ten minutes. A knock sounded on her door a second before it opened. Suki popped her head in, eyes wide with hesitation.

'I thought I'd better wake you as it's nine thirty.'

'Shit,' said Esme, scrambling out of bed.

'Don't panic. Bill's not here and I got us coffee.'

Suki was in the kitchen when Esme came down.

'I'm so sorry, Esme, about what I said at Kensington Palace. I should never have told everyone about what happened. I was nervous and the stupid story just fell out.'

She went to give Esme a hug, then stopped.

'I embarrassed you and myself,' she continued. 'Are you terribly cross?'

Esme put a teaspoon of sugar in her cup.

'It wasn't your finest moment but nothing compared to my behaviour. I deserve everything that's coming to me.' If Cece could forgive Esme her sins, then letting Suki off the hook for running her mouth seemed easy.

'What d'you mean?'

'The last thing Bill said to me was "make yourself scarce",' she said stirring her coffee, 'and I've not seen him since. I think he's going to fire me.'

'Of course he won't sack you.'

'Are you sure?'

Suki must have heard the nervousness in her voice, 'Yes, I swear.' She made a sign of the cross to reinforce the truth of her statement, then passed her an envelope with Max's name on it.

The reality of Suki's words kicked in. Bill was probably just getting Esme to tie up loose ends before he gave her her notice. But still, if nothing else, it was a temporary reprieve and she thought this way, at least she'd have chance to talk things over with Max, to get her painting perhaps, and to say goodbye.

Esme knocked on the door and went in. Flea got up from his basket and padded over, his head bowed and tail swinging lazily in submissive recognition.

'Hello, fella,' she said, stroking him whilst watching Max lost in his work and oblivious to her arrival. A large landscape was clamped upon the easel which at first glance looked to be by Guardi or Canaletto. Most scenes of Venice in this style were by one of these two and this showed the Grand Canal in winter.

'I'm sorry I didn't get to say thank you for your party. I had a ball.'

'It was fun, wasn't it?' said Max.

'Coralie and Oti were lovely, and I was more than a little surprised by your piano-playing skills.'

Max laughed, 'Hardly skilful. More like beating the shit out of the ivories, but I can bang out a tune.'

He finally turned to look at her, resembling a deep-sea creature who has learnt to adapt to the absence of light with its personal torch to attract prey. His hair stood crisp with turpentine and paint around his headlamp and he was full of a wildness of one obsessively driven to do something at the cost of all else – personal hygiene and sleep, by the look of his dark circles.

'You are the first human I've seen in days. The Uffizi is driving me mad. Left my phone off the hook so I don't need to hear that I'm two months late on delivery, every five seconds. They pay a fortune so I can't tell them to piss off.'

'I won't keep you – Bill sent me with this envelope – I haven't come to badger you about my painting. You can take as long as you like.'

'No, no, you're a heavenly distraction.'

Esme gave him a hug, taking in his chemical tang. His shirt was unevenly buttoned and despite spending most of his days inert she could feel a strength that came from good genes rather than athletic prowess.

'I just want to thank you, really.'

He raised his eyebrows, 'Oh yes?'

'You've been a rock, Max. If I'm honest, I was shit-scared about leaving home and coming to London. Scotland doesn't prepare you for the madness of this city and well…'

Max had gone back to cleaning a gondola, but he was listening.

'I wanted to thank you for making it easier. It's been lovely spending time with you and watching you work. Almost like going back to when things were…' she paused, 'less complicated. All about the art, not the art world. What you do is amazing. I mean, you are an artist in your own right and I feel lucky to have been able to see it up close, to escape…'

Putting his brush down and removing his magnifying glasses he swivelled his stool to face her.

'What have you done?'

Recognizing his master's admonishing tone but not the smile that went with it, Flea slunk to his basket.

'I've been a bit of an idiot,' she said, blushing. 'More than a bit.'

'Oh God, don't worry. We've all been there.'

'I know but I…'

'Tell me. I'm sure it's not as bad as you think. Anything you do would be like being mauled by a teddy bear.'

Esme told him. Everything. He sat quietly listening with his arms folded across his chest. At times he looked like he might laugh and at others a proud father. When she had finished, he put his hands behind his head and stretched like an idle lion.

'Thank Christ you've got it in you to go off piste. I was concerned you might toe the upper-class line too conscientiously.'

'I know, but what if Bill fires me? He'd be well within his rights.'

'He'd never do that. He's just making you stew, and rightly so. There will have been plenty of worse things he has done. No one with Bill's success could have an unchequered past. No. He won't sack you.' Max smiled.

'But I've betrayed his trust.'

'Listen, it's these kinds of things that make you more interesting as a person. You fucked up, got fucked and now you have to learn from your mistakes and move on. Find a way to make it up to him.'

Esme considered this and perhaps Max was right. She'd come to London looking for adventure and found it, albeit not in the way she hoped.

'If he sacks me I'll have to go back home. How can I convince him I'm sorry if I'm not even here?'

'It won't happen, especially when he sees your painting. Worst-case scenario is he'll want you as a client.'

'What?' Esme held her breath.

Max rose and wandered to the back of the garage. A stack of canvases lay protected under a calico dust sheet and with little consideration he tugged one out, flung it over his shoulder and returned to stand square in front of her. With no ceremony, he flipped it around to show her.

'Is this the same painting?' Esme gasped, staring at the young woman with long dark curls in a white dress.

'She's pretty stunning, isn't she? I knew she was good but once the soot came off she revealed herself to be even better than I suspected.'

Esme inched forward, almost scared to get too close.

The painting's loose, experimental brushwork surrounding the subject's head and figure gave the portrait an outstandingly atmospheric presence. The sitter's hands had been left sketchy in an unresolved manner which added to the painting's charm. Romney must have deliberated over their placement and Max had left them unfinished which enhanced the picture's impressionist quality.

'You see the lute and organ and how her hands are almost in the prayer position? I think she was depicting St Cecilia. Emma was supposed to have had a beautiful singing voice and we know she was an accomplished actress, both on and off the stage.'

Lady Hamilton's features had the regularity of a Greek sculpture and were full of immediacy and poetic expression. Romney had captured an innocence – a sense that all are children in the eyes of God – that was in contrast to her voluptuous body.

'Oh, Max, it's ravishing. You are a genius.'

'I could have made her good as new but her flaws are what makes her beautiful. All that remains is to put her back in her frame.'

'I love her. I can't believe that this is the same painting I brought in.'

'Well, it just shows that nothing broken is beyond repair.'

As valuable as the restored painting was Max's ability to see behind the mask of deliberate destruction. She wondered how the Contessa knew the picture was coming to her and if she did, had she defaced it because of Emma Hamilton's resemblance to her mother? Either way, Esme was in love with the picture. Before the renovation she assumed she would offload the painting to anyone who would take it off her hands. It had embodied everything she wanted to bury in order to move on. But now, Emma Hamilton, in all her saintly disguise, represented a future where anything was possible. The Earl had wanted her to have this painting and his gift had been there all along, hidden, just waiting for her to realize that with a little patience and willingness to look beneath the surface, she would find something closer to the truth. Lady Hamilton was a symbol of familiarity and reassurance who instilled courage.

Esme hugged Max again, 'I think Emma is my first girl crush,' she giggled.

'I wish everyone was as grateful as you, Esme,' said Max. 'Right, I'd better get on before the Uffizi turn me into meat-balls. I'll get the painting sent over with Bill's Tiepolo.'

'Thank you, Max. Really. Thank you.' And Esme retreated out of the studio and into the glare of the day. She hadn't noticed the significant drop in temperature on her way to the studio and the coolness made her feel alive, made her feel as if she'd stepped out of a painting.

'Esme!'

Esme whipped around to see Max running after her, waving an envelope.

'I almost forgot to give this to you. It was stuck on the back of the canvas – sandwiched between the painting and a layer of board.'

Esme instantly recognized the writing. It resembled the movements of an insect that had fallen into a pot of ink and taken a brisk walk across the paper – scratchy boy-writing like the letters sent to her at school.

Clutching the letter, she entered Brompton Cemetery under its pillared portico. The cemetery was vast. Acres of headstones of all sizes, tall stones higher than Esme, small ones, grand ones and weathered ones all sat alongside each other. Despite the ranks of the dead, it felt teeming with life; a continuous conversation between departed souls, birdsong, plants and sky. An avenue of lime trees seemed to go on forever. So many trees. Dozens of species. It was a revelation. This felt like a place of communion for the living as well as a resting place for the dead.

A soft breeze chased around her shoulders making her shiver a little. The slick green leaves of tall trees rustled, and a skein of ivy dangling from the branches began to wave. As the ivy blew, it cast pretty lace-like shadows on the ground which reminded Esme of banners, rippling over the dearly departed in silent celebration.

She thought of the all the thousands of people buried under her feet, their dreams unfulfilled. The countless echoes of 'could have' and 'should have'… countless books unwritten, countless songs unsung. Was this how the Earl had thought when he died? When she'd realized who it was from, she'd wanted to open the letter alone but this place, balanced between the living and the dead, felt right. Sitting on a grass bank in the shade of a headstone, she pushed her finger under the flap of the envelope, eased it open and pulled out the letter:

My dearest Esme

I write this as my life comes to a close. I have had a happy life, not in small part, thanks to my darling Diana, your mother.

Cancer is a terrible thing – but for far longer than my present illness, something else has been eating away at me. When you harbour secrets, it is they that wear you out, outlasting everything until it is only the secrets that remain.

Since your birth I have known you are my daughter. It is a terrible thing to know a child is yours and never to hear them call you 'father'. But it was not just my secret to tell. In fact, I only write this now because I fear your mother will never be able to say the words. We wanted to tell you, Esme, but your young life was the eye of a storm and we did not want you to feel its destructive force any more than you would already have to. I suppose I was lucky too because you and your dearest mama have always been such a big part of my life and Culcairn's; I have never felt the guilt of absenteeism.

I have watched you grow, the spitting image of Diana, with love and pride. You share her beauty and compassion, her gentle and forgiving nature. I do not write this a confession for absolution, but as a keepsake from your birth father who loved you very, very much.

This painting holds more value to me than all the more famous names housed at Culcairn because she reminds me of Diana. And of you. Cherish her and keep her safe.

With my enduring love
Henry Culcairn

Esme's spine was tingling as she read and reread the words. She saw the sky above her and felt the wind in her hair but her surroundings seemed as though they had turned upside down as she clung onto the grass to keep her balance. The Earl's words were balled tightly in her trembling fist. She was stunned. If there had been a fire she would have thrown the letter into the grate to watch it burn around the edges and go up in smoke.

Which pain was worse – the shock that the Earl was her father or that the man she called 'father' never was? There had been many times at Culcairn when the Earl had acted like a father, taking her in when her mother couldn't look after her, protecting her from his vicious wife. There had even been moments when she had wished the Earl *was* her father, given his kindness and patient interest in the things she did, but she'd always imagined him as some additional father figure, never in exchange for her own. This letter of confession changed all that. It showed that his acts of kindness were, in fact, acts of guilt. Everything had been a charade to appease his conscience. The Earl had never truly been there, she realized – not for her, nor her mother. Now the truth was out it filled her with unexpected anger and disappointment. What had seemed like occasional welcome flashes of kindness from a friend seemed meagre offerings when measured against what a father should do.

She found herself thinking of the man who had raised her. She had often judged him harshly, felt his absence. But in the light of this news, she saw she had been looking at her family not with clear eyes but as though through a broken window. She saw that her father had done his best, amid the cracks and sharp edges. He had taught her so much about beauty, about art. But only now did she feel his greatest lessons – about loyalty, about love and family. Dysfunctional they might have been, but Esme felt grateful that he'd showed her that family was about more than blood. Unlike the Earl, Colin Munroe had been proud to call her his daughter.

Esme longed to see him, to hold him and thank him for not rejecting her and treating her as his own to the outside world. Then she froze. Did her father know? Who else knew? Mrs Bee, Bill? The affair between her mother and the Earl was common knowledge, so he must have suspected. Esme wished she had a mirror so she could look at herself for familial similarities with fresh eyes but she had never noticed a physical resemblance with anyone other than her mother.

In a matter of minutes she had also gained three more siblings. It meant Lexi, her childhood playmate, was her half-sister. This would have been their dream come true when they were little but given Lexi's refusal to reconnect, Esme suspected she would see this as more of a poisoned chalice than a magic wand to save their friendship. She wondered now if Lexi knew – was that why she'd shut Esme out? And what about Sophia? She'd always seen her intelligence and blue-grey eyes as Munroe traits but she supposed they weren't a reliable indicator of paternity.

No wonder the Contessa had treated her as if she was contaminated. Being the daughter of her husband's mistress was bad enough, but to be his daughter, too – Esme finally understood the depth of her loathing. There was a farcical symmetry to the 'the bastard child' being another potential heiress and the fact that she, the Contessa, was driven to exact revenge by defacing the one thing the Earl had left his daughter. She had tried to destroy the Romney in the same way she done everything in her power to break Esme. It was a grand failure on both counts and Esme wanted nothing more to do with her or the Earl's fortune. The painting was legacy enough.

The letter had changed her past in a few short lines and she knew it was also a signal to change her future. Her childhood defined her yesterdays but since it was built on lies she saw it could not control who she was today. She could start over and leave her sorrow behind and all she had to do was walk forward. The actions of others may have shaped her but they didn't own her. Nor could she hide behind them as excuses.

It wasn't her mother, the Contessa, the Earl, and certainly not her father who was holding her back. She had to face her own anger, stubbornness and fears and let them go. Esme shut her eyes and mentally shuffled through the different personalities she had been trying on for size, one after another. The cool worldly young woman, the party girl, the career woman, the society, they were all just parts in a play. But the role of victim was one she had become used to and she had looked to others to shake it off. But she saw she could cast it off herself. Finally see herself as lucky. The Earl's gift was not the painting but these handwritten words, the key to her freedom.

Tilting her head back, she watched wispy clouds fly briskly across the sky, leaving a large swatch of clear indigo blue. Such clouds foretold a change in weather. They had no shape at all or every shape because they were constantly changing. She closed her eyes and sensed the warmth of the sun glowing orange on her eyelids. It was a wonderful feeling.

Chapter Twenty-Six

The door to the shop was wedged wide open with a copy of the *Yellow Pages*. She'd stayed in the cemetery as long as she could and thought she'd left it late enough for Bill to have gone home but she hadn't banked on a refurb being underway. From across the road she could see the gallery was empty, removed of all paintings. A stepladder leant idly against the far wall, fenced off by a ring of pots. It seemed the showroom was immersed in a thorough revamp. Her desk was covered in a dust sheet and Bill sat behind, feet up and crossed on top. She tried to sense his mood by the way he held his newspaper. There was no snapping or flicking of the pages, which was a good sign, and he took unhurried sips from the mug held precariously aloft.

She thought about doing a runner but her boss looked into the street and stared right at her.

'Fuck,' she said out loud and almost whipped in front of an oncoming BMW. What would Cece say?

She made her way to the entrance and stood very straight with her fingertips skimming the doorframe for balance, suspended in the moment between success and failure.

'It's OK, you can come in,' said Bill with a slight edge. He took his glasses off and twisted them between his thumb and forefinger in the way her father did when he was annoyed.

'So. Where shall we start?'

Esme looked down at the floor which had been stripped of its carpet. There was no sadness in her tears – they were the messengers only of overwhelming remorse. With the greatest effort she lifted her head, wanting to beg forgiveness.

'I'm so sorry, Bill.'

His face was impassive and nothing moved apart from his fingers manipulating his glasses which continued to stir her fear.

'Bill, I can only apologize for fucking everything up. Seriously. I behaved like an imbecile.'

'The thing is, Esme, there are no short-cuts to accomplishment. It took me fifteen years to become an overnight success. Fifteen years of making mistakes and carrying on regardless because I had the drive and bloody-mindedness to succeed, no matter what. I learnt from my mistakes and used them to further my career. You have a choice now. You can either sit in this job and wait for some rich fuck to propose, like Suki, or you can buckle down to proper work and make a go of your career.'

Esme nodded, hardly daring to let herself hope that Bill was giving her a chance.

'But if you really want the second option then you have to promise me to take responsibility, to get out there and use the famous Munroe eye to prove your worth.'

Bill was giving her a lifeline which was both thrilling and terrifying.

'Of course I want this and I will, I promise, do my absolute best. I'll work all the hours of the day and night...'

'I'm not asking you to do that – just to be accountable for the tasks and projects I give you.'

'I will. Bill, thank you. You have no idea how grateful I am. And I'll pay you back, you can take the money out of wages,' she said.

'You might not need to. If you just listen – because opportunity sometimes knocks very softly,' he said cryptically. 'It's one of the reasons why I am making some changes.'

'So what's going on here?' said Esme. 'In one afternoon, you've stripped the entire place.'

'It seems you made quite an impression on our young American friend.'

'Ollie?'

'Yes, Oliver Maxey. He brought me some contact sheets,' Bill said, pulling a sheaf of photographic paper from under the calico. 'I'm not sure you'll be too happy but I'm over the moon.'

The images were black-and-white and showed a crumpled figure sitting head bowed on a pavement. As usual, Oliver had made the familiar unfamiliar, bringing out new emotion in the way he framed the shot and almost made it abstract. Esme could see despair weighing down on the figure – a smacked-out junkie? – as if the day lay on top of their shoulders like stones, but there remained something beautiful in the heartbreak he'd captured.

'Oliver took these?'

'Yes. It's the ones on the next sheet you really need to see.'

The printed negatives continued on the next page. The girl – for Esme could now see it was a girl – looked up, eyes bruised with mascara and tears catching the sunlight. It was her. In that candid, awful moment outside his gallery, Ollie had captured the essence of her mistakes creating images that were perfectly imperfect, elegant yet provocative. From the mess of her emotions had somehow come images that played with the classical aesthetics of proportion and clean lines. She was amazed.

'Look at you!' said Bill. 'A beautiful mess.'

She scanned the next page – a record of misjudged actions in detailed precision – her bag discarded on the ground next to her, open and empty, a broken shoe and scattered dreams.

'I had no idea...'

'That's what makes them so incredible. This is what I've been waiting for, Esme.' He took hold of her shoulders and shook them, excitedly. 'These are why I'm changing the space. New pictures, new paint.'

He went on to tell her how Ollie had come to the gallery to show him the photographs of her saying it was only right that she and Bill ought to have first refusal. 'He said he couldn't resist taking them of you and he couldn't exhibit them or sell them to anyone else without your permission. He clearly knew how much you regretted missing out on the other pictures. As a matter of fact, I think he brought these to me to help you.'

'Help me?'

'These are evidence of your contrition, blossom.'

Esme would never forget the feeling of relief that swept over her or the sensation that she was being lifted from her own ashes.

'He wanted to give them to me but I refused. Instead he has a body of unseen work and, along with these, I am giving him his first solo Central London show. You will be the one to decide if these are for sale or just for display.'

'Bill, that's incredible,' Esme cried.

'Photography has never been shown here before so the gallery is having an overhaul to complement his work. Thanks to your fuck-up, I'll be exhibiting the new wonder boy.'

'Wow. What will the neighbours say?' she laughed. 'I am so pleased. For you both.'

'We're not getting married, blossom, although I admit, he's ravishing.'

'He is,' she grinned.

'This will shake up Jermyn Street. Out with the old and in with the new.' He got up with an attempted little skip. 'And you, my darling girl, are getting a promotion. I want you to be my ears and eyes.'

'Are you sure?'

'It's decided. With your youth and beauty and dedication, you will open more doors than I will. People only show me what they think I want to see. You are a blank canvas.'

Esme thought of Emma Hamilton: her intensity and ability to take today's admirers back to another time. George Romney had captured a moment and turned it into thought and feeling, and Ollie had done the same. She hoped there was a place for both of them in this gallery and that Bill wouldn't turn his back on Old Masters forever.

'Where's Suki, by the way?'

'I told her to take the next two weeks off whilst the refurb is being done. She's thrilled as it means she can read all those wedding magazines she bought. I'd love to say you could do the same but I need you here to plan Oliver's exhibition. Now I'm going to go and get some rest and I'll see you in the morning.'

Esme couldn't rest. Instead she walked down to the waterside. The tide was out, leaving behind a trove of pre-loved items and trash. It wasn't a fragrant breeze coming off the Thames but it held a welcome dampness that reminded her of Scotland. A few weeks ago, Esme had thought she could conquer London. She had imagined a whirl of art openings, rebellious nights, larky parties, bittersweet romances conducted right here on the Embankment. So much had changed but not in the ways she'd envisaged.

She looked all round her – at the two bridges, Albert and Battersea, the great trees, the grey-brown ever-flowing river. She sat on a bench, her hands in her lap folded over her jeans and smiled, thinking she had never seen anything as beautiful as this. The river was the heart of London; for centuries it had brought all the wonders of the world to the capital, and now it had transported Esme to a place where things were simple once more. The air was warm, skittish and nimble and she glanced down the long stretch of water which ran perpetually, ebbing and flowing, forgiving and renewing and reshaping the shoreline until it came to a brackish conclusion as it met the sea. And with it, she felt it carrying all her misdemeanours and her past away.

Chapter Twenty-Seven

Autumn was her favourite season and Esme was so happy she lived in a world where there were Octobers. It was the time when everything burst with its last beauty, as if nature had been saving up all year for a grand finale. The symphony of colours richer than any other month – green speaking of life and strength, orange of golden contentment and red a burning heart that would keep the world warm through winter months. Autumn carried more gold in its pockets than all the other seasons put together, she had once read. It settled you into your favourite chair, like an old friend.

Work was going really well. Bill's forgiveness and faith in her ability had given her the confidence to pick herself up and earn success. Old Masters were still her passion but as she learnt more about fine art photography, she came to appreciate that the skill of printing was as important as the composition itself. She and Ollie had spent hours in the darkroom. He had shown himself to be kind and patient, a natural teacher who could turn the ordinary into something fresh and new. Life to him was an exclamation. He shouted his talent through his work yet never felt the need to explain it to anyone. His photographs spoke for themselves. The exhibition had been triumphant and, thanks to Bill, Maxey prints were in high demand and there was a healthy waiting list of subjects wanting to be photographed by him. She loved her job and she had to admit, she was falling in love with him. She and Oliver had slept together the night of his new exhibition and had barely been apart since.

Somehow Dan had managed to crash Ollie's opening night. At a thirty-foot distance he was still attractive with the strident body of an alpha male. At close range, his inflated ego took up the gallery as if he owned the place.

'Lovely to see you, beautiful,' he said, moving in to kiss her hello. Esme recoiled, inhaling the stench of his chauvinism and lies. 'I've been thinking about you constantly,' he proclaimed, but his words struck her as empty and contemptible. There was nothing to charm or tempt her anymore.

It was incredible, that, after everything, the closest to an apology he could offer was a 'I couldn't resist you,' as if it was her fault. She had told him he was ridiculous and to fuck off. 'Ouch,' Dan had winced, then rebounded with a sleazy smile. 'That would hurt me if I believed it or even cared.' Seeing the tension from across the room, Max had subtly taken him by the arm and kicked him out.

The friendship between Max and Esme had continued to grow. Whenever she was swamped or overwhelmed she sought the tranquillity of his company and studio. Seeing him and Ollie form a friendship was a delight to her too. They were such different breeds, like a whippet and Afghan hound, she used to tease. They fought like kids over the respective superiority of each other's chosen fields, but there was also a deep well of mutual respect.

But Ollie had gone. He'd needed to go back to the States for a while and Esme couldn't deny London was not as much fun without him. He had been away too long. When Ollie got back, she was taking him to one of Max's bohemian nights of revelry and drunkenness.

On the night he'd left for New York, Cece had invited her for a drink at the new bar she was running. They'd regenerated their friendship and were taking things slowly. When she'd arrived in London, Esme had been so desperate to make friends that she'd overlooked the time needed to forge significant bonds. To date, their relationship had been built on surface appeal and convenience, but now both were keen to underpin what they shared – as strays roaming the metropolis – ready for life's surprises.

Work and Ollie may have kept her busy but Esme knew she couldn't use them as excuses not to act on the lessons of the summer. She was on her way to meet her father and as she turned into Sloane Avenue now, her heart was drumming in her chest so hard it ached, but it was the good kind of ache: excitement and effort and action. She stopped to breathe in the crisp air that smelt ever so slightly of smoke.

Her parents had become members of the club she now stood outside when they'd sold the London house. Designed as a bolt-hole for out-of-towners spending the occasional night in the city, you paid a small surcharge for a decent room and a full English breakfast. It was exactly the kind of place Cece teased

Esme for frequenting, but she understood why her father had chosen it. The antiques were subtly arranged and it was decorated with understated elegance. Bookshelves lined the walls of the room she was shown into and there was no overhead lighting, just a few lamps and a pair of picture lights showcasing a decent landscape and portrait of a Chelsea Pensioner.

Esme found an empty sofa in the corner in front of the fire and ordered a pot of tea with toast and Gentleman's Relish. It was comforting to be back in the warm arms of tradition for an hour or two. She got up to browse the shelves as if she was at home. She slipped out a leatherbound copy of *Vanity Fair* and ran her finger down the spine.

'Am I in time for tea?'

Esme turned. Her father's hair was greyer or perhaps highlighted by the sun. The suntanned face was handsome as ever and as familiar as an old pair of slippers. He wore an open shirt with a scarf looped around his neck and as she moved to face him fully, he regarded her like she was someone he knew but couldn't place.

'Esme! My God, look at you. You've become a woman!'

She laughed and went over to embrace him. He felt strong and smelt of lavender.

'Are you wearing aftershave?' she asked. 'You never wear aftershave.'

'It's this soap. Made in the village I've been staying in,' he said, handing her a brown box tied with straw, 'for you, darling.'

'How lovely. Thank you,' said Esme. 'Here, I've got us a place by the fire. London must seem cold after the South of France. And tea is on the way.'

He looked at her approvingly and joined her on the sofa.

A good-looking waiter dressed in a neat black-and-white uniform wrestled with a tray weighed down by an unnecessary array of Spode china. Sugar bowl, milk jug, teapot, plates, cups and saucers, tea strainer, cutlery, butter dish and decanted fish paste smartly filled a chunky silver tub. Keeping up appearances is so complicated, thought Esme.

'Here, let me help you.'

Esme watched her father stand to assist the young man in his struggle. He poured them each a cup, remembering that she liked two sugars.

'It seems a lifetime since I saw you. How are things?' he asked, spreading a thick layer of butter onto his toast.

'I had a bit of a rocky start. Finding my feet, learning on the job, but everything is brilliant now. Bill's been a hero.'

'You're in expert hands, just don't let him exhaust you.' He smiled, the creases around his eyes filling with sunshine.

'And I've met someone. He's gorgeous but it's early days.'

'Really? Do I know his parents?' he asked with mock casual indifference.

Esme rapped his hand with her spoon and they both laughed.

'No. You won't know him or his family. He's a photographer from New York. His show at the gallery was a sell-out.'

'Ah, Bill did mention something about that. He was raving about him,' he said leaning back into the sofa, putting his hands behind his head.

The waiter reappeared and asked, 'Would you like anything else?'

'Esme?'

'No, I'm fine, thanks.'

'So he's a Yank?'

'Yes, but he's living here for now. Although he's away for work at the moment so you can't give him the third degree about me while you're here!'

'Well, I look forward to meeting him, darling,' he said. Esme had never introduced a boyfriend to her family before, and she found herself suddenly looking forward to the encounter.

'How's everything with you?' she asked.

'Extremely well. I adore France. The people are so much more relaxed. Less prejudiced. The Brits could learn a thing or two. I'm not back for long. The Culcairn set is just too bloody restrictive. If it wasn't for visiting your mother and Mrs Bee, I'd not even have gone back there on this visit. I didn't go up to the castle while I was there. Your mother's home and The Lodge were enough for me. I know we spent a lot of time with the Culcairns when you were younger but I don't think it's a happy home for the Contessa.'

Esme had the sense that he was about to say something more but had stopped himself. There was a brief silence, and then she laughed. '*Totally* agree. London has taught me that. There's so much more to life than stilton and "Pass the port, old bean."'

'The thing is, people like the Culcairns take everything for granted. Assumption is their curse. Don't get me wrong, I still miss Scotland and your mother, of course.'

Esme could hear the sincerity in his voice, and also the inner turmoil. It really must have been so difficult for him, especially considering what she now knew, and she had to fight the temptation to lean over and hug him.

'It's true. I grew up believing that the world revolved around a candelabra-laden dining table but actually I'm happier hanging out in a greasy spoon,' Esme said.

'I'll stick to fresh croissant and kippers, thank you,' he laughed.

Esme drained her cup and set it on the table. She hadn't expected to feel quite like this, so comfortable with him, so sympathetic. She found herself seeing him in a new light, which itself cast long shadows over the way she had thought of him and treated him in the past. 'There's something I need to say...' she said.

'You're not pregnant, are you?'

'No!' she giggled nervously, and then the words came out in a rush. 'No, seriously, I just want to say that I'm sorry I was never there for you. For not understanding how difficult it must have been living with Mum and trying to cope with her illness. To be honest, there were times when I hated you for not seeming to care. It was like you brushed everything under the carpet, but now I know it was your way of coping. I was so wrapped up in my own misery that I never thought to look beneath the surface to see how you were really feeling.'

'Darling, it was hard for all of us and no one more than your mother. Her depression was a bitter pill to swallow, especially as the woman I married was such a beautiful soul. But living with me wasn't easy for her either.'

'I know you did the best you could, given the... circumstances... for me and Sophia too.'

'Is everything OK, darling? Has something happened?'

'No, everything is fine. It's good. It's just that I'm beginning to see things more clearly now.' Esme kept her eyes on her father and continued, 'I managed to get that painting restored.'

'The one Henry Culcairn left you?' There was a slight edge to his voice, but somehow she could tell it wasn't directed at her, or even Henry really. It spoke of sadness and regret, rather than self-pity or resentment.

'Yes. That one. It's very beautiful… and actually, looks a lot like Mum… but I'm not sure what to do with it.'

She paused, then said, 'The thing is, I'm not sure I want anything to remember the Earl by.'

Their eyes met and there was a moment of heavy silence. Then he leant back and folded his hands behind his head again. It was as if he was looking past her, into the distance, then he straightened again and said calmly, 'Darling, I think you should keep it. Of course you should. It's important to remember people.'

'Of course, but we should remember who they really were, not who we thought they were or even wanted them to be, when we were too young and too stupid to know any better…'

Her father reached over and took her hand. 'Squirrel, darling. I know I'm not the most demonstrative when it comes to showing my feelings, but not a day has passed when I haven't felt blessed to have you in my life and I love you dearly.'

'I know,' she said, squeezing his fingers softly, and then continued, meaning every word from the bottom of her heart, 'and I love you too, Daddy.'

As they sat and drank another cup of tea, Esme felt she'd said enough. Sometimes less was more, and there was a sense that they understood each other, just by sharing the quiet moment together. Their cups drained once again, mutual intuition made them stand at the same time to say goodbye. Esme hugged her father hard.

'Keep me posted on your progress and whereabouts, darling. I'm awfully proud of you, you know,' he said.

'And I'm proud of *you*, Daddy,' she laughed.

They promised to meet up again soon and then Esme stepped out into the early evening. The streetlamps were flickering into life, illuminating Pimlico Road in a soft electric glow. The sky was tinged with yellow and pink and held the promise of snow. Soon, families across the country would break out the decorations, place wreaths upon their doors, and sit around their fires sharing minced pies and mulled wine. Esme felt a childlike rush of excitement at the thought of Christmas. It was a time to celebrate, to come together and give thanks. To say goodbye to the year and welcome the dawn of the new. For the first time, Esme felt completely, utterly, joyously at peace. She knew the best present she was getting this year was from herself; it was crafted from all the moments of joy and love that she had known, and all the pain and doubt and stupid mistakes that she had made. It was a gift of herself, to herself, and she intended to make the most of it.

Acknowledgements

Thank you to my wonderful publisher HQ and the heavenly, kick-ass Lisa Milton. To Charlotte Mursell, who I am going to miss terribly – what the hell will I do without your pushing and prodding and exaggerations? To Caroline Michel for her Manolo's and diplomacy. To my beloved family for their understanding and patience in being an absent mum/wife during the writing process. To Genevieve Pegg, my incredible editor. Thank you for your sensitivity, your wisdom and kindness; you helped turn this novel into something I'm proud of. To Charlie and Annabel Redmayne for giving me permission to have a holiday. To Caroline and John Giddings, because I love you both and want to support Access All Areas for the Isle of Wight Festival. And finally, to Jack Lankaster. You are quite simply a literary genius and my writing rock/tutor/mentor.

ONE PLACE. MANY STORIES

Bold, innovative and
empowering publishing.

FOLLOW US ON:

@HQStories

Susannah Constantine is a television presenter and journalist. She lives in West Sussex with her husband and three children. She has co-written nine non-fiction books with Trinny Woodall. *Summer in Mayfair* is her second novel.

Also by Susannah Constantine:

After the Snow

'Though... ...'
THE TIMES MAGAZINE

'Captivating'
WOMAN & HOME

'Beautifully written ... with a dramatic, thrilling conclusion'
HELLO!

'Fans of *Downton Abbey* will love this'
DAVINA McCALL

'A tenderly absorbing tale, shades of Dodie Smith'
YOU MAGAZINE

'A modern-day Nancy Mitford'
SIR ELTON JOHN

'Brimming with secrets, scandal, shame'
THE SUN

'This touching, atmospheric story ... has
echoes of *I Capture the Castle* about it'
THE SCOTTISH DAILY MAIL

'Frank and thrilling'
S MAGAZINE